"Quite simply, this is the m.... .   n Ponzi schemes to date. It is invaluable to not only criminologists, legal experts, and students, but also should be required reading for those in the general public with financial investments. From detailed typologies of Ponzi schemes, to economic trends that facilitate them, to characteristics of both victims and perpetrators, Springer has provided us with a veritable encyclopedia of these devastating frauds."

— **Colleen P. Eren,** *William Paterson University,*
author of *Bernie Madoff and the Crisis: The Public*
Trial of Capitalism

"Springer provides an insightful analysis of Ponzi schemes in the United States that examines politics, policies, case histories, victims, offenders and legal responses. The book sheds renewed light on a costly and widespread form of white-collar crime, and will be a valuable resource for practitioners and scholars alike."

— **Henry N. Pontell,** *Distinguished University Professor, John Jay College of Criminal Justice, CUNY, Professor Emeritus, University of California, Irvine*

"A thorough, comprehensive and understandable analysis of Ponzi schemes – the types, motivations, and consequences."

—**Thomas Tornow,** *Retired Attorney, Judge and Law School Instructor*

The Politics of Ponzi Schemes

In the space of three years, from 2009 to 2012 Bernie Madoff, Tom Petters, and R. Allen Stanford were all convicted for running multi-billion dollar Ponzi schemes. These three schemes alone have had the largest financial take in U.S. history. But what role does the economy and legislation play in the occurrences of Ponzi schemes? What is the nature of Ponzi schemes and what are their tools and mechanisms? What can we know about Ponzi perpetrators?

Unraveling the answers to these questions (and many more), Marie Springer provides the first representative portrait of Ponzi schemes, their perpetrators, and their victims. Adopting a multidisciplinary approach, she begins by presenting an overview of different types of Ponzi schemes. She later explores perpetrators and victims of Ponzi schemes followed by a close examination of economic trends, regulatory changes, and the financial relationship with Ponzi schemes. Other key features include:

- A non-technical overview of both offender-based and offense-based approaches of studying this form of fraud.
- Examples of Ponzi schemes and Ponzi schemers.
- A wealth of descriptive statistics on known federal cases from the 1960s until the present to quantify this specific form of fraud.

Broadening our understanding of Ponzi schemes as a form of white-collar crime, *The Politics of Ponzi Schemes* provides an excellent foundation for students and practitioners of public administration, banking, as well as investors, finance and accounting, law enforcement officers, legislators, and regulators.

Marie Springer is an adjunct assistant professor in the Departments of Economics and Public Management at John Jay College of Criminal Justice, City University of New York. Her research interests are white-collar crimes in financial markets, affinity-fraud, banking industries, elder-fraud in financial markets, and government accountability. Her research looks at the government responses in legislation and the effectiveness of the legislation in controlling, preventing, and punishing white-collar crimes in financial markets.

The Politics of Ponzi Schemes

History, Theory, and Policy

Marie Springer

NEW YORK AND LONDON

First published 2021
by Routledge
52 Vanderbilt Avenue, New York, NY 10017

and by Routledge
2 Park Square, Milton Park, Abingdon, Oxon, OX14 4RN

Routledge is an imprint of the Taylor & Francis Group, an informa business

© 2021 Taylor & Francis

The right of Marie Springer to be identified as author of
this work has been asserted by her in accordance with
sections 77 and 78 of the Copyright, Designs and Patents
Act 1988.

All rights reserved. No part of this book may be reprinted
or reproduced or utilized in any form or by any electronic,
mechanical, or other means, now known or hereafter
invented, including photocopying and recording, or in any
information storage or retrieval system, without permission
in writing from the publishers.

Trademark notice: Product or corporate names may be
trademarks or registered trademarks, and are used only for
identification and explanation without intent to infringe.

Library of Congress Cataloging-in-Publication Data
A catalog record for this title has been requested

ISBN: 978-0-367-69067-0 (hbk)
ISBN: 978-1-138-61606-6 (pbk)
ISBN: 978-0-429-46249-8 (ebk)

Typeset in Times New Roman
by codeMantra

This book is dedicated to the Mary's in my life:
Mary Foster, Marianne Evans, and Mary Springer.

Contents

Illustrations

Figures

Tables

Acknowledgments

This book was built on the investigations and documents provided by the many federal employees in the agencies of the Federal Bureau of Investigation, the Department of Justice, the Securities and Exchange Commission, the Commodities Futures Trade Commission, the Internal Revenue Service, the United States Postal Service Investigators, the US Marshals, the US Department of Treasury, and the Secret Service. It is their professionalism, competency, and investigative skills that made this research possible.

The Securities and Exchange Commission's employees were extraordinarily helpful in accessing information throughout the research process. In particular, Robert Rand, who works with the SEC website, helped me to maximize the SEC's search engines. In addition, over years of research, there were multiple Freedom of Information Act requests made of the SEC; the staff were always very helpful and professional. They made it a pleasure to carry out the research.

There are a great many individuals in the Department of Justice, its courts and bureaus, who were helpful in finding public information on cases, great thanks to all of you. Above all, the availability and consistency of information enabled this research. As I have read the indictments and other documents, I marveled at the investigative skills and countless hours that must have gone into these cases, likewise with the SEC and CFTC complaints. Also, the E-Government Act and PACER enabled access to archives and documents through the internet that in previous decades have been too time intensive to access. Throughout this research of nine years, I saw the search engines improve and the availability of case documents increase with each agency.

I would also like to acknowledge that over the years of research I have seen the SEC, CFTC, FBI, DOJ, USPS, and IRS increase the amount of consumer education information for the general public. All of these agencies work very hard to try to educate the American public to carry out their own due diligence and to recognize fraud when they see it.

I have watched the educational sites, and the wealth of investor information that has increased dramatically over the years.

I owe considerable gratitude to Fred Gerkens, who is a walking encyclopedia of knowledge on securities law and fraud, for his insights and editing. Likewise, there are no words to thank Kim Martin, for her insights, common sense, and a lifetime of support. In addition, thanks to Jackie Kashmer, a retired federal court reporter, who has provided insight into the federal judicial system and procedures. Great thanks to Jim Leitner and his staff for their insights on hedge funds and trading practices.

I would also like to acknowledge John Jay's Lloyd Sealy librarians Kathleen Collins, and Ellen Belcher who is the archivist of the Fraud and Swindles Collection, Special Collections, Lloyd Sealy Library, John Jay College of Criminal Justice/CUNY, New York City. Thanks to the anonymous donor(s) who contributed the collection.

Great appreciation to Dr. Jeremy Porter and Dr. Sal Guajardo for their help in research design and in making quantitative methods understandable and a valuable tool. Dr. Richard Lovely inspired a passion for research 30 years ago. Most importantly, the ideas for this book have been built on the white-collar crime works of Dr. Sally Simpson, Dr. Michael Benson, and Dr. Henry Pontell. Special thanks to Dr. Pontell for his lifetime of work in the field of white-collar crime, and his practical, down-to-earth advice.

Abbreviations

AICPA	American Institute for Certified Public Accountants
A.p.	Administrative proceeding
BMIS/BLMIS	Bernard L. Madoff Investment Securities LLC
BOP	Bureau of Prisons
CBD	Cannabidiol
CD	Certificate of Deposit
CFTC	Commodities, Futures Trading Commission
DOJ	United States Department of Justice
FBI	Federal Bureau of Investigation
FCIC	Financial Crisis Inquiry Commission
FDIC	Federal Deposit Insurance Corporation
FFETF	Financial Fraud Enforcement Task Force
FinCEN	Financial Crimes Enforcement Network
FINRA	Financial Industry Regulatory Authority
ICE	United States Immigration and Customs Enforcement
ICO	Initial Coin Offering
IPO	Initial Public Offering
IRS	United States Internal Revenue Service
L.r.	Litigation release
MLM	Multilevel Marketing scheme
MUI	Matter Under Inquiry
NASAA	North American Securities Administration Association
NASD	National Association of Securities Dealers
NFA	National Futures Association
NRSI	Name Relationship Search Index
NRSRO	Nationally Recognized Statistical Ratings Organization
OIG	Office of Inspector General
PACER	Public Access Court Electronic Records
PI	Preliminary Inquiry
PIPE	Private Investment in Public Entity
P.r.	Press release

REIT	Real Estate Investment Trust
SEC	Securities and Exchange Commission
SIFMA	Securities Industry and Financial Markets Association
S.m.	Sentencing memorandum
SS	Secret Service
USAO	United States Attorney's Office
USPIS	United States Postal Inspection Service
USSC	United States Sentencing Commission
Y2K	Year two thousand

Introduction
Ponzi Scheme Research and Overview

This book comes to press 100 years after the namesake of all Ponzi schemes, Charles Ponzi, committed his fraud scheme in 1920. The goal, herein, is not to be a "how-to" for potential Ponzi schemers, but instead to educate investors so that they can recognize potential frauds before they invest. Second, I hope to provide useful information to those who investigate and prosecute Ponzi schemes. Third, I hope to add to the knowledge of legislators with regard to this one type of fraud, so that they may have an understanding of how their legislative decisions with regard to laws and regulations influence the average citizen's lives, by way of this one type of fraud. Lastly, I hope to expand the academic understanding of how social dynamics and interactions are mechanisms for financial victimization. Above all, it is hoped this book is as interesting to read as it was to research and write. There is no end to the creativity of Ponzi perpetrators; each scheme is a mystery to be unraveled. Part I looks at the Ponzi schemes; Part II is the individual level, the perpetrators, the victims, and the money. Part III is about the bigger picture, the economics, history, and legislation.

The population being studied is the known cases of federal-level Ponzi schemes included in federal databases, from the time period of January 1962 until January 31, 2020, that are publicly accessible. The criteria for determining which federal-level cases are included in the data set are the use of terms such as "Ponzi," "Ponzi scheme" "Ponzi-like," "Ponzi-style," and "Ponzi payment" in federal regulatory and law enforcement agency documents. Ponzi schemes are the units of analysis. The federal agency documents are a matter of public record, accessed through federal agency websites. Only cases that have been determined in a federal criminal court of law or by federal civil administrative proceedings to be a Ponzi in nature are included in the data sets used for this research. The data sets are a comprehensive population of known cases within federal websites from 1962 through January 2020, not an exhaustive universe of all Ponzi schemes; the latter is not knowable, documentable, or provable.

The data sets are comprehensive in that they include all known schemes using the term "Ponzi" that are included in federal agency documents from the time period 1962–2020, available on federal agency websites. The term "Ponzi" is unique; federal agency search engines are sophisticated and can find all usage of the term when used in text. The great majority of cases in the study involved actions by more than one federal agency, allowing for cross-referencing. It is known that there are frauds that technically have the actions considered to be Ponzi schemes but no federal agency used the term "Ponzi" in the text; these cases are not included in the study because the criterion is that a federal agency must designate a fraud scheme as "Ponzi" to be included in the study. The number of the known cases that have the Ponzi actions without the designation is less than 100, a quantity that would not dramatically affect the overall outcome of the analysis.

Data Collection

Federal Agencies' Databases

The documents used in coding the Ponzi schemes were collected from these federal agencies: Securities and Exchange Commission (SEC), Federal Bureau of Investigation (FBI), Department of Justice (DOJ), United States Attorney's Offices (USAO), Commodities and Futures Trading Commissions (CFTC), Internal Revenue Service (IRS), United States Postal Service Criminal Investigations (USPS). The units of analysis, the Ponzi schemes, have been collected from legal documents that are publicly available through the SEC, FBI, CFTC, and DOJ. In addition, some documents were accessed through Public Access to Court Electronic Records (PACER).

In addition, financial markets industry oversight organizations serve the purpose of licensing, examining for compliance and imposing ethical standards in securities and commodities. Brokers, traders, and investment advisers are tested and licensed through the private sector trade regulators: Financial Industry Regulatory Authority (FINRA) and the National Futures Association (NFA). These agencies also provide publicly accessible information on the professional status of broker, traders, and advisers free of charge. The databases for these entities were used to determine if the brokers and traders were licensed. Generally, this is stated in SEC and CFTC documents; however all perpetrators were checked to see if they had been licensed or if they had sanctions. Both entities can bar individuals from trading; they also report on sanctions, complaints, and convictions.

The criteria for inclusion on the data sets are:

1   Use of the following terms by federal agencies in the text of legal documents: Ponzi; Ponzi-like; Ponzi-style; Ponzi payment; any variation thereof.
2   In federal agency databases, and a matter of public record.[1]
3   Received civil federal agency administrative actions and/or criminal conviction.

This study used advanced search engines of the following federal agencies:

*   Securities and Exchange Commission (SEC)
*   Commodities, Futures Trading Commission (CFTC)
*   Federal Bureau of Investigation (FBI)
*   United States Postal Service Office of Investigations (USPIS)
*   Internal Revenue Service (IRS)
*   Department of Justice (DOJ)
*   United States Attorney's Offices (USAO)
*   United States Marshals Service (USMS)
*   United States Secret Service (USSS)
*   United States Immigration and Customs Enforcement (ICE)

The SEC and CFTC search engines are sophisticated enough to catch any use of the term "Ponzi" in all textual usage.[2] The SEC, CFTC, FBI, and DOJ are the primary agencies investigating Ponzi schemes and the primary sources used for cases. The agencies' documents cross-reference one another. DOJ and FBI documents list other agencies involved in investigations, as do the IRS and the USPIS. The SEC and CFTC documents discuss criminal actions and provide docket numbers for criminal cases.

The legal documents were reviewed at least four times, throughout the coding process by the author. Initially each document was examined to determine the "Ponzi" criteria for inclusion. Second, the documents for each scheme were again perused for the names and details of the perpetrators. Third, the documents were again analyzed for details about incorporation, the tools used, and the manner and means of carrying out the scheme. This process has been carried out by the author with a meticulous attention to detail and cross-referencing documents. Once a case was found to be designated a Ponzi scheme in federal documents, each document was then analyzed for information on the amount of money taken in the scheme, the time frame, the number of perpetrators and victims, the location, professions, incorporation, and whether or not the perpetrators were registered with the SEC or CFTC or FINRA.

Federal-level criminal and civil actions are consistent throughout the nation as well as in sentencing and reporting, and vocabulary usage, supporting the consistency and validity needed to carry out quantitative analysis. State laws vary on registration for brokers, dealers and advisers, prosecution sentencing, and reporting; it would not be appropriate to compare state- and federal-level prosecutions. The state cases do not allow for consistency in laws, reporting, or accessibility to documents and therefore were not used.[3]

The Ponzi cases that are in the data sets have been determined through criminal legal proceedings, or through an administrative judges (civil) to have occurred; they are a matter of public record. Cases that have not resulted in civil administrative actions, sanctions, or criminal guilt are not part of the study. No individuals – either the perpetrators of the fraud or the victims of the fraud – were contacted.

There is consistency in that the terms "Ponzi" and "affinity fraud" are standard terminology that has the same meaning in all federal agencies. Each agency is required to enforce the same federal laws. As such, there is consistency and reliability in the laws, the standard vocabulary, and practices followed in these federal agencies. There is consistency in reporting practices of all agencies. Likewise, all[4] cases are prosecuted by one agency: the DOJ, by United States Attorneys; there is consistency in the prosecutorial practices across the nation's offices.

Most of the Ponzi cases have taken place in several states. The majority have been investigated by more than one federal agency. There were a few cases that have been criminally investigated and prosecuted on state levels, but also received civil sanctions through the SEC or CFTC. These cases were included because there were federal-level civil sanctions imposed. In most cases, federal laws have been broken making the cases federal level. Few cases take place only within state boundaries; most are multistate and, in many cases, international in scope.

The FBI press releases are a product of the USAO, under the DOJ. They are listed through the FBI web site but originate with the USAO. The DOJ also issues the same documents under their banner and the USAO. Both the FBI and DOJ websites were searched for cases. The DOJ's main site was searched initially; then each state's United States Attorney's office websites, under the DOJ, were searched for press releases individually.

The exceptions in data collection are those cases that occurred in Hawaii. The Hawaiian FBI/DOJ office did not post written press release as consistently as the US mainland state offices. The determination of Ponzi schemes in Hawaii has been acquired from phone communications with written confirmation, with the FBI Special Agent assigned to financial crimes in Hawaii. The agent provided a list of Ponzi schemes in a phone conversation and then confirmed through an email communication. The agent also held public television press conferences stating that these cases were Ponzi schemes. In these cases, documentation has been taken from PACER, video press conferences featuring the agent, and general media news reports, and in some cases FBI press releases and SEC documents.

Federal Documents

The federal process of reporting legal actions is consistent. Only those cases stated as being affinity-fraud in federal documents are designated in coding as affinity-frauds. Whether or not the Ponzi case is a registered brokerage, dealer, or investment adviser is determined by publicly accessible federal-level documents as well as those registered with the SEC, CFTC, FINRA, and the NFA. Qualities of the schemes such as the number of perpetrators, the name of companies, the amount taken, and the months of sentences are a matter of court records and not subject to interpretation. The quantity of victims or amount taken used in the data set is the amount in final legal actions; the amount is not interpreted. The manner and means are considered qualitative because of inconsistent word usage in federal documents; this is explained in the description of the manner and means in Chapter 4. Meanings and definitions are determined by the federal agencies, and the Acts and legislative statutes governing the federal agencies and their actions are a matter of public record.

From 2002 on, the E-Government Act made federal documents easily available on federal agency websites. This requires court personnel, for federal agency to upload documents to the agency website or to PACER. Not all older documents were uploaded and easily available. In some cases, these documents were acquired through contacting court clerk's offices and requesting these documents. In most cases the documents were initially available through the SEC and CFTC, in other cases the IRS or USPS. Once a case has gone on to criminal indictment and an arrest has been made, the documents are available through the FBI and/or the DOJ. Those documents not available through the above sources were acquired through PACER.

Once federal regulatory and DOJ agency websites were exhausted, any remaining information not found was searched for through Public Access to Court Electronic Records, known as PACER, using the known names of perpetrators of business names. This federal information site includes magistrate actions, civil actions, and criminal actions for a minimal charge. In many cases, the actual sentencing information was derived from PACER. Not all court documents are available. Each court district determines what is posted on PACER. Transcripts of court proceedings are recorded and in a stenographer's notes, but not necessarily transcribed unless the court, the plaintiff, or the defendant's attorney pays to have the proceedings transcribed. The court has the responsibility to make the documents accessible, although in many cases the documents are not available because no party paid to have them transcribed.

When there has been a jury trial instead of a plea bargain, the defendants often appeal. In cases where the defendant plea bargained, part of the plea agreement is that they will not appeal the sentence. When there is an appeal, the court documents are generally publicly accessible; the court records have been transcribed in order for the defendant to appeal their conviction. Some of the most detailed information comes from these appeals.

The Ponzi schemes/units of observation were also coded for dimensions of fraudulent practices and the methods used to carry out the schemes, referred to as the manner and means in Chapter 4. These aspects are qualitative assessments because the different federal agency documents reporting the methods of the schemes vary from very general to very specific; there is no consistency in vocabulary to support reliability for a quantitative analysis or replicability. For example, an SEC document may provide specifics on the types of securities promoted; an FBI or DOJ document may just use the term "securities" in discussing the same scheme.

The schemes were coded for length of time as well as the amount of money taken in millions. At times, there were discrepancies among federal documents with regard to the amount of money taken in these schemes. It is not known how the federal agencies arrive at the amount taken. The perpetrators of fraud do not keep meticulous financial records about the money they take in and how it is used. The amount used in coding is the amount indicated in federal complaints served on the perpetrators, indictments and convictions, whichever amount is the final amount applied in the final administrative or criminal legal action. The schemes were also coded for dimensions of fraudulent practices: the tools used to carry out the schemes as well as the manner and means.

Chapters Overview

Part I discusses the Ponzi schemes and their characteristics. It examines Ponzi schemes using the offense-based approach, in researching and discussing the characteristics of the schemes. The offense-based approach looks at the crime and the qualities of the crime. Herein this refers to the Ponzi scheme, a type of fraud, not a law that is violated. Murder is an offense that is a type of violent crime; a Ponzi schemes is a type of fraud within white-collar crime that encompasses many laws and regulations.

In Chapter 2 the types and subtypes of Ponzi schemes are explained. There are two primary types of frauds: the intentional frauds and unintentional frauds. Intentional Ponzi schemes are those that were conceived of as frauds from the very beginning and carried out knowing that the activities are illegal. Unintentional Ponzi schemes are those that developed into frauds out of a legitimate business- or brokerage-failure. There are subtypes within these two types. Hedge funds and commodity pools make up a large percentage of Ponzi schemes. The nature of these funds and pools and how they may be associated with Ponzi schemes or how they are set up as Ponzi schemes are explained.

Among intentional fraud schemes affinity-fraud, false-brokerages, cybercurrency frauds, and other types of intentional fraud schemes are described and discussed. In some circumstances feeder funds were knowing participants; in others they were unwitting victims of the fraud. When feeder funds are unwitting victims, it is rarely discussed in federal documents; only those feeder funds that were charged are mentioned in federal documents.

This section explains the complexity of intentional schemes. It will also discuss the nature of hedge funds and commodity pools that are fraudulent fronts for intentional Ponzi schemes. Hedge funds and commodity pools are explained and how the organization has enabled the fraud to take place. There are a great many hedge funds and commodity pools that function quite legitimately and are able to make a profit for their participants. This section will discuss some classic cases and how they were initially legitimate businesses and how they came to be Ponzi schemes or unwitting participants in someone else's Ponzi scheme.

Unintentional frauds are those that begin as legitimate businesses or brokerages and then develop into Ponzi schemes out of some failure such as an economic downturn or incompetence of the business owner, or some personal concern such as a partnership splitting up or a nasty divorce. These schemes are generally brokerage-failures, business-failures; some feeder funds were duped and did not know they were contributing to a Ponzi scheme. Each subtype of scheme is then discussed, explaining the nature of each and how it differs from other types.

Chapter 3 will discuss the tools of the Ponzi frauds. These are the mechanisms that enable the frauds such as aliases, falsified credentials, fraudulent documents, unrealistic interest promises and guarantees, the use of offshore accounts, shell companies and multiple business entities, campaign donations, and charitable donations.

Chapter 4 discusses the manner and means of the schemes. This is what the perpetrators told investors they would be investing in, or, in some cases, what were actual investments that eventually failed. Some schemes are based in stocks, bonds, commodities, and other investment instruments. Other schemes are based in office, farm, or medical equipment. Some schemes are based in loans of every possible variety. Many schemes during the housing market bubble prior to the financial crisis were based in mortgage-backed derivatives or real estate. Mortgages, real estate property, and real estate developments have been a means of Ponzi frauds from the entirety of the time frame. One aspect of manner and means is how the schemes are based on technological advances attracting those who want to get in on the next big trend and make a fortune. There were schemes based in phones and pay phone prior to cell phones. Many schemes are based in "algorithms." As financial markets become more computerized, the options for using computer technology to commit fraud and as a basis for fraud dramatically increase. Anything of value is a basis for these frauds, wine, sports paraphernalia, Uber, and Broadway theater tickets. The only limitation is what gullible people won't fall for. The biggest trend to watch for now is cryptocurrencies. This chapter will also discuss technological trends that inspired the types of frauds and how the mechanism used to perpetrate frauds changes with technological advances.

Chapter 5 discusses aspects of the money. The fraud cannot exist without the investor-victims having some liquid funds. The perpetrator has devised a way to get that money. The key element that makes a Ponzi scheme what it is is taking money from later investors to pay interest to earlier investors. This chapter discusses the money taken, money laundering, bankruptcy, disgorgement, and restitution, the legal actions of returning the money to the victim-investors.

Part II

Part II discusses the perpetrators and the victims, the individual level. The offenders of Ponzi schemes are discussed in Chapter 5. This chapter discusses the demographics of Ponzi perpetrators. In general, Ponzi perpetrators tend to age in to crime as opposed to out of crime as in other types of crimes. For Ponzi perpetrators to be successful they must present an air of credibility and of success. No one is going to give their life savings to someone who appears to be unsuccessful. The Ponzi perpetrators use their victims' money to present themselves as being very successful.

Chapter 6 discusses how the social dynamics of trust, persuasion, and gullibility and greed enable the fraud. We might assume that those who have been taken advantage of must be gullible or naïve, but it is not always quite that simple. Some victim-investors may have been naïve, but others were quite sophisticated professional investors; others were institutional investors. This chapter discusses how the perpetrators convince their victims to invest. Theories on how we trust and how we decide whom can be trusted are discussed in relationship to Ponzi perpetrators and victims. The mechanisms that perpetrators use to instill trust are discussed such as those using religious terminology.

The offenders or perpetrators of the Ponzi schemes are discussed in Chapter 7. Generally, the perpetrators are charismatic and friendly; this chapter discusses the personality qualities that enable them to defraud their victims. The demographic information about them is available through federal documents; their age, gender, professions, and other characteristics that contributed to carrying out the fraud bring some surprising details on this specific type of fraud perpetrators. This chapter discusses familial groups of perpetrators, where it is families, siblings, or married couples that have carried out Ponzi schemes. There is very little information on female white-collar perpetrators in media or academia; this chapter has a section devoted to the female perpetrators.

Chapter 8 discusses the victims. Without contacting victims directly, this chapter discusses social dynamics that enable the fraud to take place such as the mechanisms of trust, persuasion, and social affiliation. Generally, there is an assumed trust when we are dealing with professionals such as lawyers, accountants, clergy, and stock brokers. We assume their reputation matters to them and they will be honest with us because they want our continued business.

Chapter 9 presents findings on the sentencing process and on the sentences of the perpetrators. The chapter also discusses the civil sanctions and process of the SEC and the CFTC. Clearly the 110-year sentence of Allen Stanford, the 150-year sentence of Bernie Madoff, and the 330-year sentence of Norman Schmidt were intended to send a deterrent message to others, in that a 75-year-old inmate cannot serve a 150-year sentence. Such extreme sentences may somehow make the investor-victims feel that they got their pound of flesh, but more than likely they would prefer to have their money back, discussed under the disgorgement and restitution processes (Money, Chapter 5).

Part III discusses history, the economic events, laws, and regulations that are violated, the bigger picture. Minsky's theory of financial instability explains boom economies, financial decline, then government intervention. This section discusses the laws and regulations in relationship to the economic events and trends reflecting on Minsky's theory. This chapter discusses the legal basis for what is considered a Ponzi scheme and the regulations that are violated and the laws that are broken. This also looks at history and Ponzi schemes.

Chapter 10 discusses economic theory and financial trends over the duration of the study. This chapter looks at financial events such as the dot-com era, the subprime mortgage boom, and the financial crisis and what was going on in Ponzi schemes at these times. Hyman Minsky's (1982) theory of financial instability is reflected on, in that boom and bust economies are fertile ground for frauds and then exposure of frauds, followed by government intervention. In addition, this chapter reflects on the time frame and the manner and means of Ponzi schemes with changes with technological and financial trends.

Chapter 11 is the legal framework and the legislative events, regulatory changes that have been enacted to address fraud, and how regulation has been relaxed, replaced, or ignored, increasing or reducing fraud. In Minsky's theory the government response to financial decline is intervention, generally in the form of laws or regulations. This chapter reflects on financial trends and the laws and regulations that results.

Chapter 12 is significant, unusual, and historic Ponzi schemes. There have been many Ponzi schemes of note throughout the history of the United States. This type of fraud was not referred to as a "Ponzi" scheme until Charles Ponzi's scheme in 1920. Even after Ponzi's six-month scheme this form of fraud was usually referred to as a swindle. This chapter covers those swindles that have been referred to as Ponzi schemes in history as well as more recent Ponzi schemes that relate to technological or economic trends throughout the history. Some schemes have been included for some unique or interesting characteristic.

The final chapter sums up what is known about Ponzi schemes and gives suggestions for carrying out one's own due diligence. The reality is we are most vulnerable to someone we have a social relationship with that has established trust. This chapter provides insights into how to recognize when something doesn't "pass the smell test" and to reduce one's chance of being involved in a Ponzi scheme.

This study has been in progress for nine years and continues. The federal agencies and media are searched daily for new Ponzi schemes. Ponzi perpetrators are ever adapting to new technologies and trends; these cases are continually interesting to see what makes them work – and fail. There are changes in the economy that trigger changes in the Ponzi schemes. As this goes to publish, COVID-19 affects the entire world; it will be interesting to see how that will influence the economy and what types of Ponzi schemes it will inspire.

Notes

1 Not all federal court documents are transcribed and publicly available.
2 SEC web designer Robert Rand was consulted throughout the research to maximize SEC databases.
3 The exception is when a perpetrator received a state level conviction.
4 A few cases received state level criminal convictions but had federal level civil actions and sanctions.

Reference

Minsky, H. (1982). *Can "it" happen again? Essays on instability and finance.* Armonk, NY, M.E. Sharpe Inc.

Part I

The Ponzi Schemes

Chapter 1

Ponzi Schemes and White-collar Crime

The Nature of Ponzi Schemes

The primary action that determines that a fraudulent scheme is a Ponzi is that the funds of later investors are used to pay interest or principal to earlier investors. Without this action, a fraud is not a Ponzi scheme. Not all frauds labeled as Ponzi schemes in the common media were designated as Ponzi schemes by federal agencies or law enforcement authorities. Only those cases that were determined by federal authorities to be Ponzi schemes are used in this study.

The term "Ponzi" refers to a specific type of fraud perpetrated by Charles Ponzi in 1920. Prior to that event this type of fraud fell under the general category of a swindle or confidence game. Kathy Phelps and the Honorable Steven Rhodes (2012) provide a concise list of characteristics that law enforcement and regulatory agencies use before they designate a fraud as a Ponzi scheme:

1 Deposits were made by investors.
2 The Debtor conducted little or no legitimate business operations as represented to investors.
3 The purported business operations of the debtor produced little or no profits or earnings.
4 The source of payments to earlier investors is from cash infused by new investors.

(Phelps and Rhodes § 2.03[1][b], pp. 2–8)

Some fraud cases have been falsely labeled as Ponzi schemes in the general media. These were frauds whereby the perpetrators simply stole the money of their victims, not investing it or paying other victim-investors, but instead spending the funds on what is usually an extravagant lifestyle. These were instances where there was taking of funds without Ponzi payments. These schemes are sometimes referred to as take-the-money-and-run schemes (from the Steven Miller Band song lyrics) (Huddleston, 2012, p. 57). These cases are theft by deception, not Ponzi schemes. For this reason, media designations of Ponzi schemes were not used in this study.

Fraud schemes that are designated "pyramid schemes," also known as multi-level-marketing schemes (MLMs) in federal documents, are not part of this study, unless they were also classified as a Ponzi scheme. The business structure in MLMs is different from Ponzi schemes in that there are several levels or layers of participants, sometimes referred to as "members," who each bring in their own members or clients. Whereas Ponzi schemes have primary perpetrators that control the entire scheme. Multi-level marketing entities can be legitimate businesses where each level sells an actual product and earns a profit; the profits trickle up to more senior participants. There are well-known legitimate, successful, well established multi-level marketing businesses. Ponzi schemes are never legitimate business entities.

In 2009, the term "Ponzi scheme" became a common term in media with the schemes of Bernie Madoff and Allen Stanford. Two of the three biggest Ponzi schemes in world history became public knowledge, and in the press daily. The three schemes were all international in nature with victims all over the world. The first of the two Ponzi schemes was carried out by Bernard L. Madoff. Bernard Madoff admitted that his investment advising service – Bernard L. Madoff Investment Services (BMIS/BLMIS) – was actually a Ponzi scheme in early December 2008. Six months later, he was sentenced to 150 years in federal prison at the age of 75. The second of the two major Ponzi schemes was that of Robert Allen Stanford (Allen Stanford) and his Stanford International Bank Ltd. Stanford was charged with securities violations by the Securities and Exchange Commission (SEC) on June 19, 2009, and criminally indicted on June 18, 2009. Stanford was convicted and sentenced to 110 years in federal prison.

The third of the three largest and most significant Ponzi schemes in world history was based in Russia: Mavrodi Mondial Moneybank (MMM). The MMM scheme was a global Ponzi scheme that functioned in at least 118 countries with an estimated investor base of approximately 250 million people worldwide (Hess and Soltes, 2018). The scheme originally began in Russia in the early 1990s following the move to a capitalist economy. The founder, Russian Sergei Mavrodi, died on March 26, 2018, putting an end to the scheme. The scheme became global when Mavrodi began using cryptocurrency approximately 2011. The total amount of money involved was not reported in the media; there were too many countries, and multiple cryptocurrencies being used at the time of Mavrodi's death. With Mavrodi's death there was no individual to take responsibility. Since MMM was a global scheme, and cryptocurrencies were the monetary unit, there was no law enforcement agency with jurisdiction to try to account for all of the lost funds.

A Ponzi scheme is not a specific crime, but a type of fraud. This research uses the SEC's definition of Ponzi Schemes:

> A Ponzi scheme is an investment fraud that involves the payment of purported returns to existing investors from funds contributed by new investors. Ponzi scheme organizers often solicit new investors by promising to invest funds in opportunities claimed to generate high returns with little or no risk. In many Ponzi schemes, the fraudsters focus on attracting new money to make promised payments to earlier-stage investors and to use for personal expenses, instead of engaging in any legitimate investment activity.
>
> (SEC)

Ponzi schemes are just one type of white-collar crime. The term "white-collar" symbolizes the socioeconomic level of the perpetrators, indicating professionals and corporate executives who would be likely to wear suits and ties to work as opposed to those who are in the trades, symbolized by the term "blue-collar," the attire that those in these professions are thought to wear to work. The term "white-collar crime" was initially coined by Edwin Sutherland in 1939, (1983), defined as "as a crime committed by a person of respectability and high social status in the course of his occupation" (Sutherland, 1983, p. 7). This study defines the term of white-collar criminals to include those who present themselves as being of a high social status and respectability, using the rewards of their frauds to fulfill the image of high status, in order to perpetrate the Ponzi schemes.

The study of offense-based research in white-collar crime is defined by "the illegal act or the series of illegal acts committed by nonphysical means and by concealment or guile, to obtain money or property, to avoid the payment or loss of money or property, or to obtain business or personal advantage" (Edelhertz, 1970, p. 3). This definition from Herbert Edelhertz came from his work in the Department of Justice. Edelhertz felt that the academic community (Clinard and Quinney, 1994; Cressey, 1953; Reiss and Biderman, 1980; Sutherland, 1947), approaches of offender-based definitions of white-collar crime were too narrow, too restrictive. As such, Part I of the book addresses the offense of Ponzi schemes and examines the nature and characteristics of Ponzi schemes referred to as the tools, manner, and means going forth.

This type of fraud includes many laws and regulations that are violated, commonly mail fraud and wire fraud, as well as such regulatory violations as failing to register as a brokerage, or investment adviser, or a commodity broker. The laws and regulations are discussed in Chapter 11. The term "Ponzi scheme," for the purpose of inclusion in this study, is qualified herein, in terms of requiring all four parts – offense-based, offender-based, and environment-based – and adds a fourth criterion that includes the amount of money taken to be over $100,000. The offense is defined within publicly available federal agency documents, and designated to be Ponzi schemes within the wording of the text in these documents. Herein the offenders are defined as those who carried out and were charged in the frauds, were considered of high socioeconomic status or who presented themselves as such in Ponzi schemes, by the nature of their crime. The environment requirement is that the crime takes place in what is an enterprise, corporation, or other business formation, or a brokerage entity that presents itself as a legitimate business, or that may be a legitimate brokerage or hedge fund.

The fraud triangle developed by Donald Cressey dictates that there are three primary factors: financial pressure, opportunity, and rationalization (Cressey, 1953). Cressey's theory explains that an individual perceives financial pressure that motivates them to commit fraud. The environment of being in a corporate setting or a business enterprise provides the opportunity to commit fraud. The individual then justifies their fraudulent actions, being the rationalization aspect of the fraud triangle.

Benson and Simpson (2018) also take the opportunity perspective in examining white-collar crime. With both Cressey, and Benson and Simpson, it is the opportunity that already exists that enables the white-collar crime. The perpetrator works in a corporation, or bank; it is not their corporation or business. With Ponzi schemes, the perpetrators make their own opportunity. Ponzi perpetrators are entrepreneurs; they are the Chief Executive Officers (CEO), Chief Financial Officers (CFO), or presidents of the businesses they formed. In most cases the company itself is a fraud, designed to take the funds of the investor-victims, and may consist of several shell companies. In Ponzi schemes the environment and opportunity are created by the perpetrators.

Generally, white-collar crime research incorporates the environment or setting, as a defining factor establishing the crime to be white-collar, for example the offense(s) occurred in a large corporate setting. However, this study defines Ponzi schemes as a white-collar crime having five elements:

1   The offense: taking funds from later victims to pay earlier victims.
2   The offender or perpetrator(s).
3   The environment: the business, corporation, or brokerage.
4   Multiple victims.
5   Aggregated victim's losses of over $100,000.

The offense is the Ponzi scheme, designated as such in federal documents. The offenders or perpetrators are those who have been charged civilly and/or criminally convicted by federal agencies (or federal-civil and state-criminal). The environment is the enterprise, business, or brokerage established by the perpetrator(s). For a fraud scheme to be a Ponzi scheme there must be multiple victims in order for funds to be taken from one victim and given to another victim – the defining characteristic of a Ponzi scheme. This study includes a minimum monetary amount taken from the aggregated victims for inclusion in the study. All of the Ponzi schemes included in this study took more than $100,000 from the aggregated victims; there were none found to be less than $100,000.

This study respects the presumption of innocence, understanding that the cases documented in federal agency files are those where enough evidence was found to determine violations of the law. The perpetrators received actions and sanctions civilly by administrative judges, and/or were criminally convicted or pleaded guilty. There were other cases that are not public record because they did not become formal investigations; there may not have been adequate evidence for the SEC, CFTC to commence a formal investigation, or to reach a DOJ conviction. This study covers only the known federal Ponzi cases that have been brought to criminal or civil action and are public record.

Charles Ponzi, the namesake of all Ponzi schemes, and Bernie Madoff's, Allen Stanford's, and Thomas Petters' Ponzi schemes are not the primary interest of this study; the latter three are units of analysis within the entire population of 1,359 Ponzi schemes. They are used as examples throughout because most people are familiar with these schemes. Madoff has been written about quite thoroughly (Brame, 2016; Eren, 2017; Henriques, 2011; Kirtzman, 2010; Kurdas, 2012; Markopolos and Fisher, 2010; Ross, 2009); these are just the Madoff books alone. Madoff and Stanford have been in the mainstream media nearly every week since 2009; there is nothing new to be said. Charles Ponzi and other significant and historical schemes have been addressed in a section devoted to the significant Ponzi schemes in history of this type of fraud (Chapter 12), before and after Charles Ponzi. These cases are referred to throughout the study as examples, as well as many of the other Ponzi schemes.

References

Benson, M. and Simpson, S. (2018). *Understanding white-collar crime: An opportunity perspective*, third edition. New York, NY, Routledge.

Brame, R. (2016). *Brutal takeover: The story behind the seizure of Global Stanford Financial Group and criminal prosecution of R. Allen Stanford*. Scotts Valley, CA, CreateSpace Independent Publishing Platform.

Clinard, M. and Quinney, R. (1994). *Criminal behavior systems: A typology,* third edition. New York, NY, Routledge.

Cressey, D. (1953). *Other people's money.* Glencoe, IL, The Free Press.

Edelhertz, H. (1970). *The nature, impact and prosecution of white-collar crime.* Washington, DC, US Department of Justice.

Eren, C. (2017). *Bernie Madoff and the crisis; The public trial of capitalism.* Stanford, CA, Stanford University Press.

Henriques, D. (2011). *The wizard of lies. Bernie Madoff and the death of trust.* New York, NY, Times Books.

Hess, S. and Soltes, E. (2018, April 28). Russia's greatest Ponzi mastermind is dead, but his legacy lives on in the crypto world. *Quartz.*

Huddleston, P. (2012). *The vigilant investor.* New York NY, Amacom.

Kirtzman, A. (2010). *Betrayal: The life and lies of Bernie Madoff.* Harper Perennial.

Kurdas, C. (2012). *Political sticky wicket: The untouchable Ponzi scheme of Allen Stanford.* Scotts Valley, CA, Create Space Independent Publishing.

Markopolos, H. and Fisher, D. (2011). *No one would listen: A true financial thriller.* NJ. Hoboken, NJ, John Wiley and Sons.

Phelps, K.B. and Rhodes, S. (Honorable) (2012). *The Ponzi book: Legal resource for unraveling Ponzi schemes.* New Providence, NJ, LexisNexis.

Reiss, A and Biderman, A. (1980). *Data sources on white-collar law-breaking.* Washington, DC, Bureau of Social Science Research.

Ross, B. (2016). *The Madoff chronicles: Inside the secret world of Bernie and Ruth.* Glendale, CA, Kingswell.

Sutherland, E. (1947). *Principles of criminology.* Philadelphia, PA, J.B. Lincott.

Sutherland, E. (1983). *White collar crime: The uncut version.* New Haven, CT, Yale University Press.

Chapter 2

Typological Categories of Ponzi Schemes

Few academics, regulatory, or law enforcement entities have attempted to differentiate the types of Ponzi schemes. It was only through the first year of researching Ponzi schemes that it became evident that there are different types of Ponzi schemes. Generally, regulatory and law enforcement agencies differ between "classic Ponzi" and "Ponzi-like." They will refer to some as affinity-fraud and make note of which are also considered pyramid schemes. Generally, people assume that all Ponzi schemes begin as intentional frauds and involve some sort of securities. Most Ponzi schemes began as intentional fraud schemes; however, some began as legitimate businesses or brokerages that failed and then evolved into frauds, and they are not all based in securities.

This study has categorized Ponzi schemes into several types. The first level of differentiation is between those that are intentional, and those that are unintentional, meaning they developed from what was once a legitimate business entity. The majority of schemes are intentional; however, the second category warrants attention as well. Defining these different types of Ponzi schemes will support greater understanding for legislators, regulatory enforcement, and will aid in law enforcement and civil investigations. It may also help investors to recognize the symptoms fraud.

One author who did formulate types of Ponzi schemes is Spencer Winters. In contrast, the typologies developed through this study are differentiated from Winters' typing of Ponzi schemes. In his article "The law of Ponzi payouts," Winters defines Ponzi schemes in two types: (1) "fixed-income" and (2) "equity type" Ponzi schemes (Winters, 2012, p. 123). Winters defines equity-based schemes as those in which investor-victims are asked to refinance their homes providing the Ponzi perpetrator with the refinanced funds. The victims believe the money paid to the perpetrator is being used to reduce their debt. In equity-based schemes, the investor-victims are told their funds will be used to invest in securities, commodities, futures, options, and so on. They are told they will receive a percentage based on market trends. In some cases, this is a guaranteed amount (Winters, 2012). His argument is based on claw backs in the recovering of funds and what legally constitutes "transfer of value." This is in reference to what Winters refers to as the equity-type schemes as being shares or stocks, or that the investor contracts to have their funds invested. However, in most Ponzi schemes the funds are never invested but were received under fraudulent terms from the very beginning, regardless of what a contract may have stated the intended investment would be. Winters considers Bernie Madoff's scheme to be an equity-based scheme. In the Ponzi scheme data herein, the great majority of schemes would fall under Winter's classification of equity-based schemes.

In the study herein, many Ponzi schemes have several, and overlapping, typological designations. For example, Bernie Madoff's scheme was considered an affinity-fraud that also involved hedge funds that were feeder funds that contributed to his fund. Madoff's investment firm became a brokerage-failure from early on because he simply was not very good at trading stocks by his own admission in his sentencing testimony. Bernie Madoff's words are probably similar to the thinking of most of the brokerage-failure and business-failure schemes; in Madoff's words:

> When I began the Ponzi scheme, I believed that it would end shortly and I would be able to extricate myself and my clients from the scheme. However, this proved difficult, and ultimately impossible...
> (USA v. Madoff guilty plea, 2009, March 12, p. 23, lines 21–24)

Madoff also stated that he knew what he was doing was wrong and illegal. He did not design his business as a fraud from the onset, he explained that there was a recession in the early 1990s and he could not bring in profits, hence brokerage-failure. His scheme may have begun as a brokerage-failure, but there was no attempt to end it, when he knew what he was doing was illegal all along. Instead he kept bringing on new investor-victims to keep the scheme going.

This study defines two primary types of Ponzi schemes: (1) those that were intentionally initiated and known to be fraudulent – referred to as *intentional* Ponzi schemes herein, and (2) those that became Ponzi schemes through investment or business-failure referred to as *unintentional* Ponzi schemes. There are the five secondary levels of variations of Ponzi schemes.

Figure 2.1 illustrates the subcategories that fall under intentional or unintentional schemes. The third category shows those types of entities that may fall under either intentional schemes or unintentional. For example, a hedge or feeder fund may be a legitimate brokerage entity that believes it is investing in a larger legitimate entity. Then the larger entity it is investing in is actually a Ponzi scheme that the hedge or feeder

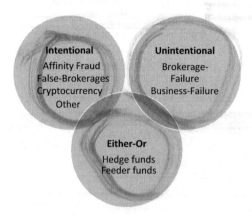

Figure 2.1 Intentional versus Unintentional Types of Schemes.

fund may or may not have known was an illegitimate enterprise. The original hedge/feeder fund was not a fraudulent entity, but it had unwittingly invested with a fraudulent entity, becoming a contributor to a Ponzi scheme.

The schemes that were intentional Ponzi schemes from the beginning and are coded in the data as "intentional." Of all of the schemes within the data set, 1,233 of 1,359 schemes were intentional Ponzi schemes, and 126 were unintentional schemes. The qualities used in coding to differentiate the two are defined below.

Intentional Ponzi Schemes

Most Ponzi schemes did originate as intentionally designed frauds. The intentional Ponzi schemes are quite strategic. The perpetrators tend to be intelligent and well spoken, oftentimes described as friendly and charismatic. They must convince investor-victims of the legitimacy of their business entity. The SEC definition of a Ponzi scheme is:

> A Ponzi scheme is an investment fraud that involves the payment of purported returns to existing investors from funds contributed by new investors. Ponzi scheme organizers often solicit new investors by promising to invest funds in opportunities claimed to generate high returns with little or no risk. In many Ponzi schemes, the fraudsters focus on attracting new money to make promised payments to earlier-stage investors and to use for personal expenses, instead of engaging in any legitimate investment activity.
>
> (SEC)

The primary activity that identifies a Ponzi scheme is the action of using the funds acquired from later investors to pay interest to earlier investors. This is differentiated from pyramid schemes, where a participant pays money for a product or service, whose members then recruit other members with the intent of the profits trickling upward through the ranks. There are legitimate pyramid-type businesses built on the practice of recruiting layers of sales people who recruit other sales personnel; these are referred to as multi-level-marketing entities. Examples of legitimate pyramid style businesses, or multi-level-marketing business entities, would be those that sell cosmetics or home goods, frequently in showcased parties. Usually, there are levels of membership depending upon how many new memberships are recruited. In illegitimate pyramid schemes, members just keep bringing layers of "members," "partners," or "agents" into the fold, but there is no legitimate product; frequently there is a membership fee. A scheme is included in this study when a federal agency uses the term "Ponzi" in legal action documents. If the case is just designated solely as a pyramid scheme it is not included.

Ponzi-Pyramid Schemes

There were 12 schemes classified as both Ponzi and pyramid in federal documents. All but three took place after 2001. Only four of the Ponzi/pyramid schemes had criminal indictments and guilty-pleas/convictions; the remaining eight had civil sanctions and penalties only. The following Ponzi schemes were also classified as pyramid schemes by the SEC:

- Sergio Tanaka of *Tropikgadget* was the founder of a scheme that was both Ponzi and pyramid, taking place from approximately 2013 to 2014. This scheme had two primary entities; one of the entities was incorporated in the United Arab Emirates and the other in the Madeira Free Trade Zone in Portugal. The primary place of business was Lisbon, Portugal. The overarching entity was referred to as the *Wings Network* that included entities in a total of six countries, including the United States (Florida and Delaware), Portugal, and Brazil. The entities were promoted through promotional events, webinars, YouTube, phone apps, websites, and other social media. The promoters/participants had rank based on how much money they brought in by the sale of memberships; this is the pyramid aspect. Second, members were charged a $94 membership fee that allowed members to find out about higher-priced packages. These packages were the only product; the sole purpose was to recruit more members. There was no actual product. As each member was recruited with the more costly packages; the funds went to the higher-status promoters, the Ponzi aspect (SEC, 2015, February 25, prg. 2). This scheme primarily targeted the Latino communities speaking both Spanish and Portuguese (SEC, 2017, February 28, l.r.). The perpetrators received only civil sanctions through the SEC.

- *eAdGear* was a pyramid and Ponzi scheme very similar to *Tropikgadget*, taking place from approximately 2010 to 2014. This scheme also sold memberships. Just as *Tropikgadget* primarily targeted Latino communities, *eAdGear* primarily targeted Chinese investor-victims, in the United States and in other countries. The primaries – Charles Wang, Francis Yeun, and Qian Zhang – incorporated *eAdGear* in California and Hong Kong. The alleged business was described as using search engines that increased visibility to potential customers for business' websites. The profits were made from recruiting new members. Many of the member-victims were family members and friends, who then recruited other friends and their families. In this case the perpetrators also received civil sanctions, and penalties through the SEC (SEC, 2016, February 1, l.r.).

- A third Ponzi-pyramid scheme was that of *DFRF Enterprises* that took place from approximately 2014 to 2015. The name came from the founder's initials: Daniel Fernandez Rojo Filho. This scheme was promoted through the internet and through online videos. The difference in this scheme is that Filho claimed there was a real product that members were investing in: gold mines in Brazil and Africa. There were no gold mines; there was no gold. Similar to *Tropikgadget*, the targeted populations were Spanish- and Portuguese-speaking people in the United States. Investor-victims participated through memberships of an initial $1,000 fee. Similar to the above schemes, *DFRF* was also promoted using YouTube. Members were told they would receive a debit card with their profits.

- DFRF was associated with another pyramid-Ponzi scheme *Universo Foneclub* (SEC, 2015, July 30). Filho was indicted criminally but was determined not competent to stand trial. The other perpetrators also received SEC civil sanctions and penalties. The pyramid-Ponzi scheme *Universo Foneclub* was short-lived, operating only for a few months in 2006. This scheme alleged to be a business of prepaid phonecards. The "phone cards" were said to be sold at cost, meaning no profit earned. If there is no profit, how would the investors gain interest? They didn't; the returns paid to investor-members were solely the fees from new recruits. This scheme targeted those in Brazilian and evangelical Christian communities; its website was in Portuguese, as was the contract.

Intentional Ponzi schemes make use of any manner of other types of fraud, including feigning to be someone else who owns a legitimate business; telemarketing; internet fraud; false promissory notes; false bank notes; document fraud; pump and dumps; the list is only limited by the creative thinking of the perpetrators. With most intentional Ponzi schemes, investigators may have found a Ponzi scheme through investigating some other aspect of the fraud taking place, such as tax evasion, unregistered securities, money laundering, or mail fraud. The methods of operation of Ponzi perpetrators are endless, each one more creative than the other. When a Ponzi scheme has multiple business entities it makes it challenging for authorities to find all the money and perpetrators.

In the intentional-scheme, the primary perpetrator may or may not have registered standing with the SEC or CFTC, or state regulatory agencies. The primary may have legitimately established a corporation, an LLC, or other formation, although the business activities are not legitimate. Generally, the perpetrators go to great lengths to appear to be a legitimate business. It is the appearance of success that attracts victims. Intentional schemes tend to be quite complex and present an image of credibility. Perpetrators generally have very convincing made-up financial reports and literature. Investors who do not know how to perform their own due diligence or to verify claims made within falsified financial documents, which is most people, are quite vulnerable to these confidence-artists.

For the purpose of this study, a differentiation between unintentional fraud and intentional fraud was determined using FBI, DOJ, SEC, and CFTC documents. The criteria for determining the primary type of Ponzi scheme were:

- Where there was indication that the brokerage was legitimately registered with federal agencies, or not.
- Or, an indication in federal documents of whether or not the business was functioning as a legitimate business and then an indication of failure (business-failure).
- Brokerage-failure schemes are determined by whether or not the business entity is properly registered with the SEC or CFTC and the primary perpetrator is a registered broker/dealer or investment adviser. The SEC and CFTC documents use wording that indicate that the individual or entity had lost funds through bad trades, and that actual trades as promised had taken place. The individual or entity must have been properly registered to qualify as a brokerage-failure.

There are different professional licenses that are required to be registered with the SEC and CFTC, such as brokers, brokerages, and registered investment adviser (Chilton, 2011). This is important to know, because if an entity or individual is not registered with the SEC, the CFTC, or the Financial Industry Regulatory Agency (FINRA), the North American Securities Administrators Association (NASAA), National Futures

Association (NFA), or a state regulatory agency, it can function illegitimately with no means of attracting notice. This means the perpetrators may not be in a position to legitimately invest in stocks, commodities, futures, or options, *for other people*. They can legally invest for themselves but not for others; this is one law classic intentional Ponzi perpetrators rarely break: they do not bother to invest their client's money! Regardless, if they say they will invest for people, without proper licensing and registration it is still a violation. There is no means for these regulatory agencies to have these entities in any kind of monitoring capacity if they are not registered. Regulatory and law enforcement agencies discover the fraud through investor complaints or other whistleblowers, primarily. In the case of Bernard Madoff, he was in business for more than 20 years, and chairman of the National Association of Securities Dealers Automated Quotations (NASDAQ); the SEC did not require him to be registered as an investment adviser until 2006, two years before he finally confessed to his fraud (Markopolos and Fisher 2010). Madoff avoided the requirement of registering as an investment adviser by not charging an advising fee (Frankel, 2012, p. 19; Lewis, 2015, p. 44).

When the purported stocks, product, or service that victims are told their funds are invested in do not exist, there is nothing for anyone to follow, monitor, or track. Ponzi perpetrators are expert at producing falsified documents that look quite legitimate, such as annual reports, account statements, and financial statements. If the perpetrator tells investor/victims that what is being invested in is proprietary, and investors go along with that, there is no way for investors or regulatory agencies to ascertain if anything is actually invested or traded. The claim that investing practices are proprietary in and of itself should be a red flag to investors.

False-Brokerages

False-brokerages are entities that functioned as investment businesses presenting themselves as registered entities but were not registered with the SEC or CFTC as required. There were 415 schemes that met the false-brokerage criteria. The perpetrators may have told investors they were not required to be registered. These entities may have carried out some investing or trading as promised, or they may not have done any investing whatsoever. In all cases, they presented themselves as legitimate brokers, traders, or investment advisers without being legally registered with the SEC, the CFTC, or FINRA. Some may have registered with state agencies as required by specific states, which varies by state. If they are required to register with the SEC or CFTC and are not, they were charged by these agencies; it is a violation that is stated in SEC and CFTC documents. Of the 1,359 Ponzi schemes in this study, only 12 percent were legitimately registered financial investment entities through the SEC and CFTC.

These schemes are classified as intentional schemes because they were not functioning as legitimately registered brokerages, investment advisers, or commodity pools. In some cases, the perpetrators did have the appropriate series licenses through FINRA, NFA, or NASAA, and may have registered with the state they lived in or traded in, but they were not registered with the appropriate federal agencies as required by law. Being registered requires a layer of reporting and accountability where federal agencies have some capacity for oversight and monitoring. The following cases are examples of false-brokerage schemes:

- Claudio Aliaga ran a false foreign exchange trading company out of Florida from 2007 to 2010. Aliaga was never registered with the CFTC in any capacity, nor was he a licensed broker, trader, or investment adviser. As is common to false-brokerages, Aliaga did invest a small portion of the funds taken in from investors in foreign exchange markets (FOREX) trades, but the great majority of the $4.5 million was used for himself and as Ponzi payments (CFTC, 2012, September 26).

- Eric Schmickle ran a commodity pool without being registered to do so; he was not registered with the CFTC in any way. This scheme made use of a registered futures commission merchant for trading, but Schmickle was not registered to run a commodity pool. Schmickle did make trades but endured heavy losses. He then resorted to a Ponzi scheme. Schmickle's scheme was a classic form of commodities false-brokerages; a commodity pool that had no formal authority to trade commodities or to accept investors' money for investing, nor qualified for exemptions under CFTC regulations (CFTC, 2012, September 24).

- Michael Regan ran a securities-based false-brokerage from 1998 until 2008. His business entity was never registered with the SEC as required, nor had he ever been licensed as a broker or investment adviser. Regan did invest a small portion of the funds received but endured losses. He used the majority of funds to pay Ponzi payments, as well as using funds to provide himself with the appearance of being very successful. This was a classic intentional Ponzi scheme, complete with false credentials and falsified profits (SEC, 2009, June 24).

Affinity-Fraud

Affinity-fraud, also known as community-based fraud, Ponzi schemes might seem more egregious than others because the primary agent preys on people he or she has some self-designated affiliation with. This is a relationship that is built on trust or builds trust through similarity in order to perpetrate the fraud. The perpetrator either belongs to a self-identifying group or finds his or her way into a group, such as joining a church. Among these groups, we see people victimized by national heritage, ethnicity, religion, sexual orientation, deafness, or professions. In federal documents many of the first victimized in many Ponzi schemes are "friends and family." They may fall into a self-identifying community, or they may be a diverse group of people who do not fall into an "affiliation," yet they are often considered affinity-frauds. This study does not categorize "friends and family" within affinity-fraud, although friends and family are the first line of victims in many schemes.

A subset of affinity-fraud are those schemes that featured immigrants who were preyed by other immigrants of the same nationality. In these communities, individuals may trust only those who speak the same language, or who share a common ancestry or history. They may be people who came to the United States as refugees, or who had endured political upheaval, such as the Khmer Rouge. The common language and history bind individuals together; they are more trusting of those from their homeland. If they have left their country of origin because of government abuses, they may not be willing to trust the government in their new home. These individuals are particularly vulnerable to their fellow countrymen and women.

Affinity Ponzi schemes are generally intentional Ponzi schemes; they are differentiated by the nature of the relationship between the perpetrator and the victim (Perri and Brody, 2012). It is specified in this study because of the social relationship that has been identified in federal documents between the victim and the perpetrator. The affiliation establishes trust, the social bond of trust being the primary mechanism used to carry out the fraud. Most affinity-fraud cases were based within religious organizations (see Figures 2.2 and 2.3). Frauds based on religious affiliation are known as faith-based frauds. Faith-based frauds of all types are in great quantity, yet it is likely not all are reported to authorities. There have been cases perpetrated within religious groups that the victims refused to believe they were defrauded; they were preyed on by their deep faith. Charles Frasca, in his book *Stock swindlers and their methods*, discussed the use of religious affiliation to acquire victims for frauds in 1931; the method of using religious affiliation to acquire victims for fraud is anything but new (Frasca, 1931). The means of using or feigning religiosity for fraud victimization has not waned with time.

Affinity-fraud perpetrators may have exploited their victims based on multiple qualities such as faith and ethnicity, or faith-nationality and profession. An example of this is a scheme that preyed on Filipinos, military and Christians (SEC, 2008, February 26). Nationality is differentiated from ethnicity because the victims self-identified with a specific

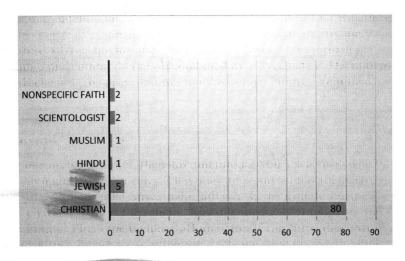

Figure 2.2 Faith-based Affinity Ponzi Schemes.

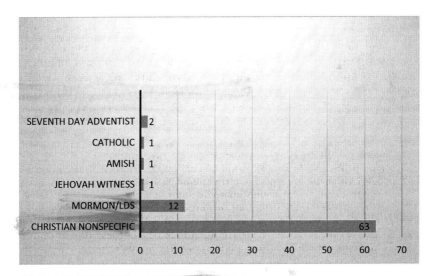

Figure 2.3 Christian Denomination Affinity Ponzi Schemes.

nation. An example of nationality-identity is Armenians, who may have come from several countries originally, but self-identify with being Armenian. Ethnicity refers to African-Americans, Asian-Americans, or Hispanics, who are Americans but not self-identifying with a specific nation in federal documents. Some schemes preyed on Brazilians and people of Portuguese nationalities, which might be classified as Latino, Hispanic for coding, but these victims were identified as being of specific nationalities in federal documents; the commonality was the language of Portuguese.

There were 133 schemes that were classified as affinity-fraud schemes. Some schemes were combinations of self-designated affiliations such as race and faith, or nationality and faith. Of the schemes designated as affinity-frauds, 91 were faith-based (Figure 2.2); 45 were nationality-based; 25 were ethnicity-based; six were profession-based other than athletes. Two schemes were perpetrated by those who were deaf targeting those in the deaf communities. There was one scheme based on sexual orientation.

Although not classified as affinity-fraud in federal documents, four schemes preyed on professional athletes, two of which had former professional athletes as the perpetrator. Professional athletes are particularly vulnerable to fraud, in general, because of their large salaries, and that they are in the public eye and can be identified. The schemes preying on athletes are covered in Chapter 8 on victims.

Affinity Faith-Based Frauds

Throughout the nine years of research on Ponzi schemes, there have been many myths about Ponzi schemes and Ponzi perpetrators that the author has been asked about, such as a predominance of one religious affiliation over another, as perpetrators. Unless a Ponzi scheme used religious affiliation to perpetrate the fraud, there is no reason for federal authorities to identify a perpetrator's religious affiliation in an investigation or in federal documents. Therefore, the demographic of religious affiliation is only noted in affinity faith-based Ponzi schemes.

Of the faith-based Ponzi schemes, federal documents sometimes specified the specific group using specific terms such as "Mormon or Latter-Day Saints" or "Jewish" or non-specific terms such as "church members" or "Christian." Some cases used only the generic "religious organization" or "faith-based" (Figure 2.3).

The following are a few of the classic faith-based Ponzi schemes:

- Julius Blackwelder was "the Bishop of the Bridgeport Ward of the Church of Jesus Christ Latter-day Saints" in Connecticut (DOJ, 2013, June 27). Blackwelder told investors from his congregation that the funds would be invested in commodities-futures contracts. However, the funds were used to pay Ponzi payments, and to build his 7,000-square-foot home. When the members of his congregation were told he was an experienced commodities trader, they believed him. It would have been socially unacceptable to question the credentials of the Bishop of their church. Blackwelder received 46 months in prison and is no longer a Bishop.

- Ronald Nadel preyed upon those within his Jehovah's Witnesses congregation (SEC v. Renaissance Asset Fund Inc., 2006). Many of his victims were elderly. In this case Nadel settled with the SEC and received only remedial civil sanctions, being barred from association with a broker-dealer for five years. This scheme used classic Ponzi tools of promissory notes and pushing investors to roll-over their principal and interest rather than to withdraw the funds with the promised profits (SEC, 2008, Nadel).

- James B. Duncan, Hendrix Montecastro, and Maurice McLeod carried out a scheme that victimized "church members," "military personnel," and members of the "Filipino community," three affiliations (SEC, 2008, February 26). McLeod had previous convictions. Montecastro held a real estate license at the time of the scheme. Duncan was associated with several companies in several states. The three used word of mouth to attract potential investors who were told they would be investing in "real-estate, business assets and accounts receivable" (SEC, 2008, February 26). The scheme pooled investors' funds, using the funds to pay previous investors and themselves. Duncan received a criminal sentence of 41 months; McLeod and Montecastro were only charged civilly.

- Tony Pough, Joseph Brunson, and Timothy McQueen called themselves the Three Hebrew Boys; it is a reference to Chapter 3 in the book of Daniel in the Christian Bible. In this verse, three men are thrown into a fire for refusing to worship the king's image. In this Ponzi case, military personnel were targeted in a scheme that was marketed as a religious debt elimination program. The three also filed documents "accusing the U.S. Attorney of treason and committing acts of war by prosecuting them" (FBI, 2009, November 20).

Faith-based fraud has a wide-ranging area of frauds, commonly embezzlement, but also other types of fraud. It seems plausible that there might be more faith-based frauds in the areas of the country that are deemed to be more religious. Faith-based fraud is a challenge to research because not all incidences are reported to authorities. Second, churches are not required to file an annual report;[1] there is no way of knowing how many incidents are handled quietly within a religious organization rather than reported to authorities.

The Bible Belt is an area of the United States considered to hold strong Christian religious beliefs. The term refers to the states of Alabama, Arkansas, Georgia, Kentucky, Louisiana, Mississippi, North Carolina, Oklahoma, South Carolina, Tennessee, Texas, and Utah. This study looked at the possibility that there may be more faith-based Ponzi schemes found in the Bible Belt states; it was found that there were not a larger percentage of faith-based Ponzi schemes in the Bible Belt states. The states of Georgia, Louisiana, Mississippi, North Carolina, Oklahoma, South Carolina, Tennessee, Texas, and Utah had a total of 25 faith-based frauds out of a total 91 faith-based frauds; less than a third. The states with the highest incidence of faith-based Ponzi schemes were California with 17, followed by New York, Texas and Utah,[2] each with six faith-based Ponzi schemes, and Illinois with five faith-based Ponzi schemes. In short, there was not a higher incidence of faith-based Ponzi schemes in the Bible Belt states than in other states. It might be expected that Utah[3] would have more faith-based schemes but the federal agency documents would need to have stated specific terms such as "Christians," "Latter-Day-Saints," or "Mormons" to be considered faith-based; that was not stated in all of the Utah Ponzi schemes; the assumption cannot be made that the schemes were faith-based.

Cryptocurrency Ponzi Schemes

The Cryptocurrency market suddenly exploded in 2017 and has continued to grow. This is considered a type of Ponzi scheme because many financial industry leaders and many government officials consider cryptocurrencies in general to be Ponzi schemes. Cryptocurrency, cybercurrency, digital-currency, digital-assets, virtual-currency, electronic-currency, and bitcoins are all names for currencies that do not physically exist as a fiat currency, minted by a government. Internet-based currencies enable a new financial transaction mechanism making Ponzi schemes possible, solely existing through internet technology. Currency is defined as monetary units minted and recognized by a government for legal tender. Cryptocurrencies are not minted or recognized by any nation as valid for legal tender; they have no physical existence or nation backing their value as fiat currency. Internet cryptocurrencies have been considered digital Ponzi schemes by World Bank group President Jim Yong Kim (Hagan, 2018). There were four cryptocurrency cases that were charged or tried as Ponzi schemes:

- The SEC took action on the first case of this kind in July of 2013; the Department of Justice filed criminal charges in November of 2014 against Trendon Shavers. Shavers' company: *Bitcoin Savings and Trust* promised investors 7 percent per month, and was an intentional Ponzi scheme; there were no investments. Shavers was sentenced to 18 months in 2016; his total Ponzi scheme take was less than $800,000, one of the lowest amounts taken in a federally convicted Ponzi scheme (DOJ, 2016, July 21).
- Dean Dillon's scheme told investor-victims that their bitcoin funds would be pooled to invest in binary options in an online exchange.

Dillon never registered with the CFTC as a pool operator. This scheme was pure Ponzi from the inception; there were no binary option investments, just Ponzi payments (CFTC, 2018, January 19, p.r.).

- Homero Garza started out with business entities that sold bitcoin mining hardware, offered a cryptocurrency, and offered shares in cryptocurrency/virtual currency mining operations. Garza was selling cryptocurrency mining operations by way of investment contracts. The contracts were called "Hashlets." Garza sold many more of these contracts than his computer systems could hold. His scheme and sales tactics used technological jargon that would pique the interest of those trying to get in on the newest technological trend (SEC, 2015, September 1).

- Nicholas Gelfman's scheme made use of both cryptocurrency in pooled funds and the alleged use of algorithms. Gelfman called this strategy "Jigsaw." It seems that it was all an intentional scheme from the onset, that what little investing may have taken place produced failures, no profits (CFTC, 2017, September 21).

Bitcoins emerged in approximately 2009, as a reaction to global economies that were in trouble, in countries where the people were afraid of bank collapses. This is a form of trading cryptocurrency or digital-currency, sometimes referred to as digital assets. There is a supplier who offers the cryptocurrency at a price with a limited supply, only online, not through a legitimate investment or currency exchange; no government entity has monitoring capacity. There are easily thousands of buyers waiting; it is an artificial market that drives cryptocurrency prices up. The cryptocurrency investment opportunities are posted online. Investors can participate from anywhere in the world, making this a difficult crime to investigate and to enforce any one nation's laws.

Cryptocurrencies require no central authority such as a government or central bank to require a bank account or identification of ownership. For those who want absolute anonymity it is a preferred currency. Cryptocurrency is not fiat money that is not stored in a central location, such as a bank or thrift, that would enable authorities to monitor transactions, enabling perpetrators to avoid taxation, regulation, and law enforcement. It is documented through blockchain that is encrypted. The funds cannot be seized if they do not physically exist, or even exist on paper such as with a stock, certificate of deposit, or a bond (Goodman, 2015).

Several cases have been presented to the courts requiring judges to determine whether or not bitcoins or cryptocurrencies qualify as money under the law. In the earliest case, United States District Court Judge Jed Rakoff determined that bitcoins are defined as money, setting a precedent for charging crimes using bitcoins for monetary transactions (USA v. Faiella et al., 2014). United States District Judge Alison Nathan determined that "Bitcoins can be accepted as payment of goods and services or bought directly from an exchange with a bank account" (USA v. Murgio, 2016). In July of 2016, Miami-Dade Judge Teresa Pooler determined that bitcoins and virtual currency do not fall under the statutory definition of a "payment instrument" under federal tax law[4] (Florida v. Espinoza, 2016). In the most recent of these cases, a state-level judge held that bitcoins are not money by federal definition, whereas two previous federal judges determined that cryptocurrency is money. Cryptocurrencies must be considered money for charges to be brought. Legislation on this is a topic that is continually being considered by law makers in order to establish cryptocurrencies' legal definitions for legal actions (Nelson 2019).

The use of cryptocurrency is becoming more common as the world market place becomes more internet-based. The ability to move money around the world electronically without any government's ability to monitor it is a perfect breeding ground for Ponzi schemes and other frauds. The following two cases were internationally based using cryptocurrency. They are significant for their magnitude, in that they cover many nations with little ability for oversight because of the international nature of cryptocurrency usage and tracking. The laws are not universal on cryptocurrency. It is not known if there were American victims in the MMM scheme:

- *Mavrodi Mondial Moneybox/Movement,*[5] or *MMM*, is the largest known Ponzi scheme worldwide in history. This scheme moved from country to country through the internet. Once this scheme came to light in Nigeria, it moved on to Ghana as of January 2017. This scheme, begun in Russia in 1994, was founded by Sergey Mavrodi. This scheme branched out to Ukraine, India, Thailand, African countries, and Indonesia. *MMM* had several versions of the scheme, each titled by the year. This ability to move money around the world through the internet will prove a challenge for governments to keep up with fraud perpetrators, money launderers, and those who evade prosecution and paying taxes. This scheme collapsed with the sudden death of Sergey Mavrodi on March 26, 2018 (mmmglobal.world).
- *OneCoin* is stated to be both pyramid and Ponzi in the federal indictment of Konstantin Ignatov (USA v. Konstantin Ignatov, 2019). The mastermind of the *OneCoin* scheme was Konstantin's sister Ruja Ignatova who stepped away from running the entity in October 2017 (DOJ, 2019, March 8; U.S., 2019, March 6). This scheme began in Bulgaria in 2014. It was promoted in "Thailand, Singapore, Columbia, Argentina, Brazil, Paraguay, Bulgaria, France, and Spain" (USA, 2019, March 6). This case became the jurisdiction of the United States when Ignatov sold *OneCoin* and met with Americans

in Las Vegas, and the Southern District of New York, where the case has been investigated and prosecuted. The pyramid aspect of this scheme involves memberships of varying levels and commissions. Konstantin pleaded guilty in 2019; one co-conspirator was found guilty; and another is awaiting trial. Ruja is at large.

This section has described the types of schemes considered to be intentional in nature. The perpetrators designed the fraud knowingly and intentionally. The following section describes those schemes that are deemed to have occurred out of broker- or business-failure: unintentional frauds.

Unintentional Frauds

Unintentional frauds are a type of fraud whereby a primary or a partnership is running a business or brokerage successfully, who then experiences some financial difficulty causing them to resort to fraud as a means of survival (Kranacher et al., 2011). Unintentional frauds are those schemes where an entity began as a legitimate business, with the intent of running a lawful business. At some point the business or brokerage failed, and the primaries turned to a Ponzi scheme in an effort to keep their business afloat. They believed they would eventually make a profit and pay their investors back. The business owners know they are breaking the law, lying to investors and falsifying documents. The category of unintentional does not diminish the culpability of the perpetrators just because they began legitimately; they all knew that fraud and Ponzi schemes are illegal. The businesses or brokerages were not formed with the intent of fraud, as in the intentional Ponzi schemes.

Brokerage-failure Ponzi Schemes

This type of Ponzi scheme evolved out of legitimate brokerages, dealers investment advisers, commodity pools, or a hedge funds that began to fail at some point, particularly with the financial crisis or earlier financial events. There were 74 brokerage-failure schemes. The broker may experience losses due to bad trades or a down market. It may be that they are not very good at trading. The primary makes the choice to "borrow" funds from new investors to satisfy the promised investment profits to earlier investors, and usually to keep the business afloat. They may have believed they would make a good trade and return the funds without anyone knowing of the losses. But the losses kept coming during the financial crisis, and once legitimate businesses then became Ponzi schemes. This is compared to other variations of Ponzi schemes that were conceived of as scams from the beginning; the perpetrators intended to break the law.

These once legitimate brokerage entities were working within the law and staying afloat prior to the financial decline. Unlike the intentional types of Ponzi schemes, these perpetrators would have been registered with the SEC, CFTC, FINRA, and state agencies, as licensed traders, brokers, hedge funds, or financial advisers and filed all of their forms on time. These legitimizing credentials are required by law at designated financial levels, and a matter of public record with the SEC, CFTC, FINRA, and state regulatory agencies. In brokerage-failure schemes, the perpetrators believed that they could recoup their losses with good trades, so they then borrowed from later investors to provide earnings for earlier investors.

When this study began, it was thought that as the 2007 financial crisis grew, many legitimate brokerages evolved into Ponzi schemes in a last-ditch effort to survive. Many of these legitimate brokerages that failed during the financial crisis may have been heavily invested in the home-mortgage market prior to the financial crisis (SEC, 2008, February 26). The Financial Crisis Inquiry Commission (FCIC) has determined the home-mortgage/subprime scandal was the primary cause of the financial crisis (FCIC, 2011). This would have caused those entities heavily invested with investments in mortgages and mortgage-backed derivatives to fail with the declining economy. They would not have been able to get their investments out soon enough to prevent losses.

The laws determining who is required to be registered and who is not required to be registered among federal and state agencies are publicly available.[6] There are reporting requirements for legitimate trading and investment adviser businesses. The shortfall is the Ponzi schemes that feign legitimate businesses aren't investing anyone's money, rendering them impossible to any form of monitoring by regulatory agencies, as they would with registered brokerages. Any individual carrying out financial investing actions with other people's money must be registered with the SEC or the CFTC and/or state regulatory agencies depending on the financial level. In many Ponzi schemes the perpetrators were not registered; this is stated in SEC and CFTC complaints. This determines which of the entities determined by federal regulatory and law enforcement to be Ponzi schemes were legitimately functioning investment businesses.

The Investment Advisers Act of 1940 states:

> Section 3(a) (4) (A) of the Act generally defines a "broker" broadly as "any person engaged in the business of effecting transactions in securities for the account of others."
>
> All "financial planners, money managers and investment consultants are regulated as 'investment advisers' in the United States under the United States Investment Advisers Act of 1940." As such, they are required to register with the SEC.
>
> (SEC)

The legal action documents within the SEC, CFTC, and sometimes the FBI and DOJ databases indicate what the entities have been charged with, and if they have been properly registered with the SEC or CFTC. The documents also indicate when the entity became a Ponzi scheme, as well as when federal authorities ended the scheme. The SEC, CFTC, and FBI designate a fraud "Ponzi" through the investigative process. The investigative process in the SEC and CFTC refers to a case that has been brought before the Commissioners and they have determined that the case warrants an official, formal investigation. These civil cases included in this study have received civil sanctions and administrative actions. Many of these cases are referred to the FBI or United States Attorney for criminal action. Some cases are initiated with the FBI, Internal Revenue Service (IRS), Secret Service, or United States Postal Inspectors. There is a presumption of innocence, understanding that the cases documented in federal agency files are those that enough evidence was found to determine a violation of the law, administratively and/or criminally. The following are examples of brokerage-failure schemes:

- A classic example of a brokerage-failure scheme is Carlin King of *Hanover Stevens*. King began *Hanover Stevens* in 2002 as retail foreign exchange brokerage in Atlanta, Georgia. His costs of doing business had become more than the profits. Also, investors began to pull their funds out. Without enough principal to make investments he could not make enough in profits to maintain the business. To meet his business expenses, he began a Ponzi scheme in 2006. When new clients were not found, the scheme collapsed; this is the pattern of most broker-failure schemes (FBI, 2009, July 17, p.r.).
- Angelo Alleca is also a classic example of a brokerage-failure. Alleca was a registered investment adviser. Alleca began his investment fund in 2004. By 2006 he started seeing losses and opened more funds to cover up the losses. He thought he could make profitable investments to repay other investors but as the financial crisis peaked, he could not recoup the losses (SEC, 2012, September 18).

Business-Failures

This classification covers Ponzi schemes that developed out of legitimate businesses that failed; there were 54. In business-failure schemes the perpetrator made an attempt at legitimate business; there were actual purchases of properties, or business activities that were other than financial market enterprises. These businesses functioned profitably at some point prior to turning into a Ponzi scheme. Most of these schemes took place during the bubble and financial crisis. Many were based in real estate and mortgages. These are a few examples of business-failure scheme cases:

- Jonathan Papa owned several restaurants. He asked investors to invest in *Papa Holdings*, his business entity, in support of his restaurants. His restaurants failed, turning the investment into a Ponzi scheme. This scheme took place from 1995 until 1999. Papa offered unregistered stocks of his four restaurants. It was originally a legitimate, functioning business that failed, turning it into a fraudulent scheme (SEC, 2006, November 30, l.r.).

- Brent Newbold had a company that sold environmentally safe cleaning products to retail businesses such as Walmart and Ace Hardware. His business owed more than it was bringing in and turned into a Ponzi scheme, eventually filing for bankruptcy. This scheme took place from at least 2008, through 2010 (DOJ, 2016, January 21, p.r.).

- Michael Morawski and his partner, John Constant, had a business in apartments and multi-family dwellings in several states. There were properties purchased but these properties did not bring in the promised revenues; therefore Morawski and Constant could not pay the interest and resorted to a Ponzi scheme. In this case, there were actual properties purchased; in many schemes, the perpetrators only said they had purchased real estate properties (FBI, 2011, March 6, p.r.).

- Michael Turnock had a business that paid insurance premiums for businesses. Investors contributed funds that were to be used to pay the insurance premiums for businesses. These businesses then paid Turnock the fees for the premiums, with the interest. The interest was to be paid to the investors. After two years, this business was not making a profit, so Turnock resorted to Ponzi payments. This scheme took place between 1996 and 2012 (DOJ, 2013, July 9, p.r.).

- Marc Dreier had been a successful lawyer who had made partner at several law firms before beginning his own law firm in 1996 (USA v. Marc Dreier, 2009, s.m.). Dreier borrowed money to start his law firm. He expanded the firm to more than 250 attorneys with several offices around the nation (Simon, 2011). As the law firm grew, he borrowed more money to fund the operations and to pay the interest on the debts. When he could no longer borrow money, he developed his Ponzi scheme based on fake promissory notes (Simon, 2011; U.S. v. Dreier, 2009, s.m.). The debts and interest were being paid with money received through the promissory notes (SEC, 2008, December 8). His scheme primarily preyed on hedge funds and corporations, with a few individual victims. Dreier also overspent in his personal life on fine art work, mansions, and yachts. He was too far in debt and could not repay the debt (Simon, 2011).

The following subcategories may have been functioning legitimately, falling in the unintentional fraud category, or they may have been the bases for, or part of, an intentional scheme.

Feeder Funds

Ponzi schemes frequently attract other investment entities such as hedge funds in the securities market, and pools in the futures and options market. These entities are sometimes referred to as funds of funds or feeder funds. There were 27 schemes that were feeder funds to other Ponzi schemes. The nature of these financial entities is quite complex, making it difficult for investors and authorities to monitor. These entities are funds that have their own clientele. Frequently they are hedge funds. Those included in the data set were charged either civilly through the SEC and/or criminally through the Department of Justice separately from the main Ponzi scheme.

Those who contribute to feeder funds may not have known where their funds were being invested, as in the case of Stephen Greenspan who invested with a fund-of funds, that then invested with Bernie Madoff (Greenspan, 2009, January 3). Greenspan did not know who Madoff was or that his money had been invested with BMIS. Greenspan wrote the book *The annals of gullibility: Why we get duped and how to avoid it* (2009). His book went to press just before Madoff's scheme was exposed; he did not know he was a victim at the time. In some cases, the primary business owner in some feeder funds were not charged civilly or criminally because they did not know that what they were investing in was a Ponzi scheme. They were victims, not co-conspirators. The following are examples of feeder funds:

- Nikolai Battoo lost his investor's money by investing in feeder funds to Madoff. Battoo was the manager of, or senior adviser for, several hedge funds. This means that hedge funds worked with him to make their portfolio investments. Battoo had to have a good performance record and must have been considered a sophisticated investment manager to achieve that status. One of his clients was a major international bank (unnamed); this bank terminated his services in 2008. This was a big client. At the same time Battoo was heavily invested with Madoff. As the financial crisis increased his hedge funds accounts diminished. A sophisticated investor, such as Battoo, had a fiscal responsibility to know that Madoff was a Ponzi scheme. It may be that Battoo hedged his bets and thought these investments would somehow improve. Regardless, with the admission of guilt by Bernard Madoff and the decline of the stock market, Battoo's fund failed (SEC, 2012, September 6).
- Another classic feeder fund case is David McQueen et al. In this case, the perpetrators were insurance salesmen who became involved in Jim Clements' scheme, without knowing it was a Ponzi scheme, originally. Clements' scheme told investors they were investing in foreign currencies (SEC, 2011, March 30, l.r.). Clements' scheme used certain

investors as account managers who then recruited other investors. McQueen was one such account manager who went on to form a second Ponzi scheme feeding into Clements' scheme. McQueen was making 10 percent in Clements' Ponzi scheme; he then involved others, promising them 5–6 percent, meaning he was making 4–5 percent off of those investor-victims he brought in to his feeder fund (DOJ, 2014, December 3, p.r.; SEC, 2011, March 30, l.r.).

Hedge Funds and Commodity Pools

Hedge funds and commodity pools are legal joint investment entities when properly registered with the SEC or CFTC, as required by law. These funds, or pools, allow for investor's funds to be jointly invested in a fund that distributes losses and gains to all fund members according to their contribution percentage to the fund. Hedge fund involvement in Ponzi scheme is complex; they may be the perpetrators of the frauds, or the victims of the frauds; in many cases they were the feeder funds to the frauds that may or may not have been willing participants. They may have been entities that only said they were hedge funds as a mechanism to bring in funds. There were 29 schemes that were indicated to be hedge funds.

In some cases, the feeder funds were legitimate hedge funds that were duped by someone they believed to be credible. Some were legitimate hedge funds that knowingly were involved in fraudulent activities. In other cases, the hedge fund itself was not a legitimate business entity but presented itself as such. Hedge funds are particularly vulnerable to the market because they often invest in higher-risk investments. Also, there are new start-up hedge funds that begin, then do poorly because they cannot bring in or maintain enough working capital (Johnson, 2010). If a hedge fund cannot bring in sizable returns for sophisticated clients, they lose the client. Hedge funds are private investment groups that generally require at least 65 percent of the investors to be accredited. An accredited investor is one who has at least $1,000,000 in assets and has an income of at least $200,000 per year. Generally, there is a minimum investment requirement of at least $250,000; the minimum amount varies by fund. Hedge funds trade in many markets including FOREX, stocks, bonds, and commodities. These funds move billions of dollars in and out of investments very quickly and can dramatically influence trading volume.

When there was no legal responsibility for hedge funds to register with the SEC, there was no reason for the SEC to monitor their activities, making them the perfect partner in Ponzi schemes. As of December 2, 2004, hedge fund managers are now required to register with the SEC as investment advisers (Downes and Goodman, 2014). The previous lack of regulation allowed some entities to legally thrive without the knowledge of the SEC.

Madoff's scheme had many feeder funds that were contributing to the greater pool of Madoff's fraudulent investment arm. After Madoff's conviction, some of the managers of these feeder funds were also convicted of participating in securities fraud, many of whom received prison sentences. Some funds were victims. It is not known how many feeder funds were considered victims and how many were accomplices.

Some hedge funds that have been caught in up in larger Ponzi schemes claim they did not know the entity they were investing in was fraudulent. However, anyone involved in the financial industry understands that guaranteed profits, especially guaranteed high profits, are a sign of something illegitimate. Anyone running a hedge fund has a fiduciary responsibility to carry out due diligence and to recognize a fraudulent investment scheme. There is also a legal expectation of performing due diligence for those who are registered brokers, dealers, or advisers. No one can guarantee a profit in investing and surely no legitimate entity can promise or deliver consistent, high-profit returns on an investment. In other words, they knew, or they should have known, something illegitimate was in play but they claimed innocence while their profits continued. No feeder fund, hedge fund, or investor files a complaint with the SEC or CFTC while they are receiving consistent profits from an entity they have invested with; they cry foul only when they lose money.

In the commodities markets, there are commodity pools: "A cooperative effort in which funds contributed by a number of people are combined in order to trade commodity futures or options contracts" (Etzel, 2003). Commodity pools function in the same manner as hedge funds, in that participants share in the profits and losses of the investments made by a pool operator. There were 56 schemes that claimed to be commodity pools. Commodity pools differ from a hedge fund in that they do not require investors to be accredited. Commodity pools are regulated under the Commodities Exchange Act 7 USC §1A, 5, definition:

Commodity Pool Operator

The term "commodity pool operator" means any person engaged in a business that is of the nature of an investment trust, syndicate, or similar form of enterprise, and who, in connection therewith, solicits, accepts, or receives from others, funds, securities, or property, either directly or through capital contributions, the sale of stock or other forms of securities, or otherwise, for the purpose of trading in any commodity for future delivery on or subject to the rules of any contract market or derivatives transaction execution facility, except that the term does not include such persons not within the intent of the definition of the term as the Commission may specify by rule, regulation, or order.

(CFTC, CEA)

Commodity pools are regulated by the CFTC. Pools are collected funds of several investors used to invest as a whole. With each case, it is a matter of determining whether or not the primary was registered with the CFTC as a legitimate investment business according to the law. As with securities fraud cases, in many cases the primary only stated that the entity was registered, providing very convincing falsified documents, when the entity was not registered.

- Such a case is Michael Gale and the *Capital Management Group*. Gale ran a commodity pool and did indeed invest in commodities under accounts in his wife's name. However, he was not registered with the CFTC; not being properly registered is a violation. When he experienced losses, he began a Ponzi scheme (CFTC, 2013, July 25). This qualifies as a false-brokerage scheme.
- Chetan Kapur began his first hedge fund, *Think Strategy*, as an investment adviser, in 2002. After one year, he established a second hedge fund: *Capital Fund*. Kapur established a third fund to contribute to the first two hedge funds in 2004: *Multi-Strategy Fund*. His companies were a feeder fund to two other Ponzi schemes (SEC, 2011, November 10). He contributed to the Ponzi schemes *Valhalla*, run by Arthur Nadel (FBI, 2010, February 24, p.r.), and *Bayou Superfund*, run by Samuel Israel III and Daniel Marino (SEC, 2005, September 25, l.r.). Kapur had a responsibility to register his hedge funds with the SEC and to perform due diligence on the entities he was investing in.

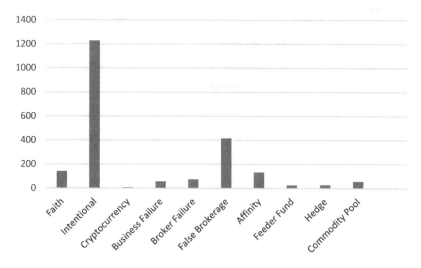

Figure 2.4 Ponzi Typologies.

In Figure 2.4 we see a comparison of the types of Ponzi schemes. The great majority were intentional Ponzi schemes, 1,225. Second to that was the false-brokerages, 415. This illustration demonstrates that approximately of one-third of the intentional Ponzi schemes were false-brokerages. Hedge funds and commodity pools combined were 85 schemes. The unintentional schemes – business-failures and brokerage-failures combined – were 128 schemes.

Conclusion

To conclude up this chapter, there are intentional Ponzi schemes, which can be any manner and means. They may have presented themselves as a legitimate brokerage, investment adviser, or legitimate business. The key characteristic is the scheme was intended as a fraud from the very beginning. This type includes affinity-frauds that prey those with similar identities. There are unintentional schemes that begin intending to run a legitimate enterprise that then failed and turned into a Ponzi scheme. Hedge funds and pools may be intentional or unintentional schemes. There are feeder funds that may have been involved in fraud with full knowledge or who may have been an unwitting victim of the fraud likewise with hedge funds. Cryptocurrency cases are considered intentional frauds, because the alleged monetary unit does not physically exist as fiat currency. Currently different countries around the world have varying laws that are ever changing (The Law Library of Congress, 2018).

Notes

1 From the IRS: Generally, tax-exempt organizations must file an annual information return (Form 990 (PDF) or Form 990-EZ (PDF)). Most small tax-exempt organizations whose annual gross receipts are normally $50,000 or less can satisfy their annual reporting requirement by electronically submitting Form 990-N if they choose not to file Form 990 or Form 990-EZ. Churches, some church-affiliated organizations and certain other types of organizations are excepted from filing. Retrieved from: https://www.irs.gov/charities-non-profits/churches-religious-organizations/filing-requirements

2 Utah had 48 Ponzi schemes; however, only six specified affinity-fraud or religious affiliation in federal documents.

3 The State of Utah has identified itself as having a problem with fraud and specifically affinity-fraud (Reyes, 2019).

4 While this case was not a Ponzi scheme, it is interesting to note that the investigating agent's name is Gregory Ponzi.

5 Originally titled: Mavrodi, Mondial, Melnikova after its originators. Now it can be referred to as Moneybox or Movement in the last word.

6 See: https://www.sec.gov/reportspubs/investor-publications/divisions-marketregbdguidehtm.html and https://www.cftc.gov/IndustryOversight/Intermediaries/registration

References

Chilton, B. Commissioner, Commodities Futures and Trading Commission. (2011). *Ponzimonium*. Washington, DC, U.S. Government Printing Office.

Commodities Futures Trading Commission v. Michael Gale (2012, July 25) Complaint.

Commodities Futures Trading Commission v. Eric N. Schmickle and Q Wealth Management Inc. (2012, September 24) Complaint.

Commodities Futures Trading Commission v. Claudio Aliaga et al. (2012, September 26) Consent order.

Commodities Futures Trading Commission v. Dillon Michael Dean and The Entrepreneurs Headquarters Limited (2018, January 18) Complaint.

Commodities Futures Trading Commission Charges Colorado resident Dillon Michael Dean and his company, The Entrepreneurs Headquarters Limited, with engaging in a bitcoin and binary options fraud scheme. (2018, January 19). Press release.

Commodities Futures Trading Commission v. Gelfman Blueprint Inc., and Nicholas Gelfman (2017, September 21) Complaint.

Department of Justice, (2014, December 3). Byron Center man sentenced to 30 years for Ponzi scheme. (David McQueen). Press release.

Department of Justice, (2016, January 21). Byron Center Man, David W. McQueen's, conviction and 30 year sentence for Ponzi scheme upheld on appeal. Press release.

Department of Justice, (2013, June 27). Former bishop of Trumbull Church sentenced to 46 months in prison for investment fraud scheme. (Julius Blackwelder). Press release.

Department of Justice, (2016, July 21). Texas man sentenced for operating bitcoin Ponzi scheme. (Shavers). Press release.

Department of Justice, (2013, July 9). Denver business owner is sentenced to 77 months in prison a part of a Ponzi scheme. (Turnock). Press release.

Department of Justice, (2016, January 21). Granite Bay man sentenced for defrauding investors in a "green" cleaning product company. (Newbold). Press release.

Department of Justice, (2019, March 8). Manhattan U.S. Attorney announces charges against leaders of OneCoin: A multibillion-dollar pyramid scheme involving the sale of a fraudulent cryptocurrency. (Ignatov). Press release.

Downes, J. & Goodman, J. (Eds.). (2014). *Dictionary of finance and investment terms*. Hauppauge NY, Barron's Educational Series.

Etzel, B. (2003). *Webster's new World finance and investment dictionary*. Indianapolis, IN, Wiley Publishing.

Federal Bureau of Investigation, (2009, July 17). Head of Atlanta-based foreign exchange brokerage firm sentenced to prison for defrauding investors. (Carlin King). Press release.

Federal Bureau of Investigation v. Tony Pough, Joseph Brunson and Timothy McQueen Three Hebrew boys. (2009, November 20). Press release.

Federal Bureau of Investigation, (2010, February 24). Former hedge fund manager Arthur G. Nadel pleads guilty in Manhattan federal court to massive Ponzi scheme. Press release.

Federal Bureau of Investigation, (2011, March 6). Two suburban men allegedly obtained $16 million from 300 investors in fraudulent real estate investment scheme. (Morawski). Press release.

Financial Crisis Inquiry Commission. (FCIC), (2011). *The Financial Crisis Inquiry Report; Final Report of the National Commission on the Causes of the Financial and Economic Crisis in the United States.* Washington D.C., Government Printing Office.

Florida v. Espinoza, Michel (2016) Circuit Court F14-2923.

Frankel, T. (2012). *The Ponzi scheme puzzle. A history and analysis of con artists and victims.* New York, NY, Oxford University Press.

Frasca, C. (1931). *Stock swindlers and their methods.* New York, NY. Charles Frasca Publisher.

Goodman, M. (2015). *Future crimes.* New York, NY, DoubleDay/Random House.

Greenspan, S. (2009). *The annals of gullibility:* Why we get duped and how to avoid it. Westport, CT, Praeger Publishers.

Greenspan, S. (2009, January 3). Essay: Why we keep falling for financial scams. *Wall Street Journal.*

Hagan, S. (2018, February 7). Cryptocurrencies are like Ponzi schemes, World Bank Chief says. *Bloomberg.*

Johnson, B. (2010). *The hedge fund fraud case book.* Hoboken, NJ, John Wiley and Sons.

Kranacher, M., Riley Jr. R., and Wells, J. (2011). *Forensic accounting and fraud examination.* Hoboken, NJ, John Wiley and Sons Inc.

Law Library of Congress, Global Legal Research Center. (2018). Regulation of cryptocurrency around the world.

Lewis, M. (2015). *Understanding Ponzi schemes, Can better financial regulation prevent investors from being defrauded?* Cheltenham UK, Edward Elgar Publishing.

Markopolos, H. and Fisher, D. (2010). *No one would listen: A true financial thriller.* Hoboken, NJ, John Wiley and Sons.

Nelson, R. (2019). *Examining regulatory frameworks for digital currencies.* Before the Committee on Banking, Housing, and Urban Affairs. Washington, DC, Congressional Research Service.

Perri, F. and Brody, R. (2012). The optics of fraud: Affiliations that enhance offender credibility. *Journal of Financial Crime,* Vol.19 No. 4 pp. 355–370.

Reyes, S. (2019). Is Utah the fraud capital of the world? Retrieved from: https://attorneygeneral.utah.gov/utah-fraud-capital/

Securities and Exchange Commission, (2005, September 25). SEC charges Samuel Israel III, Daniel E. Marino, Bayou Management, and Bayou funds for defrauding hedge fund investors and misappropriating investor assets. Litigation release.

Securities and Exchange Commission, (2006, November 30). Jonathan C. Papa sentenced to three years imprisonment for running a multi-million dollar Ponzi scheme. Litigation release.

Securities and Exchange Commission v. Universo Foneclub Corporation, Sanderley R. De VasConcelos, aka Sann Rodrigues, aka Sanderly Vasconcelos Rev. victor Sales aka Victor William (2006, May 30) Complaint.

Securities and Exchange Commission v. Renaissance Asset Fund Inc., Ronald J. Nadel, and Joseph M. Malone (2006, July 17) Complaint.

Securities and Exchange Commission, (2008, January 10). In the matter of Ronald Nadel. Administrative Proceeding No. 3-12927.

Securities and Exchange Commission v. James Duncan, Hendrix M. Montecastro, Maurice E. McLeod, Pacific Wealth Management LLC., Stonewood Consulting Inc., and Total Return Fund LLC (2008, February 26) Complaint.

Securities and Exchange Commission v. Marc s. Dreier (2008, December 8) Complaint.

Securities and Exchange Commission v. Regan & Company and Michael C. Regan (2009, June 24) Complaint.

Securities and Exchange Commission v. Trevor G. Cook and Patrick J. Kiley (2009, November 23) Complaint.

Securities and Exchange Commission v. James Clements and Zeina Smidi (2011, March 30) (also McQueen). Litigation release.

Securities and Exchange Commission v. Chetan Kapur; Lilaboc, LLC d/b/a ThinkStrategy Capital Management, LLC (2011, November 10) Complaint.

Securities and Exchange Commission v. Nikolai Battoo (2012, September 6) Complaint.

Securities and Exchange Commission v. Angelo Alleca et al. (2012, September 18) Complaint.

Securities and Exchange Commission v. Tropikgadget FZE, Tropikgadget Unipessoal LDA, Sergio Henrique Tanaka, Carlos Luis Da Silveira Barbosa, Claudio De Oliveira Pereira Campos, Vinicius Romolo Aguiar, Wesley Brandao Rodrigues, Andrew Elliot Arrambide, Julio G. Cruz, dennis Arthur Somaio, Elaine Amaral Somaio, Pablo Andres Garcia, Viviane Amaral Rodrigues, Simonia De Cassia Silva, Geovani Nascimento Bento, Pricila Bento (2015, February 25) Complaint.

Securities and Exchange Commission v. eAdGear Holdings Limited, Charles S. Wang, Francis Y. Yuen, and Qian Cathy Zhang (2014, September 24) Complaint.

Securities and Exchange Commission v. Homero Joshua Garza, Gaw Miners, LLC, and Zenminer LLC (d.b.a Zen Cloud) (2015, September 1) Complaint.

Securities and Exchange S v. DFRF Enterprises LLC, Daniel Fernandez Rojo Filho, Wanderly M. Dalman, Gaspar D. Jesus, Eduardo N. Da Silva, Heriberto C. Perez Valdes, Jeffrey Feldman and Romildo Da Cunha (2015, July 30) Complaint.

Securities and Exchange Commission v. eAdGear Inc., et al. (2016, February 1) Litigation release.

Securities and Exchange Commission v. Tropikgadget (2017, February 28) Litigation release.

Securities and Exchange Commission, (2019, August 20). SEC charges ICO Research and Rating provider with failing to disclose it was paid to tout digital assets. Press release.

Simon, M. (2011). *Unraveled: An ambitious man, an immoral plan.* (DVD, Dreier). Retrieved from: www.grandentertainmentgroup.com

United States Department of Justice, (2014, May 9). Byron Center man guilty of $46,000,000 investment fraud. (David McQueen). Press release.

United States Investment Advisers Act of 1940.

United States v. Anthony R. Murgio 209 F. Supp. 698, 707–08 (S.D.N.Y. 2016).

United States v. Bernard L. Madoff (2009, March 12) Guilty plea proceedings. 09 cr 213 (DC).

United States v. Bernard L. Madoff (2009, June 29) Sentencing proceedings. 09 cr 213 (DC).

United States v. Konstantin Ignatov (2019, March 6) Indictment.

United States v. Marc Dreier (2009, July 8) Government's sentencing memorandum.

United States v. Marc Dreier (2009, July 8) Marc Dreier's memorandum in aid of sentencing.

United States v. Robert M. Faiella et al. 39F. Supp.3d 544, 545–47 (S.D.N.Y. 2014).

Winters, S. (2012). The law of Ponzi payouts. *Michigan Law Review* Vol.111 No. 1 pp. 119–144. University of Michigan Law School.

Chapter 3

The Tools of Carrying Out
the Ponzi Schemes

This chapter discusses the mechanics of the Ponzi schemes, the tools by which the perpetrators carry out the frauds. The basic tools are what is used to carry out the frauds, such as fraudulent documents, fraudulent credentials, aliases, exclusiveness, and shell companies. Chapter 4 will discuss the manner and means of the schemes: what the perpetrators told their victims they were investing in. Some tools, such as fraudulent documents, were used in all Ponzi schemes, whereas offshore accounts and aliases were used in only some schemes.

Contact

The are several methods used by perpetrators to find their investor-victims. The initial point of contact could be someone the investor-victim already is acquainted with, or a stranger. Generally, in many schemes the first investor-victims are family and friends. When it is a family that is committing the Ponzi scheme, the initial victims may be other than family members and friends. The perpetrators may use television or radio programs, particularly those that are faith-based, or language-based in the case of nationality-based Ponzi schemes. As social media has become a part of our everyday lives, there are now YouTube promotions, webinars, phone apps, other social media; websites are now standard in most Ponzi schemes and business entities. Word of mouth is probably the most common means of promoting a Ponzi scheme: early investors – yet to be victims – tell their friends and relatives about the investment opportunity. Sometimes the initial contact was made through a professional relationship such as an insurance agent, a mortgage broker, a CPA, or an attorney. Many perpetrators held seminar events at hotels. Business entities can purchase calling lists for cold calling; frequently these lists are the elderly. The use of internet technology and online social networks is becoming a common means of contacting new and younger victims. Older investor-victims are more likely to go to seminars held at hotels. The schemes that were also pyramid schemes primarily found victims through online social networks. The following recent scheme is one of the largest to date, having made use of most contact mechanisms:

- One of the more recent and significant schemes, Robert Shapiro of *Woodbridge*, had many sales agents. They used television promotions, radio advertising, advertisements in newspapers, social media, hosted seminar events, and carried out cold calling (SEC, 2017, December 20).

The schemes based on faith made use of churches, synagogues, temples, and faith-based radio and television to find their investor-victims. The following scheme was promoted at churches:

- Thomas L. Kimmel promoted his scheme through conferences held at churches using biblical terminology and principles to convince the church members to invest in his *Sure Line Acceptance Corporation* (IRS, 2015).

Aliases

In many cases the perpetrators used aliases. They may have used several aliases to carry out several schemes at the same time or serially, one after another. In some instances, the aliases are a variation on the original name such as: Gerald Rogers or Jay Rodgers, or Stefan A. Wilson and Stephan K. Wilson. In other cases, the aliases may be completely different names. They may have had a previous conviction, or securities sanction, and therefore use a different name in a later fraud. In some cases, such as Gerald Leo Rogers and Scott Klion, there were several aliases.

- Scott Klion also operated under the names of David Tanner and James Tucker, conducting three separate Ponzi schemes, with three sets of co-conspirators and three sets of victims. Two of the schemes were going on at the same time; the third had taken place six years earlier. Klion did not receive a federal criminal conviction in any of these cases, civil sanctions only (SEC, 2006, September 14).
- In the *New Century Coal* Ponzi scheme, three of ten perpetrators used aliases. The primary, Robert Rose, used John Hankins; Robert McGregor used Jim Robinson III; Ray Spears used Brock Hamilton (USA v. Brian C. Rose et al., 2014, June 10). This scheme was based on coal mines (FBI, 2016, December 12, p.r.; FBI, 2017, January 24, p.r.).
- Gerald Leo Rogers also went by the names Jay Rogers, Jay Rodgers, Jay Kellum, Jerald Rogers Kingston, Gerald Lee Rogers, and Roger Charles Gilliam. Rogers had two previous securities felony convictions and multiple securities sanctions, before his 2004–2005 Ponzi

scheme, one of which he had served a 25-year sentence. Rogers started three companies within months after his release from prison. These companies were incorporated in Nevada and Wyoming, as well as an offshore entity said to be the parent company. It is as if his time spent in prison on the first conviction was used to plan his next fraud scheme. His conviction in this scheme got him a ten years' sentence; his partner received only civil sanctions (SEC, 2005, March 2).

- One perpetrator was never criminally tried because he could not be found. Jeff Teitelbaum, also known as Mike Picozzi, Kevi Polardi, Ed Perente, and Frank Blasetti, could not be found to be arrested and tried. The charges were dismissed in 2016 since it had been seven years since the initial indictment. His three co-conspirators all pleaded guilty and received sentences (USA v. Teitelbaum, 2016, September 6).
- Jerry Mckerac also went by three other names: Gerald F. Czewinski, Jerry J. McKormick, and Gerald J. McKerak. He also had two different residences in two states (USA v. Mckerac, 2013, March 14).

Falsified Credentials

False credentials are rampant in most fraud schemes in general. This may include using an SEC, a CFTC, or an FDIC logo on the entities' website to make it appear as if the entity were registered with the SEC or CFTC. It may mean the perpetrator presents themselves as having education and college degrees that they do not actually have. They may present themselves as being an attorney or CPA when they are not. Some name-drop the names of stars or business entities they have never met.

In most of the false-brokerage schemes the perpetrator presented themselves as a broker, a trader, or an investment adviser. In some cases, they may have taken the appropriate series exams through FINRA, but they were not properly registered to do business as required by the SEC or CFTC. In other cases the perpetrators stated to clients that they were appropriately licensed. However, the perpetrators had not taken or passed the series licensing exam enabling them to register and establishing the appropriate credentials for managing clients' funds. For this reason, the SEC, CFTC, and FINRA broker-check and the NFA have sites where consumer-investors can check if someone they want to do business with is properly registered, licensed, and in good standing. These agencies also explain in plain, understandable language what investors can and should expect from a legitimate investing company. This information is also provided in many languages (see Chapter 13).

The false representation of being properly registered with the SEC or CFTC is quite common in Ponzi schemes. Some perpetrators may have been registered at some point prior to their scheme but were not registered at the time of the scheme. A great many perpetrators claimed to have many years of experience in trading, falsely. Such classic example is the case of David L. Ortiz:

- Ortiz claimed to be both registered with the SEC and having 30 years' experience, both of which were false. He was never registered with the SEC or CFTC, nor were any of his companies registered, as he falsely represented to his clients (CFTC, 2011, February 28, p.r.; CFTC, February 23).

There were individuals in other professions that also represented themselves as being appropriately licensed for business. Some of these businesses were false banks. Others stated that they were mortgage processers or real estate brokers, but they did not have the appropriate licensing to carry out the stated business. It is also thought that some perpetrators acquired the licensing such as real estate, insurance agent, or broker's license just to perpetrate the fraud. Some simply misrepresent that they have education that has not been attained, and more commonly, that they have passed the appropriate exams through FINRA.

- Khemraj Hardat fraudulently represented himself as having a PhD. He also told investor-victims that he was acquainted with Michael Dell of Dell computers, and NBA players Shaquille O'Neal and Stephen Curry. Hardat told investor-victims that "Pepsico and Dr. Pepper Snapple owed him more than $100 million," all of which was untrue (DOJ, 2019, August 12, p.r.).
- Brian Sapp adapted the identity of someone else. He presented himself as the owner of a construction company, then produced fraudulent contracts with that business entity. Sapp was charged with fraud and identity theft (DOJ, 2018, December 4, p.r.).

Unrealistic Interest Promises

It is customary for Ponzi perpetrators to promise guaranteed interest revenues as well as high interest rates, in most cases far beyond any realistic value. Often times the term High Yield Investment Program (HYIP) is used to describe the schemes. There is generally a promise of no-risk, or a failure to honestly report the risks involved. Honest reporting is a fiduciary requirement for brokers, dealers, and investment advisers. One reason Madoff's scheme was successful was because he promised what was considered a low interest rate, about 1 percent per month, up to 13.5 percent annually. This amount was believable to his investors, considered conservative for most investors. However, any amount that is guaranteed is not credible. No legitimate broker or investment adviser can ever guarantee any profits; the market is too unpredictable. A guarantee of profits is a red flag for investors, as is a guarantee of high rates of interest. Realistically, if a business entity was capable of generating 1,000 percent profit or more, it would not need the funds of investors. The following schemes promised exorbitant returns:

- John Scott Clark promised investors in writing that they would receive 3,000 percent in returns, annually. Clark's investor-victims were told the investment was low risk, and that an individual LLC would be established in their names. The scheme revolved around payday loans that were nonexistent (SEC, 2011, March 25).
- Blake Prater promised his victims 1,000 percent annually in his internet-based Ponzi scheme. Prater's scheme victimized more than 20,000 victims through a series of related websites. Prater was also a recidivist with prior convictions for forgery and fraud (SEC, 2003, September 10, l.r.). The scheme alleged to be investing in a portfolio of businesses; there were no businesses or investing.
- C. Edmund Burton and Ralph W. Odom promised a return of 2,600 percent annually, also promising that there was no risk to the investor's capital. This was a prime-banking scheme; investor-victims were told that this was a bank-to-bank trading entity that supported humanitarian activities (SEC, 2002, April 22, l.r.).

Fraudulent Documents

Fraudulent documents are the rule in Ponzi schemes; all schemes make use of fraudulent documents. Just as the perpetrators are experts at oral deception, they are skilled at producing fraudulent documents and promotional literature. The perpetrators may send out account and financial statements that appear to be legitimate, individualized to each victim. The practice of falsifying financial statements is as old as financial statements. Charles Frasca discussed the unscrupulous accountants that would provide falsified certified financial statements in the 1920s and 1930s for stock swindlers (Frasca, 1931, p. 59). Then, as is the case now, many investor-victims did not, or do not, have the ability to recognize fraudulent statements or to check if the actual reported investments were made. It is common place for Ponzi schemes that represent themselves as brokerages to send out monthly statements with false trading information, as if actual securities, FOREX, or commodities investing had taken place, when no trading had taken place. The Dodd-Frank and Sarbanes-Oxley Acts now have sections requiring corporate executives and accounting firms to provide honest accounting and honest financial statements.

In short, anything that is a document can be fabricated, just as the information on the document is made up in Ponzi schemes. The following is a list of some of the fraudulent documents reported in Ponzi schemes; this list is by no means exhaustive:

- Fabricated purchase orders
- Falsified invoices
- Counterfeit stock certificates (with fabricated CUSIP[1] numbers)
- Promissory notes
- Account statements
- Financial statements
- Fabricated contracts
- Mortgages
- Property appraisals
- Government contracts
- Audit reports
- Falsified tax documents and IRS forms
- Falsified corporate ledgers
- Fabricated trading tickets
- Lease agreements
- Certificates of deposit

In more prominent cases, some exhibits – the falsified documents – used in prosecutions are publicly available. The Department of Justice offers many of the exhibits in these cases; however, to the untrained eye these documents look perfectly legitimate. In the Thomas Petters case, the fraudulent documents are quite lengthy. These documents are invoices to major companies such as Costco and Sam's Clubs. The untrained eye would not know how to recognize the deception (DOJ, exhibit 105, USA v. Petters, 2008). The following cases are examples of types of fraudulent documents and false information used:

- Jeremy Lundin of *Big Island Capital* told investors in promotional documents that he had $730,000 in capital, but he had not yet opened a bank account for the entity (DOJ, 2017, September 1, p.r.).
- Scott Newsholme used falsified account statements, fraudulent stock certificates, fabricated promissory notes, alleged to be for debt instruments such as bonds (SEC, 2017, September 6).
- In the *New Century* Coal Ponzi scheme based on coal mines, the perpetrators created "ghost vendor companies with valid bank accounts" to present the image that *New Century* was a viable legitimate business (USA v. Brian C. Rose et al., 2014). Fraudulent documents were created that represented expenses from exploration and mining of coal. When savvy investors asked for proof of the existence of coal mines and expenditures, the perpetrators simply fabricated false documents, including renting a mine and heavy equipment to support the illusion of a fully functioning operation.

Multiple Business Entities and Shell Companies

Many schemes have multiple business identities, oftentimes incorporated in several states, and at times in other countries. This enables the perpetrators to move funds from one business to another quite easily. It enables hiding funds and provides the appearance of legitimate transactions. Multiple business entities in multiple states give the perpetrators more opportunities to reach potential victim-investors in more locations.

Shell companies are used to launder money, and, in other cases, to give the impression that funds are being invested in what are actually shell companies. These companies usually exist in name only, for the purpose of another company's operations. The purpose of shell companies is to move money from entity to entity to make it more difficult for authorities to monitor activities and to follow the money trail and to give the impression actual business is taking place. Shell companies are used in many illegal business enterprises, not just Ponzi schemes. The process is one of moving money from one business to another, and many more to give the appearance that actual funds are legitimately being transacted through legitimate businesses. Nothing could be farther from the truth. There were 879 Ponzi schemes that had only one business entity; 313 had two business entities; 167 of 1,359 had three or more business entities. Several schemes had multiple companies or shell entities:

- Four Ponzi schemes had between 20 and 23 business entities.
- Two schemes were in the thirties range: 31 and 35.
- One had 82 business entities.
- One had 100 business entities.
- Two had 150 business entities
- One had 275 business entities.
- Larry Reynolds ran Nationwide International Resources Inc, to launder funds for Thomas Petters scheme; it was purely a shell company (FBI, 2010, September 14).
- Edward May formed more than 150 limited liability corporations; his scheme took $350 million (FBI, 2011, October 4, p.r.).
- Val E. Southwick had at least 150 Nevada corporations purported to be involved in real estate development. His entities issued promissory notes and sold unregistered securities (SEC, 2008, February 6).
- Gregory Gray Jr. of *Archipel Capital* and *BIM Management* had at least 12 business entities with variations on the name *Archipel Capital*. Gray's methodology:

  > When Investor A sought proof of the Late Stage Fund LP's ownership of Uber shares, Gray sent Investor A's business manager a fabricated stock transfer agreement that bore a cut-and-pasted signature from a prior legitimate purchase of stock by another

Archipel Entity. The purported seller of these *Uber* shares, Seller A, never owned or signed any documents related to a sale of Uber shares.

(SEC, 2015, February, 27)

- In the case of Robert Shapiro and *Woodbridge,* most of Shapiro's 275 LLCs had no actual business activities, revenues or otherwise; they were purely shell companies for the purpose of carrying out the fraud. The scheme promised investors that the funds were going to third-party borrowers, and that profits would be made in interest paid on the loans (SEC, 2017, December 20).

Incorporations and Company Formations

The state(s) in which Ponzi schemes are carried out and where they have been incorporated or formed may be the same or different states. Most schemes have victimized investors in several states and/or several countries. Table 3.1 compares the quantity of incorporations/formations per state and the quantity of federal-level Ponzi schemes that were prosecuted criminally or had SEC or CFTC administrative actions. Where the case is charged civilly or criminally is a matter of venue and jurisdiction,

Table 3.1 Ponzi Schemes, Incorporation/Formation, Population per State

State	Total Ponzi 1962–2019	Total Ponzi Incorp/Formed	Ponzi Total Incorp/Formed Ratio	State Population 2019
Alabama	9	0	9:0	4,903,185
Alaska	2	1	2:1	731,545
Arizona	23	14	23:14	7,278,717
Arkansas	3	7	3:7	3,017,804
California	**216**	**136**	**27:17**	**39,512,223**
Colorado	34	23	34:23	5,758,736
Connecticut	26	18	13:9	3,565,287
Delaware	**2**	**127**	**2:127**	**973,764**
DC	7	4	7:4	705,749
Florida	117	107	117:107	21,477,737
Georgia	37	27	37:27	10,617,423
Hawaii	16	7	16:7	1,415,872
Idaho	8	0	8:0	1,787,065
Illinois	79	51	79:51	12,671,821
Indiana	11	8	11;8	6,732,219
Iowa	4	1	4:1	3,155,070
Kansas	7	0	7:0	2,913,314
Kentucky	4	2	2:1	4,467,673
Louisiana	8	6	4:3	4,648,794
Maine	1	0	1:0	1,344,212

(Continued)

State	Total Ponzi 1962–2019	Total Ponzi Incorp/Formed	Ponzi Total Incorp/Formed Ratio	State Population 2019
Maryland	7	4	7:4	6,045,680
Massachusetts	25	12	25:12	6,892,503
Michigan	34	24	17:12	9,986,857
Minnesota	25	13	25:13	5,639,632
Mississippi	4	4	1:1	2,976,149
Missouri	20	14	10:7	6,137,428
Montana	1	5	1:5	1,068,778
Nebraska	5	4	5:4	1,934,408
Nevada	**19**	**131**	**19:131**	**3,080,156**
New Hampshire	3	3	1:1	1,359,711
New Jersey	42	29	42:29	8,882,190
New Mexico	4	2	2:1	2,096,829
New York	121	67	121:67	19,453,561
North Carolina	41	23	41:23	10,488,084
North Dakota	1	3	1:3	762,062
Ohio	31	0	31:0	11,689,100
Oklahoma	12	7	12:7	3,956,971
Oregon	12	10	6:5	4,217,737
Pennsylvania	41	26	41:26	12,801,989
Rhode Island	5	2	5:2	1,059,361
South Carolina	12	0	12:0	5,148,714
South Dakota	0	2	0:2	884,659
Tennessee	27	10	27:10	6,829,174
Texas	123	89	123:89	28,995,881
Utah	48	32	3:2	3,205,958
Vermont	1	1	1:1	623,989
Virginia	34	18	17:9	8,535,519
Washington	28	15	28:15	7,614,893
West Virginia	1	2	1:2	1,792,147
Wisconsin	12	7	12:7	5,822,434
Wyoming	**1**	**18**	**1:18**	**578,759**
Puerto Rico	3	2	3:2	3,193,694
US VI	1	2	1:2	106,405
US population 2019	1359	1120	1359:1120	328,239,523

Note: California is emboldened because it had the largest number of Ponzi schemes but also the largest population. Delaware, Nevada and Wyoming have more incorporations/formations because of their incorporation laws.

by statute. The venue is the place whereby a case is tried or administrated; the jurisdiction is the court that has the authority, determined by the law or statute that has been violated. In securities and commodities cases, the jurisdiction is determined by the regulations that have been violated, and the venue is determined by the primary place of business.

The legal structure of business formations serves to protect the officers in a company, or not, depending on the choice of entity formation. The Ponzi schemes may have had multiple incorporations, incorporations, and Limited liability Companies (LLCs), or they may have just told investors they were incorporated. The purpose of incorporation is to protect personal assets from company debts. Incorporation allows for shareholders. LLCs can have one owner or several partners; many of the Ponzi schemes were LLCs. In general partnerships, the owners take part in the managing of the company and are responsible for business debts. Limited partnerships (LP) allow for partners to share in the profits but they do not participate in the running of the business. Incorporations and LLCs were the primary formations mentioned in the federal documents.

The "nerve-center test" (Garner, 2009) is the test used by courts to determine a business entity's primary operation location for the purpose of legal actions. Many corporations incorporate in Nevada or Delaware because of tax incentives and opacity. The court determines the "nerve-center" as the location where the corporate officers reside, specifically the primary agent, for determining where a case is judicated. Delaware, Nevada, and Wyoming have greater quantities of incorporations as compared with the number of Ponzi schemes; however that is not where the cases were tried or prosecuted unless the business was run from those states. Civil and/or criminal charges are brought in the state of the primary or the location from which the business is run. The Supreme Court determined in *Hertz Corp. v. Friend et al.* (2009) that the nerve-center is generally where the primary business activities take place. Most Ponzi schemes are multi-state and often multi-country. Victims may be in many states and countries; this is especially true since more recent schemes make use of the internet to carry out the schemes.

In comparing where a Ponzi schemes was charged civilly, or criminally prosecuted with the state of incorporation/formation, we see that each state's incorporation laws influence the quantity of incorporations/formations in that state. Some states require at least one of the corporate officers to live in the state to incorporate; others, such as Delaware and Nevada, do not. In Figure 3.1 we can see that California has the most Ponzi scheme prosecutions but a comparable amount of incorporations with Nevada. New York and Texas also had more scheme prosecutions than incorporations. We can see that Delaware and Nevada have significantly more incorporations than prosecutions. All prosecutions are federal level; it is the same standard. The difference is some states have more attractive incorporation laws. It is the state law that varies, encouraging the incorporations. In Table 3.1 we see the individual states, the number of Ponzi prosecutions, and the number of incorporations/formations and the state population. California has the most Ponzi schemes, but it is also the most populated state. California has a ratio of 27 schemes to 17 incorporations, whereas Delaware has two schemes to 127 incorporations. Most states have more schemes than incorporations, except for Delaware, Nevada, and Wyoming.

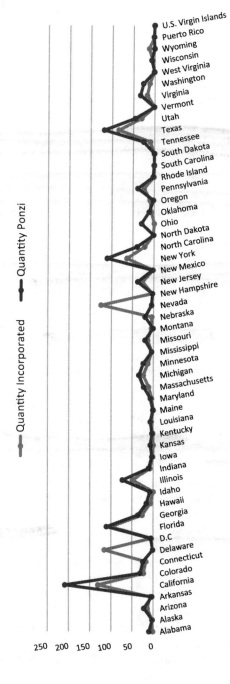

U.S. Virgin Islands
Puerto Rico
Wyoming
Wisconsin
West Virginia
Washington
Virginia
Vermont
Utah
Texas
Tennessee
South Dakota
South Carolina
Rhode Island
Pennsylvania
Oregon
Oklahoma
Ohio
North Dakota
North Carolina
New York
New Mexico
New Jersey
New Hampshire
Nevada
Nebraska
Montana
Missouri
Mississippi
Minnesota
Michigan
Massachusetts
Maryland
Maine
Louisiana
Kentucky
Kansas
Iowa
Indiana
Illinois
Idaho
Hawaii
Georgia
Florida
D.C
Delaware
Connecticut
Colorado
California
Arkansas
Arizona
Alaska
Alabama

250 200 150 100   50   0

━●━ Quantity Incorporated   ━●━ Quantity Ponzi

Figure 3.1 Quantity of Ponzi Incorporated/Formation per State and Quantity of Ponzi per State of Prosecution.

The State of Utah and its Department of Securities determined that it had a problem with fraud and white-collar crimes, establishing the White-Collar Crime Registry (HB 378, 2015). Utah State Attorney General Sean Reyes asked the question, "Is Utah the Fraud Capital of the U.S?" and answers, "Yes, yes we are" (Reyes, 2019). Utah has recognized a problem and enacted legislation to aid law enforcement in reducing recidivism, and to enable the public to carry out research to find if someone they are interested in doing business with has a white-collar crime conviction. The State of Utah requires those who have been convicted of state-level crimes listed under 77-42-105 to register with the Utah State White-Collar Crime registry. Those crimes include (not exhaustive, only selected):

- Securities fraud (61-1-2)
- Theft by deception
- Unlawful dealing of property by fiduciary
- Insurance fraud
- Mortgage fraud
- Communications fraud
- Money laundering
                 (State of Utah https://www.utfraud.com/Home/Laws)

Opaque Incorporation States

Delaware, Nevada, and Wyoming stand out for their opaque incorporation laws and corporate tax incentives. Delaware has a low franchise tax, and Nevada has no franchise tax. Nevada has gross receipts tax instead of corporate taxes. In Delaware under Title 30 § 1902 (6), "A corporation maintaining a statutory corporate office in the State but not doing business within the State" are exempt from corporate taxation (Delaware, 2019). Both Delaware and Nevada do not require officers to be residents; only a registered agent is required to receive documents; this can be an attorney hired for the purpose. Delaware does not list the primaries in corporations, or LLCs, on public record. Both Nevada and Delaware do not require that board members be disclosed publicly. In Delaware, it is very inexpensive to incorporate. Neither state requires a bank account or formal meetings to be held in the state, only requiring a registered agent address, (as of this writing). When an entity has opened a bank account in Delaware the funds are exempt from attachment, such as in divorce proceedings and by creditors (Delaware, title 8). Delaware's laws favor companies with stockholders, such as: stockholders in other states are not subject to Delaware taxes. Delaware has a court of chancery that is solely focused on business law; these are judicial only; no juries. Nevada has more protections for the officers of corporations. Nevada corporations can choose to indemnify all officers from all actions. This is not the case in Delaware.

Offshore Accounts

Offshore accounts are a means for hiding illegitimately acquired funds, and legitimately attained funds for the purpose of reducing taxes. Offshore accounts are often used by money launderers, drug traffickers, arms dealers, and other illegally obtained funding activities. Offshore accounts are a way for anyone who needs to hide funds, including legitimately attained funds that entities and individuals may want to avoid paying taxes on, or those who may want to shield from divorce proceedings. Ponzi perpetrator Allen Stanford held 29 separate offshore accounts (USA v. R. Allen Stanford 2009, June 18). Stanford had incorporations in Antigua, and Texas, in addition to incorporating the Stanford Bank in Venezuela. There are businesses that have legitimate reasons for offshore accounts, but in general, the purpose of offshore accounts is to avoid taxes, monitoring, or to hide funds; these Ponzi schemes were all intentional.

Some countries are known as tax havens or financial service centers. Generally, in these countries there are residents who sit on boards of companies incorporated within that country, as a profession; they are professional board members. These individuals may be retained by several companies as board members through licensed professional firms. For example, the Cayman Islands government website informs perspective corporations that there are professional firms licensed for the purpose of being officers in corporations:

> The most convenient way to incorporate a company in the Cayman Islands is to engage one of the many professional firms licensed for this purpose. In addition to incorporation services, these firms provide such services as registered offices, directors, nominee shareholders and other officers, and company management services.
>
> (Cayman Islands, 2020)

These boards may be required to meet at least once per year, based on the country's laws; however these board members have little capacity for oversight of a corporation carrying out business outside the Cayman Islands. The only option of oversight for the professional licensing corporation entity is to resign its service from a corporation doing business in a foreign country that is suspected of wrongdoing. The foreign company (in this case, an American company) can simply switch to another professional board of directors company.

The Cayman Islands website explains that disclosure of board members or professional agents is prohibited by law; in other words, the identities of owners and board members are opaque to the general public. These companies are allowed to have as few as one shareholder, and there are no corporate, property, or payroll taxes. As of 2020, the Cayman Islands has 109,986 companies registered with its Registry of Companies (Cayman Islands General Registry). The Cayman Islands has a population of 61,944 as of July 2020 (CIA).

• The scheme perpetrated by William Wise, and Jackie and Kristi Hoegel, made use of offshore entities, financial service centers, fraudulent banks, prime banking, shell companies, and aliases to perpetrate their fraud. They also included family members in carrying out this fraud (see Manner and Means Chapter 4) (SEC, 2009, March, 26).

Several Ponzi schemes within this study were incorporated in other countries, as illustrated in Table 3.2. *Tropikgadget* is a Ponzi and pyramid scheme incorporated in both the Madeira Free trade zone of Portugal and the United Arab Emirates, with the primary place of business in Portugal. However, the Ponzi scheme was primarily carried out in Massachusetts. This affinity-fraud case had 15 perpetrators who predominantly preyed on other Portuguese and Brazilian Americans.

Table 3.2 Ponzi Schemes Offshore Incorporation

Country	Quantity of Schemes	Country	Quantity of Schemes
Antigua and Barbuda	1	Jamaica	1
Aruba	1	Mexico	1
Bahamas	9	Montenegro	1
Belize	3	Nauru	1
British Virgin Islands	4	Netherlands	1
Canada	5	New Zealand	5
Cayman Islands	12	Panama	11
Costa Rica	2	Peru	1
Denmark	1	Portugal	1
Dominica	1	Saint Kitts & Nevis	11
Ecuador	1	Saint Vincent & Grenadines	2
Great Britain	5	Seychelles	1
Grenada	4	Sweden	1
Hong Kong	5	Switzerland	4
India	1	Turks & Caicos Islands	6
Isle of Man	1	United Arab Emirates	1
Israel	1	Venezuela	1

Exclusiveness

Most Ponzi perpetrators enhance the attractiveness of their program by giving the air of exclusiveness. This behavior provides a sort of snob-appeal to the scheme. It is likely that in most Ponzi cases, it is not that the perpetrators are trying for exclusiveness, but instead they are picking victims who are not sophisticated enough to recognize the fraud. Perpetrators are looking for the most gullible people, the myrmidon, people who will believe whatever they are told without questioning the validity of what is said, or the fraudulent statements and documents submitted by the perpetrators to their investor-victims.

Campaign Donations

It is common for perpetrators to give donations to congressional and presidential candidates' campaigns. They get photographs of themselves with candidates and elected officials for giving large donations. This is one mechanism used to enhance their credibility. Both Allen Stanford and Bernard Madoff made campaign contributions to many Democratic Party candidates (Mayer, 2008, 2009). Senator Frank Lautenberg had received a campaign contribution from Bernard Madoff (Mayer, 2008), and was also a victim of Madoff. The Lautenberg family charity – The Lautenberg Foundation – was one of Madoff's victims (Lautenberg v. Madoff, 2009). Former First Lady Hillary Clinton, Representative Charles Rangel, and Senator Charles Schumer received donations from Madoff (Mayer, 2008). Madoff's most interesting donation was to Christopher Dodd, one of the authors of the Dodd-Frank Act. Dodd's donation was received prior to 2008 (Mayer, 2008), the Dodd-Frank Act was enacted in 2010.

- Daniel Christian Stanley Powell received a photograph of himself with Bill Clinton for donating to musician Usher's *New Look Foundation* (FBI, 2014, November 13, p.r.).
- Norman Hsu was charged with securities violations as well as illegal campaign donations (SEC, 2008, October 6, prg. 7). Hsu raised $850,000 for Hillary Clinton's campaign in 2008. The money had to be returned (Willis, 2015). Hsu received more than 24 years in federal prison for his $60 million Ponzi scheme. Hsu was charged with violating the Federal Election Campaign Act in addition to several fraud charges (USAO, 2007, December 4, p.r.). Hsu asked investors to make campaign donations at $25,000, then he reimbursed them with funds from the Ponzi scheme (FBI, 2009, September 29, p.r.).
- In the Allen Stanford case, Stanford made donations to many politicians. Stanford made contributions to both Republican Senator John McCain and Democrat Senator Bill Nelson and then presidential

candidate Barack Obama. In the House, Stanford had contributed to then Speaker John Boehner (Winship, 2012).

- In Hassan Nemazee's Ponzi scheme that victimized banks, he used the funds to make donations to his local political candidates as well as state- and federal-level candidates, and political action committees. Nemazee also donated to charities (DOJ, 2009, September 21 p.r.; DOJ, 2010, July 15, p.r.).

Charities

In addition to schemes that purport to be investing in charities or supporting charitable activities, it is common for Ponzi perpetrators to donate large sums of money to charities. This helps enhance their credibility in the community and increases their ability to bring new investor-victims into their scheme. In some cases, the victim-investors are told that a portion of their investment returns will be going to charities. Generally, this charitable giving is brought to the attention of the courts during sentencing, trying to show a good side to the perpetrators. The charitable giving is just a mechanism to give the appearance of being an upstanding citizen, but their charitable donations are made with their victims' funds. Some of the investor-victims were charities.

- The Ponzi scheme of Michael and Carolyn Anderson told investor-victims that at least 12.5 percent would be used to benefit abused children and women, through their companies: *Rainbow Foundation* and *Seaoma* (SEC, 2017, November 8).
- Michael E. Gause and Charles Homa gave the *World Harvest Church* $1.8 million (World Harvest Church v. Guideone Mutual Insurance Company, S.C.G. 2010). The court-appointed receiver, Phillip Stenger, had to sue for a return of the funds. The court ruled that the church had to return $1 million. Gause also operated his scheme from the Cayman Islands; he had several offshore corporations (SEC, 2002, May 8, l.r.).
- A classic example of using charitable giving and philanthropy is stated in the government's position report in Thomas Petters' sentencing: "Throughout, the defendant carefully crafted and manipulated his image as a charitable and religious philanthropist to fool business, political and religious leaders, who in turn lent credibility to the defendant further facilitating and concealing the fraud" (USA v. Petters, 2010, Government's Position, p. 2).
- Kenneth Wayne McLeod's victims were primarily federal and state law enforcement officers. McLeod had made large donations to the Drug Enforcement Administration (DEA) Survivors Benefits Fund

(OIGDOJ, 2014, December 3). Many of his victims were DEA agents, as well as other federal law enforcement agency employees.

Ponzi perpetrators not only gave to charities to enhance their credibility in the community, but in some cases, they told their victims that the funds were to be used in humanitarian or charitable activities. Some affinity-fraud schemes told investors they were helping build businesses, or in support home of mortgages in specific ethnic or religious communities. The perpetrators preyed on the investors' desire to help others within their communities. In some cases, it is the charity or non-profit that is the victim. In Madoff's case, there were several non-profit entities that lost large amounts of money; one was Yeshiva University (Hernandez, 2008) and another was the Lautenberg Foundation (Lautenberg v. Madoff, 2009).

- In the case of John G. Bennett Jr. and *New Era Philanthropy*, in this scheme, it was the charities and non-profits that were the victims of the Ponzi scheme. Bennett offered unregistered securities that did not exist, to the charities, churches, and universities (SEC, 1996, September 30).

The earlier characteristics described the basic tools commonly used by Ponzi perpetrators to carry out the schemes. Deception and fraudulent documents are the primary tools in every Ponzi scheme. Other common tools used to carry out the frauds are falsified credentials, aliases, snob appeal, charitable giving and campaign donations, and shell companies, all of which serve the purpose of presenting an appearance of credibility, legitimacy, and successfulness – the keys to convincing investors to give up their money. The following chapter describes the types of investments that investor-victims were told they were investing in, what is referred to as the ways, manner, and means.

Note

1 Committee on Uniform Securities Identification Procedures (CUSIP), identifying all registered stocks and bonds.

References

Braithwaite, J. (1985). White collar crime. *Annual Review of Sociology* Vol.11 pp. 1–25.

Cayman Islands. Retrieved July 10, 2020, from: http://www.gov.ky/portal/page/portal/srghome/registration/flag/ownership/companiesandshipping/incorporation

Cayman Islands General Registry https://www.ciregistry.ky/

Central Intelligence Agency World Fact Book. Retrieved 2020, retrieved from: https://www.cia.gov/library/publications/the-world-factbook/geos/print_cj.html

Commodities and Futures Trading Commission vs. David L. Ortiz, Goyep International, Inc. and Royal Returns, Inc. (2011, February 23).

Commodities Futures Trading Commission, (2011, February 28). CFTC charges Florida resident David L. Ortiz and his companies, Goyep International, Inc. and Royal Returns, Inc., with defrauding customers in an off-exchange foreign currency scam. Press release.

Federal Bureau of Investigation, (2009, September 29). Former political fundraiser Norman Hsu sentenced to 292 months in prison for Ponzi scheme and related campaign finance crimes. Press release.

Federal Bureau of Investigation, (2011, October 4). Edward P. May sentenced for orchestrating $350 million Ponzi scheme. Press release.

Federal Bureau of Investigation (2014, November 13) San Diego man who ran scam that offered investments in 'reverse life insurance' policies convicted of federal fraud charges. (Powell). Press release.

Department of Justice, (2009, September 21). Manhattan U.S. Attorney Charges Hassan Nemazee in $292 million Ponzi scheme. (Nemazee). Press release.

Department of Justice, (2010, July 15). Hassan Nemazee sentenced in Manhattan Federal court to 12 years in prison for orchestrating $292 million fraud scheme. Press release.

Department of Justice, (2013, March 15). Ashburn man sentenced to 84 months for Ponzi scheme involving purchase of Beacon Hill golf course. (Amendola; McKerac). Press release.

Department of Justice, (2013, April 30). Three fraud defendants who met in prison sent back to serve new sentences in $3.6 million Ponzi scheme. (Parilli; Lauer; Andersen). Press release.

Department of Justice, (2014, June 24). Manhattan U.S. Attorney announces guilty plea of New York Accountant in connection with the massive fraud at Bernard L. Madoff Investment Securities. (Konigsberg). Press release.

Department of Justice, (2017, September 1). Big Island Capital fraudster charged with operating million dollar Ponzi scheme. (Lundin). Press release.

Department of Justice, (2018, December 4). Identity thief pleads guilty to operating $1.4 million Ponzi scheme. (Brian Sapp). Press release.

Department of Justice, (2019, August 12). Conman who posed as beverage entrepreneur sentenced to more than 7 years in Federal prison for running $7.5 million Ponzi scheme. (Hardat). Press release.

Federal Bureau of Investigation, (2010, September 14). Larry Reynolds sentenced for his role in Petters $3.7 billion Ponzi scheme. Press release.

Federal Bureau of Investigation, (2016, December 12). New Century Coal fraud ends in lengthy prison sentences for 10 individuals. Press release.

Federal Bureau of Investigation, (2017, January 27). (Rose) Unearthing a coal mine fraud. Press release.

Federal Bureau of Investigation, (2011, October 4). Edward P. May sentenced for orchestrating $350 million Ponzi scheme. Press release.

Frasca, C. (1931). *Stock swindlers and their methods*. New York, NY Charles Frasca Publisher.

Garner, B. (ed) (2009). *Black's law dictionary*. St. Paul, MN, Thomson Reuters.

Hernandez, J. (2008, December 22). Betrayed by Madoff Yeshiva U. adds a lesson. *New York Times*. New York.

Hertz Corp. v. Friend United States Supreme Court 559 U.S. 77 (2010).

Internal Revenue Service. (2015). Examples of money laundering investigations – fiscal year 2015 (Kimmel).

Lautenberg Foundation v. Bernard Madoff Investment Securities (2013, April 3).

Lautenberg Foundation, The et al. v. Madoff, 2:09-cv-00816-SRC-MCA (U.S.D.N.J. 2009) Complaint.

Lautenberg Foundation v. Madoff Order of Administrative termination-bankruptcy Civil 09-816(SRC) (U.S.D.N.J. 2011).

Office of Inspector General Department of Justice (OIGDOJ). (2014, December 3). Report of Investigation Regarding DEA's relationship with K. Wayne McLeod.

Reyes, S. (2019). Is Utah the fraud capital of the world? Retrieved from: https://attorneygeneral.utah.gov/utah-fraud-capital/

Securities and Exchange Commission v. John G. Bennett Jr. (1996, September 30) Litigation release.

Securities and Exchange Commission v. John Scott Clark (2011, March 25) Complaint.

Securities and Exchange Commission v. Charles R. Homa, Michael Gause et al. (2002, May 8) Litigation release.

Securities and Exchange Commission v. Advance Local Development Corp. et al. (2002, April 22) (Burton). Litigation release.

Securities and Exchange Commission v. Blake A. Prater and Wellspring Capital Group, Inc. (2003, September 10) Litigation release.

Securities and Exchange Commission v. Premium Income Corp., Inforex LTD., Tri-Forex International LTD. Aka Tri-Forex Ltd. And International FOREX Company, Gerald Leo Rogers aka Jay Rogers and Jay Rodgers, and Alexander Igor Shevchenko (2005, March 2) Complaint.

Securities and Exchange v. Seaforth Meridian LTD, Seaforth Meridian Advisers LLC, Seaforth Meridian Management LLC, Alain Assemi, Timothy J. Clyman, John D. Friedrich and Scot Klion aka James S. Rucker and David Tanner (2006, September 14) Complaint.

Securities and Exchange Commission v. Vescor Capital et al and Val E. Southwick (2008, February 6) Complaint.

Securities and Exchange Commission v. Next Components, LTD., and Norman Hsu (2008, October 6) Complaint.

Securities and Exchange Commission v. Millennium Bank, United Trust of Switzerland S.A., UT of S, LLC., Millennium Financial Group, William J. Wise, d.b.a Sterling Administration, d/b/a Sterling Investment Services, d/b/a Millennium Aviation, Kristi M. Hoegel, a/k/a Kristi M. Christopher, a/k/a Bessy Lu,. Jacqueline Hoegel, a/k/a Jacquline Hoegel, a/k/a Jackie Hoegel, Philippe Angeloni, and Brijesh Chopra (2009, March 26) Complaint.

Securities and Exchange Commission Digest, (2009, March 26). SEC halts $68 million Ponzi scheme involving Caribbean based bank and Swiss Affiliate. (Wise & Hoegel). Enforcement proceedings.

Securities and Exchange Commission v. Gregory Gray, Jr., Archipel Capital LLC, Bim Management LP (2015, February 27) Complaint.

Securities and Exchange Commission v. Ariel Quiros, William Stenger, Jay Peak Inc. (12 entities) Q Resorts, Inc., and AnC BioVermont GP Services (2016, April 12) Complaint.

Securities and Exchange Commission v. Robert H. Shapiro and the Woodbridge Group of companies et al. (2017, December 20) Complaint.

Securities and Exchange Commission v. Scott Newsholme (2017, September 6) Complaint.

Securities and Exchange Commission v. The End of the Rainbow Partners LLC. And the Estate of Michael F. Anderson (2017, November 8) Complaint.

State of Utah, White Collar Crime Offender Registry. Retrieved from: https://www.utfraud.com/Home/Registry, retrieved on November 29, 2019

United States Attorney Office Southern District of New York. (2007, December 4, p.r.). Manhattan U.S. Attorney indicts Norman Hsu for massive fraud scheme. Press release.

United States Department of Justice exhibit 105, U.S. v. Petters, (2008).

United States Attorney, (2009, July 17). Accountant for Bernard L. Madoff Investment Securities, LLC charged in felony information for accounting violations. Press release.

United States v. Thomas Joseph Petters (2010, March, 8) Government's position regarding sentencing.

United States v. Robert Allen Stanford aka Sir Allen Stanford, Laura Pendergest-Holt aka Laura Pendergest, aka Laura Holt, Gilberto Lopez, Mark Kuhrt and Leroy King (2009, June 18) Indictment.

United States v. Jerry J. Mckerac (2013, March 14) Indictment.

United States v. Brian C. Rose aka John Hankins, Robert McGregor aka Jim Robinson III, Dallas McRae, Hugh Sackett, James Robinson, Brent Loveall, Jason Smith, Ray Spears aka Brock Hamilton, and Jenifer Key (2014, January 10) Indictment.

United States v. Jeff Teitelbaum, aka Mike Picozzi, aka Kevin Polardi, aka Ed Perente, aka Frank Blasetti (2016, September 9) Motion to dismiss.

United States Department of Justice, (2019, April 22). Conman who pretended to be beverage entrepreneur pleads guilty to federal fraud charges stemming from $5 million Ponzi scheme. (Hardat). Press release.

Winship, M. (2012, May 9). Politicians won't return Ponzi payoffs. *Huffpost Politics*.

World Harvest Church v. Guideone Mutual Insurance Company, Supreme Court of Georgia No. S10Q0341 (2010, May 3).

Chapter 4

Ways, Manner, and Means Used to Carry Out the Schemes

The ways, manner, and means refer to what the perpetrators told their investor-victims they were investing in. They are the words that were used to entice, confuse, and defraud their victims. Braithwaite uses the term "modus operandi," more commonly known as the method of operation (Braithwaite, 1985). The term "manner and means" is commonly used in federal documents to describe the methods by which Ponzi schemers carried out their fraud scheme. The manner is the method or way something is done. Black's law dictionary defines the means as "something that helps to attain an end" (Garner, 2009). This section is not an in-depth explanation of the accounting manipulations, just an overall description of the alleged investments for the frauds – what the perpetrators told their investor-victims that the investments would be. The intent of this chapter is to familiarize the reader with some financial instruments and terminology, and to understand how those terms were used in promoting Ponzi schemes. Some schemes did not use financial market instruments but instead used other surprising types of investments.

There may have been some actual investing or legitimate business going on as stated by Ponzi perpetrators in some schemes. More commonly, there was no actual investing or business activities taking place. The perpetrators always stated there was business or investing activities happening, regardless of whether or not that was true. The method, manner, and means are described within SEC and CFTC documents, generally within the complaint. Other cases are explained within the FBI or DOJ documents such as complaints, indictments, or informations.

In some schemes there are several types of fraud taking place. The scheme is classified as a Ponzi scheme in federal documents, but may also be considered mortgage fraud, insurance fraud, bank fraud, and tax fraud. These schemes are considerably complex. In addition to defrauding individual investors, they may have also defrauded banks, pension plans, institutions, and insurers.

Most schemes involved some type of investment instruments. The perpetrators reported to investor-victims that the entity was marketing any of several instruments such as securities, promissory notes, bonds, commodities, options, binary options, annuities, warrants, FOREX, and futures. The data was recorded with every term reported in federal case documents. Some may have used several types of investment instruments. This provides a general idea of how perpetrators promoted their operations to investor-victims.

Many schemes were stated to be both mortgage and real estate investment products, just mortgage, or just real estate products. Examples would be mortgages, distressed properties, apartment complexes, mortgage-backed derivatives, and real property. More often than not, the names were just words; there was no actual investing. In the cases during the housing bubble (2002–2006), some started out as legitimate businesses then failed. Most were pure Ponzi from the beginning.

Mortgage-based Frauds

Mortgage frauds have many variations. The classic form is that the perpetrator purports to be placing investors funds in a business entity that invests in real estate or mortgages but instead is fully a Ponzi scheme from the onset. Some were part of the mortgage derivative market that contributed to the housing boom and financial crisis. One type of mortgage fraud invites investors to be part of a mortgage company that allegedly funds mortgages, but no real mortgages actually exist, unbeknownst to investors. In other cases, the mortgages did exist, at least in part, but the entity developed into a Ponzi scheme or only functioned superficially as a mortgage company. Prior to the Glass-Steagall Act of 1933, there were many mortgage frauds similar to those that took place just prior to the financial crisis during the housing boom created by subprime mortgages in the mid-2000 decade. These were two periods in history where regulations were not in effect or not enforced, allowing many mortgage frauds to occur in relationship to a booming economy and then a financial collapse. In the 1920s there were cases of mortgage securities fraud whereby the investor-victims were buying securities in mortgages companies that never actually provided loans to consumers (Frasca, 1931). This was in the time period of Charles Ponzi's fraud scheme that now is the name sake of this specific type of fraud. At that time, this specific type of fraud scheme was simply called a "swindle," a term that applied to many types of frauds.

To understand the significance of mortgage-based frauds during the housing bubble and financial crisis we need to compare the numbers. There were 86 mortgage-based Ponzi schemes in the entirety of the study.

- Sixteen of those began and ended before the housing bubble (1962–2001).
- There were 29 schemes (51 percent) that began during the housing bubble (2002–2006).

- Twenty-one schemes (37 percent) began during the housing bubble (2002–2006) ended during the financial crisis; the remaining schemes ended after the financial crisis (2007–2010).
- Thirty-three schemes that began at any time prior to the financial crisis ended during the financial crisis (59 percent).
- Three mortgage-based schemes began during or after 2011.

One scheme was unusual in that the number of perpetrators (92) outnumbered the victims (60). This scheme was a predatory lending case, of which the Ponzi aspect was only one of many fraudulent activities in the mix:

- The most classic case of mortgage fraud that came about as a result of the subprime-mortgage failure was the case known as The Enterprise (PEI). This case involved at least 92 perpetrators, 90 of whom pleaded guilty or were found guilty and sentenced. Two perpetrators were foreign nationals and are currently fugitives. Twenty-five of the 92 perpetrators were women, a very high ratio as compared with other Ponzi schemes. This scheme, centered in North Carolina, operated from 2005 until 2012, making use of predatory mortgage lending practices (FBI, 2012, October 24, p.r.). The Ponzi characteristics were only one aspect of the many fraudulent actions involved in this scheme, including straw buyers. Generally, in mortgage frauds, a straw buyer is an individual who applies for a loan on a property that someone else will live in and/or control. This scheme took in $75 million; the individual perpetrators could not have received much financially in addition to the Ponzi payments that went out.
- Ronald Luczak and his wife Lisa, and Sandra Mainardi, a loan officer, were involved in a mortgage scheme during the housing bubble. They made use of straw buyers who presented themselves as buying the properties for their primary residence. Luczak then paid the mortgage obligations of the straw buyers with the funds from other straw buyers' mortgages. This also included many falsified documents, including income statements, falsified asset documents, and inflated property values (FBI, 2009, June 30, p.r.).
- Ramon Cendana used his mortgage company to "create fictitious mortgage closings" (FBI, 2010, April 28, p.r.). Many investors refinanced their own homes, who then used the funds to invest with Cendana's companies. There was never any investing in actual mortgages, just Ponzi payments.

The housing market bubble began in 2002, just after the recession of 2001 (Dokko et al., 2009). It is no coincidence that there was an increase in mortgage- and real estate-based Ponzi schemes during the housing bubble. The peak of the housing bubble is generally considered April 2006 (Financial Crisis Inquiry Commission Report, 2011, p. 214). From that point on, the housing market declined devolving into the financial crisis. The financial crisis is considered to have begun in 2007 (Financial Crisis Inquiry Commission Report, 2011, p. 213).

Real Estate

Some schemes were based in both mortgages and real estate. This section covers the real estate aspect specifically, excluding the mortgage factor. In the real estate-based frauds, the general theme is that of stating that there was investing in real property or in distressed properties, but little or no actual investing. In a few cases there was actual investing in real estate that failed; not enough funds were brought in to satisfy promised profits and the legitimate business turned into a Ponzi scheme. Others were intentional frauds form the very beginning. There were 155 real estate-based schemes. Of those:

* Twenty-two began in 2001 or earlier.
* Seventy-three began during the housing bubble (2002 to 2006).
* Fifty-nine began in 2007 to 2010.
* Five schemes began during 2011 or later.

Of those, only six were business-failure schemes, meaning 149 were intentional Ponzi schemes. The Federal Reserve Board of Governors generally considers the onset of the financial crisis in mid-2007,[1] as does the FCIC (2011, p. 213), and the ending period December 2010 (FCIC, 2011, p. 417).

There were 11 cases that were stated to be both real estate– and mortgage-based frauds in federal documents, all but one were intentional Ponzi schemes, meaning the stated real estate or mortgage investments were fabrications; there was no actual investments in real estate or mortgages. Of those,

* Six began during the housing bubble and ended during the financial crisis.
* Two began and ended before the housing bubble.
* One began before the housing bubble and ended during the bubble.
* One began prior to the bubble and ended during the financial crisis.
* One began during the financial crisis and ended after the crisis.

Therefore, more than half began during the housing bubble and ended during the financial crisis, all of which were intentional schemes.

Two separate schemes – Fred Clarke-*Cay Club Resorts*, and Wayne Puff – had multiple entities that were purported to investors to be owned real estate by the business entity. In the Puff case, there were 82 entities purportedly used to "purchase or sell property" (SEC, 2005, September

12, prg. 12). *Cay Clubs* was a real estate development entity formed by David W. Schwartz and Fred Davis Clark Jr, with more than 100 entities, although not incorporated in any state (SEC, 2013, January 30). These real estate entities were on the books to give the impression of being fully functioning real estate investment businesses.

Securities

The term "securities" is often used to refer to stocks, bonds, and equities. Securities are specifically defined as investment instruments that indicate partial ownership in a corporation (Downes and Goodman, 2014). Generally, financial instruments of stocks, equities, bonds, options, futures, annuities, and warrants are frequently referred to as securities. However, Section 2(a) (1) of the Securities Act (1933) defines these investment tools as securities:

> The term "security" means any note, stock, treasury stock, security future, security based swap, bond, debenture, evidence of indebtedness, certificate of interest or participation in any profit-sharing agreement, collateral-trust certificate, preorganization certificate or subscription, transferable share, investment contract, voting-trust certificate, certificate of deposit for a security, fractional undivided interest in oil, gas or other mineral rights, any put, call, straddle, option or privilege on any security, certificate of deposit, or group of index securities including interest therein or based on the value thereof), any put, call, straddle, option, or privilege entered into on a national securities exchange relating to foreign currency, or in general, any interest or instrument commonly known as a "security", or any certificate of interest or participation in, temporary or interim certificate for receipt for, guarantee of or warrant or right to subscribe to or purchase, any of the foregoing.
>
> (15 U.S. Code §77b. (a) (1))

Within the SEC documents the terms "securities," "stocks," and "equities" are used interchangeably. For this study, these terms are referring to shares in a corporation. Bonds are considered debt instruments and discussed separately. Securities-based frauds are the most common means for perpetrating Ponzi schemes. There were 272 schemes specifically using the term "securities," "equities," or "stocks." The schemes may have included unregistered securities, meaning they may not be sold publicly, that they are private offerings and not subject to the usual public disclosure laws required by the SEC. Only those using the terms "securities," "equities," or "stocks" were counted as securities in the data. Some schemes may have included securities in actual trading or solely in words alone; meaning the perpetrators only stated they were making trades; no actual trades took place, more often than not.

- Michael C. Regan offered securities in his unregistered investment fund. The fund, called *River Stream*, was to invest through stock trades. However, Regan lost money early on and resorted to a Ponzi scheme. His scheme sold unregistered securities in his investment firm that was supposed to be investing in the stock market. His companies were not registered with the SEC, making this a false-brokerage that failed (2009, June 24).
- Paul Moore was an alleged investment adviser that sent his clients account statements indicating that securities had been purchased. The statements were falsifications, in that no securities had been purchased. Moore also lied about his experience, education, and registration as an adviser (SEC, 2015, July 16). Moore's scheme was a classic intentional Ponzi scheme.
- Martin T. Wegener told his clients he would invest in "publicly traded securities, publicly traded mutual funds and other investment vehicles" (SEC, 2010, June 14, p. 6). While some of the companies on Wegener's statements to clients did exist, others on the statements were fictitious companies. Had victim-investors carried out due diligence, they would have found the companies on their statements did not exist. Regardless, Wegener did not invest the funds in any of the stocks he had purported to clients. This was an intentional Ponzi scheme.

Bonds

Bonds are considered a type of security, although they are actually debt instruments, primarily issued by government entities: municipalities, counties, states, federal. Bonds are primarily used by government entities for the purpose of raising revenues for capital projects. In all, there were 47 Ponzi schemes that used the term "bonds" (not bail bonds[2]); of those 26 were non-specific as to what type of bond. Federal bonds can be purchased through the US Treasury; there were four schemes that specifically stated Treasury or T-bonds. Five schemes used the generic "government bonds" term, which could mean federal and/or municipal. Municipal bonds include city, county, state, and sometimes institutional entities such as universities, and can be purchased through a licensed municipal bond broker. Six schemes specifically used the term "municipal bonds." Bonds are rated through the ratings agencies; potential investors should check the ratings for the bonds before purchasing them as well as to carry out due diligence on the broker. Two schemes claimed to be selling German war bonds and another was selling Turkish Eurobonds.

There are corporations that issue bonds as a debt instrument, when the entity needs to borrow money. When a corporation issues bonds legitimately, the document is called a bond indenture; it can be quite lengthy with legal jargon (hundreds of pages), a challenge for any potential investor. In legitimate corporate bond issuances, there should be a corporate trustee who monitors the bond compliance. There were six schemes that specifically claimed to be selling corporate bonds.

- The *Winans Foundation Trust*, and Michael Winans Jr. told investor-victims that they were investing in Saudi Arabian crude oil bonds. This scheme raised about $8 million from 2007 to –2008 at the very beginning of the financial crisis. There were never any bonds or investing in Saudi oil. The primary purpose of bonds is to raise funding for a government entity or as a loan to a corporation. Saudi Arabia would not need Americans to buy bonds for it to produce crude oil; oil is primarily owned (98.5 percent) by the Government of Saudi Arabia. It is surprising that more than 1,000 people believed the promotions (DOJ, 2013, February 27, p.r.).
- In the case of *Abatement Corp. Holding*, Laurer and Davis promised investor-victims their money would be invested in three types of bonds:
  - International balanced bond fund.
  - Triple A corporate bonds.
  - Government bonds.

Investor-victims were also told that their funds were FDIC-insured and Securities Investor Protection Corporation (SIPC)-insured. The FDIC does not insure securities or investments; it only insures funds deposited in FDIC-insured banks. The SIPC only insures investors in member brokerages; it does not protect against fraudulent stocks or when stocks lose value, but only when a SIPC member brokerage is failing financially (in liquidation). In addition, this scheme was formed in the Turks and Caicos. This scheme was carried out by a married couple Brenda Davis and Joseph Laurer (SEC, 2014, September 10). This scheme was a fraud in every aspect.

- In Gary Lane's Ponzi scheme, he had worked for a legitimate brokerage house. He told investor-victims they would be investing in treasury bonds. Instead he routed victim's funds through his wife's trading account (SEC, 2014, November 25). Although Lane was employed at a legitimate brokerage house, and held three licenses to trade, his scheme was fully and intentionally a Ponzi scheme.
- Gregory Loles' scheme preyed on friends, his church's members as well as his church itself. Loles was on the church's endowment fund committee and invested the churches funds in his Ponzi scheme.

His scheme was based on arbitrage bonds: "bonds issued by a municipality in order to gain an interest advantage by refunding higher-rate bonds in advance of their call date" (Downes and Goodeman, 2014). However, there was no actual investing in anything. This was a classic intentional, affinity-faith-based Ponzi scheme (FBI, 2014, February 26, p.r.).

There are legitimate "church bonds"; churches and religious organizations can and do go out to bond to fund buildings and religious colleges. Legitimate church bonds come in registered bonds and private placement bonds with restrictions under SEC Regulation D;[3] they also require financial statements. Oftentimes, when it is a clergy that is proposing bonds or borrowing for a church or religious entity, the members or parishioners won't question their leader about the legality or validity of the investment they are offering to the members of the religious organization.

- Roger Williams was a pastor of a church. He asked the members of his church to purchase "church bonds" in order to pay off the debts owed by the church itself. Williams convinced parishioners to allow him to manage their IRA accounts, which he used for himself. Many of his victims were elderly parishioners. The funds went to his own largess and paying Ponzi payments (DOJ, 2018, September 13, p.r.).

Equities

"Equities" is another term for "stock," a share ownership in a corporation. A few schemes specifically used the term "equities" as opposed to "securities" or "stocks."

- James Risher and Daniel Sebastian operated what was referred to as private funds, of which one was called: *Safe Harbor Private Equity Fund.* Risher and Sebastian promised to invest through "FINRA regulated" entities. However, only a small amount of investing was carried out. Risher, had a long criminal history in several Georgia counties as well as federally in Florida. Many of their investor--victims were retirees and Florida teachers (SEC, 2011, August 29).

Many cases were also charged with selling unregistered securities, commodities, notes, or certificates of deposit. Anyone selling securities must register them with the SEC; there is a very specific process for this under section five of the Securities Act (1933). The process affords prospective investors the opportunity to carry out due diligence. It also requires regular reporting by the entity offering securities. Securities represent a share ownership in a company, commonly referred to as a stock. Unregistered securities are restricted securities acquired through a private sale. There are certain restrictions under Rule 144 (17 CFR §230.144), as to how this must be done and who is qualified. If a broker or adviser is offering unregistered securities or a private offering, the investor needs to familiarize themselves with the details of this regulation before considering investing.

Initial Public Offerings

Public companies are those where the public can own shares of a corporation. Private stocks or equities are generally entities that are owned by families or partners. The stocks or shares may stay within families. It is when a corporation goes public that the entity comes under the monitoring of the SEC. The process of taking a company public requires a company to file a registration with the SEC, and then the SEC has to declare the registration as effective. This process involves filing a prospectus delineating the nature of the business. This is something prospective investors should access and read carefully. In legal initial public offerings (IPO), the entity must file Form S-1 with the SEC, and are publicly available through EDGAR, the SEC's database on registered companies. When the SEC does declare an IPO in effect, it has been subjected to review of compliance with regulations; it is not a judgment on the soundness or viability of the entity or potential profitability. The SEC cannot guarantee the information provided in the prospectus is accurate or a full disclosure.

An IPO is the first public offering of stocks when a company goes public. Generally, there are underwriters, usually investment bankers, hedge funds, or private equity firms who are the first investors. A company has a lengthy registration process with the SEC before it can become public. Generally, in the pre-IPO stage the stocks cannot be sold until the company has passed the registration process and is officially effective. Usually the initial shareholders are the founders of the company. The shares for sale in an IPO are new shares, not usually those of the founders. Some Ponzi perpetrators say they have ownership of stocks in the pre-IPO stage and market themselves as private equity entities. Investing in the pre-IPO stage can be risky.

Private Investment Entities

Generally, in a private offering the shares might be offered to friends, family, and possibly accredited investors at first. When a company is in the pre-IPO stage investors are investing in what is known as a "start-up." Sometimes these basement- or garage-based companies legitimately look for private investors to help them get their idea off the ground. This is highly speculative and risky investing. Some are indeed legitimate entities that will develop to the IPO stage. Many will fail before they reach the level of registering to go public. There are those entities that are pure Ponzi scheme from the very beginning. Eight schemes told investor-victims they were investing in pre-IPOs or IPOs.

- John Bivona promised his investor-victims that he would invest in what was primarily pre-IPO technology start-up companies that his investor-victims had specific interests in. Instead their funds were used to purchase other stocks for earlier investors. The funds were shuffled from account to account to make it appear as if there were investments being made (SEC, 2016, March 21).
- Craig L. Berkman and John Kern also promoted pre-IPO investments in technology-based entities: Facebook (public in 2012); Groupon (public in 2011); LinkedIn (public in 2011); and Zynga (public in 2011). This scheme took place from 2010 to 2013. Berkman told investor-victims that he owned pre-IPO stocks in these companies. Berkman did not hold any pre-IPO stocks in any of these companies, with the exception of only a small amount of Facebook stocks. He told his investor-victims their funds would be backed by his Facebook shares. Needless to say, there were no actual investments; this was yet another classic intentional Ponzi scheme from the beginning (DOJ, 2013, December 16).

Private investment in public equity (PIPE) are entities that offer investing in pre-IPO companies, such as start-ups as well as already established public entities. Generally, if it is pre-IPO, there is a condition that the business will be registering with the SEC soon. There were seven schemes that told investor-victims they were investing in PIPE entities.

- Jeanne Rowzee was an attorney, working with James Halstead, a licensed insurance broker, and Robert Harvey a "venture capitalist" (SEC, 2008, September 15). The three promoted their scheme to acquaintances and clients they knew. They held lavish parties to recruit others. When they promoted their PIPE investments, they never offered their potential investor-victims information on the entities they alleged they were investing in or financial information, a realistic expectation when investing with PIPEs. The investor-victims took their word for what the PIPEs were. Harvey also offered memberships in *Harvest Income* using the Regulation D exemption.[4] This entity was feeding funds to Rowzee and Halstead's scheme. For both of these types of investments, the investors were required to be accredited investors; their investors were not accredited; they were inexperienced investors.[5] There were no investments in PIPE entities or any other investing; all funds were used for the personal gains of the three and for Ponzi payments (SEC, 2008, September 15).

Some schemes portrayed themselves as private investment entities. Private placement memorandums are also known as unregistered offerings.[6] In a legitimate unregistered offering, there will be markings that indicate it is not registered with the SEC and that there are restrictions on transfer. Under Regulation D, Rule 504 issuers can sell up to a million dollars in securities within one year's time. However, those who qualify for the exemption must file with the SEC (this can be accessed through the SEC website). Rule 505 allows for up to $5 million but can only be sold to accredited investors. Rule 506 allows selling to accredited investors with a small number of unaccredited investors.[7] There are specific rules that apply to these exemptions that can be accessed through the SEC website.

Certificates of Deposit

Generally, certificates of deposit (CDs) are purchased from a bank. They are a loan to the bank for a set amount of time and generally have low interest rates, but are considered secure when purchased through an FDIC bank. Brokered CDs are issued by banks and generally purchased in large quantities by brokers. There are individuals who promote CDs as investment instruments. Individual brokers are not required to be licensed on either the state or the federal level; (Investor.gov); this makes it a challenge for potential investors to perform due diligence. If a CD is purchased through an FDIC bank, it is covered with all of an individual's holdings in the same bank up to $250,000. There were 16 cases that were based in CDs.

- Michael Earl Hill promoted 30-month CDs to his elderly clients that were backed by thin air. CDs are generally low interest while Mike Hill promised high interest rates. Hill used the funds acquired from his elderly clients to trade in risky securities and to make Ponzi payments (SEC, 2001, November 1, l.r.).
- Malcolm Segal also promised high interest rates on CDs. Segal did purchase some CDs for his clients, but redeemed them early to fund his own expenses and Ponzi payments. Segal did purchase some CDs from FDIC-insured banks as promised; however, he put them in one name instead of the individual investors, thereby negating the individual investor-victim's protections under the FDIC (SEC, 2015, July 1).

Derivatives

These are financial instruments based on the market performance of some asset, security, or index. Most of us began to hear the term used in relationship to mortgage-backed securities during the subprime mortgage boom and then the financial crisis. The asset was the mortgages that were bundled. Each "bundle" was a security made up of several mortgages. The value was derived from that of the mortgages. Cases that purported to be in mortgaged-backed securities are discussed in the mortgage section. There were three Ponzi cases claimed to be investing in derivatives; there was no actual investing in derivatives in any of the cases.

- Thomas Lanzana and Nikolai Masanko told their clients they were investing in foreign currency derivatives (DOJ, 2019, August 27, p.r.). Lanzana and Masanko had several businesses, none of which had trading accounts nor were they registered with the CFTC. The two also told their investor-victims at different points that they were investing in securities, and at another point in a hedge fund. There was never any investing or any derivatives based on assets (CFTC, 2017, August 21).
- John Holdaway and Kevin Kyes told their Japanese investor-victims that their funds would be held in an account and used as collateral to trade in derivatives and FOREX. Instead the funds were used to make Ponzi payments to other investors in yet a different program based on gold. In this case the perpetrators also used fake names to make it appear as if their business entity had more employees (DOJ, 2018, October 5, p.r.).

Commodities

Commodities are physical goods that are traded on markets and exchanges. Commodities include agricultural products, livestock, precious metals, and minerals. There were 135 commodity-based Ponzi schemes, including commodity pools. Commodities frauds may have included actual investing in commodities, investing in part or only purported investing, similarly to securities schemes. There were many entities that claimed to be commodities pools. Some of these pools were appropriately registered with the CFTC and NFA; others only stated they were properly registered. Schemes that purported to be investing in commodities may have made legitimate investments that failed; they may have made some investments but not used all of the received funds in investing, or simply made no investments in commodities at all. Thus, commodities-based schemes fall under either unintentional frauds or intentional frauds, including false-brokerages.

Many perpetrators were charged by the CFTC with not being properly registered commodity pools. A commodity pool is a collective fund that combines the contributions from several investors to gain trading leverage. There are specific regulations in place to protect investors, such as fiduciary responsibilities and informing investors honestly. Perpetrators are often charged with failing to inform their clients truthfully about their professional licenses and experience, or lack thereof, losses, and whether or not there are actual trades taking place. Victims often believe the perpetrators when they are told the entity is registered with the CFTC or are told the entity is exempt from registration. The specifics on who is allowed an exemption can be found at Title 17 CFR Ch. I, Part 4 §4.5, Commodity Pool Operators and Commodity Trading Advisers. The following are examples of commodities-based Ponzi schemes.

- The business entities of Jose Cecilio Martinez Beltran et al. (six perpetrators) of *Alpha Trade Group and Orsa Investments* were incorporated in Panama. Beltran ran an unregistered commodity pool throughout 2009. This scheme stated that the investments were risk free and would bring returns of at least 12 percent per month. The funds were never invested, some of which were sent to an offshore account in Anguilla. The commodity pool was not registered with the CFTC, nor were the perpetrators registered as brokers. This is an example of a false-brokerage scheme; it was intentional (CFTC, 2011, September 27).
- Victor Cilli's company, *Progressive Investment Fund*, was a registered commodity pool. Cilli's pool was investing in commodities futures trading. A small percentage of the funds taken in were used for commodities futures trades, then suffered severe losses. The losses were not reported to investors, then Cilli used the funds from new investors to pay earlier investors. This scheme ran from approximately 2006 through 2007 (CFTC, 2011, June 15). This is an example of a brokerage-failure scheme.

Futures

Futures are contracts where an investment instrument is contracted to sell at an agreed-upon price on a specific date. Both the buyer and seller are obligated to carry out their part of the transaction as agreed upon.[8] There were 43 schemes involving futures, which may have been just futures, or in combination with other investment instruments such as stocks, options, and commodities. As with many Ponzi schemes, the perpetrators only said they were futures brokers and that investments would be in futures markets. It is a type of investment process that is confusing to many inexperienced investors. Futures examples:

- Dro Kholamian told his investor-victims that they would be investing in both "leveraged off-exchange" FOREX contracts and futures contracts. Kholamian was not registered as commodities trading adviser. He had accounts with futures commissions merchants but he withdrew the funds in those accounts. Kholamian did no FOREX trading with the funds. In a classic intentional scheme, Kholamian did not trade all of his clients' funds but instead made Ponzi payments and used his investor-victims' funds for his own personal expenses. His victims were primarily Armenians (CFTC, 2018, November 30).

- Scott Bottolfson carried out his futures scheme through two commodity pools. At least one of the pools was registered with the NFA as a commodity pool; however, his trades experienced losses (CFTC, 2011, January 7). A commodity pool when formed legally through the CFTC allows for the pooling investors funds in order to trade on commodities, futures, or options. In this case, Bottolfson used about one-fourth of investor funds to trade, much of which was lost; then the remaining funds were used for Ponzi payments, and by Bottolfson personally (CFTC, 2011, October 19, p.r.).
- John and Jeffrey Fowler carried out a Ponzi scheme based on gold futures. The two Fowlers, with a third conspirator, promised their investor-victims that their funds would be used to purchase gold futures. Gold futures is an agreement to purchase or sell gold at a specific agreed-upon price at a date set in the future. The investor-victims were issued promissory notes for their funds. The promissory notes were worthless, as were the alleged gold futures that never existed. This was an intentional Ponzi scheme (SEC, 2013, July 5).

Foreign Currency Exchange: FOREX

Foreign currency exchange, known as "FOREX," are investments based in foreign currency exchange markets. Those who invest in the foreign currency market are buying one country's currency with money from their own currency, or a currency for another nation, based on the fluctuating values of currencies. As the values of the currency's rise and decline investors make or lose profits. The CFTC has oversight over these markets. There were 116 foreign currency-based Ponzi schemes in the data set. These perpetrators may make some actual investments in foreign currency markets, but more often than not, there were no actual investments made, only purported investments. These are a few of the FOREX schemes:

- The scheme of Anthony Garcia, Shawn Christie, and Edward Lindsey made use of options on the foreign currency exchange. Garcia pressured victims to invest; however, trades were never actually made. This was a classic intentional Ponzi scheme complete with high pressure and telemarketing tactics. Even though this was an intentional scheme, the offenders were ordered to repay the money, since the scheme had only taken $219,000 (CFTC, 2003, April 3, p.r.).

- Eldon Gresham did engage in some trading in FOREX, but was unsuccessful. Gresham reported gains when there were actual losses to clients. Gresham also targeted Christians as investors, telling them that "the Lord had blessed him" (CFTC, 2009, July 2, p. 7, line 19). Gresham also used the tactic of exclusiveness saying he was only offering his investment to "a limited number of fellow Christians" (CFTC, 2009, July 2, p. 7). This qualifies as a faith-based affinity-fraud scheme as well. Gresham was never registered with the CFTC in any capacity as required by CFTC regulation.

General or Other Investment Instruments

These include other investment instruments such as options, binary options, warrants, annuities, and any non-specific investment tools. Documents may have specified that the schemes were based in these instruments. In the great majority of cases there was little to no real investing or trading; these terms are only what investor-victims were told their funds were being invested in. The more complex the investment tool, the easier it is for perpetrators to use semantics to pull the wool over their client's eyes.

Options

In most of the options Ponzi schemes the schemes were classic intentional Ponzi schemes, meaning investor-victims were told they were investing in options, but in reality, there were no actual investing in options and all funds went to Ponzi payments and the personal use of the perpetrator(s). With standard options, it is a right to purchase or to sell stocks, commodities, or foreign currency for a set price for a specified expiration date. More commonly, the options do not reach the expiration date, and they are usually traded on price fluctuations. If the deadline expires and the purchase has not been made, the buyer loses the money. Binary options are generally trading on whether a stock or commodity reaches a certain price by a certain date; if the option expires the buyer receives a predetermined amount or they receive nothing.

- In this typical classic intentional Ponzi scheme, Jeremy Lundin told his investor-victims, who were friends and associates, that he would invest their funds in options. He falsified account statements to the victim-investors, and put the funds from his business account for *Big Island Capital*, which were meant for trading in options, into his personal account. He never established a broker account to make it appear that he was making trades. This false-brokerage scheme took place between 2014 and 2017 (DOJ, 2017, September 1, p.r.).

Warrants

When most of us see the term "warrants" we are thinking of a judicial document asking for an arrest or to search premises. While there have been many of those issued in Ponzi investigations, we are talking about a financial instrument called a warrant. Warrants give the holder the right to buy or sell a security without an obligation; it is a right to purchase or sell, not ownership. Generally, they are issued by the company itself with an expiration date.

- In his Ponzi scheme, Ronald Olear made use of shares of stocks and warrants of shares of stock. A warrant: "entitles the holder to buy a proportionate amount of common stock at a specified price, usually higher than the market price at the time of issuance, for a period of years to perpetuity" (Downes and Goodman, 2014). In this case Olear worked as a coordinator for maintenance, shipping, and security at a company. This position gave him access to shredded materials in a security zone. Olear found shredded stock certificates and used them to fabricate falsified stock certificates, making it appear as if he owned them; he then sold warrants based on these fraudulent stocks (FBI, 2010, December 20).

Boiler Rooms

This unsavory practice uses high-pressure tactics to convince people to invest in whatever financial instrument they are promoting; oftentimes it is penny stocks. Boiler rooms are used in many fraud formats, not just Ponzi schemes. Generally, the brokers use high-pressure tactics through cold-calling. As stated throughout the book, it is possible to purchase lists of names with phone numbers and now email addresses, based on demographics and personal characteristics.

- One Ponzi scheme that used boiler-room tactics is that of Cecil Speight. Speight issued counterfeit securities complete with fabricated CUSIP[9] numbers. These counterfeit stock certificates included several different mistakes, such as the wrong person as the signatory, and one country listed as the country of incorporation on one side with a different incorporation country on the back. Speight had individuals who cold-called people using high-pressure tactics. The sellers claimed to be associated with other investment/financial firms that were successful businesses; there was no association, it was all false. Basically, everything they pushed to the 70 investor-victims was untrue. Speight hired two attorneys to receive the funds of investors to give the appearance of legitimacy (SEC, 2014, July 23). These two attorneys were also charged criminally: one received a sentence of 48 months; the other, James Schmidt, died of cancer before sentencing (USA v. James L. Schmidt, 2019, April 15, motion to dismiss). They were making 2 percent on the funds they received. In this case the business was registered as a transfer agent with the SEC. This entity was required to file annual forms (TA-2) with the SEC, but failed to do so. Second, entities registered with the SEC are required to provide up-to-date business addresses; Speight's business did not have accurate addresses listed with the SEC. These are the types of information that could be uncovered by accessing the SEC's database in a due diligence search. This scheme took place from approximately 2012 to 2013.

Hedge Funds

A hedge fund is a private fund, where funds of all investors are pooled. The primary partner has a significant investment, and other partners or investors are generally accredited.[10] It is more risk-prone investing designed to support higher returns. To be accredited, an investor should have an income that is more than $200,000 for an individual or $300,000 for a couple, with a net worth that is more than $1 million. Investors are expected to be financially sophisticated and knowledgeable about speculative practices, short selling, and leveraging. In short, investors are expected to have an understanding of the risks in investing and to be able to weather losses. Generally, hedge funds require 65 percent of their investors to be accredited. There were 29 hedge fund-based schemes in all, having been referred to in SEC documents as hedge funds (as opposed to fraudulent hedge funds in name only). Of those:

- Six schemes began before the housing bubble (2001 or earlier).
- Ten schemes began during the housing bubble (2002–2006).
- Seven schemes began during the financial crisis (2007–2010).
- Six schemes began after the financial crisis (2011 or later).

As with all Ponzi schemes in this study, there were both legitimate hedge funds that failed, and fraudulent schemes that falsely portrayed themselves as hedge funds. There were 41 entities that called themselves "hedge funds" either legitimately or illegitimately. Bruce Johnson states that "The hedge fund industry has long been prone to periodic 'die offs' where as many as 15–30 percent of all funds cease trading" (Johnson, 2010, p. xi). In some of the cases in this study, the legitimate hedge funds endured losses, then began paying investors with later investors funds rather than earned profits that did not happen. There may very well be hedge funds that tried this tactic and succeeded in earning enough funds to pay investors back; we will never know.

Dodd-Frank requires hedge fund managers with over $100 million in assets under management to register with the SEC. Mid-sized investment advisers managing assets between $25 million and $100 million are not required to register with the SEC, unless their home state does not have adequate regulation for hedge funds. For the investor, these are unregulated funds; this means that there is a lot of gray area where an investment entity can state that it is operating within SEC regulations when it is operating anything but legitimately. There are also "funds of funds," investment entities that only invest with hedge funds. These are usually hedge funds investing in other hedge funds, also referred to as "feeder funds" in earlier chapters. In the Dreier and Madoff cases, there were hedge funds that were victims of the Ponzi schemes.

- *Bernie Madoff Investment Securities* had individual investors, municipalities, charities and pension funds, hedge fund investors, and fund of funds investors. Until 2006, Madoff was a broker-dealer. In 2006 the SEC required him to register as an investment adviser. Some of the hedge funds and funds of funds were what is classified as feeder funds; they invested their clients' funds in his fund. In Harry Markopolos' 2005 submission to the SEC titled *The world's largest hedge fund is a fraud*, he explains that "third party hedge funds and funds of funds" were not allowed to use Madoff's name in their statements or marketing. There were multiple layers of funds. The actual investors in the hedge funds, funds of funds, and pension holders whose pension funds invested with Madoff had no idea where their money was invested; they never had a chance to carry out due diligence.
- Marc Dreier was a Manhattan attorney who sold fraudulent promissory notes to hedge funds (SEC, 2008, December 8). This case took place prior to the financial crisis; the notes were alleged to be based in real estate development. In the Dreier case, it was the hedge funds who were victimized. Dreier was a reputable attorney with a successful law firm. He skillfully convinced hedge fund managers, who tend to be quite financially sophisticated in general, to invest in his promissory notes.
- In their unregistered false hedge fund, John Turant and Russ Luciano convinced investor-victims that they were experts in financial markets. The three business entities whose sole purpose was to perpetrate the fraud were formed in Nevada. The alleged securities promoted for the investments were never registered with the SEC. Very little of the funds acquired from investors were actually invested in day-trading as the investor-victims were told. Turant lied to his investor-

victims about having the appropriate licenses and financial markets experience. His work experience was primarily "maintenance work, cutting hedges and ordering office supplies" (SEC, 2003, September 15). This was a classic intentional, false-broker Ponzi scheme.

Oil and Gas

Oil- and gas-based schemes have taken place throughout the entire time span of the study. As soon as there was a demand for oil and gas with the invention of automobiles, there was opportunity for fraud. In these schemes, the perpetrators stated that the investors would be investing in oil or gas enterprises, drilling, exploration, fracking, wells, and the revenues thereof. Oil and gas schemes were generally based on the claim that there were already known wells in production, the purchase of new wells, or searching for new wells. There were 53 cases based on oil or gas wells and drilling, including fracking.

- In the 1997 *Amerivest* case, Jerry Anderson, Peter Sacker, and Robert Kerns promised investors that they would be investing in securities in oil and gas wells. Anderson, Sacker, and Kerns did not own all of the oil and gas wells the stated revenues were to be collected from (SEC, 1997, October 16, l.r.). In SEC administrative proceedings Anderson and Kerns insisted they had purchased oil wells. However, they had sold the same shares of those oil wells to multiple investors (SEC, 2000, May 31).
- John Bridges and his fictitious company, *Logan Investments*, told investors that they would be investing in a private oil company and the construction of a liquid petroleum pipeline. Bridges' scheme was an intentional scheme; there were never any shares or a pipeline to invest in (FBI, 2013, July 23, p.r.).
- *Tennstar Energy/Black Gold Resources* was represented to the victim-investors that their funds would be invested "in various oil wells" and to "employ enhanced oil recovery techniques such as fracking" (SEC, 2017, August 11, p. 4). Hydraulic fracking is a process of drilling into the earth, then using high-pressure water injected into subterranean rock in order to extract oil and gas. The more recent practices have made use of horizontal drilling, although fracking has been around since 1950.

Precious Metals, Diamonds, Mining Markets, and Coins

Precious metals are gold, silver, platinum, and palladium. Their value is universally recognized and are the bases for markets, fine jewelry, and industrial uses. Frauds based on precious metals generally stated they were investing in mines or bullion. In most Ponzi cases based on precious metals or mining, there was little, if any, actual investing taking place. There were 36 schemes based on precious metals, diamonds, mining, coins, or jewelry. At least one scheme was based on diamond mines, and two schemes were based on jewelry.

- Ryan and Bita Nassbridges told investors they would be investing in bullion and coins, and that their investments would be insured against losses. Instead they used their victims' money to invest in commodity futures and options trading and lost the money (CFTC, 2014, October 24, p.r.).
- William Ison and Douglas Ellingson and *Blue Diamond Excavation* alleged that they were running a mining company. This company did not mine or produce profits (DOJ, 2014, August 27). The perpetrators also claimed that they had donated a trillion dollars to AIDS research (FBI, 2012, November 9, p.r.).
- Lawrence Heim operated a legitimate coin and gold investment company in Oregon. "In 2009, Heim fell behind in his coin purchases, as the value of gold and silver rose" (FBI, 2012, October 31). He then began a Ponzi scheme. This entity falls under the business-failure schemes. Many of his victims were elderly.
- Matthew Addy operated a retail jewelry business in Pennsylvania. He targeted those within his own religious affiliation, making this an affinity-fraud, although the specific group was not mentioned in documents. The stated investment was in wholesale jewelry and loose gemstones, none of which were actually purchased (FBI, 2013, June 7, p.r.).
- Rose Marie O'Reilly's scheme was stated as investing in pink diamonds and silver antiques. Her method of operation convinced prospective victim-investors that the specific items were significant historical silver pieces, and pink diamond jewelry alleged to have been owned by a New Orleans organized crime boss. She stated that she was trying to acquire the lost pieces to these sets, then would sell the sets for a profit (DOJ, 2016, January 15, p.r.).
- Luis Perez's scheme targeted his local Hispanic community in this affinity-fraud scheme. Perez had two jewelry businesses that the investor-victims were told they were investing in. His scheme stated that he worked with pawn shops in New York City that held diamonds that were collateral for his investments. Perez did not actually finance any pawn shops as stated, nor did he have any stones with pawn shops and did not have diamonds in safe deposit boxes as stated to his investors. The alleged diamonds were fake. Also, Perez had told his investors that he put them on his life insurance policy;

however, he had failed to pay the premiums (SEC, 2010, June 2, l.r.). Perez was also involved in a bank fraud scheme at the same time as the Ponzi scheme (ICE, 2011, February 2, p.r.)

- Michael S. Goldberg presented himself as being a diamond buyer from merchants in New York City. He told his victims he would then sell the diamonds for a profit. He also told investor-victims that he was working with JP Morgan Chase to purchase foreclosure assets. This was a classic intentional scheme in that it was never a legitimate business that all assertions were false from the onset. This was a scheme that had begun 12 years earlier but collapsed during the financial crisis (FBI, 2011, May 16, p.r.).

Technology-Based Frauds

In his 1923 book, *Confessions of a confidence man: A handbook for suckers,*[11] Edward Smith explains that all inventions and aspects of social activities are an opportunity for a fraud or scam. Even in the then immediate-post Charles Ponzi years, this was evident. This section describes those schemes that are technologically based schemes that lured investors; there were 89 schemes within this category. As technology changes, fraudulent schemes adapt. Technological products have been the vehicle to be invested in, or, in the case of cryptocurrencies, the actual means of investing. When there are new and upcoming technologies investors want to get in early and invest in the hope of buying low and selling high. The technological tools of this type of fraud have changed with the times: ATMs, pay phones, dotcoms, algorithms, internet/IP, and recent technologies: Twitter and Uber. As science makes progress and electronic technologies improve, each progression invites yet another basis for a Ponzi scheme. Now, most, if not all, Ponzi perpetrators make use of the internet and phones; as a result, most perpetrators are charged with wire fraud.

- One earlier example of a technology-based fraud was Peggy Stines in the 1980s. The scheme was based on extraction of silver halide from photographic film processing. Digital photography and home printing are quite commonplace in 2020; this type of scheme would not be successful in this time period. In Stines' scheme there was no actual extraction of silver taking place (Stines, 1984, August 2).
- Larry Ellis' scheme of 1995–2000 was one of several schemes based in automated teller machines (ATM) (SEC, 2001, July 25). These types of schemes were based on privately owned automated teller machines, with the intent that investors would be partial owners and share in the profits from fees earned through usage. In most of Ponzi scheme cases based on ATMs, there were never any machines purchased.

- Charles Edwards ran one of the pay-phone schemes in the time period of 1996–2000. Edwards' business was a legitimate business-failure scheme. Cell phones were on their way in; pay-phones were on their way out. He simply did not make the profits and turned to a Ponzi scheme instead (SEC, 2006, August 2, l.r.).
- Steven Bartko's scheme from 2003 to 2011 was based on electronics parts and circuit boards to be sold to government contractors. He provided investors with fraudulent statements and invoices on government contracts. There were no government contracts (FBI, 2012, April 16).
- Michael Garian was a classic technology scheme of the dot-com-era technology schemes in 1997–2001 (SEC, 2003, February 7, l.r.). This scheme falsely sold investors IPOs of internet and other technologically based companies. This scheme was intentional and an affinity-fraud scheme that preyed on Armenian Americans.
- Gregory Gray's scheme is known to have been active from at least June of 2014. His scheme was based on pre-IPOs of *Twitter* social media stocks. *Twitter* went public in November of 2013 (SEC, 2015, February 27). His scheme was investing in pre-IPOs of *Uber Technologies* (DOJ, 2015, March 5, p.r.). *Uber* is a phone application technology available through smart phones allowing pairing potential riders with a car service. *Uber Technologies* went public in May 2019. Gray had never owned *Uber* stock, although he told his investors he did.
- Frederic Elmaleh, also represented to his victim-investors that their investments were going to funds that would invest in technology companies such as "*Twitter, Inc., Alibaba Group Holding Limited, Uber Technologies, Inc., Square, Inc., Pinterest Inc.,* and *GoDaddy Group, Inc.*" Elmaleh and his partner Ahmad Naqvi claimed that through their venture capital connections they could place investments in privately held technology companies. A small portion of the $17 million in funds received were used to make investments that failed, producing no profit. The rest was used to support Elmaleh and Naqvi and to buy luxury vehicles and to pay Ponzi payments (DOJ, 2016, April 13, p.r.).
- Paul Gilman's business intended to promote sound technology. His businesses endeavored to "optimize sound systems in sports stadiums." Gilman claimed he could use sounds waves for oil fracking, and to reduce the viscosity of oil. His businesses failed and then became a Ponzi scheme (SEC, 2018, June 4).
- *Full Tilt Poker* is the first online poker Ponzi scheme. This online gambling site began in 2004. In 2006 Congress enacted the Unlawful Internet Gambling Enforcement Act. This Act governs payment systems in online gaming. Founder Raymond Bitar had to find more creative ways to process the funds received through the gambling

site. Eventually, the cost of doing business outweighed the profits and Bitar began a Ponzi scheme. Bitar's scheme also deceived banks. Bitar pleaded guilty and received time served due to poor health (Vaughan, 2013). This poker-based Ponzi scheme lasted from approximately 2006 until 2011, with 11 individuals charged. Ten received sentences, from time served, one week to 36 months. The individuals involved were supposed to keep separate accounts for each online player. This was not done, allowing for payments to be made from other players' accounts, hence a Ponzi scheme. This was estimated to having taken in $1 billion in the superseding indictment (USA v. Bitar, 2013, April 23). The DOJ seized five internet domain sites. Eventually, the final settlement was $731 million to be repaid to the players. Player-victims were in the United States and in other countries.

- In the *New Century Coal* Ponzi scheme based on a specific type of high-grade coal called "Blue gem" alleged to be used in the manufacture of silicon and computer electronics. This scheme was based on coal mines. The perpetrators went so far as to rent a mine and import heavy equipment to give the appearance of mining coal. Every aspect of this scheme was fraudulent: there was no high-grade coal, or coal mines. This scheme was an intentional fraud from the very beginning (FBI, 2016, December 12, p.r.).

With the general interest in climate change and in reducing fossil fuel usage, there have been extensive technological progresses. It is a bit surprising there have not been more Ponzi schemes based in energy efficiency products. These solar and bio-energy schemes were recent; the most recent large scheme was *DC Solar*, over a billion dollars.

- Clarence Counterman and Robert Loya told investor-victims they were investing in four solar energy companies: *Renewable Energy Consultants, Inc., EP Solar Technologies Inc., LITTCE Inc.*, and *Eco Global Corporation* (DOJ, 2017, February 2, p.r.). This scheme also began during the financial crisis in 2008 and was stopped in 2013. There was no indication that any of the funds had been used for the intended solar energy products or companies.
- Neal Goyal opened at least three funds beginning with the title of *Blue Horizon*, the second of which was begun in 2007: *Blue Horizon Bio-Energy Fund*. Goyal started his fund in 2006 when it still appeared the economy was doing well. The funds were alleged to be investing in specific types securities; the bio-energy fund was supposed to be investing in bio-energy securities. His fourth fund, Caldera, was established in 2009, alleged to be investing in equities. Goyal's

first fund was marketed to friends and family. Each year thereafter he began another fund; he eventually had four funds. Goyal did try to invest; however, early on he had losses and resorted to a Ponzi scheme by 2007. By this time the financial crisis had begun. Goyal may have started his business with the intent of investing; however, his timing was bad and so were his trading skills. His scheme collapsed in 2014 (SEC, 2014, May 28).

- Christopher Warren began his company *Clean Energy Advisers* in 2013. This investment was alleged to be in solar farms that *Clean Energy Advisers* owned. Warren told investor-victims that his solar farms were selling energy to utility companies. The farms Warren reported as being owned by his company were actually owned by someone else, and other reported farms did not exist. This was an intentional Ponzi scheme from the onset (DOJ, 2019, June 11, p.r.).

- Jeff and Paulette Carpoff owned the solar mobile generator companies *D.C. Solar Solutions* and *DC Solar Distribution*. In this scheme, investors were told their investments were going to manufacture and purchase generators from *DC Solutions* that were then leased to *DC Distribution*. The generators were then supposed to be leased to users. The actual generators manufactured were about one-fourth of what was told to investors. The majority of investments were the Ponzi scheme (SEC, 2020, January 24).

As technology changes, the means of carrying out the frauds change. Several Ponzi schemes of the past decade report the use of "algorithms" as tools to determine investments. Algorithms are mathematical data processing instructions designed for specific functions. Those purporting to use these techniques may or may not have an actual system for trading in place. Some cases may have been using algorithms but failed, turning to a Ponzi scheme. Others only said they were using algorithms. What is certain is that any new technology or gadget to come to the market will inspire new types of frauds as investors speculate on the possibilities of whatever is the newest trend.

Vaping products are some of the more recent technology in the market place. Vaping is using electronic cigarettes as one would use a standard cigarette. The electronic cigarette vaporizes a liquid containing nicotine so that it can be inhaled. These products began to appear in 2007. There are always those watching for the newest technology who find a way to turn an investment in it into a Ponzi scheme.

- Leonard Lombardo had previously been barred from association with National Association of Securities Dealers (NASD) members for securities violations in 2000 by NASD. Lombardo's current scheme used funds from investors who thought they were investing in improving distressed real estate. The time period was 2011, when many homes were going into foreclosure as a result of the financial crisis. However, Lombardo used those funds for *Clearette*, a distributor of e-cigarettes. In 2015 Lombardo abandoned the e-cigarettes and moved into producing e-juice, the liquid that goes in to e-cigarettes. Lombardo moved funds between business ventures without telling investors. He also used the received funds to make Ponzi payments to investors (SEC, 2017, September 29).

Current and Future Trends in Ponzi Schemes

The first two Ponzi schemes based on cannabis-related products have become a matter of public record just before this book went to press. There are currently 11 states that have legalized recreational marijuana, yet it is still illegal on the federal level. Twenty states have legalized medical marijuana use. This first cannabis-based scheme was reported by the SEC September 30, 2019.

- The scheme of Mark Ray et al. involved several business entities. This scheme promoted to investor-victims that the funds were going for cattle trading and licensed marijuana transactions. Two businesses supported cattle trading; one business, called *Universal Herbs*, had marijuana retail sites in Denver, Colorado. The fourth business was said to finance cannabidiol, an oil said to have medicinal qualities. As with all Ponzi schemes, investor funds were not used to purchase cattle or cannabis transactions but instead were Ponzi payments going to previous investors (SEC, 2019, September 30). Colorado was the first state to legalize marijuana for recreational use. This scheme began in 2016; Colorado legalized recreational marijuana in 2012. The complexity of this case is that bank accounts were set up and LLCs were formed in Illinois by co-conspirator Reva Stachniw to receive funds for the alleged investments. However, Illinois, the eleventh state to legalize recreational marijuana, was not allowing the purchase until January 2020.
- The SEC filed a complaint with the second cannabis-based Ponzi scheme in California, in January 2020. In this scheme the business entity is in Washington state but also formed in Nevada and Washington. The case is in unregistered securities in cannabis production. The scheme itself took place from 2015 to 2017 with a take of $4.8 million.

Artificial Intelligence

Artificial intelligence is being used to detect fraudulent schemes. The South Korean Seoul Special Judicial Police for Public Safety arrested two individuals for a Ponzi scheme in 2019. Artificial Intelligence was also used to locate the perpetrators. It is also just a matter of time until a Ponzi scheme is perpetrated based on investing in the development or use of artificial intelligence. Where there is a technological advance, there is someone willing it to create a fraud.

Paid-to-Click

One new form of technology that has inspired several types of fraud is paid-to-click schemes. In these internet-based schemes investor contribute a fee up-front for advertising their websites, and with the paid-to-click aspect requiring members to click on a certain amount of other member's websites. These schemes ask investor-victims to buy "adpacks" (SEC, 2017, November 7). These products ask investors or clients to purchase a membership, and then must click on other member's websites. The profits were supposed to come from memberships and from being paid to click on advertisements online, but instead were solely Ponzi payments. There is no actual product other than advertising. The following schemes are based on this format:

* Charles Scoville and his *Traffic Monsoon* used YouTube videos to promote the investment in "Banner AdPacks." This was a website where "users browse each other's websites, and a pay-per-click program, where users are paid to click on others' website banner ads" (SEC, 2016, July 26, prg. 4). This format had two different types of memberships: paying and non-paying. However, it was pure Ponzi scheme; there was no means of making a profit other than the investments made by victims. Scoville had 162,000 victims.
* Pedro Fort Berbel's scheme targeted internet investor-victim's in three different languages: English, French, and Spanish. Similar to *Traffic Monsoon*, investors purchased an advertising plan that had the option of clicking on links or another plan that did not require clicking on links. Investor-victims were told they would share in the profits, but there were virtually no profits, just investor's funds paid out as Ponzi payments (SEC, 2017, September 28).

Banking Fraud

Banking frauds as Ponzi schemes come in several varieties. In most cases the Ponzi scheme was based in prime banking or false banks. There 28 cases of bank-based frauds other than prime bank instruments. These may have been referred to in federal documents as banks, bank debenture, European or foreign banks, bank instruments, and offshore banks. In some cases, it is the banks that are defrauded, as in the case of Robert L. Bentley, who was selling privately issued CDs to small banks and credit unions. In the general bank cases, the perpetrator simply set up a bank without the authorization to do so, and it became a Ponzi scheme. Allen Stanford formed banks in other countries each with different banking laws.

- Allen Stanford's *Stanford International Bank Ltd.* was domiciled in St. John's Antigua, West Indies. This "bank" did not provide loans for its income but instead sold CDs through its US affiliate: *Stanford Group Company* (SEC, 2009, February 16, prg. 19). Stanford's banks in other countries functioned as retail banks. As soon as Stanford's empire began to crumble, Stanford's retail banks in Venezuela and Panama were seized by the governments. The banks may have functioned as legitimate banks by the legal standards of those nations; however, the basis of the funds for those entities was based in his Ponzi scheme (Associated Press, Daily News, 2009, February 19).

There were two Native American bank cases: Ron Sparks and Owen Stephenson, *First Americans Bank*; and Edward Driving Hawk Sr. et al., *U.S. Reservation Bank and Trust*. The false bank fraud schemes of Howe (discussed in Chapter 12), Driving Hawk, and Sparks were primarily affinity-fraud cases where the perpetrator appealed to those in their self-identifying groups. However, the prime banking schemes tend to prey on anyone gullible enough to believe the perpetrator's words.

- Edward Driving Hawk's *U.S. Reservation Bank & Trust* was complex because the business entity was granted licensees by Rosebud Sioux Tribe of South Dakota. The business was functioning as a bank without the federal or state governments authority to do so. The intent was a Native American financial institution that would offer investment trading for Native Americans (SEC, 2002, April 3). This scheme promised investor-victims that their investments would "leveraged profit sharing" (SEC, 2002, April 3). In this case "leveraged" refers to using the investor's funds in US Treasury bonds, or for investing, or loans to finance the business. Instead the funds were used for Ponzi payments.
- In a separate, earlier scheme, Ron Sparks also ran a Native American bank called the *First Americans Bank*. Similar to Driving Hawk, Sparks did not have the federal or state authority to run a bank. In this case, it also turned out to be a Ponzi scheme (SEC, 2000, February 24, l.r.).
- Bentley's scheme was carried out from approximately 1986 until 2001. This scheme took advantage of at least 3,000 banks, credit unions, or businesses, and individual investors. This scheme told investors that he would be investing their funds on bank issued CDs that were from FDIC-insured banks (SEC, 2002, January 9).

- Michael J. Randy sold CDs to more than 500 investor-victims in several states. Randy told his investors that the CDs were issued by banks in Montserrat and Grenada. Everything about this case was false; there were no associated banks in Monserrate or Grenada. This was more than $16 million in false CDs (SEC, 1999, March 9, l.r.; SEC, 1999, September 8, l.r. Johnston).
- William Wise, Kristi Hoegel, and Jackie Hoegel established *Millennium Bank* in St. Vincent and Grenadines. This entity was run through a financial service center in Kingston St. Vincent. *Millennium Bank* was owned by *United Trust of Switzerland S.A.*, chartered in Switzerland. United Trust of Switzerland LLC was formed in Nevada by Jackie/Jacqueline Hoegel, Kristi Hoegel, and William Wise in Nevada (Kristi Hoegel is Jackie Hoegel's daughter). Kristi Hoegel also had two other aliases. *Millennium Bank* offered guaranteed high-yield CDs. Investors mailed checks to St. Vincent and Grenadines, but then those checks were mailed to Napa California where they were electronically deposited to *Washington Mutual-JP Morgan Chase* accounts held by *United Trust LLC*. *Millennium Bank* primarily targeted US investors, but also promoted itself in thirteen other languages. Wise received a sentence of 262 months, while the Hoegels were only ordered to return funds that were traceable through *Millennium Bank* by the SEC (SEC, 2009, March 29).
- Scott Yoshizumi is a classic example of someone who is a financial markets investment fraud recidivist. Yoshizumi had two previous investment fraud convictions, had filed for bankruptcy, and did not have the experience he stated, and lied about his credentials to his customers. His scheme was an intentional Ponzi scheme in every aspect. Yoshizumi's Ponzi scheme claimed to be investing in "bank debentures" from the "top 200 world banks" (SEC, 2000, November 24, l.r.). This scheme could have been considered a prime banking scheme; however, the words were not used in the federal documents.

Prime Banking

Prime banking schemes tend to prey on anyone gullible enough to believe the perpetrator's words. "Prime banks" are generally considered the top 50 banks in the world. According to the SEC this refers to top financial institutions such as those on "Wall Street, London or Geneva, to other world financial centers."[12] These cases are pure fraud; there are no "prime bank notes." Prime banking cases tend to promise high rates of returns and may state they are endorsed by or affiliated with the International Monetary fund or the Federal Reserve Bank. The use of the term "prime" is designed to convince the victims of the status of the investment when it is not a real investment product. There were 40 prime banking schemes; many prime banking schemes took place in the late 1990s (19); nine schemes took place in the 2000–2010 decade. The more recent prime banking scheme was that of Marino and Polera:

- The scheme of Anthony Marino and George Polera had taken place from 2013 through 2015. This scheme made use of prime banking in that the perpetrators offered prime banking instruments in several forms as stated in the SEC complaint; these prime bank instruments were "fictitious" (SEC, 2017, July 25, p. 2). The prime bank instruments were offered as securities in the form of promissory notes that offered 84 percent interest. This scheme had so many red flags it only took in $615,500; someone caught on quickly.
- In Stanley Anderson's prime banking scheme, he told investors that major international banks were selling "high yield bank instruments off the books to private traders who are allowed to buy the instruments at a discount and resell them for extremely high unrealistic high rates of return" (SEC, 2008, July 28). In general "High-Yield Investment Programs," also known as HYIP, are frauds. They promise exorbitant rates of return that cannot possibly be met.
- Roy E. Matlock and Alan Root sold "prime bank instruments." There were only eight victims in the $3.5 million fraud, one of which was the Chicago Housing Authority Pension Plan. The curiosity is that a government entity pension plan should have some requirement of due diligence that would have recognized this as a fraud (SEC, 2000, November 8, l.r.). Prime bank instruments are not an actual financial instrument that exists legally.

Promissory Notes

Promissory notes are a written promise to pay money, basically "I owe yous" (IOU). Legitimate promissory notes are debt instruments used when companies need to raise money. There were 82 schemes based on promissory notes. They are securities that must be registered with the SEC and can be verified through the SEC-EDGAR database. If the seller is legitimate, he or she is licensed to sell securities. Promissory notes specify that the borrower is borrowing a certain amount of money and the terms of that borrowing, such as maturity date, and the interest that is to be paid. Promissory notes include the place that they are issued, as well as the names and signatures of the parties. The transaction becomes illegal when the borrower has no intention, or has no ability to pay back the funds that were borrowed. In many cases the schemes were intentional frauds from the onset, meaning there was never any intention of paying back the principal investment/loan.

- Robert Narvett's promissory notes specified his company *"Shield"* as the borrower and his investor-victims as the lender. The notes specified that the principal amount would be paid back at an annual interest rate of 20 percent. Narvett tried not to provide specifics but, when pressed, told investor-victims that the notes would be used as working capital to build *Shield*. *Shield* was said to be a recruiting agency. All of the funds raised went toward Narvett's personal expenses and Ponzi payments, in a classic, intentional scheme (SEC, 2013, August 16).

- Algird Norkus' scheme convinced victims to invest in promissory notes designated to his business entity. His business was alleged to insure people who had been refused insurance from other insurance companies. Higher-risk insurance companies charge higher fees, and would therefore bring in higher revenues from premiums. In this case, the promissory notes were scheduled to be repaid in five years' time. The business entity *Financial Update Inc.* was an intentional Ponzi scheme; the funds were never used in an insurance capacity, nor were there insured clients (SEC, 2010, October 14).

Unregistered promissory notes are generally those that have a term shorter than nine months that may qualify as exempt from registering with the SEC. If they are not registered, they are not under the monitoring of the SEC, and there may not have had formal due diligence carried out. In other words, they are risky and may be a fraud. Legitimate promissory notes must be registered with the SEC and the state of which they are issued, and the seller must have the appropriate license to sell them.

Medical Equipment, Medical Billing, and Pharmaceuticals and Research

The medical Ponzi frauds came in three basic versions, for the most part, one of which purports to be investing in medical equipment; a second is said to be investing in medical receivables, a third is investing in research and development of treatments, equipment, or pharmaceuticals. In truth, there was never any investing or research and development going on in any of the medical cases. There were 18 schemes based on medical/pharmaceutical terminology. The following are a few classic examples:

- Edwin Fujinaga's scheme told investor-victims their funds would be used to buy accounts receivable from medical providers, factoring. The investors were also Japanese, as was Fujinaga, making this also an affinity-fraud scheme. Fujinaga also established *Sterling Escrow* that was supposed to safeguard investor funds. Instead it was an account that received funds and paid out the Ponzi payments (USA v. Edwin Fujinaga, 2015, July 8).

- Robert Hurd and his company, *Your Best Memories*, was stated to be promoting Alzheimer's treatments that included DVDs of patient's photographs and coconut oil. Hurd had told investors that his company had received approval from the US Food and Drug Administration (FDA), another fraudulent claim. The entire scheme comprised several frauds, including unregistered securities. There was only one actual sale of the product. Hurd and partner Gross sold shares of the companies, promising that 60 percent of funds would be used for working capital, to produce the products. Only 17 percent was used; the rest went for salaries and Ponzi payments (SEC, 2014, June 11, l.r.).
- Christopher Pedras ran a New Zealand-based scheme that told victim-investors that they were investing in kidney dialysis machines, and dialysis clinics in New Zealand. Pedras also had a bank trading company as part of his fraud. Pedras lived in California and New Zealand; his victims were primarily in the United States (SEC, 2013, November 5, l.r.)

Insurance Frauds

Ponzi scheme insurance frauds are carried out in many forms. Insurance fraud in general is one of the largest areas of fraud. There were 22 insurance-based Ponzi schemes. In some cases, the perpetrators were licensed insurance agents; in others the perpetrators falsely presented themselves as being licensed agents. The victim-investors are told they are investing in insurance companies in some cases, and in other cases they are investing in insurance products, such as viaticals. Insurance companies must make a profit in order to function as a business. They make profits from investing the funds and by collecting premiums where the insured do not make claims. When the insured never make claims, the insurance company keeps the money that has been paid into the company as premiums. Some schemes were properly functioning insurance businesses that failed, becoming business-failure schemes.

One particularly egregious form of insurance frauds make use of viaticals. Viatical settlements offer legitimate insurance clients who have terminal illness the opportunity to sell the death benefit policy to someone who will collect upon their death, providing a source of income in the late stage of life. Three Ponzi schemes purported to be investing in viaticals, stating that all investors would receive a portion of the death benefits when the policy holder died.

- Frederick Brandau, with 11 other offenders, perpetrated one of the more egregious types of schemes: viaticals. Brandau's scheme took place in the late 1990s. The victim-investors were investing in a company that purported to buy viaticals; it was just a Ponzi scheme (SEC, 2002, July 8). The fraudulent documents used to perpetrate the scheme were falsified insurance policies. During the 1990s there were several of these types of schemes that preyed on the elderly and those dying with AIDS.

- James Griffin's scheme invited investors to invest in an insurance company that was allegedly selling insurance to the disabled. These schemes also told victim-investors that a percentage of their returns on their investments would be going to a charity of their choice (SEC, 2015, July 30). Griffin told investor-victims that the charitable gift annuities were backed by a major insurance company (DOJ, 2016, December 13).

- Donald Neuhaus and Kimberly Snowden told investors that their funds would be used to pay premiums on life insurance policies that were being sold. In this case, investor funds were being used to pay on life insurance premiums. Part of the process includes actuarial calculations of life expectancies. This determines how much money should be set aside for an insured individual. If this is not done correctly the premiums are not enough and the fund runs short. In addition, instead of putting the received premiums into investments, Neuhaus and Snowden used the money paid in premiums for themselves. When the money was depleted, they began to pay out as a Ponzi scheme (SEC, 2007, August 23).

- Bart Posey et al., ran several unlicensed and/or unauthorized health insurance companies beginning in 2005, in Tennessee and Arkansas, North Carolina, Indiana, Delaware, New Jersey, New York, New Hampshire, with an entity in Pakistan. The Pakistan entity, *Beema*, was the underwriter for the insurance being sold by Posey et al., and was a shell company. Posey paid health insurance claims with the premiums paid by new insurance clients. There were legitimate healthcare claims that were denied payment (USA v. Bart Posey, 2013, June 26).

Annuities

Annuities are a financial product generally purchased through insurance companies. There are times when an individual receives a large amount of money, such as from an inheritance, being paid a lump-sum on from a job retirement account, or sometimes a settlement in the case of an accident or a law suit; the recipients may choose to put the money into an annuity. Some annuities are paid in a series of payments. The primary purpose of an annuity is long-term funding, such as income in retirement. Generally, the payout is in regular installments but can also be in one lump-sum. Legitimate annuities are purchased through a reputable insurance provider. It is important to understand what annuities are, to recognize when the term is being used as a ruse for a fraud.

- Rosi Ray, also known as Gloria Lujan in court records, told her investor-victims that their investments were going to purchase the annuity settlements of accident victims. These were to be purchased at a discount, meaning there would be a profit for the investors. However, there were never any settlement annuities purchased. All funds that came in were used for Ponzi payments and to Ray and her employees (USA v. Rosi Ray, 2010, December 1).
- Joyce Allen became the primary of *Benchmark Capital* upon the suicide of its founder Charles Candler. Allen was an independent insurance agent when Candler hired her to sell annuities (USA v. Joyce E. Allen, 2015/2017). When the SEC began investigating *Benchmark* and Candler, he killed himself. Allen and Candler sold investor-victims fraudulent securities in the form of annuities, annuities that were completely non-existent. Their victims were told their funds were going into annuity accounts. Instead the funds went into Joyce Allen's account. The funds were paid out into Ponzi payments to the other annuity investors and to Allen and her employees for personal use (USA v. Joyce Allen et al., 2012, July 17, indictment). The annuities were never invested in anything to earn interest as promised, or as would be expected if they had been purchased through an insurance company. The victims thought their money was going into an annuity account.

Debt Service

Ponzi perpetrators prey on both individuals and businesses, in debt service schemes. In one type of debt scheme, the mechanism is debt consolidation where the individual victim or business victim pay into a debt service that will allegedly negotiate for lesser fees to debtors. However, the Ponzi perpetrator does not pay into the debts for long; if at all, they simply take the money. In these cases, the investors to the debt consolidation entity receive Ponzi payments. Generally, there is no actual payment into debt or actual debtors. One scheme was based in credit card debt collections; there were no actual debt collections. At least one Ponzi scheme was a case of what is known as "distressed-debt," meaning a company is in financial difficulties, or stress. The mechanism for making a profit is that some investors specialize in buying the bonds or securities of troubled companies. When the company rebounds there is a profit to the investor, or the investor may move to gain control of the company.

Factoring is another form of service management. Generally, this is the purchase of "factored" accounts receivables from companies, the purchase of the debts owed to them. For example, there may be a time lag between when a debt is incurred, such as a medical charge, and when the debt is settled by the patient or the insurance company. Factoring takes over the collection of that debt, and pays the business entity a percentage. When factoring is used as the bases of a Ponzi scheme the perpetrator says the company is involved in factoring; they are telling investors that their funds will be used to buy the cases that when collected will provide a profit for investors. However, there is usually no purchase of receivables, just Ponzi payments.

- Donald Bader and five of his family members ran a factoring operation in Colorado in the late 1980s. This scheme took in $9 million from what was said to be going toward accounts receivables for medical clinics and physicians. This case was civil only; there were no criminal charges (SEC, 1990, November 20).
- A more recent case of factoring involved post-dated checks from Brazil, of which Antonio Buzaneli purported to purchase the checks at a discount. Buzaneli's investors were told their funds were being used to purchase the post-dated checks. Buzaneli also opened this same business operation in London, Taipei, Shanghai, Singapore, and Panama (DOJ, 2019, April 9, p.r.)

In the following case, the funds brought in through investors were not used to toward distressed debts as stated, but instead were used toward Ponzi payments.

- The Damian Valdez scheme promised to purchase "low-risk debt obligations" (SEC, 2011, August 10, p. 2). The funds were not used to purchase debt obligations guaranteed by the US government as promised, but instead were used to invest in "strips." Strips entitle the holder of a debt to a portion of the "interest paid on a loan" (SEC, 2011, August 10, p. 2, prg. 3). These were high-risk investments; when the loans that the strips were based on defaulted, the value of the investment was nothing. The perpetrators then resorted to Ponzi payments.

There were six cases that were some form of debt-based fraud. Of those cases, two took place between 2003 and 2009. The remaining three began during or after 2008, during the financial crisis. One scheme was prior to the year 2003. The housing boom inspired two cases. During the financial crisis there was greater concern over debt, inspiring the debt services schemes. Debt service schemes often involve the practice of combining the debts of someone who is deeply in debt, then negotiating a lesser fee from the creditors. However, in a Ponzi situation, the perpetrators use the money from later investors to pay other investors; there has not been an actual debt service that paid down anyone's debts in the Ponzi data set.

Loans

In the cases of loan-based frauds, there was rarely a legitimate business that failed; they were predominantly intentional Ponzi schemes. There were 62 schemes using the term "loans"; some of these also used the term "mortgages." Oftentimes schemes stated several investment platforms in their marketing to investor-victims. In most cases the perpetrators only told investors the company was providing loans. Many were affinity-fraud cases where the perpetrators told investor-victims that the business was making loans to people from their own specific nationality or ethnic group.

- Sona Chukhyan's case involved investors making short-term loans to individuals who might not qualify with a traditional loan entity. The scheme included third-party loans, meaning investor-victims were told their investments would be loaned out and their profits would come from the interest paid on the repayment of those loans. The funds were never used as loans, but instead were Ponzi payments to previous investors. Her scheme also involved flipping real estate; she falsely told investor-victims that she already had buyers set up to flip properties (FBI, 2013, October 23).
- In the civil case of Veros Partners, Matthew Haab et al., the Ponzi schemers told investor-victims that their investments would be supporting private "short-term operating loans" to farmers as well as bridge loans (SEC, 2015, April 22). The funds were not used for new loans but instead used to pay off previous farm loans. Veros was registered with the SEC as an investment adviser. This scheme had taken place between 2013 and 2014. Many of the farmers who were originally loaned funds did not do well and were delinquent in paying back their previous loans. When the farmers could not repay their loans, Veros could not pay the funds due to investors; a Ponzi scheme was begun (SEC, 2015, April 22). This type of fraud is a business-failure scheme.
- Lydia Cladek ran a company that was supposed to be funding high-interest motor vehicle loans. She used promissory notes for these transactions and promised an interest rate as high as 20 percent (FBI, 2010, November 23, p.r.). Originally this business entity was successful. Then Cladek began using investor funds to pay her own expenses rather than the interest to investors (USA v. Lydia Cladek, 2014, Crt of Ap.).
- A recent case based on professional athletes was perpetrated by a former NFL football player and a former bank executive. The former National Football League player, Will Allen, had played with the New York Giants, the Miami Dolphins, and the New England

Patriots. The scheme was based on making short-term loans to professional athletes. The few loans that were made were smaller than the amount reported to investors. The funds were used to perpetuate the Ponzi scheme (DOJ, 2017, March 1, p.r.) (Allen and Daub).

EB-5 and Immigration

The schemes involving immigrants were generally affinity-frauds. Previous research by the author on affinity-fraud and immigrant communities found that immigrant communities were particularly vulnerable because they are new to the country and tend to trust others from their native land. The immigrants tend to trust those who speak the same language. Many are not fluent in English and do not know that there are government agencies available to help them. Some of the immigrants came as refugees from areas of political upheaval, where the governments were not trusted.

The second aspect of immigrant focused Ponzi schemes is a new tool for preying on the vulnerability of immigrants, and comes from the EB-5 program. There were three EB-5 Ponzi schemes. Similar to cryptocurrency, this is new, so there are only a few cases that are Ponzi schemes. The EB-5 program was established by Congress in 1990 to stimulate the economy through foreign investors. The EB-5 immigrant investment program is for immigrants who want to invest in commercial business in the United States to earn residency through investing. "The EB-5 immigrant investor program gives foreign investors the opportunity to earn permanent residence in the United States, through investing" (SEC, 2016, April 12, prg. 5). These investors must invest in an established business or start a new business. This legitimate federal program was soon used by fraudsters to take advantage of immigrants, in many fraudulent means, not just Ponzi schemes.

- One scheme primarily victimized Columbians and Americans of Columbian descent; the scheme is classified as an affinity-fraud. The title of the company, Immigration General Services, was supposed to invest in immigration bail-bonds. In the classic mechanism of falsifying federal credentials common in Ponzi schemes, Jenny Coplan told her victim-investors their funds were FDIC insured. The FDIC only insures up to $250,000 per individual in banks and savings associations that qualify. It does not insure investment services, brokers, or hedge funds (SEC, 2013, September 30).
- The *Jay Peak* EB-5 scheme of Ariel Quiros promised investment in a Vermont ski resort. *Jay Peak* was at least 15 companies, owned by *Q Resorts*, incorporated in Delaware. The schemers targeted individuals who wanted citizenship. Funds were also stated to be used for a

biomedical research center (SEC, 2016, April 12, prg. 6). There were legitimate *Jay Peak* businesses; however, there was little management of the invested funds, resulting in a Ponzi scheme. This scheme raised "more than $350 million from more than 700 investors in 74 countries" (SEC, 2016, April 12, prg. 41). The SEC settled with Jay Peak in early 2019.

- The *USA Now* scheme of Marco and Bebe Ramirez, promoted their investment scheme first to Mexican investors, then to immigrants from Egypt, and Nigeria. The scheme promised to hold immigrants' funds in escrow until the immigrants received their EB-5 visas. Marco and Bebe Ramirez' traveled to other countries trying to recruit investors. According to SEC documents, no investors received any US Citizen and Immigration Service (USCIS) documents, or the return of their original investments (SEC, 2013, September 30, prg. 4).

This concludes the chapter on ways, manner, and means. This is just an over view; there are many more themes used to perpetrate fraud that have not been covered in this chapter. Securities-based schemes are the most common, followed by commodities and FOREX. The most glaring red flag is that any technology or trend that is new is going to be the most likely means of carrying out a Ponzi scheme. When there is very little information available, it is easier for perpetrators to use jargon and technical vocabulary to convince investor-victims that the perpetrators are experts on the investment mechanism. Chapter 12 discusses the manner and means of Ponzi schemes over the study time frame.

Notes

1 https://www.federalreserve.gov/monetarypolicy/bst_crisisresponse.htm
2 One scheme was reported to invest in bail bonds.
3 See: https://www.sec.gov/oiea/investor-alerts-bulletins/ib_privateplacements. html
4 Regulation D exemption: https://www.sec.gov/fast-answers/answers-regdhtm. html
5 Securities Act 17 CFR § 230.501, Rule 501 of Regulation D:
6 https://www.sec.gov/oiea/investor-alerts-bulletins/ib_privateplacements. html
7 Accredited investors are individuals who have an earned come over $200,000 for at least two years, $300,000 for couples, or have a net worth over $1,000,000, without the value of the primary residence (SEC).
8 Futures Commission Merchants must register with the CFTC.
9 Identifying numbers for stocks under the Committee on Uniform Securities Identification Procedures.
10 For information on the Securities and Exchange Commission specifics on hedge funds and accredited investors see: https://www.sec.gov/investor/alerts/ib_ hedgefunds.pdf   https://www.sec.gov/fast-answers/answers-accredhtm.html https://www.investor.gov/additional-resources/general-resources/glossary/

rule-506-regulation-d and https://www.investor.gov/additional-resources/
general-resources/glossary/regulation-d-offerings
11 *Fraud and Swindles Collection.* [collection of published and unpublished
works on subjects relating to fraud and swindles, broadly defined]. Special
Collections, Lloyd Sealy Library, John Jay College of Criminal Justice/
CUNY, New York City.
12 https://www.sec.gov/divisions/enforce/primebank/howtheywork.shtml

References

Associated Press. (2009, February 19). Venezuela government seizes local
Stanford bank. *Daily News.*
Braithwaite, J. (1985). White collar crime. *Annual Review of Sociology* Vol.11
pp. 1–25.
Commodities Futures Trading Commission, (2003, April 3). Federal court or-
ders Georgia Foreign currency firm and its president to repay customers in
CFTC fraud action. (Garcia). Press release.
Commodities Futures Trading Commission v. Eldon Gresham Jr d/b/a The
Gresham Company (2009, July 2) Complaint.
Commodities Futures Trading Commission, (2009, July 9). CFTC charges
Georgia man with operating a multi-million dollar FOREX Ponzi scheme.
(Gresham). Press release.
Commodities Futures Trading Commission v. Increase Investments, Inc., Spirit
Investments, Inc., and Scott Bottolfson (2011, January 7) Complaint.
Commodities Futures Trading Commission v. Victor Eugene Cilli and Progres-
sive Funds LLC. (2011, June 15) Complaint.
Commodity Futures Trading Commission v. Alpha Trade, S.A. a/k/a Revolu-
tion network LTD., Jose Cecilio Martinez Beltran, Welinton Bautista Castillo,
Maria Alvarez Gutierrez, Yehodiz Padua Valentin, Maria Asela Rodriguez
and Francisco Amaury Suero Matos (2011, September 27).
Commodity Futures Trading Commission, (2011, October 19). CFTC obtains
permanent injunction against California resident Scott Bottolfson and his two
companies for defrauding customers in multi-million dollar commodity pool
Ponzi scheme. Press release.
Commodities Futures Trading Commission, (2014, October 24). Federal court
orders resident Ryan Nassbridges and his California companies to pay over
$18 million in civil monetary penalties in a commodity pool precious metals
scheme. Press release.
Commodity Futures Trading Commission v. Thomas Lanzana individually and
d/b/a Unique Forex, Nikolay Masanko, Blackbox Pulse LLC, and White cloud
Mountain LLC. (2017, August 21) Complaint.
Commodity Futures Trading Commission v. Dro Kholamian; and Blue Star
Trading, LLC. (2018, November 30). Complaint.
Department of Justice, (2013, February 27). Maryland resident sentenced to 14
years in prison for $8 million Ponzi scheme. (Winans). Press release.
Department of Justice, (2013, December 16). Florida investment fund manager
sentenced in Manhattan federal court to six years in prison for $13 million
securities fraud scheme. (Berkman and Kern). Press release.

Department of Justice, (2014, August 27). Financier steals millions by falsely claiming investor funds secured by billion dollar mining company. (Ison and Ellingson). Press release.

Department of Justice, (2015, March 5). Managing director of venture capital firm arrested and charged in Manhattan federal court in connection with multimillion dollar Ponzi scheme. (Gray). Press release.

Department of Justice, (2016, January 15). Former Austin resident sentenced to federal prison in connection with an estimated $1.4 million Ponzi scheme. (O'Reilly). Press release.

Department of Justice, (2016, April 13). Two executives at investment advisory and management firm charged in Manhattan federal court in connection with multimillion-dollar securities fraud scheme. (Elmaleh and Naqvi). Press release.

Department of Justice, (2016, December 13). Cazenovia man sentenced to 5 years on fraud and money laundering charges. (Griffin). Press release.

Department of Justice, (2016, December 14). Berkeley wine shop owner sentenced to six and a half years in prison for running a wine Ponzi scheme. (Fox). Press release.

Department of Justice, (2017, February 2). El Paso duo sentenced to federal prison for an estimated $2 million Ponzi scheme. (Counterman, Loya and Parra). Press release.

Department of Justice, (2017, March 1). Former NFL Player and former bank executive sentenced for Ponzi scheme and money laundering. (Allen, Will & Daub, Susan). Press release, District of Massachusetts.

Department of Justice, (2017, September 1). Big Island Capital fraudster charged with operating million dollar Ponzi scheme. (Lundin). Press release.

Department of Justice, (2018, September 13). Roger Dale Williams sentenced to 63 months in prison for phony investment scheme. Press release.

Department of Justice, (2018, October 5). Convicted fraudster sentenced to five years in prison for $7 million Ponzi scheme. (Holdaway & Kyes). Press release.

Department of Justice, (2019, April 9). Florida executive sentenced to 20 years in prison for orchestrating $150 million international Ponzi scheme. (Buzaneli). Press release.

Department of Justice, (2019, June 11). Florida man sentenced to federal prison in $28 million Ponzi scheme. (Warren). Press release.

Department of Justice, (2019, August 27). South Carolina man indicted for running $1.1 million foreign currency scheme. Press release.

Dokko, J, Brian, D., Kiley, M., Kim, J., Sherlund, S., Sim, J., and Van den Heuvel, S. (2009). *Monetary Policy and the Housing Bubble*. Washington, DC, Federal Reserve Board. Retrieved from: https://www.federalreserve.gov/pubs/feds/2009/200949/200949pap.pdf

Downes, J. and Goodman J. (eds) (2014). *Dictionary of finance and investment terms*. Hauppauge, NY,Barron's Educational Series.

Federal Bureau of Investigation, (2009, June 30). Cape Coral man sentenced for role in $30 million mortgage fraud case. (Luczak). Press release.

Federal Bureau of Investigation, (2010, April 28). Orlando man sentenced for role in mortgage frauds scheme. (Cendana). Press release.

Federal Bureau of Investigation, (2010, November 23). $100 million Ponzi scheme Indictment returned. (Cladek). Press release.

Federal Bureau of Investigation, (2010, December 20). Mentor man charged with securities fraud and filing a false tax return. (Olear). Press release.

Federal Bureau of Investigation, (2011, May 16). Connecticut man sentenced to 10 years in federal prison for operating a $100 million Ponzi scheme. (Goldberg). Press release.

Federal Bureau of Investigation, (2012, April 16). Ponzi scheme operator sentenced to 24 months in prison. (Bartko). Press release.

Federal Bureau of Investigation, (2012, August 23). Former Howard County man sentenced for $8 million cattle fraud scheme. (Asbury). Press release.

Federal Bureau of Investigation, (2012, October 24). Seventeen Members of a North Carolina Racketeering enterprise indicted on investment fraud, mortgage fraud, and related charges. Press release. Western District of North Carolina. (Tyson). Press release.

Federal Bureau of Investigation, (2012, October 31). Former gold coin dealer sentenced to 51 months. (Heim). Press release.

Federal Bureau of Investigation, (2012, November 9). Two charged in Ponzi scheme that netted more than $2.8 million from San Diego victims. (Ison and Ellingson). Press release.

Federal Bureau of Investigation, (2013, June 7). Pennsylvania jeweler sentenced to 51 months in prison for running $3.4 million Ponzi scheme. (Addy). Press release.

Federal Bureau of Investigation, (2013, October 23). Former Glendale resident arraigned on charges alleging she defrauded investors of $3.9 million using suspended real estate license. (Chukhyan). Press release.

Federal Bureau of Investigation, (2014, February 26). Connecticut Ponzi scheme operator who stole $27 million sentenced to 25 years in Federal prison. (Loles). Press release.

Federal Bureau of Investigation, (2016, December 12). New Century Coal ends in lengthy prison sentences for ten individuals. (Rose et al.). Press release.

Financial Crisis Inquiry Commission (FCIC). (2011). *Financial Crisis Inquiry Report; Final report of the National Commission on the causes of the financial and economic crisis of the United States.* New York, Public Affairs.

Frasca, C. (1931). *Stock swindlers and their methods.* New York, Charles Frasca Publisher.

Garner, B. (ed) (2009). *Black's law dictionary.* Thomson Reuters.

Immigration Customs Enforcement, (2011, February 2). 9 South Florida residents charged in $12 million bank fraud scheme. (Perez). Press release.

Investor.gov, *Certificates of deposit (CDs)* retrieved from: https://www.investor.gov/introduction-investing/investing-basics/investment-products/certificates-deposit-cds

Johnson, B. (2010). *The hedge fund fraud case book.* Hoboken, NJ, John Wiley and Sons.

Markopolos, H. (2005). *The world's largest hedge fund is a fraud.* Retrieved from: https://www.sec.gov/news/studies/2009/oig-509/exhibit-0293.pdf

Securities Act of 1933.

Securities and Exchange Commission v. Peggy D. Stines, individually and d.b.a Garland film Buyers Group and North Texas Film Processors (1984, August 2).

Securities and Exchange Commission v. Donald Bader et al. (1990, November 20) News Digest 90-224.

Securities and Exchange Commission, (1997, October 16). Amerivest case, Jerry Anderson, Peter Sacker and Robert Kerns. Litigation release.

Securities and Exchange Commission v. Michal J. Randy, et al (1999, March 9) Litigation release.

Securities and Exchange Commission, In the matter of David A. Johnston, (1999, September 8). (Michael J. Randy). Litigation release.

Securities and Exchange Commission v. Amerivest case, Jerry Anderson, Peter Sacker and Robert Kerns (1999, September 30) Administrative proceedings.

Securities and Exchange Commission v. Robert Dalton, James L. Masini, and George J. Bodlak (1999, September 30) Litigation release.

Securities and Exchange Commission v. Jerry W. Anderson and Robert M. Kerns (2000, May 31) Initial decision.

Securities and Exchange Commission v. First Americans Ltd., et al. (2000, February 24) Litigation release.

Securities and Exchange Commission v. Larry W. Ellis (2001, July 25) Litigation release.

Securities and Exchange Commission v. Michael E. Hill (2001, November 1) Litigation release.

Securities and Exchange Commission v. Concord Capital Enterprises, Scott Yoshizumi, Ann Ta, and Dionisia Pappas (2000, November 24) Litigation release.

Securities and Exchange Commission v. Roy E. Matlock and Alan Root (2000, November 8) Litigation release.

Securities and Exchange Commission v. Robert L. Bentley, Bentley Financial Services, Inc. Entrust Group (2002, January 9).

Securities and Exchange Commission v. U.S. Reservation Bank & Trust; Higher Investment Technologies, Inc., Global-link Capital Markets, LYD., Edward Driving Hawk Sr., Leo R. Driving Hawk Sr., John My Adams, Edmund J. Smedley, Kenneth Harrison, William J. Heresko and Thomas T. Emerton III (2002, April 3) Complaint.

Securities and Exchange Commission v. Frederick Brandau, Raphael "Ray" Levy and Jeffrey Paine (2002, July 8) Litigation release.

Securities and Exchange Commission v. National Investment Enterprises and Michael Garian a/k/a Melkon Gharakhanian a/k/a Bika Balian (2003, February 7) Litigation release.

Securities and Exchange Commission v. John F. Turant, Jr., Russ Luciano, JTI Group Fund, LP, J.T. Investment Group Inc., Evergreen Investment Group, LP, and New Resource Investment Group Inc. (2003, September 15) Complaint.

Securities and Exchange Commission v. NJ Affordable Houses Corp. an Wayne Puff (2005, December 12) Complaint.

Securities and Exchange Commission v. ETS Payphones, Inc., and Charles E. Edwards, defendant (2006, August 2) Litigation release.

Securities and Exchange Commission v. Secure Investment Services, Inc., American financial Services, Inc., Lyndon Group, Inc., Donald Neuhaus, and Kimberly A. Snowden (2007, August 23) Complaint.

Securities and Exchange Commission v. CFO-5 LLC, Trinity International Enterprises, Inc., Stanley W. Anderson, Edwin A. Smith, Charles L. Kennedy,

Michael d. Norton, individually and d/b/a Global Asset Services, and Michael R. Fair (2008, July 28) Complaint.

Securities and Exchange Commission v. Jeanne M. Rowzee, James R. Halstead and Robert T. Harvey (2008, September 15) Complaint.

Securities and Exchange Commission v. Marc S. Dreier (2008, December 8) Complaint.

Securities and Exchange Commission v. Stanford International Bank, LTD., Stanford Group Company, Stanford Capital Management, LLC., R. Allen Stanford, James M. Davis, and Laura Pendergest-Holt (2009, February 16) Complaint.

Securities and Exchange Commission v. Millennium Bank et al. (2009, March 26) (Wise and Hoegel). Complaint.

Securities and Exchange Commission v. Regan & company and Michael C. Regan (2009, June 24) Complaint.

Securities and Exchange Commission v. Luis Felipe Perez (2010, June 2) SEC charges Miami man in $40 million Ponzi scheme. Litigation release.

Securities and Exchange Commission v. Martin T. Wegener, Wealth Resources, LLC. and Wealth Resources Inc. (2010, June 14) complaint.

Securities and Exchange Commission v. Algird Norkus and Financial Update, Inc. (2010, October 14) Complaint.

Securities and Exchange Commission v. Evolution Capital advisers, LLC, Evolution Investment Group I, LLC, and Damian Omar Valdez (2011, August 10) Complaint.

Securities and Exchange Commission v. James Davis Risher and Daniel Joseph Sebastian (2011, August 29) Complaint.

Securities and Exchange Commission v. Kenneth A. Dachman, Scott A. Wolf, and Stone Lion management Inc. (2012, February 6) Complaint.

Securities and Exchange Commission v. Barry J. Graham, Fred Davis Clark Jr., Cristal Clark, David W. Schwartz, Ricky Lynn Stokes (2013, January 30) (Cay Clubs) Complaint.

Securities and Exchange Commission v. John Henley Fowler, Jeffrey Robert Fowler, and Julianne Chalmers (2013, July 5) Complaint.

Securities and Exchange Commission v. Robert Narvett and Shield Management Group, Inc., (2013, August 16) Complaint.

Securities and Exchange Commission v. Jenny E. Coplan (2013, September 30) Complaint.

Securities and Exchange Commission v. Marco A. Ramirez, Bebe Ramirez, USA Now, LLC, USA Now Energy Capital Group, LP, and Now Co. Loan Services LLC (2013, September 30) Complaint.

Securities and Exchange Commission v. Christopher A.T. Pedras et al. (2013, November 5) Litigation release.

Securities and Exchange Commission v. Neal V. Goyal, Caldera Advisors, LLC and Blue Horizon Asset management, LLC. (2014, May 28) Complaint.

Securities and Exchange Commission v. Robert Hurd, Your Bets Memories International Inc. and Kenneth Gross (2014, June 11) Litigation release.

Securities and Exchange Commission v. Abatement Corp. Holding Company Limited, (2014, September 10) (Brenda Davis and Joseph Laurer). Complaint.

Securities and Exchange Commission v. Gary Harrison Lane, (2014, November 25) Motion for enforcement for summary disposition.

Securities and Exchange Commission v. Gregory W. Gray Jr., et al. (2015, February 27) Litigation release.

Securities and Exchange Commission v. Veros Partners, Inc., Matthew D. Haab, Jeffery B. Risinger, Veros Farm Loan Holding LLC. Tobin Senefeld, farm Growcap LLC, and Pincap (2015, April 22) Complaint.

Securities and Exchange Commission v. International Stock Transfer, Inc., and Cecil Franklin Speight (2014, July 23) Complaint.

Securities and Exchange Commission v. Malcom Segal (2015, July 1) Complaint.

Securities and Exchange Commission v. Paul Lee Moore (2015, July 16) Complaint.

Securities and Exchange Commission v. James P. Griffin, John Wolle, 54Freedom Securities Inc. 54Freedom Tele Inc. MoneyIns Inc. 54Freedom Foundation Inc. 5 Ledyard Avenue LLC, 5 Ledyard Corporation, and IICNet LLC. (2015, July 30) Complaint.

Securities and Exchange Commission v. N.J. Affordable, Inc., and Wayne Puff (2015, September 12) Complaint.

Securities and Exchange Commission v. John V. Bivona; Saddle River Advisers, LLC., SRA Management Associates, LLC., Frank Gregory Mazzola (2016, March 21) Complaint.

Securities and Exchange Commission v. Traffic Monsoon LLC. A Utah limited liability company and Charles David Scoville (2016, July 26) Complaint.

Securities and Exchange Commission v. Joseph Meli, Matthew Harriton, 875 Holdings, LLC, 127 Holdings, LLC, Advance Entertainment, LLC and Advanced Entertainment II LLC. (2017, January 27) Complaint.

Securities and Exchange Commission v. Anthony Joseph Marino, George Frank Polera, and, United Business Alliance, LLC. (2017, July 25) Complaint.

Securities and Exchange Commission v. Tennstar Energy Inc. f/k/a Black Gold Resources Inc., David R. Greenlee, David A Stewart, Jr., and Richard "Pic" I. Underwood (2017, August 11) Complaint.

Securities and Exchange Commission v. Pedro Fort Berbel, Fort Marketing Group LLC. (2017, September 28) Complaint.

Securities and Exchange Commission v. The Leonard Vincent Group, Leonard Vincent Lombardo, and Brian A. Hudlin (2017, September 29) Complaint.

Securities and Exchange Commission Investor Alert: Beware of paid-to-click (PTC) scams. (2017, November 7).

Securities and Exchange Commission v. Ash Narayan, the Ticket Reserve Inc. a/k/a Forward market Media, Inc., Richard M. Harmon and John Kaptrosky (2016, May 24, Amend. 2018, January 4) Complaint.

Securities and Exchange Commission v. Sparks Trading Group LLC., and Niket Shah (2018, March 12) Complaint.

Securities and Exchange Commission v. Paul Gilman, Oil Migration Group LLC., WaveTech29, LLC., and Gilman Sound (2018, June 4) Complaint.

Securities and Exchange Commission v. Daniel Rudden, Financial Visions Inc., et al. (2018, July 19) Complaint.

Securities and Exchange Commission v. Ariel Quiros, William Stenger, Jay Peak Inc Q Resorts et al. (2016, April 12) Complaint.

Securities and Exchange Commission v. Mark Ray, Reva Stachniw, Ron Throgmartin, Custom consulting & Product Services, LLC., RM Farm & Livestock, LLC., Mr. Cattle Production Services, LLC., Sunshine Enterprises, Universal Herbs, LLC., DBC Limited, LLC. (2019, September 30) Complaint.

Securities and Exchange Commission v. Jeffrey P. Carpoff and Paulette Carpoff (2020, January 24) Complaint.

Smith, E. (1923). *Confessions of a confidence man: A handbook for suckers.* New York, NY, Scientific American Publishing.

United States Code 15 §77b. Definition; promotion efficiency, competition, and capital information. (a) Definitions (1).

United States Code Title 17 CFR Ch. I, Part 4 § 4.5.

United States Code Title 17 CFR §230.144.

United States of America v. Bart Sidney Posey Jr. William Worthy II, Richard Hall Bachman, Angela Slavey Posey (2013, June 26) Indictment.

United States of America v. Edwin Fujinaga, Junzo Suzuki and Paul Suzuki (2015, July 8) Indictment. 2:15-cr-00198-ldg-njk.

United States of America v. James L. Schmidt (2019, April 15) Motion to dismiss.

United States of America v. Lydia Cladek (2014, September 22) Eleventh Circuit Court of Appeals 13-10024.

United States of America v. Raymond Bitar and Nelson Burtnick (2013, April 23) 1:12 cr 00529. Southern District of New York.

United States of America v. Rosi Ray (2010, December 1) Indictment.United States v. Joyce E. Allen (2017, November 2) Sixth Circuit Court of Appeals (USDS, EDT, 2015).

Vaughan, B. (2013). Former Full Tilt Poker CEO pleads guilty, avoids prison time. *Reuters.* Retrieved from: https://www.reuters.com/article/net-us-poker-fraud-sentence/former-full-tilt-poker-ceo-pleads-guilty-avoids-prison-time-idUSBRE93E12J20130415–

Chapter 5

The Money

Ponzi schemes are all about money. Money comes in, money goes out. Sometimes it goes offshore. The money is illegally obtained, therefore "dirty" and must be laundered. When the fraud comes to the attention of authorities there is the effort to return the money to the victims. This chapter discusses the process, how the money comes in, and how the perpetrators use others' money to carry out the scheme and to attract other victim-investors. In some schemes the funds were solely used for Ponzi payments and the expenses of the perpetrators. Other schemes had funds that had to be laundered. Bankruptcies are inevitable, and frequently it is not the first bankruptcy for many perpetrators. As with all money transactions, there is governmental and institutional responsibilities. The banks where the funds are deposited have responsibilities to watch for suspicious activities and to report them. Throughout the life of a Ponzi scheme there are always financial institutions and government agencies that have the opportunity and responsibility to catch and stop the fraud.

Ponzi perpetrators present themselves as wealthy in order to attract others with money to invest. The first step is the appearance of success; this generally includes being well dressed, having a prestigious address, at least one mansion and luxury car. This includes the appearance of being knowledgeable in financial matters and presenting an image of financial wealth. No one is going to give money for someone to invest who is living in their parents' basement. The curiosity is how do the perpetrators attract the first victim? Frequently the first victim is a friend or family member. The trappings of wealth can be leased in prestigious looking addresses and offices, as well as luxury cars. The first step is presenting the image of financial success.

Once the perpetrators begin to bring in the money from their investor-victims, it usually goes into a bank account. Some may be invested; it may be put into actual trading accounts, as opposed to trading accounts established in name only. Some funds may be invested, as stated, and lost. In many cases the money is shuffled through shell companies or offshore accounts. In all cases the money is used to pay earlier investors and the personal expenses of the perpetrators; that is what makes the fraud a Ponzi scheme instead of just theft.

Eventually, the perpetrator cannot bring in enough new investors to make the payouts and the scheme collapses, or else investors force bankruptcy, demanding their funds back. Bankruptcy is an inevitable part of the process. Authorities are then involved, leading to disgorgement, restitution, clawbacks, and penalties. At this point, federal regulators and law enforcement step in. The court appoints a receiver or a trustee. Determining how much is taken, returned, or considered a loss is no simple task for federal authorities, the receivers, and trustees. It is highly unlikely that the perpetrators of fraud keep meticulous financial records about the money they take in and how it is used.

For the purpose of this study, the dollar amount taken used in coding the data is the latest amount indicated in federal complaints served on the perpetrators, the indictments, and convictions. Whichever amount is the final amount applied in the final administrative or criminal legal action was the amount coded in the data set. Throughout the investigative process, documents may state different amounts. One amount is the total amount taken in principal from the victims. In some cases, the amount represented in federal documents varies depending upon "profits" that may have been paid out, or there may have been principal that was returned to the victims. The federal documents do not report consistently on the amounts that have been returned to victims. For this reason, the amount considered in this study is the final total amount taken from victims as stated in federal documents. The final amount recovered by the trustee/receiver is rarely a matter of public record; therefore, only the amount taken in principal is the amount reported herein.

There is the initial principal investment, and then there is interest, and roll-overs. Documents refer to "the losses"; this could mean the funds that were received as principal from later investors then paid out to earlier investors. It could also refer to funds the perpetrator accepted as investment but used for his or her own personal spending or lost in bad investments. For later investors, their entire principal may be lost in "interest" payments that were paid to earlier investors. The term "losses" is not clearly defined or used with a consistent meaning in the documents; it could mean many things. For this reason, the "losses" are not discussed herein, only the original amount taken before the court, receiver, or trustee recovers funds.

The total amount taken in the schemes refers to the total amount money received by the perpetrator, the principal, towards the alleged or promised investment instrument. This amount does not include the promised or received interest; the amount taken is the amount calculated in the data sets. The total amount taken in known federal-level Ponzi

Table 5.1 Largest Quantities of Money Taken

Name	Quantity in Billions	Year Started	Year Ended	Duration in Years
Robert Shapiro	1.2	2012	2017	5
Scott Rothstein	1.2	2005	2009	5
Joel Steinger	1.25	1994	2005	11
Edwin Fujinaga	1.5	1998	2013	15
Martin Nordlicht	1.7	2003	2015	12
Jeff & Paulette Carpoff	2.5	2011	2019	8
Gregory Bell*	2.6	2002	2008	6
Martin A. Armstrong	3	1992	1999	7
Thomas Petters	3.65	1995	2008	13
Allen Stanford	7	1985	2009	24
Bernard Madoff	19	1992	2008	16

* Bell is a feeder fund to Petters.

schemes since 1962 is $92,476,090,000, as of January 31, 2020. The average amount taken per scheme is $68,050,000.

These largest 11 schemes had been active for many years, enabling them to take in larger quantities of money. Five of these schemes ended during the financial crisis, when they could no longer bring in new investors to keep the scheme running. Two schemes ended before the financial crisis, and four ended after 2010 (Table 5.1). By comparison, Phillip Barry's scheme was not one of the largest schemes, but it lasted for 31 years, only taking $40 million. Barry's scheme was the longest-run scheme of all, also ending in 2009 during the financial crisis. In Barry's scheme, it is likely the smaller financial take over a longer period of time decreased the likelihood of being exposed as a Ponzi scheme.

Madoff, the Largest Scheme in US History

The initial amount stated as taken in federal documents taken in the Madoff case was $65 billion. This amount included the bogus profits. As of June 2019, the approved claims amount of lost principal is $19 billion. The difference of $46 billion was falsified profits. Through restitution, clawbacks, and disgorgement, as of July 2020, approximately $14.352 billion (75.5 percent) has been recovered by the trustee, Irving Picard (Madofftrustee.com). Of that, $13.931 billion (73 percent) has been distributed from the customer fund to investor-victims (Madofftrustee.com). There are still committed funds in the process as legal proceedings continue (Madofftrustee.com). Those victims who had claims one million dollars or less have been made whole (Larson and Cannon, 2018).

Bankruptcy

Almost all Ponzi perpetrators file for bankruptcy at some point. Some are forced bankruptcies initiated by victim-investors. The victim-investors, or creditors, petition the court for an involuntary bankruptcy when they feel they will not be paid unless there is a legal requirement of payment through the bankruptcy court. Generally, this is because the fraud perpetrator has refused to give investors back their principal. Voluntary bankruptcy is initiated by the perpetrator of the fraud when they cannot pay their investors their principal. Many perpetrators had previous bankruptcies prior to initiating the fraudulent scheme. Almost all Ponzi perpetrators end up in bankruptcy once they are caught. In some cases, there is nothing left to pay back to the victims; the funds have all been spent. There is usually at least one mansion, oftentimes several mansions, private jets, yachts, jewelry, and luxury vehicles that can be sold.

Trustee/Receiver

The SEC, CFTC, or SIPC may ask the court to appoint a receiver or trustee. The receiver is a "disinterested office of the court" who has the responsibility of finding the funds, recovering the funds, determining who has legitimate claims to the funds, and distributing the funds. The trustee is the administrator in a bankruptcy. They are appointed by a federal judge; they are not employees of the SEC or CFTC. The receiver's responsibility is to the investor-victims in a Ponzi scheme and to the court. The SEC and CFTC have links within their websites for investor-victims to contact. There are also those who would try to victimize investor-victims again by feigning to be a receiver. These charlatans charge victims a fee. A receiver appointed by the court will not charge victims anything for pursuing their losses; it is their fiduciary responsibility to return the victims' funds to them. Usually, the receiver is paid through the funds and assets acquired from the estate of the perpetrator.

Each receiver establishes a receivership weblink through the SEC's or CFTC's websites. This provides the victims with a contact to file a claim for reimbursement of funds. There are deadlines by which claims must be submitted to be considered for reimbursement. Receivership applicants submit an application to the agency. The process is competitive in that the court determines receivership based on the experience of the foremost applicants and their team.

When the receiver tries to claw back funds that were paid out to the earlier investors, it must be determined what was the initial principal and what was "interest" payments. The interest payments are the funds from later investors, of which the earlier investor is not entitled to. It must also be determined who are genuine victims. In criminal only cases, it is the

United States Marshals that have the responsibility of locating and auctioning the property of Ponzi perpetrators in criminal proceedings. The SIPC also has responsibilities in recovering assets in failed brokerages. In the Madoff case, Irving Picard was appointed by the federal court to serve as the SIPC Trustee to resolve liquidation of Madoff's assets and to return funds to the victims (Madofftrustee.com).

Asset Forfeiture

Asset forfeiture is the taking of property by a government agency without compensation. Asset forfeiture is differentiated between civil forfeiture, criminal forfeiture, and administrative forfeiture. This may be the confiscation of illegally obtained monetary gains or property that has been purchased with illegal gains. There are three types of forfeiture on the federal level:

- In criminal proceedings there is a criminal conviction or guilty plea. This is a request for forfeiture of any and all illegal gains or property that may have been used in the commission of a crime, or that may have been obtained as a result of the criminal activity. For example, property such as real estate, luxury vehicles, and art work that were purchased with the gains from a Ponzi scheme can be confiscated. Computers that were used in the commission of a crime can be seized (US Department of Justice, 2019, p. 28).
- On the federal level, the civil proceedings are against the property (DOJ, 2020).
- Administrative forfeiture is seizure by a federal agency without the need of a judge. It includes money or property under the value of $500,000 (DOJ, 2020).

Disgorgement

Disgorgement is an equitable remedy, taking back the wrongful gains of a Ponzi scheme. The SEC or CFTC orders someone who has been judged as violating securities or commodities regulations to return ill-gotten gains. It is civil action requiring business entities and individuals associated with the perpetrator to give back the money to the harmed investor-victims. This may be relatives who received funds, jewelry, cars, or homes from the ill-gotten gains. This could be shell companies to other businesses related to the perpetrators. In SEC and CFTC complaints relief defendants are named. Relief defendants are individuals or businesses that may not have been directly involved in the carrying out of the fraud but may have received or hold funds or assets from the deception. They are named in the complaint in order to facilitate the return of funds. The term "relief" is used in the complaint because financial relief is sought for those who lost their money. In addition to disgorgement and restitution, the SEC and CFTC customarily impose penalties, in most cases. The purpose of penalties is to both punish and deter; however, it is likely that there is very little left to pay those penalties after disgorgement, restitution, and bankruptcy. There are criminal penalties imposed as well, under the Department of Justice.

- The Supreme court decision in *Kokesh v. SEC* ruled that "disgorgement is penal in nature (rather than equitable) and as such subject to the five-year limitation" (Clayton, 2019). The argument is that the SEC is not authorized to require disgorgement, with no time limit. The Supreme Court determined that under 28 USC. § 2462 "action[s], suit[s] or proceeding[s] for the enforcement of any civil fine, penalty or forfeiture" that in the *Kokesh* case, disgorgement is technically a penalty as a result of having violated a law. A five year limit is problematic in that cases such as time limit, then a case such as Madoff or Stanford that went on for much longer than five years, the perpetrators and relief defendants would not be required to return illegally obtained funds prior to the five years. This would force the SEC and CFTC to find Ponzi schemes sooner in order to return funds appropriately under the law (Kokesh v. SEC, p. 11).

The current argument on disgorgement is a result of the US Supreme Court decision *Kokesh v. SEC*. This was followed by the Investment Protection and Capital Markets Fairness Act, H.R. 4344, passed by the House, November 2019, and submitted to the Senate. The argument in *Kokesh v. SEC* is that disgorgement is considered a fine or penalty. The definitions in H.R. 4344 state very clearly:

Section 2 ADDITIONAL RELIEF(a)(7)(B) RULE OF CONSTRUCTION - Additional relief sought under this paragraph may not be construed to be a civil fine, penalty, or forfeiture subject to chapter 163 VI of title 28 United States Code.

It defines a time frame of 14 years, and defines "additional relief":

Section 2 (a)(7)(C) STATUTE OF LIMITATIONS. - A federal court may not issue relief under this paragraph if the action proceeding brought or instituted by the Commission was commenced more than 14 years after the alleged violation."
Section 2 ADDITIONAL RELIEF.

(a)(7)(A) IN GENERAL- In any action or proceeding brought or instituted by the Commission under provision of the securities laws, the Commission may seek, and any Federal court may grant the following additional relief:

(i)   Disgorgement in the amount of any unjust enrichment obtained as a result of the act or practice with respect to which the Commission is bringing such an action or proceeding.
(ii) Injunctions, including officer and director bars.

Both the Supreme Court decision and the Investor Protection and Capital Markets Fairness Act (H.R. 4344, 2019)[1] put time constraints on the time frame receivers and federal courts can demand disgorgement, civilly. For example, a current Ponzi case began in 1995; it is currently in the investigative process. The company has been charged by the SEC; however, the primaries have yet to be charged. Assuming this case makes it to civil action in 2020, based on the Supreme court case, the receiver may only be allowed to request disgorgement as from five years back. Assuming the Investor Protection and Capital Markets Fairness Act is passed by the Senate, this Act will allow disgorgement as far back as 2006. That means that civilly anyone who received profits before 2006 cannot be required to return them.

Restitution

Restitution is the monetary remedy intending to recover and restore the illegally obtained funds to the rightful owner in criminal cases. This amount is stated in the sentencing by the sentencing judge. An order of restitution is active for 20 years. The United States Marshals have the responsibility of asset forfeiture; they identify and value property that has been confiscated in order to compensate the victims. There is generally a court-appointed trustee/receiver who has the responsibility of determining who the victims are, how much each victim lost, what was their principal investment, and the amount of interest payments. Oftentimes the money is gone and the perpetrator is bankrupt. Sometimes the perpetrators or their family try to hide money or property. Ponzi perpetrator Scott Rothstein's wife Kimberly attempted to hide jewelry he had given her. Kimberly Rothstein pleaded guilty to conspiracy to commit money laundering and obstruction of justice; she was not involved in the Ponzi scheme.

Clawbacks

Clawbacks are the process of retrieving the interest payments paid to earlier investors from later investors' funds. Many earlier investors may feel that they invested in good faith and that they earned the profits they received. In reality their profits are actually the principal of later investors, not interest earned from actual investments. Under "fraudulent transfer" litigation, funds that were paid out to earlier investors as profits, donations to charities, or gifts to family members may be sought for financial relief to later victim-investors who are trying to get their principal back.

Fair Fund

A fair fund[2] is a fund established to collect funds acquired through clawbacks, disgorgement, or restitution that is designed to be returned to the victims of a fraud. Those who have been victims must register with a receiver or trustee that has been appointed by the federal agency.

Banks

In some cases, the investors have filed suit against the banks used by the Ponzi perpetrators for failure to monitor for suspicious activities. Generally, the claim against the bank is that they knew or should have known that their client was carrying out fraudulent activities. The investors have to prove that the bank knew the perpetrator – their client – was committing fraud (Aguilar v. PNC Bank, 2017; Rosemann v. St Louis Bank, 2017). The suit must prove that the bank knew there were fraudulent activities going on. Also, the banks are making profits on service fees. A third party can bring suit against a bank claiming negligence or breach of fiduciary duty; however, the bank has no obligation to those who are not its customers.

There have been criminal cases brought against the banks used by the Ponzi perpetrators. In the Petters and Madoff cases the Department of Justice did file criminal charges against the banks for their responsibility in the frauds. The banks received deferred prosecutions; it is the deferred prosecution that makes it all go away; the banks pay a penalty and all is forgotten.

- *JP Morgan Chase Bank* was criminally charged for its actions in Bernie Madoff's Ponzi scheme. The bank was charged with violations under the Bank Secrecy Act and agreed to pay a $1.7 billion penalty (DOJ, 2014, January 6, Criminal Information). The bank was charged with failing to have adequate money laundering policies and procedures in place, and that they failed to report suspicious activities as required under the Bank Secrecy Act (1970). In 2006 and 2007, the London Branch *of JP Morgan* was considering directly investing $1.3 billion into one of Madoff's feeder funds, but a wise chief risk officer nixed the deal because it was suspected that

Madoff was running a Ponzi scheme. Later that year, the London office carried out due diligence on Madoff's enterprise and determined that they could not prove trading had taken place, and that for such a large entity to have a small accounting firm was indicative of something questionable going on. The London branch filed a report with the UK regulators but not with the US SEC. The London *JP Morgan Chase Bank* office sent their report and concerns to the *JP Morgan Chase* in the US compliance office, but the US office failed to act. *JP Morgan Chase* received a deferred prosecution agreement that dictated that if the penalty and requirements were met, that the Department of Justice would dismiss the charges after two years. Those conditions were a civil forfeiture of $1.7 billion that would go to the Madoff victims, acknowledgment of responsibility in the Madoff Ponzi scheme, and reforming the bank's anti-money laundering program and procedures. Another bank that Madoff used had filed a suspicious activity report in 1996, and then closed Madoff's account (DOJ, 2014, January 7, p.r.).

- In the Petters' Ponzi scheme *BMO Harris Bank* was required to pay $10 million to address actions carried out by a bank it had acquired, for actions involving the Petters Ponzi scheme. The bank that was involved with Petters was *Marshall & Isley Bank*. The bank had signed an agreement that they would monitor accounts associated with Petters' business; however, the agreement was worthless. That investors believed that there was some oversight, because of the agreement, that would protect their investment, thereby allowed the Ponzi scheme to continue and investors to lose their funds (DOJ, 2018, October 12, p.r.).

- The United States Treasury Financial Crimes Enforcement Network (FinCEN) fined *TD Bank* for failure to report suspicious activities in the Scott Rothstein case. *TD Bank* was fined $37.5 million. The SEC also charged *TD Bank* civilly and ordered the bank to pay a penalty of $15 million (SEC, 2013, September 23, a.p.). In addition, in the Scott Rothstein case, a *TD Bank* regional vice president, Frank Spinosa, provided investors with false assurances that the accounts that held their funds had restrictions in place that would prevent their funds from being transferred. There were no such restrictions in place; Rothstein could move funds as he pleased. Spinosa's false statements allowed the Ponzi scheme to continue. *TD Bank* agreed to pay $15 million through SEC administrative proceedings (SEC, 2013, September 23, p.r., 2013-192). Frank Spinosa was charged with SEC civil violations and received a 30-month sentence for his criminal involvement. Spinosa pleaded guilty to conspiracy to commit wire fraud (DOJ, 2015, December 18, p.r.).

- In the Ponzi scheme of Keith Franklin Simmons, "*Community-ONE Bank* turned a blind eye to criminal conduct occurring under its nose" (DOJ, 2011, April 27, p.r.). The bank was required to pay $400,000 in a deferred prosecution agreement. The Simmons scheme took in $40 million from investor-victims.

If the banks were paying penalties as high as $1.7 billion with the *JP Morgan Chase*, and combined penalties $52.5 million in the Rothstein case, how much must the banks have made in profits to take the risk of getting caught allowing fraudulent activities? At least in the Rothstein case, a bank executive received a prison sentence.

Fraudulent Transfers or Concealment

Fraudulent transfers[3] are the moving of assets with the intent to conceal, when it is suspected that the perpetrator might or will be investigated. This is often done when bankruptcy is anticipated. This might be moving funds into relative's accounts or changing title of ownership on real estate. It differs from money laundering in that in money laundering the funds were obtained illegally. In fraudulent transfer the funds or property may have been legally acquired.

There is disagreement on whether or not college tuition payments for the children of Ponzi perpetrators is subject to clawbacks. In the case of the Palladino's Ponzi scheme, they used the money they received in their Ponzi scheme to pay college tuition for their adult child. Many Ponzi schemers have used the money received to pay tuition for private schools and college tuition for their children. In the Palladino case the bankruptcy court ruled in favor of the university, that they would not have to return the funds received for the college tuition for Palladino's child's tuition. The First Circuit Court of Appeals reversed the decision saying that the paying of children's tuition is a benefit of reasonable equivalent value and subject to clawbacks (DeGiacomo v. Sacred Heart University, 2019).

Money Laundering

Money laundering refers to the many ways the illegally obtained funds are processed through legitimate entities/opportunities with the end goal of making the money appear "clean" or legitimately obtained, in order to avoid detection by authorities. Money laundering (18 USC § 1956(b)) is a frequent charge in many Ponzi schemes. Would-be investors supply their principal investment to the would-be fraud perpetrator. The investor-victims are entitled to their original principal. However, their interest payments received are actually the principal of later investors, therefore illegal gains. This is also applied to commissions of brokers and investment advisers. If they received commissions on fraudulent investment transactions, their commissions are the fruits of ill-gotten gains. Any attempt to legalize ill-gotten gains can fall under money laundering laws.

One mechanism for processing illegally obtained funds is using the funds from investor-victims to purchase jewelry, valuable art work, or classic cars, items that hold or increase in value that could be sold, with or without profit, at a later date. These items serve the dual purpose of providing the image of wealth; they hold value, but were purchased with illegal gains. Three of the more well-known examples are Scott Rothstein and his collection of watches and luxury cars, Marc Dreier and his art collection, and the Carpoff's 185 classic car collection.

- In the case of the Le-Nature beverage company Ponzi scheme, the Podlucky family had purchased three diamonds and seven sapphires with the gains from their Ponzi scheme. They then sold those gems at a Sotheby's auction for $2.9 million. Karla and Jesse Podlucky (mother and son) were convicted of money laundering. This scheme also victimized banks and lenders (DOJ, 2011, November 29, p.r.; USA v. Tammy Andreycak, 2008, April 4).

The money laundering statute was addressed in the Supreme Court decision *United States V. Santos*. The main argument is the use of plurality of whether the funds brought in through illegal activities are "proceeds or profits" and if the funds that are used to run the enterprise are considered money laundering. This caused Congress to revisit the statute amending it in 2009 defining proceeds: "to include 'gross receipts," 18 USC § 1956 (9). Gross receipts are the total receipts from sales or other business practices. In the federal statute: 18 USC § 1956 "makes it a crime to engage in a 'financial transaction' involving 'the proceeds of specified unlawful activity' with the intent to 'promote carrying on' of the [illegal] activity" (USA v. Keith Franklin Simmons, 2013, December 11, Fourth Circuit).

- Keith Simmons had appealed his conviction of money laundering charges based on the Santos case and his case came to trial before Congress had amended the law. Simmons had used some of his Ponzi proceeds for gambling. The Santos case was based on gambling. The ruling in Simmons' case was partially reversed, partially affirmed and partially vacated (USA v. Keith Franklin Simmons, 2013, December 11, Fourth Circuit).

Structuring

Some Ponzi perpetrators are charged with structuring. Structuring is the action of avoiding required currency transactions reporting under the Bank Secrecy Act, (31 USC § 5324), and the Federal Deposit

Insurance Act. This includes Currency Transaction Reports (CTR) and Report of International Currency Monetary Instruments (CMIR). This involves reporting transactions over $10,000.00. The Bank Secrecy Act defines the following as the elements of structuring regulations:

> A person structures a transaction if that person, acting alone, in conjunction with others, or on behalf of other persons, conducts or attempts to conduct one or more transactions in currency in any amount, at one or more financial institutions, on one or more days in any manner, for the purpose of avoiding CTR filing requirements.

A perpetrator may deposit smaller amounts under $10,000 in several banks, or over several days to try to avoid bank reporting requirements. Some Ponzi perpetrators have bank accounts in different states or offshore accounts for the purpose of avoiding detection by banking authorities, and reporting of monetary transactions.

Conclusion

In conclusion, the defining characteristic that makes a fraud a Ponzi scheme is the act of taking the money from later investors to pay earlier investors. The minimum amount taken in aggregate of the known federal Ponzi schemes is: $92,476,090,000. The perpetrators try to hide the funds in a myriad of ways. In Ponzi schemes, the federal agencies, trustees, and receivers have the responsibility of finding the money taken and returning it to investor-victims. These funds are deposited into bank accounts and trading accounts. Banks have a responsibility to watch for suspicious activities and to report them to authorities. Banks must be held accountable not just by government agencies, but by the consumers who use their services. Legislators have a responsibility to make sure that federal authorities have the legal tools they need to protect investors. In part three the laws, regulations, and legislation and their history will be addressed.

Notes

1 Passed by the House November 19, 2019. Submitted to the Senate; on hold because of COVID-19 as of May 2020.
2 Internal Revenue Code (IRC), 26 U.S.C. §§ 1.468B.1-1.468B.5.; Rule 1103 17 C.F.R.§ 201.1103 Fair fund and Disgorgement.
3 Fraudulent Transfers or Concealment (18 USC § 152).

References

Aguilar, Richard et al. v. PNC Bank, N.A. (2017) United States court of appeals for the eighth circuit.
Bank Secrecy Act, (1970). 12 USC §1829b; 31 USC § 5311; 31 USC § 5324

Civil Asset Forfeiture Reform Act of 2000, 18 U.S.C. 981.
DeGiacomo v. Sacred heart University, Inc. No. 17-1334 (2019) United States
Court of Appeals for the First Circuit 17-334. (Palladino).
Department of Justice, (2011, April 27). North Carolina bank agrees to pay
$400,000 in restitution to victims of investment fraud scheme it failed to detect
and report. (Simmons). Press release.
Department of Justice, (2011, November 29). Karla and Jesse Podlucky found
guilty on money laundering charges related to the $680 million Le-Nature's
fraud scheme. Press release.
Department of Justice, (2014, January 6). Criminal Information. JP Morgan
Chase Bank N.A. Deferred Prosecution Agreement, Exhibit 99.1.
Department of Justice, (2014, January 7). Manhattan U.S. Attorney and FBI
Assistant Director charge announce filing of criminal charges against and
deferred prosecution with JP Morgan Chase Bank, N.A. in connection with
Bernard L. Madoff's multi-billion dollar Ponzi scheme. Press release.
Department of Justice, (2015, December 18). Former bank vice president sen-
tenced in connection with Rothstein case. (Spinosa). Press release.
Department of Justice, (2018, October, 12). BMO Harris Bank pays $10 million
to resolve fraud allegations. (Petters). Press release.
Federal Bureau of Investigation, (n.d.). *Asset Forfeiture.* Retrieved May 19, 2020
from: https://www.fbi.gov/investigate/white-collar-crime/asset-forfeiture
Investor Protection and Capital Markets Fairness Act, H.R. 4344.
Kokesh v. Securities and Exchange Commission, United States Supreme Court
16-529 (2017, June 5).
Larson, E and Cannon, C. (2018). Madoff's victims are close to getting their $19
billion back. *Bloomberg.*
Rosemann v. St Louis Bank (2017) United States court of appeals for the eighth
circuit.
Securities and Exchange Commission in the matter of TD Bank N.A., (2013,
September 23). Administrative proceeding.
Securities and Exchange Commission (2013, September 23). SEC charges TD
Bank and former executive for roles in Rothstein Ponzi scheme in South
Florida. Press release 2013-192.
United States Code 18 USC § 152.
United States Code 18 U.S.C. § 1956(b) 18; § 1956 (9).
United States Department of Justice, (2019). *Asset Forfeiture Policy Manual.* Re-
trieved from: https://www.justice.gov/criminal-afmls/file/839521/download
United States Department of Justice, (2020). Types of federal forfeiture. Re-
trieved from: https://www.justice.gov/afp/types-federal-forfeiture
United States v. Keith Franklin Simmons (2013, December 11) United States
court of appeals for the fourth circuit.
United States v. Tammy Andreycak (2008, April 4) (Podlucky/Le-Nature).
Indictment.

Part II

The Perpetrators and Victims

Chapter 6 addresses individual-level aspects of the victims and perpetrators that can be known from federal documents. In addition, this chapter examines the social dynamics of trust, persuasion, gullibility, and greed, in relationship to Ponzi schemes. Lastly, this chapter looks at the sentences and sanctions. Sanctions are the civil-level punishments, and prison sentences are the criminal punishments. In high-profile cases the perpetrators tend to get very long sentences, and other cases seem lenient by comparison. The Federal Sentencing Guidelines were the basic sentencing rules that were followed prior to the Supreme Court *Booker* decision that changed federal sentencing.

Chapter 6

Trust, Persuasion, Gullibility, and Greed

The foremost of the five components that enable fraud is money; the investor-victim has it and wants more, and the perpetrator wants their money. The secondary component of fraud is trust: the investor-victim must be willing to trust the perpetrator with their money. One party must have money and be willing to trust another with their money. The third component is persuasion, the ability of one person to convince another to part company with their money. The fourth component is gullibility; the investor-victim must be willing to believe the perpetrator. The fifth component is greed; both perpetrators and victims want more money than they have. Why is it that an individual who has money feels the need to make interest or profits on their money? Why are they not willing to simply leave it in a bank savings or thrift account where it is safe? The answer to the latter may be the need to keep up with inflation, or it could simply be greed: the desire for more money. Is the desire to make a profit on our money such a bad thing? A great many people do simply leave their pensions and discretionary funds in banks, particularly banks that are Federal Deposit Insurance Corporation insured. Not everyone is willing to risk losing their money. This chapter discusses the nature of trust, persuasion, gullibility, and greed, the social-dynamics that enable fraud.

Trust

Financial markets and investing could not exist without the social dynamic of trust. This section looks at the social dynamic of trust and the relationship to financial markets, investing, and how trust enables the frauds to take place. Trust is defined as a culturally recognized behavior within a community that has a generally agreed-upon understanding of honesty and integrity, and that people well behave within the expected norms for that society. It is the act of having absolute confidence in someone or something. It is an expectation of truthfulness and honesty in financial transactions; it is fiduciary responsibility.

Theories of social connections and trust have been well studied among academics in sociology and psychology. Bart Nooteboom states that "Trust requires interdisciplinary analysis, a combination of economics, sociology, social psychology and cognitive science" (Nooteboom, 2012). This study has taken that approach, finding the social dynamic of trust overlapping these disciplines and a significant part of human social and financial interactions.

It is the economic fabric of any community to have an exchange of products or services for money. There is an element of trust that we accept that a service or product is worth what the seller says it is. If the product or service is not worthy of the value of the money exchanged, we are not likely to do business with that individual again. Financial markets and investing could not exist without the social dynamic of trust.

It is the social connections that enable the fraud to occur. Among those, Frijters and Foster explain that individuals can be members of several groups at once in social identity theory (Frijters and Foster, 2013). Hence, we will see in the data that some perpetrators used their belonging to a nationality or ethnic race, such as: Fijian-Indian (DOJ, 2014, October 30, Singh, p.r.), as well as their religious affiliation and to find their victims, such as: Persian-Jews (SEC, 2012, April 11, Neman) and African American Christians (Austin, 2004). It is likely that perpetrators would have included individuals from other groups, were they willing participants, but the initial contact method to perpetrate the fraud was based on a relationship of affiliation. The relationship of an affiliation supports the concept of trust within individuals in self-identifying groups. The sense of trust within groups, especially those that hold two affiliations such as both religiousness and ethnicity, is likely to be a stronger bond that renders the group members more vulnerable to the fraud.

Academics have attempted to classify and define trust in social relationships (Castelfranchi and Falcone, 2001; Fiske, 2004; McNight et al., 2006). Anthropologist Alan Fiske developed the relational models theory, applying the concept of trust to social relationships (Fiske, 2004). His theory implies that people relate to each other in four ways. These models suggest how individuals in groups can be victimized by their trust of others they perceive to be similar to themselves. The "communal sharing model" suggest that members of a group self-identify, distinguishing themselves from others. Fiske's second model is that of "equality matching," meaning members of a group participate in reciprocal behavior: "you do for me; I do for you." The third model is that of "authority ranking" (Fiske, 2004). In this model members of a group have some recognized hierarchy. This concept applies to religious groups who would recognize someone to be an authority within the group such as a rabbi, a minister, or a pastor. In some affinity-frauds, the pastor was the perpetrator that took advantage of parishioners. The fourth model component explains that the group recognizes something of value such as currency. This may seem obvious but Fiske is an anthropologist using this model to explain human social interactions revolving around trust. A society must hold a mutual concept of financial value in order for there to be actions such as investing, theft, or fraud. Basically, Fiske is saying there must be communally accepted values in place for a community to build a sense of trust from within itself.

Castelfranchi and Falcone explain that there are boundaries between when trusting is a rational act and when it is actually "overconfident and risky" (Castelfranchi and Falcone, 2001). The authors have quantified trust in an attempt to bring a logical format to the concept of trust. Their argument uses basic logic formulas (if X then Y), in order to measure the concept of trust as well as different types of trust. It all boils down to one's ability to determine whether or not acquaintances or strangers can be trusted and if trust is a logically knowable, predictable occurrence. In their discussion, Castelfranchi and Falcone explain that trust requires shared values that two parties are aware of. This is the basis of the trust in affinity-fraud. Potential investors assume that their shared affiliation with another means that the individual will be functioning under the same moral values that they themselves would have. This concept has been discussed by other authors as well (Frijters and Foster, 2013).

Baker and Faulkner (2004) discuss social connections and how they foster economic gain. It is their contention that social connections are based on culturally recognized values that allow for economic trans-actions to take place. They clarify that sociology tends to concentrate on the positive qualities of social interactions as they relate to financial transactions, and criminologists concentrate on the negative social qualities that may contribute to criminal financial transactions. These authors argue that the views of economic sociologists and white-collar criminologists oppose one another. It would seem in the case of affinity-fraud the criminologists are winning the argument; in that it is the social connections that render the victims vulnerable to the predatory behaviors of the perpetrators of the frauds – the negative outcome.

Charles Tilly addresses trust in relationship to transnational migration. Tilly states that "trust consists of placing valued outcomes at risk to others' malfeasance, mistakes or failures" (Tilly, 2005). This is exactly what immigrants who have been victims of affinity-fraud have done; they trusted someone from their homeland and lost their money as a result. Tilly explains that "trust networks" are made of "interpersonal; connections, consisting of mainly strong ties," that may leave those within the social bond, vulnerable to "malfeasance, mistakes or failures of others" (Tilly, 2007).

Croall has discussed the issue that the perpetrators are carrying out their crimes in the environment of a business situation where the victims have a reasonable expectation of being able to trust (Croall, 2016). Trust is a commonality among most authors reporting on white-collar crime. Croall also points out that the victims in white-collar crimes do not always consider themselves victims. One point that Croall makes, that was also made by Benson and Simpson (2015), is that what information there is on white-collar crime studies does not differentiate between civil actions by regulatory agencies and criminal actions by law enforcement agencies. The study herein does address both the civil and criminal aspects of Ponzi schemes. Croall also makes note that the victims of white-collar crimes are not just the individuals affected, but also organizations such as pensions, institutions, and charities. Again, in corporate crimes and environmental crimes entire communities can be affected. As a result of the real estate and mortgage boom that came before the financial crisis, it was individuals and global markets that were affected by the subprime mortgage failure. It affected individuals, then affected the financial markets, which then affected the overall economy. Croall's point is well taken that victims are also communities; the victims can be both micro and macro levels.

In most white-collar crimes, a legitimate business has been established; it is the environment that affords the opportunity to commit a fraud. However, in the case of Ponzi schemes the business entity is rarely a legitimate business, only in the case of unintentional frauds. In standard businesses that go bad, there are already relationships established that foster trust, or at least the appearance of trust, that enable the fraud. Fraud can take place only when there is trust. In Ponzi schemes, the perpetrators make the opportunity.

Shelly Jackson has defined financial fraud/exploitation victims by types (Jackson, 2015). Jackson uses the term "age-based victims" to discuss those victims who are generally elderly and frequently the victims of many exploitive and fraudulent acts, oftentimes at the hands of their own relatives. Ponzi perpetrators frequently victimize their friends and relatives first. Vulnerability is also a category Jackson uses indicating that some victims pose a specific vulnerability to exploitation or fraud, such as individuals with dementia. Jackson defines a trust relationship, meaning there is a relationship of trust established between the victim and the offender such as a caretaker, or a member of the clergy. Fiduciary relationships present an opportunity for exploitation and fraud. In all Ponzi schemes, all cases had some level of a fiduciary responsibility, in that the perpetrators were expected to carry out some investment. Some perpetrators were attorneys, accountants, and stock brokers or advisers who have a legal fiduciary responsibility. Others were family members or friends. Jackson differentiates between fraud and exploitation in that fraud involves breaking the law and deception, whereas exploitation might be simply taking advantage of a relative (Jackson, 2015).

The great majority of us are now internet users. We send and receive information through the internet daily. We have become quite dependent on the internet. This level of trust could develop only out of knowledge, or belief, that the information on the internet, or transmitted through the internet, cannot be tampered with, has not been tampered with, or changed in some way. We now execute securities trades through the internet at incomprehensible speeds. We are moving large and small sums of money through the internet because we trust it. We have made the decision to trust technology and those who program and control the technology.

Not only do investor-victims trust the perpetrator of the fraud, but they also trust that our government agencies charged with monitoring securities and commodities are all-knowing and have the ability to monitor all transactions, and that the enacted legislation is effective. The reality is, if there are no actual securities, commodities, futures, or real estate being traded or bought and sold, there is nothing for authorities to have within their ability to monitor. In such cases, in order for authorities to catch a fraud, someone must report it to them. There are limitations to what our government agencies can know and monitor without the help of the public. In addition, legislation changes with the times; what was legal in 2000 may not be legal now, after Dodd-Frank. Now, with the prevalence of internet trading and cryptocurrencies, legislation, monitoring, and enforcement must also change to keep pace with technology.

Persuasion

The power of persuasion is how Ponzi perpetrators convince their victim-investors that what he or she is promoting is a secure, guaranteed investment. Persuasion is as important a psychological mechanism as trust is in perpetrating Ponzi schemes. Persuasion is using influence to convince the investor to act as the perpetrator wants. Persuasiveness and cunning give the intentional fraud perpetrator an unfair advantage. Trust, lack of knowledge and experience, and gullibility make investors easy prey. Many investor-victims want to believe what they are told; they believe what they want to hear without question.

The skills with which the perpetrators pursue their prey is evident in the number of victims they accrue. In legitimate investing, the investors have a 50/50 chance of gaining or losing. In Ponzi schemes, there is 100 percent chance of losing. Maybe the investor-victims will get a percentage of their principal investment back, maybe not. The investor-victims are persuaded to trust and persuaded to invest. The tools of persuasion in Ponzi schemes include the physical image of being a financial success, that the investment is a sure thing, and that the perpetrator is trustworthy. These qualities are all falsities in Ponzi schemes. The perpetrators are glib, charming, and exude self-confidence; investors want to believe they are all that they say they are.

In the following case both perpetrators had successful careers that would have provided them with the experience and credentials to persuade investors that their business entity was credible. The two did provide some loans to athletes to carry out this fraud.

• William Allen and Susan Daub's scheme claimed to be making short-term loans to professional athletes (DOJ, 2017, March 1, p.r.). Allen was a former professional football player with the New York Giants, Miami Dolphins, and New England Patriots (SEC, 2015, April 1). Allen's scheme was based on loaning funds to professional athletes while they were waiting for their contracts to pay out. This would have required an inside knowledge of how the finances of professional football athletes are carried out as well as the loan industry. There were some loans made to athletes but not nearly to the degree that Allen and Daub reported to investors. Daub was a former bank executive. This scheme relied on Allen's knowledge that professional athletes need temporary funds and the banker's knowledge of the loan business. They then marketed their scheme to individuals who would want to fund professional athletes, a bit of a snob-appeal approach.

During times of financial booms, people have discretionary funds that they want to invest, safely, in an investment that will provide the maximum interest return. Investors want to make sure they will be able to withdraw their funds when they need it. They want their investment to be safe, ideally, and guaranteed. The perpetrators know this and construct their sales pitch to accommodate these concerns.

The "house-money effect" is such that when investors experience profits they feel confident and want to continue or invest more (Nofsinger, 2016). Ponzi perpetrators know this effect and use it to their advantage. When investor-victims first invest, they get their interest right on time, consistently, as promised. This causes the victims to feel confident so that they roll over their earnings, invest more, and tell all their friends about the great investment.

Faith-based Ponzi schemes add another layer of deception to the persuasion. Victim-investors are persuaded with words of faith and belief to buy into the fraud. In most religious organizations it is considered "bad-faith" not to trust fellow worshipers or to doubt the integrity of the religious leader. Religious members might be ostracized for doubting or being suspicious of a fellow believer or the organization's leader. In some faith-based Ponzi schemes, the members of the churches who were taken advantage of did not believe they had been defrauded. They believed the government had falsely convicted their church member or clergy. Among the faith-based Ponzi schemes, it is references to God and God's showing preference, by favoring them for being devoted believers, that are a common practice as a mechanism to persuade. People want to believe that their deep faith will pay off in the here and now.

- One such case is that of David Souza who used his affiliation with his church to attract investors. Souza used the line "obvious favor of God," suggesting that his investments were successful because God made it so, that somehow God was showing favor to him and his investors because of their faith (SEC, 2009, August 28, p. 3).

- A second case example is that of Charles Leif Erickson of Massachusetts. Erickson, a church elder, told victim-investors that he believed "that the 'Holy Spirit' gave him a proprietary system for trading," enabling him to use the method he used in futures contracts. Apparently, Erickson deviated from his "system" and ended up with a 24-month prison sentence (USA v. Erickson, 2015, September 1, affidavit, p. 4).

- Eldon Gresham ran a FOREX scheme in Georgia. In his scheme, he targeted Christians telling them, "the Lord had blessed him." He also used the action of exclusiveness that he was offering his investments only to a "limited number of Christians for a limited time" (CFTC, 2009, July 9, p.r.).

- In the Ponzi-pyramid scheme *Universo Foneclub*, Sanderley De Vasconcelos and Reverend Victor Sales preyed on those within the Brazilian evangelic Christian community. Sales told member-victims that "God did not want them to be poor," that "God wanted them to be prosperous" (SEC, 2006, May 30, p. 6, prg. 14). The product was phone cards that were alleged to be sold at a lower cost than more well-known phone card companies. In this scheme, members paid memberships fees of varying ranks. There was no product to sell, no phone cards. The profits were solely from memberships.

- In *TriEnergy*, Lowell Decker, Robert Jennings, Henry Jones, and Arthur Simburg used phrases such as "deistically inspired or divinely guided" (SEC, 2006, August 9, p. 2, prg. 4).

- Richard Wyatt Davis Jr. targeted an interesting variety of people in the area of Charlotte, North Carolina. His victims were professional athletes, members of his church, and "prepers." Survivalists and other "prepers" are individuals and families who do not trust the economy or the government. Prepers are people who tend to stock pile necessities and foods because they believe that government failure or financial decline are just around the corner. Davis understood their financial fears and used that and their shared religious faith to persuade them to trust in him (DOJ, 2018, June 25, p.r.). Davis had 19 business entities (SEC, 2016, June 2).

Gullibility

The other side of persuasion is gullibility; it is that some people are easily persuaded and others not at all persuadable. When we believe what is told to us at face value, without questioning, we can be easily deceived. If we do question, we believe what is told to us without validating what we are told or presented with. As Stephen Greenspan defines gullibility, "Gullibility can be defined as an unusual tendency toward being duped or taken advantage of" (Greenspan, 2009, Annals, p. 2). Gullibility refers to accepting what someone tells us at face value, without question, being easily deceived.

> Gullibility builds on credulity (which may be considered a largely cognitive factor), but has a coercive element that also takes advantage of effective factors (in the case of a Ponzi scheme, greed) and also has situational elements (such as a sales person making false claims or a neighbor telling you how much money he made in a scheme).
>
> (Greenspan, 2009, Annals, p. 3)

Stephen Greenspan holds a doctorate in psychology. The interesting thing about Greenspan is that he was one of Bernie Madoff's victims. His book *The annals of gullibility* went to press just before Madoff confessed his massive Ponzi scheme to authorities. Even those more knowledgeable can be duped. He was one of the many who had invested with a fund of funds that had invested with Madoff. Greenspan trusted that his investment adviser had done due diligence (Greenspan, WSJ, 2009). Not only did he not know his investment was going to Madoff's fund, he did not know who Bernie Madoff was; it is likely that many of Madoff's victims were in a similar situation. Just as many of those who invested with Madoff were educated, and more sophisticated in investing, their money was lost due to trust. Trust and gullibility go hand-in-hand.

The difference between being an uneducated or inexperienced investor and gullibility is that the gullible want to believe that something that seems unreasonable is indeed true, because they are told that it is the truth. The uneducated and inexperienced can still be suspicious and cautious. The gullible want to believe the best in people; they want to believe what is told to them or submitted to them in writing. Ponzi cases are full of fraudulent documents presented to the investor-victims; it was in writing, it went to court, and they still lost their money.

Sometimes gullibility is simply believing that someone else would not do something harmful or deceitful because the investor-victim would not cheat or harm someone else. I call this: "Just-like-I-am" syndrome; the belief that someone who is like I am, looks like "I do," goes to the same church, speaks the same language as "I do," could not possibly be deceitful or predatory, because "I am not." Someone who is "just-like-I-am" could not possibly defraud someone because "I" could not defraud someone. It is the belief that the predator has our best interests at heart, solely because they are like us and they said that we could trust them.

Greed

Many US attorneys and US district court judges have commented that the Ponzi perpetrators are simply greedy; it is doubtful that anyone would argue with that. But what about the victims, is it gullibility that someone believes they will receive 3,000 percent in interest or is it greed? It is greed. There is nothing logical or believable about a promise of 3,000 percent interest. Greed is what enables the fraud scheme to occur; this applies to both intentional and unintentional Ponzi schemes. Both the perpetrator and the victims want money. Greed is an insatiable, ego-driven need for more money, and more possessions. It is one of our most primitive characteristics, with the need for status – the pecking order. The desire to be perceived as very successful affects perpetrator and victim alike.

Animals commonly steal food from one another even though they may not be hungry, but because it is their instinct to take more than they need. The difference is humans can reason and have free choice; we can choose not to be greedy. We can understand that we have more than we need. Animals also have pecking orders; in every species that survives in herds, flocks, packs, or colonies there are usually levels of status established. Humans are no different; it is the trappings of wealth that make us feel we are of higher status than others. We use the term "the haves and the have nots." The desire to "have" and to be perceived as "having" are great motivators that render us vulnerable to predators.

Ponzi perpetrators justify their actions in their beliefs that their victims are also looking for a quick, easy profit, that they are just as greedy as the perpetrator. In her book *The Ponzi scheme puzzle*, Tamar Frankel discusses that Ponzi perpetrators justify their actions, because the perpetrators feel that their victims are just as greedy as they are (Frankel, 2012, p. 129). Some perpetrators justify their actions in that the victims had a responsibility to be savvier, more educated, more perceptive; they weren't, so they deserve to lose their money.

Savings accounts pay little in interest; our rainy-day funds must be stored somewhere. Our culture encourages us to invest our discretionary funds.

We have retirement accounts, inheritances, trust funds, all of which must be put in a safe place, ideally earning interest. When we realized that Social Security would not be adequate to support the baby-boomer generation we started IRA and KEOGH accounts to save for our elder years. Those accounts have to be kept in a place that provides enough profit to keep up with inflation. Finding a safe place for our savings is not greed; it is very practical, a necessity.

Justifying taking advantage of victims based on greed is victim blaming. That being said, in some Ponzi schemes the victims were accredited investors. By the Securities Act of 1933, accredited investors are required to have a high financial worth and to be financially sophisticated. These are individuals or financial entities such as insurance companies or pension funds that are required to perform due diligence and to have an understanding of trading practices and laws. These are people who are considered educated, experienced, knowledgeable professionals and of whom we would think could recognize that something was amiss. Did their need for profits cloud their judgment, or were the perpetrators so skilled to fool the most sophisticated among us? Sometimes the perpetrators are that skilled; and sometimes it is just plain greed. In *History of greed*, David Sarna also explains that the greed of investors enables the fraud to happen (Sarna, 2010). Perpetrators believe anyone willing to invest with them wants something without working to earn it and therefore deserve to be taken advantage of.

When a Ponzi perpetrator promises their victims outrageous profits, such as 100 percent or 3,000 percent, the victims must know on some level that it is not feasible. If the individual pushing their investment was so successful, why would they need anyone else's money? The potential investor-victims in many schemes must have known that something did not pass the "smell test" when such high interest rates were promised. It seems quite irrational that anyone would knowingly contribute funds that they have any inclination they might lose. The Ponzi perpetrators go to great lengths to convince their potential and current investor-victims of the legitimacy of their product. The perpetrators guarantee profits and return of the principal; the investors want to believe them. The perpetrators are experts at deceit and fraudulent documents. While the victims are not completely to be blamed, when such extreme interest rates are guaranteed, there should at least be suspicion.

In some cases, it is the status of having luxurious possessions that assuages the needy ego of the perpetrator. Most Ponzi perpetrators are listed as having used the illegally obtained funds for mortgage payments and more often than not, the purchase of at least one mansion. The lists of luxury vehicles in many Ponzi schemes is quite beyond the pale; some of the top perpetrators have many.

- Scott Rothstein had a collection of watches as well as these luxury cars:

1 Two Ferraris
2 Two Rolls Royces – one a convertible
3 A Corvette
4 A Lamborghini
5 A Bentley
6 A Cadillac Escalade
7 A Limousine Ford Expedition
8 A Mercedes
9 A Bugatti Veyron

- In a recent scheme under the responsibility of the United States Marshals, the perpetrators had 185 luxury and classic cars; some of the vehicles were antiques from the 1920s and 1930s (U.S. Marshals, 2019, annual report, p. 40). The Marshals had the responsibility of auctioning off the vehicles to regain the funds lost in the Ponzi scheme (U.S. Marshals, 2019, October 15, p.r.).[1] The Carpoffs also had a private jet, a minor league baseball team, and sponsored a NASCAR racecar (DOJ, 2020, January 24, p.r.).
- Marc Dreier had at least 150 art pieces that were described in the indictment and forfeiture. The collection included pieces by Henri Matisse, Andy Warhol, David Hockney, Keith Haring, Jasper Johns, Roy Lichtenstein, Mark Rothko, and many more artists (USA v. Marc Dreier, 2009, January 29).
- It is quite common for Ponzi perpetrators to buy at least one, and often several, mansions. One example is Frederick Daren Berg who had: two condominiums, one for $1.95 million in Seattle and a $1.4 million condominium in San Francisco. He had a $1.25 million house in La Quinta, California, and a $5.475 million house on Mercer Island. He also had two Lear jets, and yachts (FBI, 2012, February 9, p.r.)

Mesly's theory of financial predation explains that a predator is "cold, calculative, self-centered and sneaky" (Mesly and Levy Mangin, 2012, p. 146). Mesly et al. theorize that financial predators exploit their victims' naiveté in financial matters in what they have referred to as a "predatory web" (Mesly and Levy Mangin, 2012, p. 146). Mesly et al. identify five elements of predation, the first of which is that the predator identifies a victim as being vulnerable in some way, possibly lacking in experience or just gullible. Second, the predator "establishes trust" (Mesly and Levy Mangin, 2012, p. 146). In Mesly's third criterion there is a component of time-pressure, such as a limited offer. Mesly's fourth component is some action is taken, such as the prey signs a contract. The fifth predatory-web component is a transfer of assets, such as providing the predator with funds to invest (Mesly and Levy Mangin, 2012, p. 146). Mesly's theory explains how the Ponzi perpetrators carry out their frauds, particularly the intentional Ponzi schemes. The Ponzi perpetrators know they are taking the funds of others; it was their intent; they are financial predators.

In the end, the investor-victims trusted someone they should not have trusted. In others it was a trusted professional that the investor-victim had known for years. Many victims trusted friends or family members; it was the close relationships that enabled the fraud in the first place. Maybe the victims would not have invested if the perpetrator was a total stranger. In many professional situations, when we are looking for a plumber or an electrician or other professional, we ask a friend, a relative, or a neighbor who they would use. We believe that if people we trust have done business with good results we also will have good results. At times we want to see the good in people, so we are easily convinced. We want to believe those we are close to. We do not want to miss out on something; to be left out. This is the basis for Ponzi schemes to occur; trust by association. The following chapters discuss qualities of the perpetrators and victims that enabled the frauds to take place.

Note

1 The October 2019 United States Marshals press release stated 149 cars. The 2019 Annual report stated 185 cars.

References

Austin, D. (2004). "In God we trust": The cultural and social impact of affinity fraud in the African American church. *University of Maryland Law Journal of Race, Religion, Gender and Class* Vol.4 p. 365.

Baker, W. and Faulkner, R. (2004). Social networks and loss of capital. *Social Networks* Vol.26 pp. 91–111. doi: 10-1016/jsocnet.2004.01.004

Benson, M. and Simpson, S. (2015). *Understanding white-collar crime: An opportunity perspective* (3rd ed.). New York, NY, Routledge.

Castelfranchi, C. and Falcone, R. (2001). "Social trust: A cognitive approach", in Castelfranchi, C. and Yao-Hua, T. (Eds.), *Trust and deception in virtual societies* (pp. 55–72). Netherlands, Springer-Science+Business Media.

CFTC v. Stephen Walsh, Paul Greenwood, Westridge Capital management, Inc., WG Trading Investors LP, WGIA, LLD (2006, February 25) Complaint.

Commodities Futures Trading Commission, (2009, July 9). CFTC charges Georgia man with operating a multi-million dollar FOREX Ponzi scheme. (Gresham). Press release.

Croall, H. (2016). "What is known and what should be known about white-collar crime victimization." in Van Slyke, S., Benson, M., Cullen, F. (Eds.), *The Oxford handbook of white-collar crime*. New York, NY. Oxford University Press.

Department of Justice, (2014, October 30). Former Elk Grove man sentenced to 15.5 years in prison for $20 million investment fraud and false statements in bankruptcy. (Singh). Press release.

Department of Justice, (2017, March 1). Former NFL Player and former bank executive sentenced for Ponzi scheme and money laundering. (Allen & Daub). Press release.

Department of Justice, (2018, June 25). Charlotte investment fund operator sentenced to 7.5 years for securities fraud and tax evasion. (Richard Davis). Press release.

Department of Justice, (2020, January 24). Top executives plead guilty to participating in a billion dollar Ponzi scheme—the biggest criminal fraud scheme in the history of the Eastern District of California. (Carpoff). Press release.

Federal Bureau of Investigation, (2012, February 9). Mercer island man sentenced to 18 years in prison for Ponzi scheme and bankruptcy fraud. (Berg). Press release.

Fiske, A. (2004). "Relational models theory 2.0", in Haslem, N. (Ed.), *Relational models theory: A contemporary View.* Mahwah, NJ, Lawrence Erlbaum Associates.

Frankel, T. (2012). *The Ponzi schemes puzzle: A history and analysis of con-artists and victims.* New York, NY, Oxford University Press.

Frijters, P. and Foster, G. (2013). *Economic theory of greed, love, groups and networks.* Cambridge, UK, Cambridge University Press.

Greenspan, S. (2009). *The annals of gullibility.* Westport, CT, Praeger Publishers.

Greenspan, S. (2009, January 3). Essay: Why we keep falling for financial scams. *Wall Street Journal.*

Jackson, S. (2015). The vexing problem of defining financial exploitation. *Journal of Financial Crime* Vol.22 No.1 pp. 63–78.

McNight, D.H., Cummings, I.L., and Chervany, N.L. (2006). "Initial trust formation in new organizational relationships", in Kramer, R.M. (Ed.), *Organizational Trust.* New York, NY, Oxford University Press.

Mesly, O. and Levy Mangin, J.P. (2012). Financial predation: A contemporary problem. *The International Journal of Finance* Vol.4 pp. 144–151.

Mesly, O. and Racicot, F. (2012). A note on financial predation: A market assessment. *The Journal of Wealth Management* Vol.15 No.1 pp. 101–103.

Nofsinger, J. (2016). *The psychology of investing.* New York, NY, Routledge

Nooteboom, B. (2012). *Dynamics of trust: Communication, action and third parties.* Sasaki, M. and Marsh, R. (Eds.), *Trust comparative perspectives* (pp. 9–30). Leiden, the Nethrlands Brill Academic Publishers

Sarna, D. (2010). *History of greed.* Hoboken, NJ, Wiley.

Securities and Exchange Commission v. Capital Consultants, LLC., Jeffrey Grayson, and Barclay L. Grayson (2002, April 25) Litigation release.

Securities and Exchange Commission v. Universo Foneclub Corporation, Sanderley R. DeVasConcelos, aka Sann Rodrigues, aka Sanderly Vasconcelos Rev. Victor Sales aka Victor William (2006, May 30) Complaint.

Securities and Exchange Commission v. TriEnergy Inc., H&J Energy Company, Inc., Marina Investors Group Inc., Lowell Decker, Robert Jennings, Henry Jones, Arthur Simburg, Mildred Stultz, DJM, LLC., Financial MD, Inc.,

Financial MD and Associates, Inc., Daniel J. Merriman, Global Village Records, and La Vie D'Argent (2006, August 9) Amended Complaint.

Securities and Exchange Commission, (2009, August 28). Securities and Exchange Commission vs. David A. Souza and D. A. Souza Investments LLC. Complaint.

Securities and Exchange Commission v. Shervin Neman and Neman Financial, Inc. (2012, April 11) Complaint.

Securities and Exchange Commission v. Capital Finance Partners LLC., Capital Finance Holdings LLC., Capital Financial Enterprises LLC., William D. Allen, and Susan C. Daub (2015, April 1) Complaint.

Securities and Exchange Commission v. Richard W. Davis Jr. (2016, June 2) Complaint.

Tilly, C. (2005). *Trust and rule.* New York, NY, Columbia University Press.

Tilly, C. (2007, March). Trust networks in transnational migration. *Sociological Forum* Vol.22 No.1 pp. 3–24.

United States v. Charles Leif Erickson (2015, September 1) Affidavit in support of application for a search warrant and arrest warrant.

United States v. Marc Dreier (2009, January 29) Indictment.

United States Marshals, (2019, October 15). U.S. Marshals auctioning collection of 149 classic, luxury vehicles from California case involving DC Solar. Press release.

United States Marshals Service FY 2019 Annual Report.

Chapter 7

The Ponzi Perpetrators

This chapter discusses the individuals who perpetrated the Ponzi schemes and characteristics about them that can be known from federal documents. Many of us cannot imagine how anyone could knowingly take advantage of others, taking their last dime. The question begs asking: what enables someone to victimize their family and friends, to take advantage of the elderly and the cognitively vulnerable? This chapter discusses characteristics and theories about human behavior to try to understand how the perpetrators prey on others. The most interesting aspect of this data is the finding of the diversity in perpetrators; they are not just one personality type, gender, race, religion, age, or profession. A Ponzi perpetrator can be anyone. A perpetrator can be someone we believe we know well or a total stranger who convinces us to trust them.

Ponzi perpetrators are experts at deception. Interviewing or surveying was not considered for this research because Ponzi perpetrators are skilled at lying; there would be no way to determine the validity of their words. Producing fraudulent documents is a standard modus operandi for Ponzi perpetrators, as is blatantly and intentionally lying to their victims; they are masters of fraud. Ponzi perpetrators may be pathological liars or simply very good at lying. Ponzi perpetrators are in prison for deceit; it is questionable how valid or reliable interviews or surveys with them might be. White-collar criminals, in general, are unlikely to admit guilt.

Why the Ponzi perpetrators carry out their frauds is as individual as they are, and their schemes. Clearly, they want money, as do their investor-victims. What makes one person more likely to be a perpetrator and another to be a victim? We can theorize but we cannot definitively know why some individuals choose to take advantage of others. They do it because they can. This chapter will discuss the American dream, the *gambler's fallacy*, and how they may be motivations, or the perpetrator's justification for committing these frauds. This chapter suggests that certain psychological and sociological theories might explain the motivations of the Ponzi perpetrators. We will look at what the data tells us about the characteristics of the perpetrators, in an effort to understand the people who have carried out Ponzi schemes.

Antisocial Personality Disorders

Academic researchers have attempted to define and quantify psychopathological qualities in white-collar offenders. With any type of crime, psychological factors of the individual cannot be ruled out as a cause. The studies that do exist (Alalehto, 2016; Collins and Schmidt, 1993; Listwan et al., 2010) look at extroversion, neurosis, and recidivism in white-collar criminals. Ragatz et al. (2012) use the research of others in a study to measure psychopathology in white-collar offenders. Their study makes use of the *Psychological inventory of criminal thinking styles* study by Walters (2010); the *Lifestyles criminality screening form* (Walters et al., 1991); and *the Psychopathic inventory revised* (Lilienfield and Widows, 2005). Their study sample was taken from white-collar and non-white-collar inmates in Eastern United States federal prisons. The population was made up of 226 individuals who had volunteered for a drug abuse program. The study measured for a difference between white-collar and non-white-collar offenders in psychopathological traits. The results were more indicative of substance abuse–related traits (anxiety, alcohol use), and treatment thereof, than in qualities that define psychopathology in white-collar offenders.

Blickle et al. (2006) tested for narcissistic and hedonistic tendencies in 76 white-collar inmates, and 303 who had committed white-collar offenses (no mention of incarceration). The comparison population was 150 white-collar managers from German companies. This study measured for gender, social desirability, narcissism, conscientiousness, and behavioral self-control. Basically, they found that white-collar criminals were more conscientious (by German standards), more hedonistic, and more narcissistic than the compared population of white-collar management participants. While differences were found, these studies do not present a convincing argument that white-collar criminals are psychopaths or sociopaths.

Adrian Raine and Andrea Glenn make the observation that "unsuccessful psychopaths" have criminal convictions, versus those who have not drawn the attention of law enforcement and are "successful psychopaths" (Glenn and Raine, 2014, p. 9). This suggests that there are individuals who meet the criteria for psychopathy who never have an encounter with the law but still have the characteristics of the disorder. These individuals may function quite well in corporate settings without drawing the attention of the law (Babiak and Hare, 2006; Hare, 1993). Raine and

Glenn explain that there is no biological test or predictor of psychopathy. In short, there is no gene that determines psychopathy or antisocial behavior disorders in criminals (Glenn and Raine, 2014).

In the end, these studies measured small populations that were incarcerated with variables that do not necessarily measure for psychopathic qualities. The participants were voluntary; true psychopaths may or may not agree to participate in such studies. They may want to see if they could deceive the researchers, or more likely, if there was nothing to be gained, they would not agree to participate. Measuring for psychopathic tendencies in white-collar criminals or non-white-collar criminals must be carried out by qualified psychological researchers. Psychopaths may be experts at deceit; only qualified researchers with appropriate training and experience would be able to determine validity of responses by participants. Again, ethically speaking, such studies can be undertaken only on a volunteer basis and true psychopaths may not be willing to participate unless they saw some gain, thereby negating the objectivity of the study.

In some cases, this type of extreme egocentric behavior of white-collar criminals in general has been described as psychopathic or sociopathic (Babiak and Hare, 2006; Hare, 1993). The commonly used phrase in the psychiatric field is "antisocial personality disorder." The *Diagnostic and Statistical Manual of Mental Disorders* lists the following qualities as the criteria for diagnosing antisocial disorder (American Psychiatric Association, 2015, p. 659):

A   "A pervasive pattern of disregard for and violation of the rights of others occurring since the age of 15, as indicated by three or more of the following":

1   "Failure to conform to social norms with respect to lawful behaviors, as indicated by repeatedly performing acts that are grounds for arrest." The behaviors of the Ponzi perpetrators are unlawful. In many cases, the perpetrators were professionals who had passed bar exams, public accounting exams, and passed the FINRA series exams to be brokers or advisers. Some had real estate licenses and others had insurance licenses. All of these exams have questions about the laws involved with doing business that test takers must pass in order to get their licenses. The Ponzi perpetrators know they are breaking the law.

2   "Deceitfulness, as indicated by repeated lying, use of aliases, or conning others for personal profit or pleasure." What is evident in all Ponzi schemes is dishonesty: every Ponzi perpetrator has lied to his or her victims and produced fraudulent documents. Many perpetrators use aliases, in some cases several aliases.

3   "Impulsivity or failure to plan ahead." The third indicator of antisocial disorders is impulsiveness or failure to plan ahead. In some cases, Ponzi perpetrators meticulously plan ahead. They can be extremely strategic in their manipulation of their victims. Most cases have indicated extreme self-indulgence in luxury items such as watches mansions and expensive cars; this could be an indicator of impulsiveness.

4   "Irritability and aggressiveness, as indicated by repeated physical fights or assaults." None of the Ponzi cases indicated any tendency toward violent[1] or aggressive tendencies or activities. Ponzi perpetrators are experts at being charming and friendly in order to build trust. Someone who is irritable or abusive would not succeed. If we were to profile potential Ponzi perpetrators by their charm, pleasant demeanor, and friendliness we would mistake a great many honest people for Ponzi perpetrators.

5   "Reckless disregard for the safety of others." The Ponzi perpetrators show a complete disregard for the financial well-being of their victims. They know they are taking their victims' money. Remorse is demonstrated when required to do so in court at sentencing.

6   "Consistent irresponsibility, as indicated by repeated failure to sustain consistent work behavior or honor financial obligations." The Ponzi perpetrators present themselves as being successful legitimate business people. Appearing responsible is part of keeping up the image of success. Some schemes go on for many years, even decades, because the perpetrator keeps the image of being a successful business man or woman. Ponzi perpetrators honor their financial obligations early on and as consistently as possible for as long as possible, in order to keep the scheme going. It is only when they can no longer bring in enough new investors that the scheme fails. Some cases were functioning quite well when authorities found the scheme to be fraudulent.

7   "Lack of remorse, as indicated by being indifferent to or rationalizing having hurt or mistreated, or stolen from another." Some perpetrators are noted for their lack of remorse. It is the Ponzi perpetrator's lack of empathy that enables them to commit the fraud. Tamar Frankel explains that perpetrators feel their victims are greedy (Frankel, 2012, p. 129). If they were not greedy the victims could not be so easily fooled. White-collar criminals in general tend to reject that their actions are criminal (Benson and Simpson, 2015, p. 61). Ponzi perpetrators are no exception.

B   "The individual is at least age 18 years." The youngest Ponzi perpetrators were both 19 years of age when they started their separate schemes. The majority of Ponzi perpetrators were between the ages of 45 and 55.

C   "There is evidence of conduct disorder with onset before age 15 years." The case documents do not discuss behaviors prior to the Ponzi scheme, unless the perpetrator is a recidivist. All recidivist perpetrators were over the age of 18. Documentation of criminal activity before the age of 18 is not a matter of public record.

D   "The occurrence of antisocial behavior is not exclusively during the course of schizophrenia or bipolar disorder." There was no mention of these disorders in any of the Ponzi scheme documents. However, there were 15 suicides among the perpetrators. Whether the suicides are due to remorse, or fear of prison, is not known. One Ponzi perpetrator was declared mentally incompetent to stand trial.

For an individual Ponzi perpetrator to be considered as having antisocial personality disorders (or sociopathic/psychopathic), they must demonstrate at least three of the above criteria. The perpetrators demonstrated the first criterion by the consistency in unlawful behavior in that their schemes may have gone on for many years and are repeated on multiple victims. The Ponzi perpetrators are the experts in deceit of every possible kind; the methods of deception seem to be limitless and creative; this satisfies the second criterion. The fifth criterion is showing blatant disregard for the well-being of others; the Ponzi perpetrators knowingly and intentionally take their investor-victims' money with no regard to how their lives will be devastated. The Ponzi perpetrators willfully steal from their victims demonstrating the seventh criterion. They know the victims will not get their money back. The perpetrators may state remorse, as required for sentencing, but rarely do their actions show real remorse. Oftentimes the sentencing memorandums discuss how much charitable work the individuals have done, as if this should diminish the harm they have caused or reduce their sentence; the charitable works were carried out with their victim's money.

One hundred percent of the intentional scheme perpetrators have demonstrated the first, second, and seventh criteria, at the very least. In the unintentional schemes, there may be individuals who did not fit the seventh criterion; they may indeed harbor deep remorse. In aggregate, the Ponzi perpetrators fit the criteria of antisocial personality disorders; individual perpetrators may vary in these criteria.

David Kotz was the Inspector General at the Security Exchange Commission who carried out the investigations of the Madoff and Stanford cases failures by SEC employees. In his book *Why Ponzi schemes work and how to protect yourself from being defrauded* (2014), he discusses the psychology of fraudsters. Kotz had interviewed Bernard Madoff and Russel Wassendorf for his book. In his view, he felt that Madoff's, Wassendorf's, and Stanford's actions demonstrated the behaviors of antisocial disorder (Kotz, 2014, p. 62). While Kotz did not interview Stanford for the book, through his investigation of the Stanford case he found what he believed to be indicators of antisocial personality disorder. Kotz is not a psychiatrist and is not making a diagnosis, but stating that in his view their actions demonstrate similarity to the behaviors of antisocial disorder.

McMasters, the journalist who interviewed Charles Ponzi, suggested that Ponzi had a phobia about money, stating that "no sane person would do what he is doing" (McMasters, 1962, pp. 145–146). McMasters, like Kotz, is not a psychiatrist; he was just a journalist observing behaviors he thought a normal, psychologically balanced person would not demonstrate.

The psychiatric medical profession has standards by which they diagnose antisocial disorders, psychopathy, or sociopathy. However, establishing a willing sample or population of possible white-collar criminals to interview and survey for social science research has ethical and practical limitations. Likewise, a population that does indeed fit the criteria for antisocial personality disorder, psychopathy, or sociopathic may not provide honest answers in interviews or surveys, by nature of the second criterion of deceitful behavior. In short, it is virtually impossible to carry out valid and reliable studies on white-collar or non-white-collar criminals for these psychological conditions. In the unlikely event that there was some scientific means of determining that someone is likely to be a fraud perpetrator, individuals have rights, and the science could be wrong.

Gambler's Fallacy

Several perpetrators were involved in gambling. The perpetrators may have begun the scheme out of a debt from a gambling obsession, or began gambling the funds taken in from investor-victims; regardless they believed they would recoup their losses. This section also uses the gambler's fallacy in relationship to investing losses. The gambler's fallacy is the belief that the next good poker hand or other method of gambling will be a turn of luck recuperating the gambler's losses. Here it is applied to investing in financial markets.

In the business-failure and brokerage-failure cases, the perpetrators may have believed that they would be able to produce profits in the investments or bring the business into profitability. The Gambler's fallacy is the behavior demonstrated by gamblers when they have had losses in gambling but continue because they feel that one more game will change their luck and they will win a large profit; it is suggested herein that same behavior applies in brokerage-failure schemes. The brokers have experienced successful trades in the past, but then they endure severe losses.

They then borrow from investors in an effort to try to recuperate the losses, always feeling they are just one trade away from success when they will be able to pay back their investors' principal.

Granero et al., in *Gambling on the stock market: an unexplored issue,* address investing in the stock market as it relates to pathological addiction (Granero et al., 2012). Their study included 1,470 individuals who had been diagnosed with gambling addiction, in Barcelona, Spain. Their study interviewed the individuals to determine lifestyle choices that would be characteristic of gambling addiction such as lying about funds lost, obsessive-compulsive, reward dependence, and many other indicator variables. Their findings did not support their hypothesis that the consequences are more severe for those who are stock market gambling addicted. Their study only included those who sought treatment for gambling addiction. The study is novel in that few studies have attempted to measure stock market investing as a gambling addiction (Granero et al., 2012).

This study also looks at what is known as "the gambler's fallacy" to explain behaviors in brokerage-failure Ponzi schemes. The gambler's fallacy is "a phenomenon whereby people inappropriately predict a reversal" (Shefrin, 2002, p. 46). Gamblers are absolutely certain they will make that one good game or make that one good bet and win big, turning around a losing streak. It may also be that this is the thinking process with the brokerage-failure schemes. He, or she, makes trades that fail to make profits, hide the losses from their clients, and then try another investment. When that also fails, the brokerage or hedge fund begins to pay back interest or principal to the earlier investors from the funds of new investors. The broker continues to believe they will have successful trades and pay everyone back.

Rabin (2002) explains that in investing, the Gambler's fallacy is demonstrated when an investor or investment adviser has had several losses in the market, they believe the law of probability is such that there must be a gain coming for them. Rabin suggests that people mistakenly assume that they can relate small batches of phenomenon to large batches of phenomenon, meaning a relationship between the entire stock market to the performance of one investment product, or that previous experiences in the stock market will be indicative of current stock market performances. Individual stocks can go up or down regardless of what the stock market is doing (Rabin, 2002). This applies to those schemes that tried to function as brokerages but failed.

When there is a binary, or 50/50 chance that an investment or market will go up or down, individuals believe they can predict what will be next. Generally, when the financial market has several consecutive declines, investors tend to believe there will be a correction, somehow naturally or magically occurring. With legitimate investments, there is not just up or down trends but also staying even; an investment may continue at the same performance rate. Ponzi schemes are doomed to failure; there is no 50/50 option because there is always a point when there are not enough new victims contributing to pay the earlier victims.

According to the *Diagnostic and Statistical Manual of Mental Disorders*, one of the behavioral descriptions of a pathological gambling disorder is:

> A pattern of "chasing" one's losses may develop, with an urgent need to keep gambling (often with larger bets or the taking of greater risks) to undo a loss or series of losses. The individual may abandon his or her gambling strategy and try to win back losses all at once. Although all gamblers may chase for short periods, it is the long-term chase that is more characteristic of individuals with Pathological Gambling (Criterion 6).
> (American Psychiatric Association, 2015, p. 585)

Hersh Shefrin describes the Gambler's fallacy in relationship to investing. The gambler's fallacy dictates that when an individual experiences something repeatedly, such as five coin tosses of heads in a row, they feel certain that the sixth toss is bound to be tails (Shefrin, 2002, p. 17). With brokerage-failure Ponzi schemes, the broker sees loss after loss and feels certain a good trade must be coming, and they keep trying. Shefrin also explains that some individuals have loss-aversion: they simply cannot accept a loss and hold on even when there is no reasonable chance of success. Shefrin calls this "get-evenitis" (Shefrin, 2002, p. 107), the meaning being that individuals feel that if they hold on long enough, they will eventually bring their investments back up to a profit.

This study suggests that in the brokerage-failure schemes, the brokers suffered from "get-evenitis" (Shefrin, 2002, p. 107), and succumbed to the gambler's fallacy. Once this has occurred the brokers continued to borrow funds from later investors to keep earlier investors satisfied. They could not just admit they had failed to their investors; they are loss-averse, unable to accept the financial losses, and the Ponzi scheme begins.

General Strain Theory

In sociology, general strain theory basically suggests that stressors cause people to commit crimes (Agnew, 2001; Merton, 1938; Sutherland, 1947). In the cases of Ponzi perpetrators, the desire to fulfill the American dream, achieving financial success in the cases of intentional frauds, and fear of failure is the stressor in unintentional frauds. Social-criminological theorists Steven Messner and Richard Rosenfeld (2013) discussed the American Dream and white-collar crime in their book *Crime and the American Dream*. Messner and Rosenfeld's theory is that Americans are ingrained with the belief that they must be financially successful in order to fit into society. Their theory particularly lends itself directly to those in the broker-failure schemes: the perpetrators fear a loss of status and evolve into a fraudulent scheme to remain a part of the social group they have achieved. It would also apply to most perpetrators who use their victims' money to present themselves as being financially successful. More than likely, all of the perpetrators were trying to find a way to establish themselves in the affluent, upper-economic status of the American populace. One scheme that specifically used the terminology of achieving the American Dream in marketing was that of Seng Tan.

• Seng Tan's scheme was an affinity-fraud that primarily targeted investor-victims of Cambodian descent. Tan's marketing documents stated that her company "urges you to sign up now or you will miss your best chance of fulfilling your American dream" (SEC, 2006, January 24, prg. 19). Her investor-victims were from Cambodia; achieving the American Dream would be a desired goal. Those born in America also want the American Dream, but the same terminology might not be as effective as it would on someone from another country. Tan also told investor-victims that the monthly payments would continue going to their children should they die (SEC, 2006, January 24). Tan received a sentence of 240 months at the age of 59, her husband James Bunchan, also 59, received a sentence of 35 years. Bunchan tried to hire a hitman to kill witnesses in his case. This was the only indication of violence in all of the Ponzi cases (FBI, 2009, August 13, p.r.)

This study attempted to find indicators of "strain" in federal documents. Indicators of strain would be the perpetrators stating their fear of loss of finances or social status in their pre-sentencing letters to the judge. However, these pre-sentencing reports or memoranda documents are not always transcribed and are not consistently available to the public; not enough of these documents were available to carry out a quantitative analysis. The sentencing memorandums, or letters to the judge from defendants, that were available were from Bernard Madoff, Allen Stanford, Tom Petters, Scott Rothstein, Francisco Illarramendi, Marc Dreier, and Samuel Israel. These were analyzed qualitatively for indicators of strain theory in the Messner–Rosenfeld context of a need to be financially successful.

• Francisco Illarramendi was originally from Venezuela. Illarramendi became accustomed to the American culture as a child while his father served as an embassy official from Venezuela and chose to live in the United States. Illarramendi is responsible for a $723 million scheme that lasted for at least five years. Coming from an upper socioeconomic class in Venezuela, as well as holding a master's degree in economics, indicates that Illarramendi would have fit into an upper-middle-class group in America and possibly a wealthier class in Venezuela. Illarramendi's sentencing memorandum to the court describes that he was pressured into a sizable international trade business that was not successful, leaving Illarramendi with a $5 million loss. He felt backing out of this business would have jeopardized his family's reputation and social status. His memorandum also disclosed the paying of bribes in order to carry out business in other countries. Illarramendi would be a classic example of strain theory that also includes not just the American Dream but social pressures within his own Venezuelan culture (USA v. Illarramendi, 2015, January 13, s.m.).

- Marc Dreier had graduated from Yale University and Harvard Law School. He began his law career with a socioeconomic advantage of having attended prestigious Ivy League universities. It is likely that his Ivy League pedigree, with the connections that come with his professional status, enabled him to make the connections he needed to target his victims: hedge funds. In his sentencing memorandum he explained that the mounting debt from the operations of his own law firm, and paying the interest on borrowed funds to maintain operations, became overwhelming. In his sentencing memorandum to the court he did not mention his extensive fine art collection nor his mansions or yacht. Dreier had achieved the American Dream but he borrowed money to keep it afloat and to afford the trappings of success: his artwork collection, mansions, and yacht. In his sentencing memorandum he explained that a failed marriage and mounting debt caused him to make the bad decisions resulting in his fraud. Dreier had achieved beyond the status quo and was trying to maintain it by borrowing money, then paying back the borrowed money with more borrowed money. This would be an example of strain theory using Messner's and Rosenfeld's theory of the American Dream.
- Scott Rothstein came from a "tight-knit family" (USA v. Scott Rothstein, 2010, June 4, s.m.). He went to law school, passed the bar exam, and had a successful law career. There were no indicators of failure, or fear of failure. Rothstein had achieved the American Dream. He gave generously to charities before and during his criminal acts. Rothstein appeared to be clearly of upper-socioeconomic status and was quite accomplished but still felt the need to commit fraud. There is no indicator of fear of loss or of strain theory in the sentencing documents. He had an insatiable desire for more money and the trappings of material wealth as exemplified by his expensive watch collection and his luxury automobiles. His statement did

not indicate feeling pressure to succeed; however, his accumulation of material objects of status may be an indicator of his idea of the American Dream.

- Allen Stanford denied he had perpetrated a Ponzi scheme, then appealed his conviction. Stanford was sentenced to 110 years' in federal prison for his $7 billion scheme. Stanford insisted there were actual investments taking place and that he had created banks in Panama, Ecuador, Venezuela, and Peru. Stanford still felt he ran legitimate businesses and that he had been wrongly convicted. There was no fear of failure or loss simply because in Stanford's view he successfully ran many legitimate businesses (USA v. Robert Allen Stanford, 2012, June 13, s.m.).

- Tom Petters started with nothing; his sentencing memorandum discusses achieving the American ideal of success. Petters impressed upon others that his was a classic case of someone who had humble beginnings and then achieved success through hard work. Petters' sentencing document would demonstrate Messner and Rosenfeld's discussion of strain theory and the desire to fulfill the American Dream. His sentencing memorandum was quite religious in nature and asked for mercy. The document does not mention a fear of failure or loss; it just reiterates the notion of achieving success through hard work (USA v. Petters, 2010, March 8, s.m.).

- In Bernard Madoff's sentencing memorandum, he admitted he knew what he was doing was illegal. Madoff stated:

> As I engaged in my fraud, I knew what I was doing wrong, indeed criminal. When I began the Ponzi scheme, I believed it would end shortly and I would be able to extricate myself and my clients from the scheme. However, this proved difficult, and ultimately impossible, and as the years went by, I realized that my arrest and this day would inevitably come.
> (USA v. Bernard Madoff, 2009, pp. 23 and 24, lines 21-1, s.m.)

Madoff stated that the country was in a recession when he began his scheme in the early 1990s. Madoff stated that "While I never promised a specific rate of return to my clients, I felt compelled to satisfy my clients expectations at any cost" (USA v, Bernard Madoff, 2009, March 12, p. 25, lines 18–20). Madoff came from a middle-class family; he had gone to Hofstra University and Brooklyn Law school (he did not complete the law degree). Madoff's admissions at his sentencing would indicate a fear of disappointing his clients. The fear of disappointing his clients could represent a fear of loss of business and loss of social status indicative of strain theory. Also, his admission of starting the Ponzi scheme out of failure, believing he would be able to stop it early on, then realizing the scheme could not stop, is the classic brokerage-failure scheme. In this case, the scheme went on for at least 18 years.

- Samuel Israel III came from five generations involved in commodities. In his sentencing memorandum he stated that he was afraid to admit his failings to his investors. He wanted to meet his father's approval, and he wanted to uphold his family's professional reputation. Israel had come from a successful family, and did not set out to commit fraud. He had losses, then lied about them, in his words. His case is one of fearing the loss of status socially and professionally. (US v. Israel, 2008, April, 8 s.m.)

Cressey's Fraud Triangle

Donald Cressey hypothesized that for a fraud to occur there had to be: (1) a perceived non-shareable financial need (need, sometimes referred to as pressure); (2) a perceived opportunity; (3) rationalization. In his 1973 edition of *Other people's money; a study of the social psychology of embezzlement*, Cressey theorized that an individual would have had an initial non-shareable problem that caused the financial need, later referred to as "pressure." Second, there is a perceived opportunity afforded by a relationship of trust, such as a bookkeeper or other fiduciary responsibility. In the third stage, the perpetrator of the fraud justifies or rationalizes their actions.

In the case of Ponzi schemes, there are two options. In the intentional Ponzi schemes the perpetrator designs or develops the opportunity in order to perpetrate the fraud. In addition, the perceived non-shareable problem or "pressure" does not apply because in many cases the perpetrators sometimes included several people who all knew that what they were doing was a fraud. In the third stage, that of rationalization, the perpetrators knew what they are doing is illegal; it is likely there are as many justifications or rationalizations as there are perpetrators. Cressey's fraud triangle does not apply to intentional Ponzi schemes.

In the unintentional Ponzi schemes, the opportunity is there in that the business or brokerage is established. It is likely that the individual perceived pressure in that the business or brokerage was failing and the Ponzi scheme evolved out of that perceived pressure. They rationalize that they will earn back the money they believe they are just borrowing, and will pay everyone back. Cressey's fraud triangle applies to unintentional Ponzi schemes.

Ponzi scheme perpetrators are different from other white-collar criminals in that they are entrepreneurs, establishing their own corporations and businesses. Some of the Ponzi perpetrators were fraud and securities violation recidivists. The perpetrators must know something about the business their scheme is based on, to make their Ponzi scheme believable.

Characteristics of Ponzi Perpetrators

The character and nature of Ponzi perpetrators may surprise the reader. We have seen Madoff, Stanford, Rothstein, and Petters in the public eye for the past decade. We get the impression that Ponzi perpetrators are Caucasian males, generally over 50, who are educated or at least appear to be educated. In truth, Ponzi perpetrators are an interesting variety of individuals and groups of people that are intriguing and make it clear we cannot make assumptions about who might commit fraud. Some schemes have been perpetrated by individuals; others were carried out by groups of people.

It's a Family Affair...

In at least 48 cases the scheme was perpetrated by family members, excluding those cases that were solely husband and wife teams. Generally, family and friends are the first victims in Ponzi schemes. In the cases discussed in this section it is family members such as father and son, or multiple family members, involved in carrying out the fraud. There may have been father-son-daughter teams; brothers, their wives and children; cases where the child is the primary who brought a parent in, and vice versa – a parent who is the primary that brought their children in to the scheme.

There were several cases that included brother teams, the most famous of all was Bernie and Peter Madoff. There were two sets of twins perpetrating Ponzi schemes, all males; the third set of brothers discussed below were not twins:

- Thomas and James Mulholland had a real estate business that was doing well until 2009, basically the time period of the financial crisis. This business had investors through "securities" called "Mulholland Notes." When they began to have financial problems, they started a Ponzi scheme that took place from 2009 to 2010. The brothers also held insurance licenses that were revoked because of the Mulholland Notes (SEC, 2012, November 22). This scheme raised about $2 million from 75 victims between 2009 and 2010. The two brothers ended up with Michigan state-level sentences from 10 to 20 years (Michigan v. Thomas and James Mulholland, n.d.).
- Rodney and Roger Wagner also carried out a foreign currency Ponzi scheme in 2010. This was a classic Ponzi scheme in that it was conceived as such, and carried out as such, with little-to-no investing; the

funds were solely used to make Ponzi payments. The brothers were 52 years of age at conviction; each received 48 months. This scheme took $2.1 million from 99 victims in less than one year (CFTC, 2013, February 6, p.r.; DOJ, 2017, March 9, p.r.).

- Kevin and Keelan Harris carried out their foreign currency Ponzi scheme from 2006 until 2008. Kevin is the elder brother; he received an 87-month sentence and Keelan received 120 months. Their scheme victimized more than 400 people who lost $15.6 million. Both brothers had previous non-securities criminal convictions. There was another co-conspirator, Karen Starr, who is a fugitive (CFTC, 2013, May 13, p.r.; DOJ, 2014, December 12, p.r.).

There were 11 cases that had multiple family members such as a father and two or more children, or possibly the parents and a child. There were four cases that had five family members or more:

- Donald Bader and his family ran a $9 million scheme in the late 1980s involving factoring (the purchase of receivables). The scheme involved his wife Minnie, and three other Baders, presumably children of the couple, not specified in the early SEC documents. The group entered into a civil consent order without admitting or denying guilt (SEC, 1990, November 2).
- In the Akbar Bhamani family scheme, five individuals received criminal sentences or probation. Two other non-family individuals were involved, one of whom received a federal sentence. In this real estate-based case, not all properties were purchased as stated, and in those cases that included a purchased property, each deed had been attributed several investor-victims' names and were "leveraged by as much as 300 or 400 percent" (FBI, 2010, August 13, p.r.)
- Gregory Setser carried out a faith-based fraud, with his wife, son, sister, and his brother-in-law. Gregory was a self-proclaimed minister (DOJ, 2007, January 31, p.r.). The scheme targeted evangelic Christian religious organizations, their leaders, and members (SEC, 2003, November 18, l.r.). Their *IPIC* companies were stated to carry out import/export activities selling to such retailers as JC Penney, Pier One, Costco, and other big names in retailers. However, no product was ever sold to these retailers from *IPIC*; it was solely an intentional Ponzi scheme (DOJ, 2006, June 12, p.r.). The Securities and Exchange Commission complaint included two more family members who were in-laws that were not in the criminal indictment. This scheme included three incorporated companies, that were incorporated in Delaware, Nevada, and Florida; the scheme was prosecuted in Texas.
- Joseph Lawler's scheme told investors they were investing in precious metals and real estate. Lawler had his two sons open separate

accounts to receive funds, in different states using their names, not his, although he controlled the accounts. Lawler told investors that one investment entity was a real estate investment trust (REIT). Investors were told that they could put their individual retirement accounts (IRAs) into his investment entity *Pojaris*. (When rolling over an IRA to self-directed accounts, real estate, or promissory notes, there are many risks; investors would do well to check with Investor. gov before moving their IRA.[2]) Joseph Lawler received a 36-month sentence (SEC, 2017, March 6, a.p.).

- In Larry Bates' scheme he involved both his sons and his daughter-in-law. All four received criminal sentences. This scheme was promoted through Christian radio and television, as well as the Jewish Voice. Larry Bates also falsified his education; he awarded himself a doctorate in economics; Bates had not earned a doctorate from a recognized university. Bates also held "conferences" on the impending economic collapse (DOJ, 2017, p.r.). This scheme took place from 2002 to 2013. The Bates told investors they were investing in precious metals. This was an intentional, faith-based scheme. Larry Bates received a federal sentence of 21 years.

Generally, when there are multiple family members involved it is usually the father who is the primary, although in some cases it is the son, such as James Tyson Jr., who is a primary in *PEI* (referred to as the *Enterprise* in FBI press releases) (FBI, 2012, October 12, p.r.). *PEI* had at least four family members and extended family members among the primary perpetrators. Many other perpetrators were related by marriage. This scheme also had at least one primary perpetrator who was a foreign national.

Married Couples

There were 68 schemes that the husband and wife were both perpetrators. In 13 of those cases the wife was the primary or an equal partner to the husband in the fraud.

- Rachelle and Perry Griggs' scheme was carried out while he was in prison; it is discussed below under recidivists. She contacted family members of inmates to carry out the fraud while he was in prison.
- William Apostelos told investors that he was registered as a securities broker, and that he also had a degree in mathematics, both of which were false. He and his wife, Connie, managed several businesses through which they funneled the $70 million they received in their Ponzi scheme. This scheme operated in 37 states, telling investor-victims that the funds would be used toward real estate, securities, and precious metals. Instead of investing the funds as they

said they would, they spent the money on race horses, luxuries, and Ponzi payments. Some of their victims were pension funds. He received a sentence of 180 months, she received 30 months, and a third co-conspirator, who "used his position as an attorney" to aid in committing the fraud, was sentenced to 14 months (DOJ, 2017, June 30, p.r.; DOJ, 2017, August 2, p.r.).

• In the case of Scott Rothstein, his wife Kimberly was convicted of attempting to conceal jewelry and assets of more than one million dollars in worth. Rothstein's wife, Kimberly, was not a participant in the fraud but tried to hide assets after the fact. Kimberly received an 18-month sentence for conspiracy to commit money laundering and the obstruction of justice (USA v. Kimberly Rothstein, 2013, November 11).

Demographics

While the family members as perpetrators are one form of Ponzi conspirators, we now look at the overall demographic picture of Ponzi perpetrators. Social science generally expects some discussion of demographics. The study of race and ethnicity, in general, is not an exact science. The determination of race, for this study, was taken from the Bureau of Prisons' (BOP) inmate locator for those perpetrators that received federal sentences. The racial designation allows for only: White, Black, Asian, and Native American. The inmates self-designate their race. The BOP data is the only public record that allows identification of individual perpetrators. There is no designation for those of Hispanic or Latino heritage in the BOP inmate locator. The US Census reports that Hispanics or Latinos are 18.5 percent of the population, as of 2019. (US Census, 2020). If this study left out Hispanic and Latino offenders, it would be a glaring omission. Therefore, this study used Hispanic surnames as means of determining Hispanic/ Latino heritage. Hispanic tends to refer to Spanish speaking, that includes Spain. Latino tends to refer to Latin America which includes Brazil, that is Portuguese speaking. This is an imperfect solution; there are many adoptions, and international adoptions, an individual may have been adopted from Asia, may have a Hispanic or Anglo last name; this is not knowable. Similarly, someone who is of Hispanic heritage may have been adopted by someone with an Anglo last name. The results herein should be considered a suggestion of ethnic demographics, but not in any way scientific.

That being said, affinity-fraud schemes that are based on race, nationality, or language require that there must be an indication of nationality or ethnicity, in this case Hispanic/Latino origin. There cannot be an affinity-fraud scheme that is based on victims and perpetrators that are Spanish or Portuguese heritage and language without an indication of Hispanic/Latino heritage. The question became, how to determine Hispanic ethnicity or nationality if not included in the BOP publicly available information. The answer was to make an educated guess based on surnames. This method is not ideal, but until the BOP includes a Hispanic/Latino option for self-designation, it is the best option for including Hispanic/Latino heritage.

The United States Sentencing Commission (USSC) reports use the race categories of: White, Black, Hispanic, and others. This data is aggregated; there is no option to search for individual white-collar crimes or individual perpetrators. Reports from the years 2015, 2017, and 2018 are used herein because the data is not reported uniformly from year to year, in the annual USSC reports. The USSC report for 2017 demographic reports that in 230 securities and investment fraud cases:

- 92.2 percent were males.
- 79.9 percent were White.
- 9.6 percent were Hispanic.
- 5.7 percent were Black.
- 4.8 percent were other races.
- The average age was 51.
- The average sentence was 52 months.

By comparison for all federal offenders sentenced in the year 2018:

- 21.2 percent were White.
- 20.6 percent were Black.
- 54.3 percent were Hispanic.
- 3.8 percent were other races.

(USSC, 2018, p. 48)

For fraud/theft/embezzlement it was:

- 42.2 percent White.
- 29.9 percent Black.
- 21.7 percent Hispanic.
- 6.3 percent other races.

(USSC, 2018, p. 48)

In the same category of fraud/theft/embezzlement, women were 31.3 percent and men 68.7 percent (USSC, 2018, p. 49).

The Ponzi scheme data for all known race demographics of perpetrators shows:

- 78.59 percent were White.
- 10.26 percent were African American.
- 6.14 percent were Hispanic surname.
- 4.77 percent were Asian.
- 0.27 percent were Native America (five individuals).

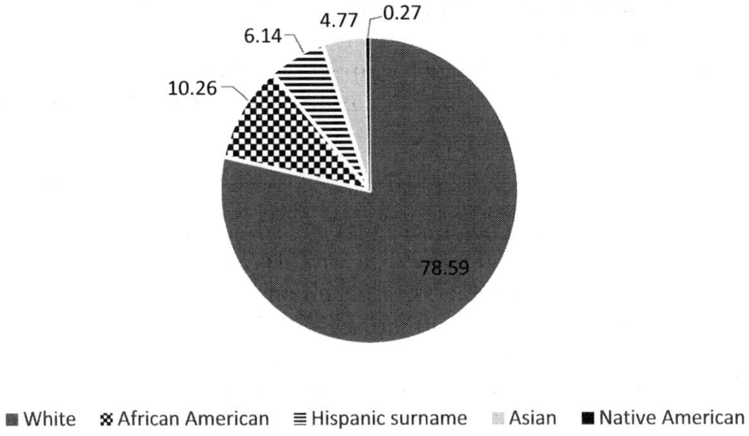
4.77
0.27
6.14
10.26
78.59
White
African American
Hispanic surname
Asian
Native American

Figure 7.1 Known Ponzi Perpetrators Race Percentages.

There were 1,210 perpetrators with no known race (39.9 percent of 3,029). In those cases where race was not known, the perpetrators may have received only civil sanctions through the SEC and CFTC, they may have been sentenced on the state level, or their case has not yet arrived at arrived at criminal sentences. Race is only known for those individuals who received federal sentences and is self-designated within BOP publicly available information (Figure 7.1).[3]

Of 3,029 Ponzi perpetrators, 362, or 12 percent, were women, as compared to 7.8 percent in the USSC demographic report (USSC, 2017). It seems that women are more prevalent in Ponzi schemes than in other types of securities frauds. Of all Ponzi perpetrators, 88 percent, or 2,667, were males. Of the 2,245 males whose age was known, the average age was 50.7 years (Figure 7.2).

Women

One of the first fraud schemes on record, now considered a Ponzi scheme, but then considered a 'swindle," was that of Sarah Howe's Banking fraud, discussed in Chapter 12 on significant schemes and Chapter 4 on banking schemes as a manner and means. Howe was the primary in what is one of the first known Ponzi/swindles on record (1879–1880). Her scheme was not considered serious enough to have the fraud named after her (Howe schemes instead of Ponzi schemes). The female perpetrators are sometimes the primary agent, also referred to as the principal agent or principal,[4] being the leader and designer of the scheme. The female primaries, meaning those cases where a woman was the founder

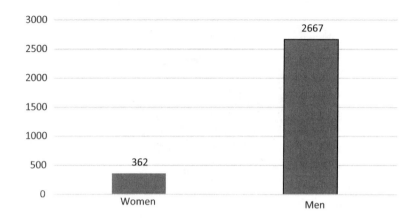

Figure 7.2 Ponzi Perpetrator's Gender.

and designer or equal partner, were 120. Of those cases, those in which a woman was the sole proprietor, there were 53 (just the woman, no employees or partners that were charged). In other cases, the women have been brought into the scheme by husbands, fathers, sons or brothers, and employers. There were 68 wives involved in schemes, five mothers of perpetrators involved, three girlfriends, nine daughters, and ten sisters. Of those women who were just employees in a scheme, there were 193. Women are at greater risk of being involved in a scheme through employment, rather than family; in either case, they made a choice to participate.

There were three women recidivists, including Howe. Howe was a recidivist, as was Laura Bauman and Susan Werth.

• Lauren/Laura Bauman/Baumann is a recidivist who was the primary in two schemes. Baumann's first scheme took place from 1997 to 1998; she was 30 years old at the time. It was based in mortgages making use of promissory notes (SEC, 1998, May 20). With her first scheme she received a federal sentence of 41 months. Her second scheme, from 2007 to 2011, was based on Christian rock groups and concert promotion. She also told investors that the funds were going toward distressed real estate. Baumann was 43 at the time of her second sentencing when she received a federal sentence of 57 months (FBI, 2012, March 6, p.r.).
• Susan Werth had been convicted of a felony theft and elder abuse in a previous 2013 case. She had also been sued for fraud in two cases.

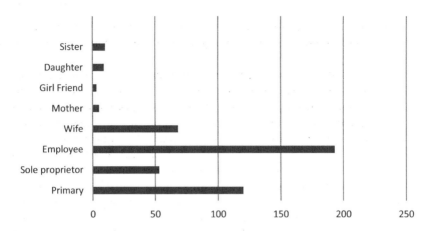

Figure 7.3 Female Ponzi Perpetrators.

Werth had three companies in her second fraud, the Ponzi scheme. She was 57 years old at her second conviction; she received 70 months (SEC, 2018, November 2) (Figure 7.3).

As discussed above, the study of racial demographics is not an exact science. This is particularly relevant when women are the perpetrators because they often take their husband's surname when married; this skews the results when using of the surname as an indicator of Hispanic nationality or ethnicity. With the caution to the reader that this data is not scientific and merely a suggestion of the race (using the BOP terminology and data) of the female perpetrators, the women self-identified as: 161 as White, 41 as African American, 21 Asian, one identified as Native American. Thirteen women were identified as Hispanic or Latina, by using their surname.[5] There were 125 women of no known race, meaning they had not been sentenced federally, may have received probation only, or received only civil sanctions; in these cases, there was no federal indicator of race, and they did not have a Hispanic surname.

Women are 12 percent of all Ponzi perpetrators; 362 out of 3,029 total perpetrators. The average age of those women, whose age is known, is 48.54; 312 out of 362. The youngest was 21 years of age and the eldest was 80 years of age. The eldest of female perpetrators is Carol Wayland, who was 80 years of age at the time of the SEC complaint in 2017.

- Wayland's case was civil only as of January 2019, meaning only SEC charges and sanctions at that point in time. Her 2014–2016 fraud, based on oil wells, was committed with her son, John C. Mueller; Wayland was the primary. They employed several people using boiler room tactics to take $2.4 million from at least 41 known victims. Wayland and Mueller's business was located in California but formed in Wyoming. She held a real estate broker license in California, but neither she nor her 53-year-old son was licensed or registered through FINRA or the SEC to sell securities (SEC, 2017, July 6).
- Karen Bowie, aged 61, received a Texas state sentence of 80 years, while her co-conspirator, Thomas Irby II, who was listed as the primary in SEC documents, received a state sentence of 24 years. Bowie is a Canadian citizen; she was named as a relief defendant in SEC documents but received the much longer sentence in the state of Texas criminal case than her male co-conspirator (TexasSSB, 2013, February 4).

Women Primaries

Women that were the primary agent or equal partner in the development of the schemes, were 120 of all of the women Ponzi perpetrators. This means that they were either the originator of the fraud, or an equal partner in the design and carrying out of the fraud or a sole proprietor. There may be an increase in women as the lead in white-collar crimes as women reach parity in the upper echelons of the white-collar professions. If Cressey's fraud triangle (opportunity, pressure/need, rationalization) (Cressey, 1973) is correct, as women have greater opportunity, they may also feel pressure and rationalize fraud, keeping pace with their male counterparts. In *Trusted criminals*, David Friedrichs also presents the theory that as women reach higher levels of acceptance in corporate America, they will have increasing opportunity to commit fraud and white-collar crime (Friedrichs, 2004, p. 15). Ponzi schemes are entrepreneurial businesses; women must have credibility in order to be perceived as capable of investing for clients (Figure 7.4).

Kathleen Daly hypothesized that "women are less likely than men to work in crime groups" (Daly, 1989, pp. 773, 789). Her study *Gender and varieties of white-collar crime* found that in three out of four white-collar crimes women were more likely to work alone. The three crimes were embezzlement, postal frauds, and credit fraud; the exception she found was false claims, that women were more likely to work with others (Daly, 1989, p. 789). By comparison, in the Ponzi study data, 61 women of 362 were sole proprietors; the remaining 301 were involved in group Ponzi schemes. This study proves the opposite of Daly's hypothesis, that in Ponzi schemes women are more likely to work with others. Daly's study

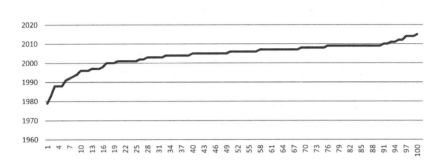

Figure 7.4 Women Primaries Time Trend.

was published in 1989, approximately a decade after the women's equality movement. Prior to 1989 there were very few female Ponzi perpetrators. It is likely that 30 years has made a difference in women being accepted into positions that provide the opportunity to commit white-collar crimes.

In order to carry out a Ponzi scheme, the individual must present an image of success, knowledge, and experience. As women are increasingly recognized in the fields of insurance, mortgage brokering, banking, real estate, law, stock brokers and investment advisers, financial planning, and accountancy, there will be greater opportunities to achieve the status that enables white-collar crime commission. To succeed at a Ponzi scheme, the perpetrator must present the image of success, knowledge, expertise, and must exude confidence. The average age for the women perpetrators is 48.54 years, approximately two years less than the average of all Ponzi perpetrators at 50.43 years.

Of the 120 Ponzi schemes that had women as the primary, 20 were based on securities or commodities; the remaining 100 were other manner and means, such as real estate, mortgages, internet, internet shopping, handbags, antiques and jewelry, annuities, health care products, cleaning/janitorial products, loans and promissory notes, green energy, and interior design. The following schemes are those where the women that had the longest federal sentences:

- Peggy Stines had the longest sentence, 99 years. However, she was released after serving ten years. Stines is discussed more fully in Chapter 12 (SEC, December 26, n.d.).
- Joyce Allen is one of the more known female Ponzi perpetrators. Allen was an insurance agent when originally hired by the originator of the fraud scheme, Charles Candler, to sell annuities in 2002. When the SEC began to investigate the company *Benchmark Capital* in 2012, Candler committed suicide. Allen took over the running of

the company. Allen was found guilty and received a sentence of 360 months, she was 67 at the time of sentencing. In her appeals she insisted she was not aware that *Benchmark* was a Ponzi scheme (USA v. Allen, 2017). This scheme took over $20 million, a comparatively low amount in comparison with her sentence of 30 years. The *Benchmark* scheme included five other employees, four of whom were women. Three women received sentences of 25 months, 21 months, and four months. The remaining female received probation of 24 months. The one male employee, Brian Murphy, received a sentence of 45 months (FBI, 2015, January 12, p.r.).

- Dawn Bennett was 56 years old when sentenced to 240 months. Her scheme began in 2014, made use of what she called "Convertible Notes" (SEC, 2017, November prg. 26). These notes alleged to be financing internet high-end sportswear (DOJ, 2019, July 31, p.r.). Many of her victims were elderly and knew of Bennett through a radio show she hosted where she provided financial advice called "Financial myth busting with Dawn Bennett" (SEC, 2017, December 1, prg. 3). The irony is that Bennett used her victim's funds to "to pay a website operator to arrange for priests in India to perform religious ceremonies to ward off federal investigators; to purchase astrological gems, and for cosmetic medical procedures" (DOJ, 2019, July 31, p.r.).
- Lydia Cladek's scheme was based in subprime auto loans, lasted from 2003 to 2010, and took in approximately $100 million. Cladek, who was 67 at the time of sentencing, received a sentence of 364 months (FBI, 2010, November 23, l.r.).
- Marian Morgan received a sentence of 396 months while her husband John Morgan received a sentence of 120 months. John pleaded guilty and Marian went to trial. Their scheme that took place from 2005 to 2009 was a high-yield prime bank scheme. This scheme took in $28 million. The Morgans were arrested in Sri Lanka. Marian was originally sentenced to 35 years, but the court of appeals reduced it to 33 years. Her age at sentencing was 55 years; she would be 88 when she is released (FBI, 2013, December 18).
- Bich Quyen Nguyen exemplifies the theory that many white-collar criminals do not accept that what they did is illegal, or at least wrong. Nguyen was the chief executive of *Sun Investment Savings and Loan*. Nguyen never showed remorse, she never took any responsibility, she lied throughout her trial. During her trial she blamed someone who was dead for the fraud scheme. Nguyen never invested any of the funds she received. Her scheme took $24 million from at least 200 investor-victims. Nguyen employed a male as chief operating officer. She was 60 years old when she received a sentence of 151 months (DOJ, 2015, February 2, p.r.). Delilah Proctor ran a second arm of the Sun Groups: *Sun Empire* and *Empire Capital Asset Management*

that employed a third female participant. All four worked together to perpetrate the fraud, holding events at the *Desert Palm Hotel and Suites* in California, as well as other hotels in other states. The fraud was also a multilevel-marketing/pyramid scheme (SEC, 2009, April 2, prg. 3).

- Sandra Venetis may have had the longest-running Ponzi scheme for a female primary. Her scheme began in 1997 and collapsed in 2010. Venetis' scheme was quite intentional. She established a business, *Systematic Financial Associates*, that was said to invest in "alternative investments" (DOJ, 2011, April 26, p.r.). These alternative investments were alleged to pay the premiums for doctors to their pension payments. Venetis pleaded guilty and received 168 months; she was 60 at sentencing.

Mortgage-based frauds include those that were said to be registered or unregistered securities in mortgage-backed securities; mortgages, mortgage pools, and real estate-based frauds would include properties distressed properties, apartments. Of all of the women primary cases, 31 out of 102 were based in mortgages or real estate. These schemes are examples of the real estate– or mortgage-based frauds carried out by female primaries:

- Jewel Hinkles also went by the alias Cydney Sanchez. Her scheme took place from 2008 to 2010 during the financial crisis. Her scheme was based on rescuing "financially distressed homeowners," meaning those who are at risk of foreclosure. There were many home owners going into foreclosure between 2008 and 2010. Hinkles' scheme preyed on home owners who were in danger of foreclosure. The complex scheme filed fraudulent documents to forestall foreclosure proceedings, giving the impression that there were investors contributing financially. Her business also employed one woman and two men. Hinkle, whose scheme took in $4.9 million, was 67 at sentencing, received 60 months (DOJ, 2014, September 29, p.r.).
- Barbra Alexander, aged 63, Beth Piña, aged 44, and Michael Swanson, aged 62, were partners in a scheme based on real estate investments from 2006 to 2009. This scheme told investors they were investing in short-term fixed-rate loans for real estate (SEC, 2010, October 7). Alexander received 108 months, Piña received 36 months' probation, and Swanson 37 months.
- Bonnie Lynn Recinos was a classic real estate-based scheme that began at the height of the housing bubble. She told investors their funds would go toward investing in real estate projects. In reality the funds went toward her expenses and Ponzi payments. Recinos' scheme collapsed in 2009. Recinos was 56 when she received a federal sentence

of four years for her scheme that took more than $1.5 million (DOJ, 2017, April 11, p.r.).

- Laurie Schneider ran her Ponzi scheme on Long Island from 2006 until 2009. Schneider had two shell companies; one was said to buy janitorial equipment from China. The second shell company was Eager Beaver Realty that was alleged to buy and sell foreclosed properties. Schneider used the $6.9 million for Ponzi payments, the appearances of success, including a country club membership (FBI, 2014, February 28, p.r.). She was one of the youngest of the female primaries at 39; she pleaded guilty and received a sentence of 36 months.

Age

Generally, in non-white-collar crimes, the perpetrators are thought to age out of crime by the time they are in their 40s. In white-collar crimes the perpetrators generally begin their criminal careers in their 40s or older. For Ponzi perpetrators to be successful they must be able to present themselves as experienced; people under 40 cannot present themselves as having decades of experience. Hence, the propensity to age into the crime of Ponzi schemes.

In this study, the perpetrator age recorded in the data was the age at the time of sentencing or when sanctioned in civil actions. The Department of Justice documents generally include the age, as does the SEC documents. The CFTC does not include the age of the perpetrators; only when there were criminal charges in CFTC cases were the ages known. At least half of all Ponzi perpetrators were charged or sentenced after the age of 50. Some perpetrators are beginning the criminal careers in their 50s and 60s.

The USSC categorizes all types of fraud under economic offenses. However, the category of §2B1.1 includes theft, property destruction, and fraud. In this category the most prevalent age range is 41–50 (23.8 percent), with 51–60 second (18 percent), over 60 was 10.4. The combined percentage is 52.2 percent, of over the age of 41 and 28.4 percent over the age of 51. Fraud must be its own category for a more accurate depiction of white-collar crimes. For all federal crimes, those sentenced who are over 51 years of age are 24.1 percent (USSC, 2018, p. 155).

The USSC reports that:

> Older offenders were substantially less likely than younger offenders to recidivate following release. Over an eight-year follow-up period, 13.4 percent of offenders age over 65 or older at the time of release were rearrested compared to 67.6 percent of offenders younger than age 21 at the time of release. The pattern was consistent across age

groupings, and recidivism measured by rearrest, reconviction, and reincarceration declined as age increased.

(2017, p. 3)

The average age of all perpetrators, whose age is known, is 50.55 years (2,550 out 3,029). The average known age for women perpetrators is 48.54 years. The average known age for men perpetrators is 50.80 years. The youngest perpetrator was age 19; the oldest was age 86 at sentencing. There were ten perpetrators who were 80 years of age or older at sentencing. The oldest to be charged civilly was a male of 90 years (Figure 7.5).

Of those 80 years of age or older, six received sentences, averaging 127 months or approximately 10.5 years. One individual, John Heath, received a state sentence of 28 years and four months. John Heath was 81 years of age at sentencing in 2008. Heath was sentenced in February of 2008, but had died by September of 2008. John Heath had also committed the fraud with his son Daniel, who was 51 years old; in this case it was Daniel that was the primary. Daniel Heath received a 127-year

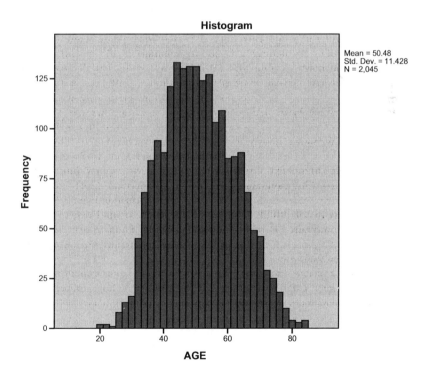

Figure 7.5 Ponzi Perpetrators' Age Histogram.

county-level sentence. Their victims were primarily senior citizens; they were also charged with elder abuse by the Riverside County prosecutor.

- Richard S. Piccoli was 83 when sentenced in 2009. His federal sentence was 240 months. Piccoli is 94 years old at this writing and serving his sentence. He is expected to be released in 2026, when he will be nearly 100 years old. Piccoli's scheme went on for 29 years. He would have been in his 50s when he began the fraud.
- The eldest of all perpetrators was Hugh Sackett, who was 86 at the time of sentencing. Sackett received a one-year sentence. He was not the primary in this scheme based on coal. Sackett was one of ten perpetrators in the *New Century Coal* Ponzi schemes (DOJ, 2016, December 12).

Education

The federal data rarely discusses the education of the perpetrators. The USSC 2018 report shows that those who have committed fraud/theft/embezzlement 21.9 percent were college graduates. The highest ratio of college graduates for federal crimes were those who committed antitrust violations, at 64.2 percent with college degrees (USSC, 2018). What is known about the Ponzi scheme perpetrators is that 176 have at least achieved a juris doctorate, or a CPA which generally requires at least a bachelor's degree in most states. At least one perpetrator was a university business professor and another held a doctorate in economics:

- Charles Cathcart held an actual doctorate in economics, unlike Larry Bates who self-awarded his doctorate in economics. Cathcart's scheme used shell companies in other countries in what was referred to as a "90 percent loan program." Investors were told they were investing in a company as third-party lenders; not at all true, it was pure Ponzi from day one (DOJ, 2009, November 24, p.r.).
- Satyen Chatterjee (aka Chattopadhyay) had taught in the University of Washington Business School at some point in his career. His scheme was based in what he referred to as fixed-rate securities. His was one of the smallest schemes, only taking in $600,000 from about five victims, over a six-year period (DOJ, 2015, May 18, p.r.).

Professions

In order to carry out a white-collar crime, specifically a fraud, the perpetrator must be in a position of trust in order to attract victims. There must be some quality that inspires trust. Some perpetrators were in professions we generally think can be trusted: clergy, CPAs, and attorneys.

Most perpetrators were self-appointed presidents, chief executive officers (CEOs), or chief financial officers (CFOs) in their own companies. In others it was the profession or the professional relationship that attracted the investor-victims.

Religious Leaders/Clergy

For the purpose of this study, the terms "clergy" and "religious leaders" refer to any individual that is the leader of a faith or spiritually based organization, such as, but not exclusive to pastors, ministers, bishops, reverends, priests, rabbis, monks, and imams. One aspect of faith-based fraud and specifically frauds perpetrated by "clergy" is that some of the perpetrators were legitimate clergy who went astray, and others became clergy or self-appointed themselves as clergy in order to carry out the fraud. Some would argue that no individuals of true faith would carry out a fraud and, therefore, all perpetrators claiming to be religious leaders were also fraudulent clergy. This study makes no judgment in that respect, but instead coded for those cases where the perpetrator was referred to as some type of clergy in federal documents. Of all perpetrators, 29, or 1 percent, were clergy; all clergy were men. Of those, three perpetrators were church pastors, ministers, or associate pastors and also registered as investment advisers or brokers. These schemes were faith-based affinity-frauds; the victims were members of the church, temple, or synagogue, or affiliated with a religious group, denomination, or houses of worship.

- The *Sunbelt Development Corporation* scheme took place from 1993 to 1994. Donald Hammond and Wendell Rogers were both ministers of their respective churches. Both failed to provide their investor-victims, church members and their relatives, with full and accurate information about the investments in Sunbelt Development (SEC, 1998, January 13, l.r.). In this scheme the two also took advantage of relatives of church members, friends, as well as members of other churches within the same denomination (SEC, March 7, l.r.). This scheme sold $3.5 million in unregistered securities to at least 200 investor-victims. Only Wendell Rogers received a criminal sentence of 105 months.
- The scheme carried out by Pastor Charles Kennedy Jr. with Stanley Anderson and Edwin Smith between 2005 and 2008 took in approximately $5 million from at least 100 investor-victims. Pastor Kennedy targeted fellow pastors and their parishioners. This was an intentional scheme that never had a basis in any business activities. Anderson, who was 70, received the longest sentence of 51 months; Smith, who was 63, received 30 months, and Kennedy, who was 71, received the shortest sentence of 12 months (FBI, 2014, January 28, p.r.).

• Luis Serna was a pastor whose foreign currency scheme targeted Spanish-speaking people. Serna did make a small amount of investments but the majority of the $4.6 million taken in was used for Ponzi payments and his own personal use (DOJ, 2014, November 11, p.r.)

Attorneys and Accountants Who Were Also Brokers

Ten perpetrators were both attorneys and broker/trader/investment-advisers. Nine perpetrators were both CPAs and broker/trader/investment-advisers. Two perpetrators were CPAs, attorneys, and licensed as broker/trader/investment-advisers. Who would not trust someone with all three credentials? These individuals had to pass bar exams, certified public accounting exams, and FINRA broker-dealer exams, all of which have legal questions and ethics questions. Law school is very costly; both the CPA and bar exams are not easy to pass. It boggles the mind why these individuals would risk such accomplishments and achieved status for fraud; they must have believed they were too clever to get caught.

Attorneys Who Were Also Accountants

It is no small feat to pass the CPA exam or the bar exam; to do so suggests an above-average intellect. To have additionally passed one or more broker or investment adviser exams would not be difficult but is uncommon. What this means is that for each of these exams these gentlemen (all were males) passed, they had to answer legal and ethics questions that would have required them to know that what they were doing was illegal. It seems incomprehensible that anyone would achieve both CPA and pass the bar to risk it all on fraud. When attorneys are convicted of a felony they are usually disbarred.

• Jeffrey L. Goldberg was an attorney, a CPA in Illinois, and was also a certified financial planner who had passed three broker/investment adviser exams, one of which was the series 65, the Uniform Investment Adviser Law Examination. His scheme took place from 1998 to 2002. Goldberg's scheme took in $6.1 million and earned him a sentence of 52 months. He claimed that his company was a holding company that provided funding for other companies. He told his investor-victims they were investing in the common stock that would be offered through the merger of two companies – one was public and the other was private (SEC, 2003, April 7).
• Kenneth Ira Starr had passed the series 63 series exam, the Uniform Securities Agent State Law Examination, in addition to being an attorney and a CPA. Starr's scheme took place from 2005 until 2010. Starr's partner in the scheme was Jonathan S. Bristol, also an

attorney, who had "served as a member of the New Jersey Supreme Court's office of Attorney Ethics" (SEC, May 13, prg. 23); how ironic. Starr received a 90-month sentence for his $9 million scheme. Bristol did not receive a criminal sentence (SEC, 2013, May 13).

Attorneys

Of the 133 perpetrators who were attorneys at the time of the fraud they were involved in, 25 were individual attorneys who were the sole perpetrator in their Ponzi scheme. There were 17 groups that had more than one attorney involved in the scheme. Of those schemes that had two or more attorneys, there was more than one person that should have recognized that what was going on was quite illegal, but they participated any way. There were six women attorneys involved in schemes. The following are a few schemes with attorneys as perpetrators that were more well known:

- Charles H. Evans Jr and Jon Christopher Evans were brothers, and both attorneys in Mississippi. Their mortgage-based scheme was quite complex involving 30 shell companies. In addition to shell companies they worked with several banks and appraisers enabling the scheme to go on for longer. This scheme secured "mortgage proceeds from banks by misrepresenting legal descriptions, title and lien history, and ownership of real estate" that the brothers said they were purchasing (FBI, 2011, December 19, p.r.). This enabled the brothers to receive bank funding beyond what they qualified for. Their victims were almost 50 banks and financial institutions. This scheme took place during the subprime mortgage bubble from 2003 to 2009.
- Peter Madoff is the brother of Bernie Madoff. Peter completed law school unlike his brother Bernie. Peter Madoff was the chief compliance officer at his brother's company *Bernard L. Madoff Investment Securities LLC*. Peter's part in the Ponzi schemes was to create fraudulent compliance reports that were submitted to the SEC. As a compliance officer it was his responsibility not only to make sure the business entity was complying with federal law but also to file the accurate statements and documents with the SEC; he knowingly falsified submissions to the SEC. Peter Madoff is scheduled for release in 2020, when he will be 75. Peter Madoff was disbarred for felony convictions associated with the Ponzi scheme (Meyerowitz, 2013).
- Marc Dreier was an attorney who was the founder of his law firm *Dreier LLP*. His law firm employed more than 270 attorneys (DOJ, 2009, July 13, p.r.). His scheme, which took place from 2002 to 2008, used fraudulent promissory notes that he sold to hedge funds (DOJ, 2009, November 2, p.r.).

- Carlos Uresti was a Texas state senator at the time of his indictment and conviction. The *FourWinds* Ponzi scheme was carried out by Gary L. Cain and Stanley P. Bates. The investment told to investor-victims was in hydraulic fracking. Even though a Texas state senator, Uresti, who was an attorney, acted as the Fourwinds "counsel, escrow agent, and unlicensed securities broker" (SEC, 2018, September 28). Texas is a state that allows legislators to have dual or employment outside of the official office (NCSL, 2018).
- Scott Rothstein takes the prize for most attorneys involved in a Ponzi scheme: seven. In addition to Scott Rothstein, Russell Adler, Stuart Rosenfeldt, David Boden, Douglas Bates, Christina Kitterman, and Steven Lippman were all attorneys at the law firm *Rothstein, Rosenfeldt* and *Adler.* All received federal criminal sentences. There were 22 total convictions in this case; the law firm had many more attorneys who were not charged in the case. There were five women convicted in this scheme.
- Jeanne Rowzee was one of the female attorneys who were convicted of carrying out a Ponzi scheme. Rowzee told her investor-victims that they were investing in "private investment in public equity" what is referred to as PIPE. Legitimate PIPE investing may include start-ups, or fixed or variable prices of stocks that are already public. Generally, these are offered to accredited investors. In this case there were no PIPE entities being invested in; it was all fraud. Rowzee claimed to be an "experienced securities attorney" (FBI, 2010, May 13). Rowzee worked with an accomplice James Halstead. He received a ten-year sentence and Rowzee received a seven-year federal sentences.

Fake Attorneys

- Richard Hicks operated a company, *Elder Advisory Services*, with his wife. Hicks did not just carry out a Ponzi scheme, but he also used the name of an attorney, presenting himself as an attorney and providing legal advice, quite illegal, and not just as identity theft. The State of Texas issued an injunctive order for practicing law without a license. He began investing his *Elder Advisory Services* client's funds in *National Note*, said to be involved in real estate, but was the main entity involved in the Ponzi scheme. Hicks' scheme was a feeder fund to *National Note*, a Ponzi scheme run by Wayne Palmer (SEC, 2012, June 25; SEC, 2013, August 13, a.p.). Hicks only received a cease and desist order; no criminal charges were filed on the federal level. His scheme took $1.8 million from 12 victims.
- Both Brett Amendola and Jerry Mckerac falsely presented themselves as attorneys in order to facilitate their fraud scheme. Their scheme

asked for funds to purchase a golf course. Apparently, they thought feigned status and a more elitist theme for their scheme would bring in wealthier investors. This was a smaller scheme, only taking in $2.8 million from approximately 12 victims. This scheme was short-lived, from 2010 to 2011 (DOJ, 2013, March 15, p.r.).

Former Judge

- Bryant E. Behrmann had been a magistrate judge in Idaho 20 years prior to his Ponzi scheme. He was suspended by the Idaho Supreme Court and disbarred. Behrmann carried out his scheme with Larry E. Hunter. The two men told investors they were investing in "distressed" inventory that would be sold at flea markets. This business did not generate profits and became a Ponzi scheme (FBI, 2009, June 9, p.r.). Both men received sentences of 72 months each.

Former Law Enforcement Officers

- John Robert Graves was a former FBI special agent. He was a registered investment adviser, sold insurance, and carried out financial planning. His wife Sara worked in real estate. The two had legitimate businesses, yet they acquired their investor-victims through those businesses, taking in $1.3 million, some of which was used for the businesses and some was used to pay Ponzi payments. He received a sentence of 137 months and she 36 months (DOJ, 2012, December 11, p.r.).
- John Bravata was a former police officer. His scheme with Richard Trabulsy was presented to investor-victims as real estate investment fund. Instead, the $50 million taken from 440 victims was used for Ponzi payments, jewelry, vacations, and a Ferrari (SEC, 2009, July 26). Bravata's son received a five year sentence and co-conspirator Richard Trabulsy received three years. Bravata received a 20-year sentence (FBI, 2013, September 23).
- Another former police officer was Matthew H. Anselmo. Anselmo had been "officer of the year" when he was an officer at Papillion Police department in Nebraska. His initial victims were family members and business associates. Anselmo's scheme purported to be involved in clothing contracts. Instead he used the funds to pay Ponzi payments, his own debts, and for gambling. He was sentenced to 48 months (FBI, 2010, March 19, p.r.).
- The third former police officer was Raymond Thomas, who had been an officer in the Warrensville Heights Police department in Ohio. Many of his victims were retired police officers and firefighters. He told his investors they were investing in three businesses, one

of which was investing in stocks and options. He specifically targeted those from his former profession, making this a profession-based affinity-fraud scheme. Thomas' sentence was 72 months (FBI, 2010, June 3, p.r.).

- One former Sheriff's deputy, David Hawkins, was carrying out FOREX trading while he was a deputy sheriff in El Paso County, Colorado. His investor-victims were other law enforcement officers and his family, making this a profession-based affinity-fraud. He initially started out carrying out FOREX trades properly, then began to move investor funds to his own accounts. Hawkins was sentenced to 30 months; his scheme took in approximately $1.2 million (FBI, 2014, February 5, p.r.).

The Unhumorous Scheme

There is nothing funny about being involved in a Ponzi scheme. However, this scheme carried out by executives at National Lampoon could be a theme for a movie. Timothy Durham, James Cochran, and Rick Snow were the officers in the *Fair Finance Company/Fair Holdings* that was successful in purchasing discounted consumer receivables before the company was purchased by the three in 2002. Once the three purchased the company they began investing in businesses that failed. Durham was also CEO of National Lampoon Inc. and Snow, who was a CPA, was interim CFO of National Lampoon (SEC, March 16, prgs. 11–13). National Lampoon had nothing to do with the Ponzi scheme, and probably found no humor in sharing their chief executives with a Ponzi scheme. The three actually received comparatively long sentences: Durham received 50 years, Cochran 25 years and Snow received a ten-year sentence (DOJ, 2015, July 26, p.r.).

Other Characteristics

Deaths

Many of the perpetrators are over 50 years of age when committing the fraud, and even older when sentenced. It is not surprising that some die in the process of investigations, trials, and sentencing. However, there were 17 known suicides, and one unsuccessful attempt, at some point in the prosecutorial process. The perpetrators cannot bear the thought of going to prison. Other than the cases of suicides, there were 22 deaths of unstated causes, meaning they may have been suicides or natural causes; specifics were not disclosed. One case was a fugitive who died in a French prison. When an accused Ponzi perpetrator dies, the criminal charges are dropped against that individual. There are usually civil actions that continue against the estate and co-conspirators.

Faked Suicides

Two perpetrators faked their deaths in order to avoid prison. Both had already been sentenced. They were caught and did serve their sentences.

- Samuel Israel III had been sentenced to 20 years. In 2008 he was supposed to surrender to authorities to begin serving his sentence. Instead he wrote the words "suicide is painless" on the hood of his car parked near Bear Mountain in New York State. Israel then left in a recreational vehicle. He managed to put off going to prison for one month (DOJ, 2009, March 16, p.r.).
- Aubrey Lee Price succeeded in hiding out for 18 months, after he avoided turning himself into authorities to begin his 30-year sentence. Initially Price had been a Christian minister-turned-financial adviser. He had given seminars to fellow Christians on investing. Price had sent his family and investors suicide letters and then faked his death on a boat in Florida. He then began supporting himself as a drug dealer (FBI, 2014, December 18, p.r.).

Fugitives, Escapes, and Health

There were 34 fugitives, who were generally foreign nationals. One perpetrator, Morris D. English Jr., is listed in the Bureau of Prisons as escaped. There were four individuals who received time served or house arrest because of severe health issues, including two strokes, multiple sclerosis, or heart conditions. One perpetrator was found to be mentally incompetent. A second perpetrator was found to suffer from post-traumatic stress disorder and his sentence was time served; he had a documented history of mental illness.

Recidivism

Recidivism is the propensity to repeatedly commit crimes that are similar in nature, after having received sanctions, penalties, or incarceration. Recidivism is qualified by rearrests and conviction in the case of criminal actions, and in the case of SEC and CFTC, civilly of securities or commodities violations. There were 20 individuals that were fraud recidivists on the federal level. These perpetrators carried out multiple schemes, sometimes years apart, sometimes concurrently. All had previous securities violations and/or felony convictions. Some perpetrators had several aliases.

- Salvatore Renaldi was a securities fraud recidivist having been previously convicted in a loan scheme, and then pleaded guilty in a pump-and-dump scheme. In his third fraud scheme, a Ponzi scheme,

Renaldi told investors they would be investing in a publishing and marketing entity (SEC, 2015, September 29). This entity, *Sanctum*, was a $1.5 million fraud. He was permanently barred from serving in investment businesses in any capacity (SEC, 2016, January 27).

Some perpetrators had previous felonies:

- One case is Perry Griggs who had a previous federal conviction for wire fraud and money laundering was stated to have been a Ponzi scheme committed in California. While he was serving a term of 96 months for the previous scheme, Griggs and his wife then solicited his fellow prisoners and their families for the new Ponzi scheme (CFTC, 2010, October 28, prg. 26). Many of the prisoners he conned were from Hawaii, where his second scheme was indicted and convicted. Griggs conned the convicts. He and his wife told their investor-victims that he was in prison for tax offenses, not mail fraud from the first fraud scheme (CFTC, 2010, October 28, prg. 32). His second sentence was 87 months; his wife Rachelle was sentenced to 48 months (CFTC, 2010, October 29, p.r.).
- The most perplexing of recidivists is Scott L. or F. Klion (CEN-TEX), aka as James S. Tucker, aka David Tanner (*Seaforth Meridian and Capital Enhancement Club*). Court records cross-reference each name. While three Ponzi schemes under three entities are attributed to Scott Klion, there were no criminal charges for any scheme, only civil charges through the SEC. Klion is also referred to in Chapter 3 in the section on aliases (SEC, 1998, June 3; SEC, 2005, May 4; SEC, 2006, September 14).
- Kurtis Keith Lowe with Robert Blackburn received criminal sentences for a scheme from 2004 to 2014 (DOJ, 2015, October 26, p.r.). The earlier scheme resulted in only civil sanctions from the SEC in 2002; this was a permanent injunction that clearly had no impact because the perpetrators began another scheme within two years of the first scheme. The first scheme primarily targeted the elderly (SEC v. Kurtis Keith Lowe et al., 2002).
- Barry Minkow is probably the most well known of Ponzi scheme recidivists. His first fraud scheme, *ZZZZ Best*, was a carpet cleaning business. After his release from prison in the first scheme he founded a non-profit, *Fraud Discovery Institute*, with the purpose of preventing and detecting fraud. Minkow had also submitted testimony to the US Senate Special Committee on Aging (USA Senate, 109th Congress, 2006). Minkow had become a minister while in prison for his first fraud scheme. He began a ministry upon his release. Minkow wrote three books on his experiences. Minkow then embezzled over $3 million from the church. Minkow had established the *Fraud*

Discovery Institute, a for-profit entity purported to aid in preventing and discovering fraud in businesses. All the while he was manipulating stock prices and evading taxes. He was released from his second prison sentence in 2019 (FBI, 2014, April 28).

- Larry Reynolds has earned the title of career criminal fraudster. Reynolds aided Tom Petters in his Ponzi scheme from 1998 through 2008, by establishing a shell company to launder funds through. Reynolds also helped in providing false documentation of a sham warehouse for invoices and insurance for what was alleged to be Petters' wholesale business. Reynolds began his criminal career as an attorney in his father's law firm in 1968; he had submitted fraudulent insurance claims for vehicle accidents that didn't happen. He served a criminal sentence and was disbarred. In 1984 Reynolds pleaded guilty to a scheme involving phony checks. In addition, at that time, there was an incident in Massachusetts involving Reynolds cooperating in an organized crime investigation. There was a threat on his life and he went into witness protection. While under protection he became involved in insurance scams around property damages during the Rodney King riots in 1994 Los Angeles. Reynolds began working with Petters in 1998. True to form, when Reynolds was arrested in connection with Petters' Ponzi scheme he became a cooperator explaining the details of the fraud to federal investigators for a reduced sentence (USA, 2010, July 30). In 2010, Reynolds received a 130-month sentence at the age of 68 (FB, 2010, September 14, p.r.).

Concluding Thoughts

The most outstanding quality of Ponzi perpetrators is that they can be anyone. They can be family members, couples, and individuals. The age range is 19 to 90 years old. They can be of any race, gender, or sexual orientation. They can be any religion. National heritage, ethnicity, or race can have everything to do with who a perpetrator chooses to victimize or nothing to do with it. We are probably more vulnerable to those who we already have a relationship of trust with than those who are strangers because we are less likely to trust a stranger.

The qualities we do know about Ponzi perpetrators are: they tend to be charismatic, skilled at deception, and good at presenting an image of success. They are glib and sound knowledgeable. They are skilled at making us feel as if we are part of something special by investing with them. We may be made to feel as if we might be left out of something big, and that we are stupid or foolish for not taking advantage of their offer. We may be subjected to snob-appeal, that only those of us who are of a certain status deserve to invest with them. They play on our emotions.

We see that some perpetrators are career criminals. Is someone who commits one fraud for many decades in the same category as a career criminal, considering their entire career was a fraud? Or is it that we only classify repeat offenders as career criminals? Certainly, someone who carried out a Ponzi scheme for 30 years should be considered a career fraudster.

What we do know is that more than half of all Ponzi perpetrators were over the age of 50. As other types of criminals age out of crime, Ponzi perpetrators and other white-collar criminals age into crime. As we move on to the next chapter on the victims, we can see that age is also a factor, in that older people are believed to be the ones with the money, therefore, they are targeted. Ponzi schemes are the crime that oftentimes preys on older people, and that the majority of the perpetrators are also older people.

Notes

1 Except for James Bunchan who tried to hire a hitman to kill a witness.
2 See: https://www.investor.gov/additional-resources/news-alerts/alerts-bulletins/investor-alert-self-directed-iras-risk-fraud
3 One exception was Scott Rothstein who received a 50-year federal sentence but is not listed in the BOP inmate locator. His race was determined through media images.
4 The term "principal" can mean either the initial funds contributed to an investment, or the primary person who initiates the fraud. To avoid confusion this study uses "primary agent," and the term "principal" refers to money, not a person.
5 This only includes the women who received federal sentences who were in the BOP inmate locator.

References

Agnew, R. (2001). Building on the foundation of general strain theory: Specifying the types of strain most likely to lead to crime and delinquency. *Journal of Research in Crime and Delinquency* Vol.38 p. 319. doi: 10.1177/0022427801038004001

Alalehto, T. (2016). Economic crime: Does personality matter? *International Journal of Offender Therapy and Comparative Criminology* Vol.47 pp. 335–355.

American Psychiatric Association. (2015). *Diagnostic and statistical manual of mental disorders* fifth edition. Washington, DC, American Psychiatric Publishing.

Babiak, P. and Hare, R (2006). *Snakes in suits, when psychopaths go to work*. New York, NY, Harper.

Blickle, G., Schlegel, A., Fassbender, P., and Klein, U. (2006). Some personality of business white-collar crime. *Applied Psychology: An International Review* Vol.55 No.2, pp. 220–233.

Collins, J. and Schmidt, F. (1993). Personality, integrity and white collar crime: A construct validity study. *Personnel Psychology* Vol. 46 No.2 pp. 295–311.

Commodities Futures Trading Commission v. Aloha Trading Company, Inc., Perry Jay Griggs and Rachelle Griggs (2010, October 28) Complaint.

Commodities Futures Trading Commission, (2010, October 29). CFTC charges Perry Jay Griggs, Rachelle Griggs and Aloha Trading Company, Inc. with Operating a multi-million dollar Ponzi scheme. Press release.

Commodities Futures Trading Commission, (2013, May 13). Federal court orders Ohioans Kevin and Keelan Harris, Canada-based Karen Starr, and their companies, Complete Developments, LLC and Investment International Inc., to pay over $23 million for fraud in foreign currency Ponzi scheme. Press release.

Commodities Futures Trading Commission, (2013, February 6). Federal court orders Rodney Wagner and Roger Wagner, and their company GID group, Inc., to pay over $2.4 million for foreign fraud in foreign currency (FOREX) Ponzi scheme. Press release.

Cressey, D. (1973). *Other people's money.* Montclair NJ, Paterson Smith Publishing.

Daly, K. (1989). Gender and varieties of White-collar crime. *Criminology* Vol.27 No.4, pp. 769–794.

Department of Justice, (2006, June 12). Federal jury convicts Gregory Earl Setser and his sister. Press release.

Department of Justice, (2007, January 31). Judge sentences family members who defrauded churches, ministries and religious organizations of approximately $62 million. (Setser). Press release.

Department of Justice, (2009, March 16). Former investment advisor Samuel Israel III pleads guilty to failing to surrender to begin a 20-year sentence. Press release.

Department of Justice, (2009, July 13). Marc Dreier sentenced to 20 years in prison for fraud. Press release.

Department of Justice, (2009, November 2). Marc Dreier co-conspirator Kosta Kovachev pleads guilty to fraud charges in Manhattan federal court. Press release.

Department of Justice, (2009, November 24). California court permanently enjoins develop of the "Derivium" "90% Loan" tax scheme. (Cathcart). Press release.

Department of Justice, (2010, May 13). Orange county man sentenced to over 10 years in federal prison for role in $61 million Ponzi scheme. (Halstead and Rowzee). Press release.

Department of Justice, (2011, April 26). Investment advisor pleads guilty to $13.6 million fictitious investment program scam. (Venetis). Press release.

Department of Justice, (2012, December 11). Husband and wife sentenced in Virginia for investment fraud scheme. (John Robert Graves). Press release.

Department of Justice, (2013, March 15). Ashburn man sentenced to 84 months for Ponzi scheme involving purchase of Beacon Hill Golf Course. (Amendola and Mckerac). Press release.

Department of Justice, (2014, September 29). Foreclosure rescue scheme defendants sentenced. (Hinkles). Press release.

Department of Justice, (2014, November 11). San Fernando valet pastor sentenced to over 10 years in prison for running $7 million Ponzi targeted Spanish speaking investors. (Serna). Press release.

Department of Justice, (2014, December 12). Warren man sentenced to 10 years in prison for $15 million Ponzi scheme. (Harris). Press release.

Department of Justice, (2015, June 16). Case updates: USA v. Timothy S. Durham, James F. Cochran, and Rick D. Snow. Press release.

Department of Justice, (2015, February 2). Bay area woman who ran $24 million investment scam sentenced to over 12 years in federal prison. (Nguyen). Press release.

Department of Justice, (2015, October 26). Tarrant County men sentenced for running $2.4 million Ponzi scheme. (Lowe and Blackburn). Press release.

Department of Justice, (2015, May 18). Former faculty member at UW business school pleads guilty to wire fraud in connection with Ponzi scheme. (Chatterjee). Press release.

Department of Justice, (2016, December 12). New Century Coal ends in lengthy prison sentences for ten individuals. (Rose; Sackett). Press release.

Department of Justice, (2017, April 11). Ponzi scheme manager sentenced to over 4 years in prison for scheme that stole over $1.5M from victims in Visalia and elsewhere. (Recinos). Press release.

Department of Justice, (2017, September 7). Bates family sentenced to 627 months imprisonment for gold and silver Ponzi scheme. Press release.

Department of Justice, (2017, March 9). Dallas county twins sentenced in foreign currency trading scheme. (Wagner). Press release.

Federal Bureau of Investigation, (2009, June 9). Directors of company in La Grande plead guilty to federal money laundering charges thousands of North American investors lose millions of dollars. (Behrmann). Press release.

Federal Bureau of Investigation, (2009, August 13). Man sentenced to 25 years for trying to hire someone to kill a witness in a federal case. (Bunchan and Tan). Press release.

Federal Bureau of Investigation, (2010, March 19). Bellevue man sentenced for mail fraud. (Anselmo). Press release.

Federal Bureau of Investigation, (2010, June 3). Former police officer charged with $889,000 Ponzi scheme. (Thomas). Press release.

Federal Bureau of Investigation, (2010, August 13). Eight charged in real estate investment scheme. (Bhamani). Press release.

Federal Bureau of Investigation, (2010, September 14). Larry Reynolds sentenced for his role in Petters' $3.7 billion Ponzi scheme. Press release.

Federal Bureau of Investigation, (2011, December 19). Two Jackson lawyers sentenced for money laundering conspiracy and federal bank fraud. (Evans). Press release.

Federal Bureau of Investigation, (2012, March 6). Promoter of Christian rock concerts sentenced to nearly five years in federal prison in Ponzi scheme that took $1 million from victims. (Baumann). Press release.

Federal Bureau of Investigation, (2012, October 12). Seventeen members of North Carolina racketeering enterprise indicted on investment fraud mortgage fraud and related charges. (Tyson/PEI). Press release.

Federal Bureau of Investigation, (2013, November 12). Two individuals sentenced in plot to conceal and dispose in connection with Rothstein case. Press release.

Federal Bureau of Investigation, (2013, December 18). Sarasota Ponzi schemer Marian Morgan resentenced to more than 33 years in prison. Press release.

Federal Bureau of Investigation, (2014, January 28). Pastor sentenced to federal prison for wire fraud in connection with $5 million Ponzi scheme. (Kennedy). Press release.

Federal Bureau of Investigation, (2014, February 5). Former El Paso county sheriff's deputy to 30 months in federal prison as part of Ponzi scheme. (Hawkins). Press release.

Federal Bureau of Investigation, (2014, February 28). Oceanside woman pleads guilty to defrauding investors of $6.9 million real estate Ponzi scheme. (Schneider). Press release.

Federal Bureau of Investigation, (2014, March 21). Defendant sentenced in plot to conceal and dispose of assets in connection with Rothstein case. Press release.

Federal Bureau of Investigation, (2014, December 18). The fraudster who faked his own death. (Price). Press release.

Federal Bureau of Investigation, (2015, January 12). Brian Murphy sentenced to 45 months in prison for conspiracy to commit mail and wire fraud through Benchmark Capital Ponzi scheme. (Allen). Press release.

Frankel, T. (2012). *The Ponzi schemes puzzle: A history and analysis of con-artists and victims*. New York, NY, Oxford University Press.

Friedrichs, D. (2004). *Trusted Criminals: White-collar crime in contemporary society*. San Francisco, CA, Wadsworth Cengage Publisher.

Garner, B. (ed) (2009). *Black's law dictionary*. New York, NY, Thomas Reuters.

Glenn, A. and Raine, A. (2014). *Psychopathy, an introduction to biological findings and their implications*. New York, NY, New York University Press.

Granero, R., Tarrega, S., Fernandez-Aranda, F., Aymmai, N., Gomez-Pena, M., Moragasw, L., Custal, N., Orekhova, L., Savvidou, L., Menchon, J., and Jimenez-Murcia, S. (2012). Gambling on the stock market: An unexplored issue. *Comprehensive Psychiatry* Vol.53 pp. 666–673.

Hare, R. (1993). *Without conscience, the disturbing work of psychopaths among us*. New York, NY, Guilford.

Kotz, H.D. (2014). *Why Ponzi schemes work and how to protect yourself from being defrauded*. New York, NY, Thomas Reuters.

Lilienfield, S. and Widows, M. (2005). "Psychopathic personality inventory", In Cutler, B.L. (Ed.), *Encyclopedia of psychology and law,* Vol.1, 641–642. Los Angeles, CA, Sage Publications.

Listwan, J. S., Leeper Piquero, N., and Van Voorhis, P. (2010). Recidivism among White-collar crime sample: Does personality matter? *Australia and New Zealand Journal of Criminology* Vol.43 No.1 pp. 156–174.

McMasters, W. H. (c1962). *The story of Ponzi: America's most baffling swindler*. Unpublished manuscript. Fraud and Swindles Collection, Special Collections, Lloyd Sealy Library, John Jay College of Criminal Justice/CUNY, New York, NY.

Merton, R. (1938). Social structure and anomie. *American Sociological Review* Vol.3 pp. 672–682.

Messner, S. and Rosenfeld, R. (2013). *Crime and the American dream*. San Francisco, CA, Wadsworth Cengage.

Meyerowitz, S. (2013, December 19). Madoff brother, convicted and jailed, now is disbarred. *LexisNexis*.

National Council on State Legislators (NCSL), (2018, February 6). Dual Employment: Regulating Public jobs for legislators.

Rabin, M. (2002, August). Inference by believers in the law of small numbers. *Quarterly Journal of Economics* Vol.117 No.3, pp. 775–816.

Ragatz, L., Fremouw, W., and Baker, E. (2012). The psychological profile of white-collar offenders: Demographics, criminal thinking, psychopathic traits, and psychopathology. *Criminal Justice and Behavior* Vol.39 No.7 pp. 978–997.

Robert Allen Stanford, v. United States of America (2015, October 29) United States Court of Appeals for the Fifth Circuit. No. 12–2041.

Robert Allen Stanford v. United States of America (2016, October) Supreme Court no.15–1490.

Shefrin, H. (2002). *Beyond greed and fear: Understanding behavioral finance and the psychology of investing.* New York, NY, Oxford University Press.

State of Michigan v. James C. Mulholland Jr. and Thomas Mulholland (No date) *Mulholland Brothers sentenced up to 20 years in prison for running $18 million real estate Ponzi scheme.*

Securities and Exchange Commission, (1984, December 26). Peggy Stines receives 99-year sentence. News Digest 84–249.

Securities' and Exchange Commission, (1990, November 20). Permanent Injunction against Donald Bader. SEC News Digest issue 90–224.

Securities and Exchange Commission v. Sunbelt Development Corporation, Wendell Rogers, Donald Hammond, and Willis Davis (1998, January 13) Litigation release.

Securities and Exchange Commission v. Scott L. Klion, Cen-Tex Alchemy Guild, and Elizabeth Alaniz (1998, June 3) Litigation release.

Securities and Exchange v. Accelerated Funding Mortgage Corp., Lauren Baumann, Bali Financial Inc. Odyssey Financial Group Inc. (1998, May 20). Litigation release.

Securities and Exchange Commission v. Kurtis Keith Lowe et al. (2000, May 31) Litigation release.

Securities and Exchange v. Jeffrey L. Goldberg (2003, April 7) Complaint.

Securities and Exchange Commission v. IPIC International, Inc., et al. (2003, November 18) SEC halts massive Ponzi scheme that targeted evangelical Christian congregations by filing emergency civil action. (Setser). Litigation release.

Securities and Exchange v. David Tanner, Capital Enhancement Club, Rocky D. Spencer, Marroc Corp. and Richard Kringen (2005, May 4) (Klion/Tucker). Litigation release.

Securities and Exchange Commission v. WMDS Inc., aka World Marketing Direct Selling Inc., One Universe Online Inc., aka UIOL, Seng Tan, Christian Rochon, and James Bunchan (2006, January 24) Complaint.

Securities and Exchange Commission v. Sunbelt Development Corporation, Wendell Rogers, Donald Hammond, and Willis Davis (2006, March 7) Litigation release.

Securities and Exchange Commission v. Seaforth Meridian, Alain Assemi, Timothy Clyman, John Friedrich, Scott Klion a/k/a James S. Tucker and David Tanner (2006, September 14) (Tanner/Klion) Complaint.

Securities and Exchange Commission, (2008, January 24). Defendants convicted of 522 felonies after Commission action against securities fraud scheme targeting senior citizens and elderly victims in Southern California. (Heath). Litigation release.

Securities and Exchange Commission, (2008, September 29). Man sentenced to over 127 years in prison for orchestrating a massive securities fraud scheme that targeted seniors; two others also sentenced. (Heath). News Digest Issue 2008–189.

Securities and Exchange Commission v. Sun Empire LLC, ECAM, LLC aka Empire Capital Asset Management, Delilah A. Proctor and Shauntel A. McCoy (2009, April 2) Complaint.

Securities and Exchange Commission v. John J. Bravata, Richard J. Trabulsy, Antonio M. Bravata, BBC Equities, LLC and Bravata Financial Group, LLC. (2009, July 26) Complaint.

Securities and Exchange Commission v. Titan Wealth Management (2009, August, 25) Complaint.

Securities and Exchange Commission v. Barbra Alexander, Beth Piña, Michael E. Swanson, and APS funding Inc. (2010, October 7) Complaint.

Securities and Exchange Commission v. Kenneth Ira Starr, Starr Investment Advisors LLC, Starr & company, LLC, and Jonathan Star Bristol (2010, December 16) Complaint.

Securities and Exchange Commission v. Timothy S. Durham, James F. Cochran, and Rick D. Snow (2011, March 16) Complaint.

Securities and Exchange Commission v. National Note of Utah and Wayne LaMar Palmer (2012, June 25) Complaint.

Securities and Exchange Commission v. Thomas Mulholland and James Mulholland Jr. (2012, November 22) Complaint.

Securities and Exchange Commission v. Richard D. Hicks (2013, August, 13) Administrative proceeding.

Securities and Exchange v. Sanctum Publishing and marketing Limited, Sanctum Media Group Inc., and Salvatore Renaldi (2015, September 29) Complaint.

Securities and Exchange Commission, (2016, January 27). Salvatore Renaldi. Administrative proceeding.

Securities and Exchange Commission v. Joe Lawler (2017, March 6) Administrative proceeding.

Securities and Exchange Commission v. Carol J. Wayland, John C. Mueller, Kentucky-Tennessee 50 Wells/400NNLPD Block, Limited partnership. HP Operations, LLC, C.A.R. Leasing LLC, Mitchell B. Dow, Barry Liss, and Steve G. Blasko (2017, July 6) Complaint.

Securities and Exchange Commission v. Dawn Bennett, and DJB Holdings LLC. (2017, December 1) Amended Complaint.

Securities and Exchange Commission v. Carlos Uresti and Stanley Bates (2018, September 28) Complaint.

Securities and Exchange Commission v Susan Werth, aka "Susan Worth" Corporate Mystic LLC. Commercial Exchange solutions, Inc. and Exchange solutions Company (2018, October 1) Complaint.

Sutherland, E. (1947). *Principles of Criminology*, Philadelphia, PA J.B. Lippincott.

Texas State Security Board (TSSB), (2013, February 4). Foreign notes scammer sentenced to 80 years in state prison. (Karen Bowie). Press release.

United States of America v. Bernard L. Madoff (2009, March 12) Bernard Madoff's sentencing appearance.

United States of America v. Bernard L. Madoff (2009, June 26) Government's sentencing memorandum.

United States of America v. Francisco Illarramendi (2015, January 13) Francisco Illarramendi's sentencing memorandum.

United States of America v. Joyce E. Allen (2017, November 2) United States Court of Appeals for the Sixth Circuit.

United States of America v. Kimberly Rothstein (2013, November 12) Sentencing.

United States of America v. Larry Reynolds (2010, July 30) Defendant's sentencing memorandum.

United States of America v. Samuel Israel III (2008, April 10) Defendant's sentencing memorandum.

United States of America v. Marc Dreier (2009, July 8) Government's sentencing memorandum.

United States of America v. Marc Dreier (2009, July 8) Marc Dreier's memorandum in aid of sentencing.

United States of America v. Robert Allen Stanford (2012, June 13) R. Allen Stanford's sentencing memorandum; doc 875.

United States of America v. Scott Rothstein (2010, June 4) Scott Rothstein's sentencing memorandum; doc. 272.

United States of America v. Thomas Joseph Petters (2010, March 8) Defendant Petters' sentencing memorandum.

United States Census (2020) Quick Facts. Retrieved from: https://www.census.gov/quickfacts/fact/table/US/RHI725219

United States Attorney's Office, (2014, April 28). Notorious conman-turned-pastor Barry Minkow sentenced to five years in prison for bilking congregation of more than $3million. Press release.

United States Department of Justice, (2013, April 30). Three fraud defendants who met in prison sent back to serve new sentences in $3.6 million Ponzi scheme. (Parilli; Lauer; Andersen). Press release.

United States Senate Special Committee on Aging 109th Congress, (2006, March 29). *Not born yesterday: How seniors can stop investment fraud*. 109–20.

United States Sentencing Commission, (2017). Quick facts; Securities and investment fraud offenses.

United States Sentencing Commission, (2017). The effects of aging on recidivism among federal offenders.

United States Sentencing Commission (2018). Annual report and sourcebook of federal sentencing statistics.

Walters, G. (2010). *The psychological inventory of criminal thinking styles (PICTS)* professional manual. Allentown, PA, Center for Lifestyle Studies.

Walters, G., White, T., and Denney, D. (1991). The lifestyle criminality screening form: Preliminary data. *Criminal Justice Behavior* Vol.18 pp. 406–418.

Chapter 8

The Victims

Ponzi scheme victims start out as investors and become victims. The term "investor-victim" is used throughout because the former investors lost their money to the frauds; they are no longer investors but instead the victims of fraud. This chapter discusses what can be known about the investor-victims from federal documents. It is doubtful that any investor has ever filed a complaint with the SEC, the CFTC, or the Department of Justice because they are making too much in profits; therefore, the broker or investment adviser must be running a scam. As long as the profits are coming in, investor-victims have no reason to contact authorities. It is when they lose money and they are now a victim that they contact the SEC, CFTC or law enforcement.

How is it that we become victims of fraud? Why is it that we convince ourselves that what seems to be too good to be true is indeed true when common sense would tell us that it could not possibly be true? In short, what makes an investor a victim? Are those who lose their wealth in legitimate investments that have gone bad victims? Or are they just unlucky? Risk is inherent in investing; there are no guarantees. We can only imagine the potential investors who spotted something that did not "feel right" or that they knew something was obviously amiss, that prevented them from getting involved in what turned out to be a fraudulent scheme. This chapter will discuss some of the qualities that contributed to turning investors into victims.

Even the most sophisticated among us can be fooled. According to FINRA, "Typical fraud victims are financially knowledgeable (victims scored higher on financial literacy tests than non-victims), are college educated, have above average income and are self-reliant when it comes to making decisions" (FINRA, n.d.). What about the victims who are accredited investors, hedge fund operators, or law enforcement personnel? How is it that the wisest of us can also be duped? Eventually, it is the investor-victims who report the fraud to the authorities. The perpetrators are experts at deceit and in putting together financial reports and other financial documents that look legitimate. In many of the Ponzi cases, it takes a very sophisticated eye to spot fraudulent documents, or experience to know how to check trades. More simply: when we have made the choice to trust someone, we tend to believe what they say is the truth. We need to believe that we have the intelligence to recognize a confidence schemer, even when we may not.

The notion of the emperor's new clothes syndrome is a common concept that illustrates that many of us are unwilling to recognize that something is wrong when it is right in front of our eyes. We may be unwilling to speak up out of fear of seeming uneducated or unsophisticated, or simply out of fear of being left out of something. Many victims are suckered into Ponzi schemes because friends, family, or colleagues are investing; they do not want to be left out.

In Ponzi schemes, the victims are from all socioeconomic levels, but the perpetrators always present themselves as financially successful; no one is going to consider investing with someone who appears to be struggling financially. The façade of success is part of the fraudster's tool kit. The perpetrators are using their victims' funds to present the image of success. It is a misconception that most of the people victimized in Ponzi schemes are wealthy. Even if they started out wealthy, once they have lost their funds to a Ponzi schemes it is unlikely that they are still in the upper socioeconomic levels.

The perpetrators have many ways of contacting and recruiting their investor-victims. One method of contacting potential victims is to host events with free lunch while perpetrators hawk their program. These events are generally held in hotels and oftentimes referred to as "seminars." The FINRA report *Baby Boomers and investment fraud research findings* reports that "Among older investors, identified victims of fraud were three times more likely to attend a free lunch seminar" (FINRA, n.d.). This same report emphasizes that older fraud victims "did not check the registration status of a financial professional (65 percent) or a financial professional's background for any broken laws or violations (78 percent)" (FINRA, n.d.).

In many cases the perpetrators begin with their family, friends, acquaintances, and social networks, such as religious affiliations. In some cases, they have targeted specific ethnic communities through language-based media, newspapers, and radio. Similarly, some faith-based schemes used Christian radio programs. Now, almost all schemes have a website that gives the appearance of a legitimate business entity. It may have falsified logos and emblems of federal agencies to present the image of being properly registered. Some perpetrators had established businesses such as insurance agencies or accounting services that simply targeted their clientele.

When the perpetrators are family, friends, or religious affiliates investor-victims may be afraid of insulting them. We fear being ostracized. We often want to support those in our social community, especially if they have an investment program that appears to be in support of a charity. We want to trust; we want to believe people. It is not just greed alone; we want to be part of something bigger. We want to feel included. Ponzi perpetrators recognize these qualities and use them to manipulate their victims.

In Ponzi schemes, the perpetrators know their victims, in most cases. In other white-collar crimes, it is less likely that the perpetrators know their victims personally. Oftentimes the perpetrator of a white-collar criminal act does not know the victim or victims, nor has ever seen, or will ever see, them. White-collar crimes are generally considered minor or victimless crimes because there is not always a face-to-face encounter between the perpetrator and the victims (Nash et al., 2017). There is little research on the victims of white-collar crimes. Generally, this is because there are usually many victims, and the names are protected in legal documents, making it impossible to find them for interviewing. However, Ponzi perpetrators generally know their victims, and have very skillfully manipulated them into being victims. Oftentimes they have socialized together at weddings and other formal and informal gatherings. In Ponzi schemes, the family members and friends of the perpetrators are frequently the first victims. One exception to the perpetrator having a face-to-face familiarity with victims is when the victim is a pension fund, hedge fund, or an institutional victim that has many sub-victims who had no idea where their money was being invested. Another exception is when the scheme is solely carried out online.

In academic literature, the study of victims of white-collar crimes is even more rare than white-collar crime research. Trahan, Marquart, and Mullings attempted to survey victims of Ponzi schemes in Harris County, Texas[1] (2005). Their study shows that all 434 victims approached agreed to be interviewed anonymously. The authors look at one scheme that took place in the 1990s, Jack Barnes, as a case study, to study characteristics of the victims. In this case, the victims received profits early on, then told their friends about the investment opportunity and, true to Ponzi form, they all wanted in as well. Of the victims in the Texas study "44 percent were males, 25 percent were females and 31 percent were couples"; the median age of victims was 47 (Trahan et al., 2005, p. 607). The authors also applied the theory of Messner's and Rosenfeld's concept of the pursuit of the American Dream (2001), being the prime motivating factor for the victims.

The Victims in This Study

In this study, the information on victims has been solely taken from information of federal documents. Federal documents offer no specific information on victims; their identities are protected. The information is generally limited to the quantity of victims and in some cases only an estimate of the total number of victims. Rarely is information on the demographics of victims offered, except in the cases of affinity-fraud, or when the victims are elderly. Very few documents provide individual information on the victims. Specifics are usually limited to the victim's initials, or: investor A; investor B, in indictments or complaints. Thus, there will be only general discussion of the victims herein, simply because there is no consistency in reporting on victims to allow for reliable and valid quantitative results.

For Ponzi schemes to function there must be multiple victims; the scheme's longevity is dependent on bringing in new victim-investors. In most Ponzi cases, the victims have a face-to-face encounter with the perpetrator(s) at some point. However, when the investor-victim is a pension fund that has invested with a hedge fund that is a Ponzi scheme, or that invests in a Ponzi scheme, there are many faceless victims. One scheme had eight victims, each one was a pension fund, each pension fund had countless individuals who had paid into the pension plan. This is also the case in feeder funds and hedge funds; the individual investors never got the opportunity to carry out due diligence. In short, there are many more individual victims than have been listed in federal documents.

Many investor-victims are suckered in with the promise of exorbitant interest rates. When a Ponzi perpetrator promises their victims outrageous profits, such as 100 percent or 3,000 percent, the victims must know on some level that it is not feasible. With such high interest rates, if the individual pushing their investment was so successful, why would they need anyone else's money? The potential investor-victims in many schemes must have suspected that on some level that something does not pass the "smell test." There should be some sense of incredulity with outlandish interest rates.

In this study, the number of victims was determined through the number stated in the latest federal document. As cases are processed through criminal and administrative courts, the number of investor-victims becomes more defined. Generally, when the SEC or the CFTC brings about an action, there is an estimated number of victims; the documents may say "dozens" or "hundreds" or thousands." Those cases were coded for the minimum mentioned; therefore, "dozens" was coded as 12, because there is no way to know how many "dozens" it referred to. What this means is there are more investor-victims than tallied because of the nonspecific terms used in some documents. In addition, a few cases never made mention of the quantity of victims. Because there must be at least two investors for a Ponzi scheme to occur, where there was no indication of the quantity of victims, two was used as the default amount. The final number of victims in a case is determined be the claims filed with receivers, however, that information is not always provided in the public records. Therefore, as of January 2020, there are a minimum of 2,631,043 victims in aggregate of the federal-level schemes. The per-scheme average number of victims is 1,934. The following are the schemes with the greatest quantity of victims:

- One scheme, *Zeekrewards*, carried out by Paul Burks was reported to have at least 900,000 victims (DOJ, 2016, July 21, p.r.). *Zeekrewards* was an internet-based scheme from 2010 to 2012; that was also a pyramid scheme (SEC, 2012, August 1). This scheme encouraged current victim-investors to recruit others; this is the pyramid aspect of the scheme. It is a Ponzi scheme because the actual returns were the funds from later investors paid to earlier investors. Victim-investors were recruited through events and through electronic media. The pyramid aspect incorporated weekly conferences calls among the leadership and members. This scheme also made use of investment seminars called "Red Carpet Events" (DOJ, 2016, July 21, p.r.).
- The second largest number of victims was Pedro Berbel's *The Fort Marketing Group*. This online investing entity victimized 150,000, during 2014–2016 (SEC, 2017, September 28, prg. 2). This scheme offered three separate business opportunities online, taking in approximately $38 million.
- Robert Shapiro and his 275 *Woodbridge* entities took in more than $1.29 billion from at least 9,000 victims (DOJ, 2019, August 8, p.r.). This scheme began after Bernie Madoff's and Allen Stanford's schemes; both had been in prison for at least two years. It is a bit surprising that so many people were taken in, to such a degree, when both Madoff and Stanford schemes were still in the news media weekly. Shapiro made use of boiler-room, high-pressure sales tactics (DOJ, 2019, August 8, p.r.).
- The *Bernard L. Madoff Investment Securities* (BMIS) was set up as an investment adviser that also managed client's investments. Specifically, they told investors that they would be investing their funds in securities; this was never done, however. The original amount considered taken was stated in federal documents as $65 billion, with at least 8,000 victims. Many of the victims were feeder funds, and institutional investors; therefore, the exact number of individual investors who lost money is not clear. It is not known publicly how many feeder funds there were nor how many investors may have invested in those feeder funds.

The above schemes were known for the sheer quantity of victims; and in Madoff's case the largest amount of funds taken. The following scheme is unique in that the perpetrators were initially victims of a Ponzi scheme, who then turned the tables and began their own Ponzi scheme:

- In the case of the Merkle brothers, Eric and Jay were taken advantage of in a scheme in Michigan. Rather than report their loss to authorities, they began a scheme of their own. They had been in their community for many decades and had the reputation of being up-standing members of the community. It was easy for them to convince fellow church members and friends to invest in their scheme. They learned the skills of running a fraudulent scheme from being taken advantage of, then used those skills to take advantage of others. The brothers then established their own oil- and gas-based Ponzi scheme, establishing several shell companies to perpetrate their fraud. This one case would demonstrate the social-learning theory of crime, in that the brothers learned how to perpetrate a fraud by being victims of a Ponzi scheme (FBI, 2010, January 19).

Generally, in Ponzi schemes, there is a trustee or receiver's website that victims must contact to be considered for reimbursement. The receiver has names of victims, but the names are not a matter of public record. The receiver has the responsibility of finding all of the victims and de-termining how much each individual invested with the perpetrator. The receiver must also determine who are legitimate victims and who are not victims, but who may instead pretend to be victims in the hopes of receiving funds.

Ponzi schemes are based on trust. In order for the fraud to take place the perpetrators must persuade the victims to trust them. As Benson and Simpson have stated, "the gendered nature of white-collar crime victim-ization patterns mirrors the gendered nature of white-collar offending" (2015, p. 220). This is not an accurate depiction of Ponzi scheme victims. Most Ponzi perpetrators do not prey on one specific gender; everyone is vulnerable. There are two exceptions:

- Sarah Howe victimized women.
- Kenneth Crumbley preyed on elderly men; Crumbley was 55 years old. In addition, most of his staff had "extensive criminal back-grounds" (SEC, 2016, January 21, prg. 13).

Trahan et al. state that "fraud affects all persons regardless of race, age, or socioeconomic status" (Mizell, 1997; Trahan et al., 2005). At most, the gender of victims in Ponzi cases is not knowable; in most white-collar crime cases there is little documentation of gender of the victims.

How Do the Perpetrators Find Their Victims?

The previous chapter discussed the perpetrators and how they present themselves as successful in order to attract investors. We would think the first criterion for victimization is having money to take. But it is also accessibility and vulnerability that make potential investors targets. In some cases, the perpetrators target their victims by identifiable qualities such as professions, or physically identifiable qualities such as race. Call lists, (lists of names) can be easily purchased providing demographics, geographic location, such as age, including contact information.

In Ponzi cases, many perpetrators attracted their victims through show-case events or seminars sometimes held at hotels. In other Ponzi cases, the victims were personal acquaintances or family members. Some victims were acquired through websites. Other perpetrators had a professional relationship established such as CPA, insurance agent, or attorney. More often than not, the victims were acquired because someone they trusted, trusted the perpetrator: word of mouth.

Radio and television are another means of communicating with potential investor-victims. In some of the nationality-based affinity-frauds, the promotion of the scheme went out through nationality-language-based media: radio shows and news media that are language specific. Many of the faith-based schemes promoted their victims through Christian radio; in fact, some perpetrators were Christian radio hosts.

Asians in Asia

The following schemes targeted their victims in other countries, although the perpetrators were charged in the United States. They may have used intermediaries or co-conspirators in other countries to make the initial contact, who were also fluent in the language of the nation targeted.

- Brian D. Fox promoted his oil investments to Asian investors, primarily in Asia, through a colleague in Singapore. Targeting investors in Asia would reduce the possibility of the victims carrying out due diligence, or ascertaining the credibility of the investments. Some of the revenues reported to investors were from properties Fox did not own. This is a common occurrence in Ponzi schemes based on oil and gas revenues. The company *Powder River Petroleum International* was organized in Oklahoma but headquartered in Canada. This scheme took place in the mid-2000 decade during the housing bubble (SEC, 2011, April 8).
- Edwin Fujinaga, an American, also targeted Japanese investors in Japan. Fujinaga's scheme took $1.5 billion from more than 10,000 victims who were in Japan (DOJ, 2019, May 23, p.r.). His partners were in Japan marketing the securities in medical receivables from America, to investors in Japan. Medical receivables would not be an easy security or investment to carry out due diligence, especially from another country (SEC, 2014, July 24).

Victimizing the Deaf Community

The following two cases targeted victims based on hearing impairment, and the secondary qualities of nationality (Japanese), and in the second case also faith-based victimization.

- Marvin Cooper targeted both deaf individuals and those who were Japanese. His scheme, based on FOREX, took advantage of 125 deaf people (CFTC, 2010, September 2, p.r.). Cooper himself is deaf. He made use of live investment seminars to recruit his investor-victims (CFTC, 2009, February 18). This is an affinity-fraud scheme based on hearing impairment and Japanese heritage.
- Marc Perlman's scheme was a commodity pool that functioned from 2009 to 2011 taking advantage of least 17, the majority of whom were deaf. Perlman also used scripture and words of faith to convince his victims to invest (CFTC, 2012, November 29, p.r.). Marc Perlman is also deaf; he used social connections within the communities to attract investor-victims (CFTC, 2012, August 28). This was an affinity-fraud scheme based on two affiliations: hearing impairment and religious affiliation.

Hedge Funds

In the following cases, it was the hedge funds that were the victims of the fraud. Note that in the Madoff case, some of his victims were also hedge funds as discussed above. Generally, the individuals that run hedge funds tend to be financially sophisticated, having the skills to check the validity of trades and understand trading strategies. Hedge funds are known for taking on riskier investments with the possibility of higher returns.

- Jason Konior represented to at least three hedge funds that his companies would "provide up to nine times the amount of the investors capital contribution". Konior targeted new hedge funds that were small; they may not have had the experience to recognize the fraudulent claims he was making (USA v. Jason Konior, 2013, February 7). If a hedge fund operator had nine times the amount of a potential investor's contribution, why would he or she need the investor's contribution?
- Marc Dreier's Ponzi scheme is one of the more complex schemes involving hedge funds as victims. Dreier offered "bogus securities of unwitting legitimate issuers to hedge funds" (DOJ, 2009, July 13, Dreier). Dreier was a successful attorney who had his own law firm. His scheme alleged to be in promissory notes in real estate development. This scheme began in at least 2002, when the

subprime-mortgage bubble was beginning. Dreier also told victims that promissory notes were purported to have been issued by a "Canadian pension plan and a Canadian company" (DOJ, 2009, July 13, Dreier). One victim-hedge fund did catch on and demanded their funds be returned; they were successful. Dreier pleaded guilty and was sentenced to 20 years in federal prison.

Unions and Pensions

Unions and pensions as institutional investors hold the financial responsibility of securing and investing member's contributions to ensure they will receive the promised payments upon retirement. In many Ponzi cases, the victims were pension funds, but ultimately it was the individuals who had contributed to the pension funds who were the end victims who lost their retirement funds. The following are examples of pension-victims or union member victims:

- Paul Greenwood and Stephen Walsh ran an entity called WG trading/ Westridge. This entity was registered with the SEC as a broker-dealer and with the CFTC as a commodity pool. The partners solicited funds as early as 1996; the scheme ended in 2009 amid the financial crisis. This was one of the larger schemes, purported to take in as much as $7.6 billion. The victims were institutional investors such as pensions, retirement plans, and universities (USA v. Greenwood and Walsh, 2009, July 24). This scheme inspired an Office of Inspector General investigation because the SEC's Los Angeles Regional office had missed "red flags" that should have been referred to that SEC's Boston Regional Office. Had this been done, it was concluded that the scheme would have been uncovered and ended sooner (SEC OIG, 2010, October 26).
- Stafford Mew, Morreon Rude, Rodney Kim, Jack Gonzales, and Charles Andrews took advantage of *Unity House*, and entity that "provided benefits to current and retired members of an employees union" (SEC, 1995, October 11, l.r.). This was an intentional, prime bank scheme that targeted individual members of a union. Both Gonzales and Kim were attorneys. All defendants received federal criminal sentences.
- Jeffrey and Barclay Grayson primarily targeted union pension funds, but also individual investors. In this complex case, the Grayson business entity, *Capital Consultants LLC*, made a multimillion-dollar loan to a credit corporation that went bankrupt. The Graysons then made Ponzi payments, not disclosing to investors that the initial investment was lost. Barclay Grayson, the son, received a 24-month sentence; his father, Jeffrey, did not receive a criminal sentence (SEC, 2000, September 21, l.r.).

Professions

Some schemes targeted individuals based on their profession. The perpetrators may have been part of that profession in some way, such as an agent, or a former member such as a veteran. In order for a perpetrator to victimize people based on profession, there must be some inside knowledge or connection to establish the element of trust. With athletes, military, and veterans, there is a sense of team-culture that renders the victims vulnerable.

Athletes

Professional athletes make particularly attractive victims to target for frauds because of their high salaries. Professional athletes are vulnerable to a great many fraudsters, not just Ponzi perpetrators. There were eight Ponzi schemes that targeted professional athletes. Professional athletes my not have the time or skills to manage their own finances; it is likely they hire financial advisers or managers. They must trust the professionals they hire. In the more egregious cases they were preyed upon by former athletes, managers, or agents.

- Ash Narayan's investor-victims included professional athletes: "a former Major League Baseball (MLB) player"; "a current National Football League (NFL) player" (SEC, 2016, May 24). Narayan entered into agreements with these professional athletes to be their financial adviser, falsely presenting himself as a CPA.
- Kenneth Cleveland specifically targeted National football League player Cory Redding, right after Redding graduated from college. Cleveland was introduced to Redding through one of his former college professors. Cleveland acted as Redding's accountant and financial adviser throughout his football career. In actuality, Cleveland was using Redding's money to pay other investors, as well as his own personal expenses. In the end Cleveland had used up all of Redding's money (DOJ, 2018, June 8).
- William H. Tank Black and James Franklin Jr. scammed more than 20 professional athletes. Black was a professional sports agent; this is a professional relationship that requires trust and fiduciary integrity. Franklin was an attorney for Black's sports agency. Black encouraged his clients to invest in another Ponzi scheme, *Cash 4 Titles*, run by Charles Homa et al. Black also directed his clients' funds to offshore entities in the Cayman Islands. Eventually, Black received a 60-month sentence and Franklin received a 54-month sentence (SEC, 2002, May 8, l.r.).
- Louis Martin Blazer III operated investment advisory businesses that targeted professional athletes and others who have high incomes.

He was initially a registered investment adviser with appropriate licenses. He asked his investment clients to invest in movies projects; some agreed, some did not. Blazer took funds from those clients who rejected the film project anyway. He then took funds from other clients to repay some clients. His fraud also included forging signatures to transfer funds from client's accounts (SEC, 2016, May 6).

Bus Operators

- Thomas Mitchell targeted bus operators of the Los Angeles MTA. The investor-victims were those who would be retiring soon or who had recently retired. Mitchell encouraged these individuals to take their retirement in one payment as opposed to a monthly annuity and to then invest the funds in a custodial IRA with his business entities: *Mitchell, Porter Ind Williams Inc.,* and *AAA Trust*. Mitchell acquired his investor-victims through word of mouth through those with in the Los Angeles MTA (SEC, 2010, March 3).

Military

- Karola Jamison was the wife of a high-ranking military officer. She used her husband's status to acquire her victims. Jamison marketed her promissory notes to those in the military and their families. Her scheme took place in 1988–1989 (SEC, 1996, April 16, l.r.). She received a sentence of 71 months.
- William E. Burbank targeted military personnel and their families with a scheme based on off-exchange foreign currency trading and the Iraqi dinar (DOJ, 2018, October 2, p.r.). Burbank had an exceptional military career, receiving commendations, and awards for his skills (U.S.D.C. 2020, March 5).

Teachers

- Anderson Scott Hall was a licensed insurance agent whose scheme took place from 1999 until 2011. The victims were predominantly in the states of Florida, North Carolina, and Georgia, who were participants in a retirement program for retired teachers and school administrators. This scheme made use of an offshore shell company incorporated in the Turks and Caicos (FBI, 2013, December 27).

Law Enforcement and Fire Fighters

- Vincent Falci started out his scheme in the early 2000 decade with his first investor-victims as family and friends. Falci had been a chief in the Middletown, New Jersey, fire department. Many of his

200 victims were police and firemen that he knew through being the fire chief. Falci later targeted victims who were wealthier. His scheme took in $10 million, and he was sentenced to 15 years (DOJ, 2019, May 22, p.r.).

- Kenneth McLeod has been discussed at length in Chapter 3. The significance of his victims is that they were primarily federal and state law enforcement officers, in a scheme that went on for at least 20 years. McLeod targeted these individuals through seminar events. The federal government paid Mcleod $15,000 for each presentation (SEC, 2010, June 24). McLeod was also allowed to present seminars at the DEA training academy (DOJ-OIG, 2014, December 3). Eventually a DEA employee recognized that McLeod was giving bad financial advice. McLeod had promised that the investments were in government bonds, yet there were no actual investments.
- Raymond Thomas was a retired police officer. He targeted retired police officers, retired firefighters, and his own family and friends. His connections were made through word of mouth. This scheme took place from 1997 to 2006. The funds were not invested in stocks and options as promised, but instead used to run his other companies: real estate, trucking, cars, and a title business, and, of course, to make Ponzi payments (SEC, 2008, October 22).

Farmers

- Cathy Giesecker and her husband originally had a trucking company that transported grain from farms to grain terminals. Giesecker had a working knowledge of the grain industry through her and her husband's grain transport company; this also provided the connections to acquire her victims: 180 farmers. She began selling grain on behalf of farmers promising the farmers above-market price when she was only getting the spot price for grain. The promised profits were paid through later sales of other grain sellers, not the current sales, hence the Ponzi scheme (FBI, 2009, July 20, p.r.). Giesecker ended up with a 108-month prison sentence.

Factory Workers

- Ricardo Rojas scheme targeted factory workers and evangelic Christian groups in Puerto Rico. His connections were made through word of mouth and through presentations to groups. He told investor-victims he would invest their funds in commodities and securities, but it was all Ponzi payments. Typically, as is common in Ponzi schemes, he promised risk-free, high-yield returns in a short time frame (SEC, 2012, August 21, l.r.).

Elderly

Many federal documents used in this research stated that many or most victims were "elderly" or "seniors" or "retirees." Because these terms are never defined or quantified in federal documents, this indicator of demographics has only been included as a qualitative consideration. Of all Ponzi schemes, 10 percent were documented as indicating that victims were elderly, senior citizens or retirees. This demonstrates the percentage of cases that indicated elderly or retired victims. This is in no way exhaustive, in that few documents clarified the nature of the victims, nor quantified how many victims were elderly, nor what age qualifies as being elderly, retired or a senior citizen. It should be noted that senior citizens are targeted because they tend to have funds to invest due to inheritance, pensions, and, in some cases, a lifetime of savings. It is likely that a greater percentage of victims are over the age of 55, but proving that scientifically is not possible because of lack of specific information in federal documents.

The problem of increasing fraud targeting elders is a result of an increasing elderly population. Those who are elderly will become more vulnerable to fraud schemes, in general, and specifically those frauds based in financial markets and financial services as they age. Many sources have predicted that there will be a dramatic increase in the elder population in the next ten years (Burnes et al., 2017; Connolly et al., 2014; US Census, 2018). The Securities Industry and Financial Markets Association, a securities trade organization, predicts that by the year 2030, at least 18 percent of the US population will be over 65 years of age (SIFMA, 2019).

When people over the age of 55 suffer devastating financial losses, they cannot simply go get a job and recuperate their losses. The job market is not friendly to older people; even if they could get a job it is not likely that they will earn enough to replace a lifetime of savings. Many may not be capable of working. Those elders who lose everything to fraud will be in need of financial assistance from relatives and government. With increasing elder populations and increasing elder frauds, society, government, and families will be responsible for their support.

The Federal Bureau of Investigation (2019) has identified that "fraudsters buy trade 'lead lists' on the internet with senior citizens' names, phone numbers, and other personal information." These lists enable fraudsters to cold-call the elderly, one type of "stranger-based" fraud connections. Those elderly who have dementia are particularly vulnerable to cold-callers. In other situations, the perpetrator targeted the elderly through seminars, show-case events, radio, newspapers, and websites; these are "stranger-frauds" where the perpetrator builds trust of an elder unknown to them. All people, in general, and especially the elderly tend to trust those they are familiar with: relatives, friends, religious affiliations, and financial services and legal professionals, "affiliation-frauds." Our elderly population is vulnerable to family, friends, and strangers.

Congress has recognized that elder fraud and elder abuse have reached a significant level requiring legislation by enacting the Elder Abuse Prevention and Prosecution Act (2017, October 18), with the intent of establishing Elder Justice Coordinators, and working groups in each federal judicial district, for the purpose of addressing elder abuse (34 USC 10101, Title I §101 (b) 2), and "financial schemes or scam[s] that was either targeted directly toward or largely affected elders—" (34 USC 10101, Title I §101 (c)2).

The Securities and Exchange Commission,[2] Commodity Futures Trading Commission,[3] and the Federal Bureau of Investigation and the Department of Justice[4] provide a wealth of information designed to aid the elderly and their families in preventing victimization through financial services and investing fraud. If the perpetrator of the fraud is a family member, a friend, or religious affiliate, the elderly individual is likely to trust them; they would not be so likely to research their credentials or professional experience through SEC-EDGAR, National Futures Association (NFA) or Financial Industry Regulatory Authority (FINRA). Many states have enacted legislation and established programs to protect the elderly and prevent victimization (Morton, 2017). It may be that an elderly person would be concerned with offending or insulting someone who is close to them by carrying out due diligence. That sentiment is exactly what enables the fraud and renders elders' easy prey to fraud perpetrators. Second, some elderly individuals are not technologically savvy and unskilled with using computers for research. There are people who will not use them at all. If elders cannot or will not use a computer, they cannot access the SEC, CFTC, NFA, and FINRA databases.

The Securities and Exchange Commission recognizes the vulnerability of older adults in financial markets. The SEC has made public the most significant research to date, concentrating on elder financial exploitation, but just within the purview of the SEC's jurisdiction: *Elder financial exploitation; Why it is a concern, what regulators are doing about it, and looking ahead* (Deane, 2018). Deane identifies three key factors contributing to an increase in elder fraud: changing demographics: a larger population of older Americans; changes in pension plans, and as people age their cognitive abilities decline, as does their health in general (Deane, 2018). Deane recognizes that we have a dramatic increase in our elderly population as the baby-boomers age, combined with naturally occurring decline in cognitive abilities, and those who develop any of several dementias, as causing a large percentage of the aging population to be vulnerable to financial exploitation. The Elder Justice Roadmap (Connolly et al., 2014) also recognizes that an escalating problem is the "brain health" of our elderly population (Connolly et al., 2014, p. 1). Currently the National Institute of Justice has promoted research in preventing elder fraud and elder abuse.

Conclusion

In the end, the victims of Ponzi schemes can be anyone, just as Ponzi perpetrators can be anyone. The more money one has, the more desirable a target they are for many types of frauds, not just Ponzi schemes. Athletes and the elderly are prized targets. Those we share a social affiliation with can be our victimizers. Sadly, it is the people whom we are closest to that may take advantage of us first. We should not forget that many victims in Ponzi schemes are institutions that invest for the benefit of the organization such as universities and pension funds. When institutions are victims, it means there are many more victims who are the individuals.

Notes

1 These are state- or county-level prosecutions; the state listed is Texas.
2 https://www.sec.gov/investor/seniors/guideforseniors.pdf; https://www.investor.gov/seniors; https://www.investor.gov/additional-resources/specialized-resources/caring-loved-ones/elder-fraud
3 https://www.cftc.gov/ConsumerProtection/FraudAwarenessPrevention/index.htm
4 https://www.justice.gov/archives/stopfraud-archive/securities-commodities-and-investment-fraud-resources-how-protect-yourself; https://www.justice.gov/elderjustice/file/900221/download; https://www.fbi.gov/scams-and-safety/common-fraud-schemes/seniors

References

Benson, M. and Simpson, S. (2015). *Understanding white-collar crime: An opportunity perspective*, 3rd ed. New York, NY, Routledge.

Burnes, D., Henderson, Jr., C., Sheppard, C., Zhao, R., Pillemer, K., and Lachs, M. (2017). Prevalence of financial fraud and scams among older adults in the United States: A systematic review and meta-analysis. *American Journal of Public Health* Vol.107 No.8 e13-e21.

Commodities Futures Trading Commission v. Billion Coupon Inc., a/k/a Billion Coupons Investment a Hawaii corporation and Marvin R. Cooper an individual (2009, February 18) Complaint.

Commodities Futures Trading Commission, (2010, September 2). Honolulu-based Marvin Cooper and his company, Billion Coupons, Inc., ordered to pay more than $6.2 million in sanctions in connection with Ponzi scheme targeting the deaf community. Press release.

Commodities Futures Trading Commission v. IGlobal Strategic Management LLC and Marc Perlman (2012, August 28) Complaint.

Commodities Futures Trading Commission, (2012, November 29). Federal court in New York orders Marc Perlman and iGlobal Strategic Management LLC to pay over $2 million for solicitation fraud and misappropriation involving off-exchange foreign currency and commodity pool Ponzi scheme. Press release.

Connolly, M.T., Brandt, B., and Breckman, R. (2014). *The Elder Justice Roadmap. A stakeholder initiative to respond to an emerging health, justice, financial and social crisis.* United States Department of Justice.

Deane, S. (2018). *Elder financial exploitation; Why it is a concern, what regulators are doing about it, and looking ahead.* White paper. Securities and Exchange Commission Office of Investor Advocate.

Department of Justice, (2009, July 13). Marc Dreier sentenced to 20 years in prison for fraud. Press release.

Department of Justice, (2013, March 15). Ashburn man sentenced to 84 months for Ponzi scheme involving purchase of Beacon Hill golf course. (Amendola). Press release.

Department of Justice Office of Inspector General, (2014, December 3). Report of investigation regarding the DEA's relationship with K. Wayne McLeod.

Department of Justice, (2016, July 21). Former ZeekRewards CEO is convicted of federal charges for operation $900 million internet Ponzi scheme. (Burks). Press release.

Department of Justice, (2018, June 8). Financial Advisor sentenced to seven years in federal prison for defrauding former Colts player. (Cleveland). Press release.

Department of Justice, (2018, October 2). Virginia man arrested and charged in Manhattan federal court with $2 million Iraqi dinar fraud. Press release.

Department of Justice, (2019, May 22). Middletown, New Jersey, investment manager and former fire chief sentenced to 15 years in prison for running Ponzi scheme to steal more than $10 million. (Falci). Press release.

Department of Justice, (2019, May 23). President and CEO of Las Vegas investment company sentenced to 50 years in prison for running a $1.5 billion Ponzi scheme. (Fujinaga). Press release.

Department of Justice, (2019, August 8). Mastermind of $1.3 billion investment fraud (Ponzi) scheme- One of the largest ever—sentenced to twenty-five years in prison on conspiracy and tax evasion charges. (Shapiro). Press release.

The Elder Abuse Prevention and Prosecution Act, Public law 115-70; 115th Congress October 18, 2017.

Federal Bureau of Investigation, (2009, July 20). Owner of T.J. Giesecker Farms and Trucking indicted on federal charges involving multi-million dollar Ponzi scheme. Press release.

Federal Bureau of Investigation, (2010, January 19). A pair of victims become a couple of cons. (Merkles). Press release.

Federal Bureau of Investigation, (2011, October 4). Edward P. May sentenced for orchestrating $350 million Ponzi scheme. Press release.

Federal Bureau of Investigation, (2013, December 27). Jacksonville man pleads guilty to operating a fraudulent investment scheme. (Hall). Press release.

Federal Bureau of Investigation, (2019, March 7). Foiling an Elder Fraud Scam.

Financial Industry Regulatory Authority (FINRA), (n.d.). *Baby Boomers and investment fraud research findings.* Retrieved on May 19, 2020, from: https://www.

saveandinvest.org/sites/saveandinvest/files/Baby-Boomers-and-Investment-Fraud-Research-Findings_0.pdf

Madoff recovery initiative, Retrieved October 10, 2019, from: https://www.madofftrustee.com/

Mizell, L. (1997). *Masters of deception*. New York, NY, John Wiley and Sons.

Morton, H. (2017). *Financial crimes against the elderly*. National Conference of State Legislatures. Retrieved from: http://www.ncsl.org/research/financial-services-and-commerce/financial-crimes-against-the-elderly-2017-legislation.aspx

Nash, R., Bouchard, M., and Malm, A. (2017, January). Social networks as predictors of the harm suffered by victims of a large-scale Ponzi scheme. *Canadian Journal of Criminology and Criminal Justice* Vol.59 No.1 pp. 26–62. doi:10.3138/cjccj.2014.E16

Securities and Exchange Commission v. Stafford, Y.L. Mew, Rodney H.S. Kim, Morreon B. Rude, and Charles E. Andrews (1995, October 11) Litigation release.

Securities and Exchange Commission v. Karola E. Jamison (1996, April 16) Litigation release.

Securities and Exchange Commission v. Capital Consultants, LLC., Jeffrey L. Grayson, and Barclay Grayson (2000, September 21) Litigation release.

Securities and Exchange Commission, (2002, May 8). Former professional sports agent William H. "Tank" Black sentenced to 60 months in prison and ordered to pay $12 million in restitution following parallel criminal prosecution. Litigation release.

Securities and Exchange Commission v. Raymond Thomas and Strictly Stocks Investment Co. Inc. (2008, October 22) Complaint.

Securities and Exchange Commission v. Mitchell, Porter and Williams Inc., The Adivanala AA Investment Trust, AB3 Inc. and Thomas L. Mitchell (2010, March 3) Complaint.

Securities and Exchange Commission v. Estate of Kenneth Wayne Mcleod, F&S Asset Management Group Inc. and Federal Employee Benefits Group Inc. (2010, June 24) Complaint.

Securities and Exchange Commission Office of Inspector General, (2010, October 26). Investigation of the failure of the SEC's Los Angeles Regional Office to uncover fraud in Westridge Capital Management notwithstanding investment adviser examination conducted 2005 and inappropriate conduct on the part of senior Los Angeles Official. OIG-533.

Securities and Exchange Commission v. Brian D. Fox (2011, April 8) Complaint.

Securities and Exchange Commission v. Rex Venture Group, LLC d/b/a ZeekRewards.com, and Paul R. Burks (2012, August 17) Complaint.

Securities and Exchange Commission v. Ricardo Bonillas Rojas and Shadai Yire, Inc. (2012, August 21) Litigation release.

Securities and Exchange Commission v. Edwin Fujinaga, et al. (2014, July 24) Complaint.

Securities and Exchange Commission v. Kenneth W. Crumbley, Jr. and Sedona oil & gas corporation (2016, January 21) Complaint.

Securities and Exchange Commission v. Louis Martin Blazer III (2016, May 6) Complaint.

Securities and Exchange Commission v. Pedro Fort Berbel (2017, September 28) Complaint.

Securities and Exchange Commission v. Ash Narayan, The Ticket Reserve Inc. a/k/a Forward Market Media, Inc. Richard M. Harmon and John A. Kaptrosky (2016, May 24) Complaint.

Securities Industry and Financial Markets Association, (SIFMA) (2019). Senior investment protection. Retrieved from: https://www.sifma.org/explore-issues/senior-investors/

Trahan, A., Marquart, J., and Mullings, J. (2005). Fraud and the American dream: Toward an understanding of fraud victimization. *Deviant Behavior* Vol.26 pp. 601–620.

United States Census Bureau, (2018). Older people projected to outnumber children for the first time in U.S. history. Retrieved from: https://www.census.gov/newsroom/press-releases/2018/cb18-41-population-projections.html

United States Code 34 USC 10101, Title I §101 (c)2) and (b) 2).

United States District Court Southern District of New York, (2020, March 30). Sentencing of William E. Burbank.

United States v. Jason Konior (2013, February 7) Information.

United States v. Paul Greenwood and Stephen Walsh (2009, July 24) Indictment.

Chapter 9

Sentencing and Sanctions

The legal actions may be civil, criminal, or both; most Ponzi perpetrators received both civil sanctions and criminal charges or convictions. In a criminal action, the convicted receives a prison sentence, probation, or home detention. The federal sentencing guidelines became effective in 1987, are advisory, not mandatory. With these guidelines, judges take into consideration the level of the offense and the perpetrator's previous history, and whether or not the perpetrator has pleaded, and cooperated, with authorities.

When the perpetrators only receive civil penalties, the sanctions are generally disgorgement and being banned from brokering, advising, or investing. In a few cases, when a perpetrator does not comply with an ordered civil remedy such as disgorgement, the perpetrator will be jailed for non-compliance, as in the case of Ronald Holt (CFTC, 2004, p.r., 4975-04).

- Ronald Stephen Holt was held in civil contempt for refusing to reveal the location of victims' funds. Holt was sentenced to federal prison until he revealed where three million dollars went, and he "Dismisses Frivolous Lawsuits He Filed" (CFTC, 2004, August 17, p.r.). No other federal criminal charges were filed against Holt.

In a few cases the perpetrators did not live to be sentenced, or committed suicide. If the perpetrators die while under investigation, their life insurance policies are subject to being confiscated in order to pay back investors (SEC v. ISC and Holzhueter, 2015, June 17). The perpetrators are older; more than half of all perpetrators are older than 50 years of age, and 475 were 60 years or older at sentencing. Three perpetrators are documented as having succumbed to cancer shortly after being sentenced, or imprisoned. Two individuals had strokes. There were 22 deaths that documents did not designate a cause, either suicide or natural causes.

The USSC reports that 94.9 percent of all federal cases for 2018 were guilty pleas; 5.1 percent were jury trials (USSC, 2018, Sourcebook, p. 172). In the Ponzi data set over the entire time period, many cases start out as trials, then most perpetrators take a plea before the trial finishes. Others take a plea of guilty early on. Of 3,032 perpetrators, 402 had trials (13.26 percent); all except one were found guilty. Those Ponzi schemes that had civil sanctions only, as of January 2020, were 936, (30.8 percent) of all Ponzi perpetrators. Ponzi schemes have a much higher percentage of jury trials: 13.26 percent, in comparison to the current national percentage of 5.1 percent for all federal criminal cases, more than double. There were 148 perpetrators that received probation only; the average was 37 months. Of those who received probation, 37 were women, (25 percent). Those cases that were only civil actions at that time of the analysis may result in criminal charges later.

The USSC categorizes all types of fraud under economic offenses. However, the category of: §2B1.1 includes theft, property destruction, and fraud. On this category the most prevalent age range is 41–50 (23.8 percent), with 51–60 second (18 percent), over 60 was 10.4 percent. The combined percentages is 52.2 percent over the age of 41 and 28.4 percent over the age of 51. Fraud must be its own category in the USSC statistics for a more accurate depiction of white-collar crimes. For all federal crimes, those sentenced who are over 51 years of age are 24.1 percent (USSC, 2018, p. 155).

Federal Sentencing Guidelines

The Federal Sentencing Guidelines were developed as a result of the Sentencing Reform Act of 1984 (SRA). The Guidelines became effective in 1987. The purpose of this Act is to provide a base for similar sentencing when there are similar circumstances in crimes, in order to eliminate unfairness in sentencing that might be based on race, geographic regions, or socioeconomic factors (DOJ, 2006). In short, the SRA was enacted to ensure consistency and fairness in sentencing of federal crimes, specifically to ensure that in white-collar crimes, perpetrators of color would receive the same sentence that White offenders would receive for equal crimes.

United States v. Booker

The 2005 *United States v. Booker* Supreme Court case impacted federal sentencing practices. This ruling by the Supreme Court established that the SRA can only be an advisory in sentencing practices. According to the DOJ 2006 fact sheet on *US v. Booker*, "Judges overwhelmingly use their authority under *Booker* to impose sentences below the range suggested by the guidelines" (DOJ, 2006, p. 3). Within a year's time since the *Booker* decision, the DOJ found that "more than 8,100 defendants were sentenced to lower terms than the sentencing guidelines" recommended (DOJ, 2006, p. 3). The change in federal sentencing standards is presumed to be the cause of reduced sentence ranges from 2006 hitherto.

In Jillian Hewitt's research on sentencing in white-collar crime cases, she found sentencing differences between the time periods prior to and post-*Booker* federal criminal case sentences (Hewitt, 2016). Her results show that how cooperative defendants are may reflect on the severity of the sentences. Hewitt also suggests that there may be disparities in post-*Booker* sentencing in geographic areas where judges see more white-collar criminal cases, such as the Southern District of New York, compared to other geographic cases where there would be fewer white-collar cases (Hewitt, 2016, p. 1066). Hewitt explains that there are many reasons that may influence the length of sentences: the amount of money taken, the number of defendants in a case, and geographic region. It is Hewitt's opinion that geographic areas with fewer cases may impose higher sentences.

Cases with extreme sentences may have intended to send a deterrent message, as well as to punish the offender. A 2008 Colorado case involving Norman Schmidt of Capital Holdings is an example of extreme sentencing (USA v. Schmidt, 2008, May 1). Schmidt, convicted of taking $40 million in a Ponzi scheme, received a sentence of 310 years.[1] In 2009, Bernard Madoff pleaded guilty to taking $19 billion (at the time the number was thought to be $65 billion), and was sentenced to 150 years in prison. Clearly cooperation and a plea did not earn Madoff a reduced sentence. Madoff's 150-year sentence was the maximum term sentence for each count, consecutively. In both of the Madoff and Schmidt cases the sentences are quite extreme, considering both sentences are longer than a lifetime. Madoff was a high-profile case; Schmidt was not a high-profile case. Norman Schmidt's trial was in 2007; he died in 2013. Madoff is currently 82 years old, with a release date of the year 2137. Extreme sentences may have served as a deterrent to some; however, it did not serve as a deterrent to the perpetrators of 274 Ponzi schemes that began after Madoff was sentenced in 2009.

From the descriptive results from the data, 1,799 of 3,029 perpetrators received sentences. Those sentences range from one month to 3,720 months, or one month to 310 years. The average for all sentences is 97.24 months. The longest sentences were after the *Booker* decision (Table 9.1); the *Booker* decision changed mandatory sentences into advisory sentences, allowing judges to use discretion in sentencing. However, of the 504 sentences prior to the *Booker* decision, the average sentence was 102 months. The average sentence, of the 1,239 sentences after the *Booker* decision, was 94 months. The change after the *Booker* decision is reduced sentences, despite the extreme sentences of Madoff and Schmidt. The average for sentences during and after 2015 is 91 months.

Norman Schmidt's Ponzi scheme took place from 1999 to 2004; however, the trial wasn't until 2007, after the *Booker* decision. Allen Stanford's scheme took place from 1985 to 2009. Madoff's scheme went from 1992 until 2008 (at least); he pleaded guilty in 2009. Andrew Williams'

Table 9.1 Longest Sentences

Name	Length of Sentence in Years	Amount Taken	2006 and Earlier	2007 and Later	State or Federal Sentence
Karen Bowie	80	$3.1 million	–	X	S
Mark Shapiro	85	$930 million	X	–	F
Irving Stitsky	85	$930 million	X	–	F
Peggy Stines	99	$17 million	X	–	F
Edward S. Digges Jr.	99	$15 million	X	–	F
Richard M. Harkless	100	$60 million	X	–	F
R. Allen Stanford	110	$7 billion	–	X	F
Daniel William Heath	127	$187 million	–	X	S
Bernie Madoff	150	$19 billion	–	X	F
Andrew H. Williams Jr.	150	$78 million	–	X	F
Norman Schmidt	310	$40 million	–	X	F

scheme took place from 2005 to 2007, a mortgage-based scheme, but the trial and sentencing were in 2012.

Deferred Prosecution

Deferred prosecution is an outcome of removing the charges after an individual or an entity has been charged. This process generally requires that the individual or entity admit guilt and agree to some additional process such as community service, or paying a penalty. Generally, it is applied to more minor crimes. Deferred prosecution was used with *JP Morgan Chase* for the bank's responsibility in the Bernard Madoff case.

•   *JP Morgan Chase* was required to admit culpability, to enhance their money laundering compliance procedures, and to pay a criminal penalty of $1.7 billion. This is a case of institutional deferred prosecution and an example of a corporation being criminally convicted (2014, January 6).
•   William Kwasnik received a deferred prosecution on the individual level because his was a minor role in the scheme. William, who was 68 at the time, is the father of Michael. Michael is the primary in the scheme and awaits sentencing. As a requirement for pretrial diversion, William had to admit to his part in the scheme, and meet the

six-month supervision requirement. Once completed, he received a deferral and the charges of money laundering, and mail fraud were dismissed (USA v. Kwasnik, 2019, October 24, Pretrial Diversion; USA v. Kwasnik, 2019, November 6, Dismissal).

Pre-trial Diversion

Pretrial diversion is a program that may be offered to select individuals before their trial begins. The offender is required to take responsibility for their actions but are not required to admit guilt (Justice Manual 712-F).

* One perpetrator entered into a pretrial diversion program, meaning the US Attorney agreed to defer prosecution based on Ray Spears completing an 18-month diversion program with the United States Probation Office. Spears completed the 18-month program; therefore, the counts against him were dismissed[2] (USA v. Ray Spears, 2017, December 7).

Nolle Prosequi

When an individual dies or commits suicide prior to the beginning or completion of a trial, the charges are dropped. There were 15 known suicides prior to conviction or sentencing. Other deaths may have been suicides, but specifics could not be found in all cases.

* One of the more known deaths was Frank DiPascali, Bernie Madoff's most significant co-conspirator. DiPascali died of cancer before his sentencing. Prior to sentencing, he helped federal authorities unravel the Ponzi scheme.

In the event of a death, the SEC, CFTC, and investor-victims may sue the estate. Some suits have been filed for life insurance policies.

* One example of this is Loren W. Holzhueter who was an insurance agent. Holzhueter had been under criminal investigation by the IRS, when he died of pulmonary fibrosis. He was also under investigation with the SEC. In this case, Holzhueter had promised his investor-victims that their funds were to go toward bonds, securities, and buying other insurance companies. Instead Holzhueter had used his investor-victims funds to pay for $9.2 million in life insurance policies payable to his wife and son, in addition to Ponzi payments

(SEC, 2015, June 17). Eventually his estate was sued for the insurance policy.

- Another case is where authorities used civil forfeiture after the death of Ashvin Zaveri, and also sought relief from his life insurance policies to return the funds to his investor-victims (FBI, 2012, November 29, p.r.).
- In one case, one primary, Robert Pribilski, died shortly before his sentencing. It is not known if his death was a suicide (U.S. v. John T. Burns, 2016, p. 3). His partner Fancois/Mahmut Durmaz is a fugitive. Both escaped sentencing.

Fugitives

Other circumstances where the charges are dropped is when a perpetrator is a fugitive and cannot be found. There are currently 33 fugitives. There were 12 that were foreign nationals; the remaining 21 were Americans. Some cases are still open because the authorities continue to look for them.

- One former fugitive was Leroy King, a citizen of Antigua. He was recently extradited to the United States to be held accountable for his part in the Allen Stanford Ponzi scheme. King had been a fugitive for ten years. Federal authorities knew where he was; he fought extradition. King was extradited in November of 2019, and pleaded guilty in January of 2020; he awaits sentencing (DOJ, 2020, January 30, p.r.).

Civil Sanctions

In the majority of cases the perpetrators received both civil sanctions and criminal convictions. In some cases the perpetrators received only civil sanctions. Some perpetrators may be criminally indicted later. There were 936 perpetrators that received only civil sanctions through the SEC or CFTC. Of those, 77 were women (8 percent). The following explains what those sanctions are.

Civil Default

Civil default judgment is a judgment that is entered when an entity or individual does not comply with a previous order by a court, such as a penalty, or it may entered against someone or a business that fails to respond to a plaintiff's claim. The following case is a classic with civil actions by the Commodities and Futures Trading commission:

- Kevin P. Whylie and Matthew James Zecchini failed to comply with the CFTC summons and complaint, making them in "default" of the CFTC's previous order. The defendants received a permanent injunction, enjoining them and prohibiting them from trading and commodities transactions. They were also ordered to pay restitution and required to pay a monetary penalty to the CFTC (CFTC, 2018, November 13). As of this writing, this case was just a civil case; no criminal charges had been filed.

Civilly Enjoined

Civilly enjoined refers to being "legally prohibited or restrained by injunction" (Garner, 2009). In the SEC and CFTC cases, perpetrators were enjoined in most, if not all, cases. It generally means that they are prohibited from selling stocks or commodities in any way. In some cases it is permanent, and in others it is temporary.

Disbarment

The SEC and the CFTC may bar someone found to have violated a regulation from serving as a corporate officer, from selling securities or working for a broker; they can also bar accountants and attorneys from appearing before the SEC. This will be indicated in FINRA BrokerCheck and on the SEC's or the CFTC's website or the NFA website. Disbarment may be temporary or permanent. This revokes their privilege of practicing as a broker, dealer, or adviser, or appearing before the commissions in any capacity. The Financial Industry Regulatory Authority (FINRA) also permanently bars individuals, not only from holding licenses and trading, but also from working for some who is licensed or associating with members of FINRA.

Injunction

An injunction is a court order preventing someone from doing something, such as selling securities, selling non-existent securities, making Ponzi payments, and embezzling. Part of the criteria for an injunction is it must be evident that injury, in this case financial injury will occur or continue to occur if an entity is not required to stop what they are doing (Garner, 2009). Cease-and-desist orders serve the same purpose.

Penalties

In most Ponzi schemes the perpetrators may receive financial penalties by the SEC or CFTC, in addition to disgorgement and restitution. After authorities claw back funds, seize and sell off assets, return funds to the victims, and bankruptcy proceedings, it is doubtful there is much money left to pay penalties. The extent to which penalties are actually paid is not public record.

Conclusion

As this book goes to print, COVID-19 dominates the media. Several incarcerated Ponzi perpetrators have asked to be released because of COVID-19. Bernie Madoff was refused early release, as was Glen Galemmo. Nevin Shapiro did receive early release/home confinement. Scott Farah was set to serve his remaining three years in home confinement but the decision was rescinded because of victim complaints.

This closes the chapter on sentencing and sanctions. The important takeaway is that not all cases are criminally prosecuted; some are just processed civilly invoking sanctions and penalties. Other cases are solely criminal with no SEC or CFTC involvement. Most cases are both civil and criminal cases. In Part III, Chapter 11, the history of the regulations and laws and their relationship to fraud are discussed in more detail.

Notes

1 The US Attorney Schmidt press release states 330 years; PACER docket report states 310 years.
2 Spears was still included in the data set because he had to acknowledge his actions as related to the fraud; he was not acquitted.

References

Commodities Futures Trading Commission, (2004, August 17). Mesa Arizona Ponzi scheme operator, Ronald Stephen Holt, held in civil contempt for refusing to reveal location of victims' funds. Press release.

Commodities Futures Trading Commission v. Algointeractive Inc., Kevin P. Whylie, and Matthew James Zecchini (2018, November 13) Order and Default Judgment.

Department of Justice, (2006, March 15). Fact Sheet: The impact of United States v. Booker on Federal sentencing.

Department of Justice, (2020, January 30). Last defendant convicted in Stanford International Bank $7 billion investment fraud scheme. (King). Press release.

Federal Bureau of Investigation, (2012, March 30). Owner and founder of MetroDream Homes sentenced to 150 years in $78 million mortgage fraud scheme. (Williams). Press release.

Federal Bureau of Investigation, (2012, November 29). Approximately $9 million to be returned to victims of oil and gas Ponzi scheme. (Zaveri). Press release.

Garner, B. (ed) (2009). *Black's law dictionary.* New York, NY, Thomson Reuters.

Hewitt, J. (2016). Fifty shades of gray: Sentencing trends in major White-collar crime cases. *Yale Law Journal* Vo. 125 p. 1018.

Securities and Exchange Commission v. The Estate of Loren W. Holzhueter and ISC. Inc. (2015, June 17).

United States of America v. Booker, 543 U.S. 220 (2005).

United States of America v. Norman Schmidt et al. (2008, May 1).

United States of America v. John T. Burns No. 15-2824 (N.D. of Ill. 2016) Seventh Circuit Court of Appeals (Pribilski).

United States of America v. Ray Spears (2017, December 7) Motion to Dismiss against defendant Ray Spears.

United States of America v. William Kwasnik (2019, October 24) Pretrial Diversion.

United States of America v. William Kwasnik (2019, November 6) Dismissal.

United States Attorney's Office, (2008, April 29). Norman Schmidt sentenced to 330 years in federal prison for multi-million dollar "high-yield" investment fraud. Press release.

United States Sentencing Commission, (2010). Demographic differences in federal sentencing practices: An update of the Booker Report's multivariate regression analysis.

United States Sentencing Commission, (2014, November). *Guidelines Manual*, §3E1.1

United States Sentencing Commission, (2015). *Annual Reports and Source books.* Table 6.

United States Sentencing Commission, (2015, August). Federal *Sentencing: The Basics.*

United States Sentencing Commission, (2018). Annual report and sourcebook of federal sentencing statistics.

United States Sentencing Commission, (2018). Sourcebook Organizational datafile, CORPFY18.

Part III

Laws, Economics, and History

Part III discusses the bigger picture: the economics, laws, history, and insights learned from the Ponzi scheme research. Minsky's theory of financial instability explains the relationship between legislation and Ponzi schemes (Minsky, 1982). Chapter 10 explains the economic trends of Ponzi schemes by the manner and means. This demonstrates trends over time. Minsky's theory sees boom economies, then financial crisis, then government intervention. Chapter 11 discusses the laws and regulations and the investigative process. In addition, it explains the criminal laws and civil regulations that Ponzi perpetrators violate. Chapter 12 goes over significant Ponzi schemes in history, reflecting on the economic trends or technical trends that have influenced the Ponzi schemes, as well as unique Ponzi schemes. The concluding chapter offers suggestions in recognizing when something might be a red flag and explains how to use the many resources offered by government agencies to prevent one from being taken in a fraud scheme.

Chapter 10

Economic Theory and Financial Trends

History has shown a pattern of economic booms and bust periods throughout the history of the country. With financial trends come failure, frauds, and a need to regulate in order to stabilize the American economy. This chapter discusses those economic trends and the pattern of regulation and deregulation as theorized by Hyman Minsky, as they relate to Ponzi schemes.

Hyman Minsky and His Theory of Financial Instability

The primary economic theory that most appropriately applies to financial events and to Ponzi schemes in the context of this book is Hyman Minsky's theory of "financial instability" (Minsky, 1982, p 15). Minsky's theory of "financial instability" explains that first, there is some "acceleration in the economy." Second there is "financial crisis." Third, there is "a sharp thrust towards lower income." Fourth, there is "intervention by the government." These steps all occurred with the housing market boom and the financial crisis as well as the Great Depression. This chapter will discuss the economic events and how the government addressed the problems caused by economic down turns and frauds.

It can be suggested or believed that the financial crisis caused Ponzi schemes to develop out of businesses and brokerages failing, but it cannot be quantitively proven because there will always be an unknown cause on the individual-level Ponzi cases, such as divorce or a failed business partnership, or possibly environmental factors. Other unknown causal factors cannot be ruled out; therefore, quantitative causality cannot be determined. Descriptively, we can say that Ponzi scheme beginnings peaked for an all-time high in 2007, while Ponzi scheme endings peaked in 2009 as depicted in Figure 10.1 (see page 215).

Regardless of bull or bear financial markets, there will always be the businesses that cannot make money following laws and regulations that were designed to prevent fraud and to keep the economy stable. They will try to find ways to circumvent the laws; they will find "loopholes." Regulators and law enforcement can only enforce the laws and regulations that are in place. When the economy is doing poorly, there will be those who lobby for deregulation, believing that less regulation increases profitability.

Legislators may feel the fury of their constituents, and then will pare down the regulations. The corporations and businesses will increase their profitability, and eventually there will be losses again; it is Minsky's theory of financial instability played out over and over. The part of the equation that has not been proven, but will be pursued in continuing research with the Ponzi scheme data sets, is the relationship to boom-economies/bull markets, bust-economies/bear markets, and white-collar crimes.

Libertarian Economic Policies

The administrations of Presidents Bill Clinton and George W. Bush implemented economic policies that contributed to the economic boom of the 2000 decade prior to the financial crisis, illustrating Minsky's theory of acceleration in the economy. Some policies were already in place to increase home ownership for the population that had not been able to afford home loans (Fannie Mae and Freddie Mac). Alan Greenspan had promoted libertarian economic policies under Ronald Reagan, George H.W. Bush, Bill Clinton, and George W. Bush. All four administrations kept Greenspan on as Chair of the Federal Reserve. Greenspan was the policy maker who influenced the laissez-faire trend toward deregulation that fueled the financial boom, which then resulted in the collapse of 2007. Under President Clinton's administration Congress had repealed the Glass-Steagall Act of 1933, enacting the Financial Services Modernization Act/Gramm-Leach-Bliley Act of 1999. The Glass-Steagall Act had separated commercial banks from investment banks, in an effort to prevent the type of financial failure that happened during the Great Depression. Glass-Steagall was the legislative government action that Minsky referred to. The Financial Services Modernization Act of 1999 allowed commercial banks and investment banks to merge.

This change in legislation allowed commercial banks and investment banks to pool mortgages to what became known as "bundling." Mortgage originators began to securitize their mortgages. Securitization turns a group or bundle of mortgages into a security of which investors purchase shares. The availability of housing loans with minimal proof of ability to pay the loans caused a boom in the housing market; these were called subprime mortgages. Everyone seemed to think the prices of houses would continue to go up. The Report on the Financial Crisis indicates that "excess liquidity" was the first step in the financial crisis. This was characterized by a "credit bubble" brought on by global investors and low interest rates (FCIC, p. xxv). Mervyn Lewis, a very perceptive academic from the University of South Australia, explains that "investment fraud flourishes in market bubbles" (Lewis, 2011). The primary conclusion in the FCIC is that this was brought on by deregulation in the Clinton and Bush administrations that allowed for the subprime mortgages (FCIC, 2011). The dissenting argument in the FCIC felt that the cause of the financial boom was a global credit bubble, whereby there were excess funds available for borrowing. This allowed for cheaper loans and riskier loans. In the dissent, it is indicated that high oil prices globally produced more money availability for lending to home buyers (FCIC, 2011).

The second stage of Minsky's theory is a "financial crisis" that did indeed happen in the time frame of 2007 until 2010 (FCIC, 2011; Minsky, 1982, p. 15). It became clear that a great many of the home buyers who bought during the housing boom could not pay their mortgage payments. Many of these purchases were fraudulent in and of themselves. There was a practice of buying the homes and then flipping them: the act of buying and then selling a house immediately for profit. One of the conditions for purchasing under the more relaxed regulations was that the buyers had to live in the homes to receive the specialized subprime loans. There was little authority checking on these home purchases to determine that the people who bought the homes were actually living in them. Some purchases were made by straw-buyers, individuals making a purchase for someone else. The loans on these homes were then securitized, meaning they were bundled together and then sold together, good loans and bad, which proved disastrous for the economy.

The third phase of Minsky's theory is a "sharp thrust toward lower income" (Minsky, 1982, p. 15). As the economy fell in 2007, a great many people began to lose their jobs and were not able to make mortgage payments. The banking entities responsible for those loans had set them up as securitized investments that then declined as the borrowers began to default on their loans. This triggered a domino effect in the stock market (herein: the market). As the market spiraled downward many investors began to pull their money out of investments, causing many Ponzi schemes to become evident. However, this is the difference: this is the time when some legitimate businesses became Ponzi schemes out of desperation, the brokerage-failures, and business-failures.

This financial decline peaked in September 2008 when Lehman Brothers went into bankruptcy and Merrill Lynch was taken over. Ben Bernanke, Chair of the Federal Reserve, considered the time period of September and October 2008 the "worst financial crisis in global history, including the Great Depression" (FCIC, p. 354). This led to the next step in Minsky's theory: government intervention.

The fourth phase of Minsky's theory is intervention by the government (Minsky, 1982, p. 15). The government intervention was the Dodd-Frank Act, the bail-outs, and Troubles Asset Adviser Program (TARP). Several authors present arguments in favor of much stronger regulation (Dheshi, 2010; Henriques, 2011). Ideas on what the regulatory legislation should be vary. In September 2008, the government-sponsored enterprises of Fannie Mae and Freddie Mac were put into conservatorship, meaning what were pseudo-government entities were now put under guardianship of the federal government to prevent further decline. At that time, American International Group, known as AIG, was bailed out to the tune of $182 billion by the Federal Reserve and the Department of the Treasury. Several of the biggest investment banks were bailed out by the federal government, regardless of whether or not they wanted to be bailed out. Later, in 2010, the Dodd-Frank Act was enacted in the hopes of providing legislation that would prevent such an extreme financial catastrophe from happening again. Within the Dodd-Frank Act, it required an amendment to the Truth in Lending Act that applies to lending practices, stating:

Subtitle B: Minimum Standards for Mortgages

Section 1411 Ability to Repay

129C. (A) Ability to Repay (1) In General. - In accordance to regulations prescribed by the Board, no creditor may make a residential mortgage loan unless the creditor makes a reasonable and good faith determination based on verified and documented information that, at the time the loan is consummated, the consumer has the reasonable ability to repay the loan according to its terms, and all applicable taxes, and insurance (including mortgage guarantee insurance) and assessments.

This amendment goes on to require income verification, and Internal Revenue Service tax returns as proof of adequate income, and specifies under what conditions the buyer must dwell within the purchased home. This is to prevent flipping properties. The goal of this amendment is to require lenders to perform due diligence on potential borrowers. In theory, this will prevent the lending practices that set the financial crisis in motion. Subtitle D Section 945 requires due diligence and disclosure in asset-backed securitization, meaning those buying securitized loans have to perform due diligence to determine the soundness of loans that are bundled. Mortgage buyers are required to know if they are buying bad loans with good loans.

Dodd-Frank itself is the fulfillment of the fourth step in Minsky's theory of financial instability. These measures mentioned here are designed to address what has been determined by the FCIC as the cause of the financial crisis: the subprime mortgage failure. Subtitle B Increasing Regulatory Enforcement and Remedies Section 922 allows for incentives for whistleblowers. Whistleblowers who provide information on fraud in a case, that is over one million dollars, can receive 10–30 percent for tips that result in bringing fraudulent acts to legal action. The financial incentives for whistleblowers provide financial motivation for potential whistleblowers such as Harry Markopolos[1] (Markopolos and Fisher, 2010), who have everything to lose by bringing fraud to the awareness of authorities.

Our legislators recognized the need for legislation to protect the citizenry and the economy with Glass-Steagall. It was a mistake to repeal Glass-Steagall. Our legislators enacted both Sarbanes-Oxley and Dodd Frank in an effort to protect the economy of our nation. When we do not recognize our mistakes, learn from them, and of course remember them, we are likely to repeat our mistakes (Santayana, 1905).

Financial Trends

We can compare the Ponzi scheme time trends and the economic events trends with the charts 10.1 and 10.2. Figure 10.1, below, demonstrates the timeline of when Ponzi schemes began in black and when they ended in grey. The chart depicts the number of schemes that began and ended in each year. It shows that the most Ponzi schemes began in 2007, while the most Ponzi schemes ended in 2009. As the financial crisis began, Ponzi schemes began to collapse.

It is clear that during the financial boom peaking between 2004 and 2007 (as indicated by the Federal Financial Stress index, Figure 10.2) that at this same time period the greatest number of Ponzi schemes were beginning. As the financial crisis peaked in 2009, so did the quantity of Ponzi schemes that ended. It is not a surprise that the two peaked during this time. What it does mean is that when there was a financial boom there was excess money; people looked for places to invest their excess funds. They invested in what they thought were legitimate investments only to find they lost their investments, not so much to the financial crash but to fraud. Then when the economy collapsed, investors ceased to invest and withdrew their funds from investments. As Ponzi perpetrators were called upon to return principal investments to their investor-victims, and they were unable to recruit new investor-victims, the schemes then collapsed.

The Federal Reserve financial events stress chart uses the black line as a base line at zero. When the indicator line goes above zero it indicates financial stress and is indicative of an economic decline. The higher

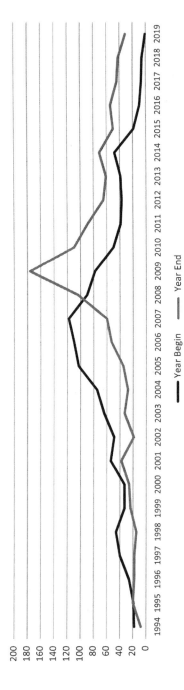

Figure 10.1 Ponzi Schemes Year Begin and End.

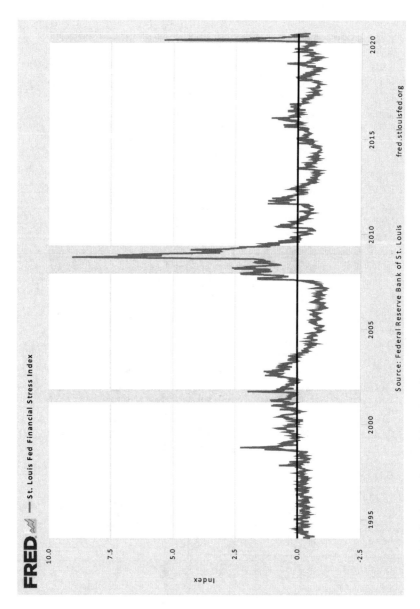

Figure 10.2 St. Louis Federal Reserve Financial Stress Index.

the blue line, the greater the financial decline, or recession. When the indicator line goes below zero it indicates the economy is doing well.

Manner and Means

Figure 10.3 illustrates the quantities of each type of manner and means. The Y axis indicates the number of schemes based on the type of manner and means. We can see that securities (SEC) schemes were the greatest number of schemes. The schemes that were "other" (Othr) schemes, those that were non-financial market investment tools or did not fit into one of the other categories, were second most. Real estate (RE) is third most as a result of the housing bubble in the mid-2000 decade. The least is cryptocurrency (Cryp), a manner and means that has been in existence a little more than a decade. Investment tools (IVT) include investment tools such as those referred to as private offerings, warrants, annuities, and CDs. Prime banking schemes are indicated by PB. Oil and gas schemes are indicated by OG. Medical- and pharma-based schemes are indicated by MdPh. Chapter 4 discusses the individual manner and means as well as subcategories, providing examples of how the manner and means were used to perpetrate the fraud. Faith-based schemes were not included in this chart because it is not a manner and means, meaning the perpetrator was not asking investors to invest their money in faith, but that faith was used to make contacts or persuade. Faith-based frauds are included in the time frame charts just as a matter of comparison.

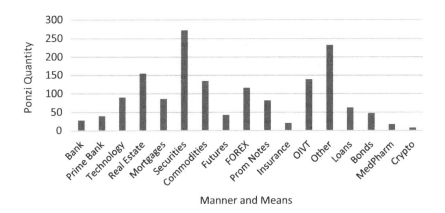

Figure 10.3 Manner and Means.

Manner and Means Time Frame

The manner and means of the Ponzi schemes were explained in Chapter 4. This is defined as what the perpetrators told their victims they were investing in. The terms that were coded into the data sets were the specific terms used in federal documents such as securities and equities; FOREX, and commodities. Many schemes were described as using multiple manners and means; there may have been three or four terms stated in federal documents. All of the terms were coded for each scheme, then analyzed using crosstab in SPSS to determine the quantity of each manner per year. One exception is that faith-based schemes; no scheme was investing in "faith" per se. Faith-based is usually considered a tool for perpetrating the frauds; however, in a few schemes the manner and means were funding for churches. Faith is included in this section to compare trends in faith-based frauds over time. The purpose of this analysis of manner and means was to demonstrate that there are different trends at different periods in time.

The year the scheme began was used because it is the political, technological, and economic trends that foster the climate to bring about the Ponzi scheme. The time frame may have been one of financial plenty, such as in boom economies. There may have been other political influences such as an oil embargo or a change in legislation. There may have been technological/economic trends such as the dot-com explosion in the late 1990s, and Uber, social networking, and cryptocurrency that enabled the fraud for the current time period.

The study includes all schemes found in federal documents beginning with 1962. However, the reader is cautioned that the term "Ponzi" may not have been commonly used in all federal cases that were technically Ponzi schemes in the 1962–1990 time frame,[2] and that not all documents are available for cases before 1990. The following charts indicate what is known for the cases where there is available information. Each chart indicates the trends in number of Ponzi schemes per year over the study period.

The vertical, or Y, axis, indicates the number of schemes that began per year. The horizontal, or X, axis indicates the year the schemes began. Please note that the quantity of schemes per year, the vertical axis, changes in each chart.

Banking-based Ponzi Schemes

In Figure 10.3a we see the numbers of schemes based on the term "bank." This would have included all schemes using the term "bank" other than "prime bank." These schemes may have been false-banks where perpetrators started up banks without the appropriate licensing, or banks may have been the victims. Others stated the investors were investing in banks. The chart shows that there were schemes based in banking in the 1985–1986 and in 1997–1998. The savings and loan crisis had taken place between approximately 1985 and 1990.

The time period between 2000 and 2011 saw a range of bank-based schemes, including schemes that were based on fraudulent banks. The Gramm-Leach Bliley Act of 1999 repealed Glass-Steagall Act allowing the merger of banks, and other financial institutions, that eventually contributed to the financial crisis.

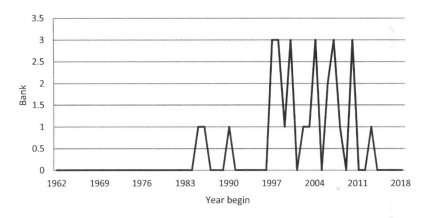

Figure 10.3a Bank by Year Begin.

Prime Banking

The mid- to late 1990s and early 2000 decades saw the greatest use of Ponzi schemes based on prime banking. As discussed in Chapter 4, prime banking refers to alleged investing in top banks around the world. This can take any form of financial instruments said to be investing in "prime banks" or investing in notes produced by prime banks; these are financial instruments that do not exist. In the late 1990s, there was a surge in prime banking schemes, whereas during the financial crisis time frame, prime bank schemes were at a low compared to other manners of schemes (Figure 10.3b).

Faith-based

Faith-based Ponzi schemes began to increase in 1997, then began to drop with the failing market around 2009–2010. There was no event or

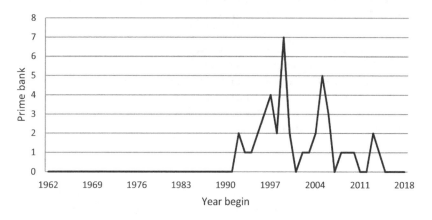

Figure 10.3b Prime bank by Year Begin.

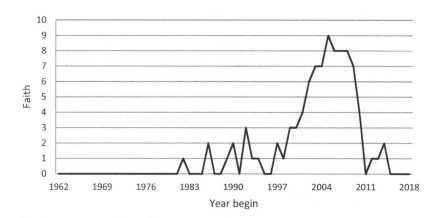

Figure 10.3c Faith-based by Year Begin.

legislative change that would have influenced an increase or decrease in faith-based frauds. This increase was in keeping with the economic trends that influenced all types of Ponzi schemes in the 2000 decade. Again, faith is not what perpetrators told their investors they were investing in but instead the mechanism used to instill trust. While faith is not a manner and means but instead a tool used to persuade, it is included in this section to compare quantity and time frame. The chart, Figure 10.3c is similar to the general securities Ponzi trend (see Figure 10.3g).

Technology-based

The theme of technology-based Ponzi schemes covers a wide range of topics, from ATM machines and phone booths in the late 1990s to current trends in algorithms. In the years leading up to the year 2000 (aka Y2K), there were concerns about financial collapse in that banking systems and other computer related processes might fail as a change from the year 1999 to 2000. In addition, there were schemes based in computer parts as computers became mainstream.

In 1982 the AT&T system was the recipient of an antitrust consent decree that prohibited business activities that were considered to be part of the monopoly on phone technology (Antitrust Consent Reform Act of 1995; U.S. v. AT& T, 1982). As a result, in the late 1990s there was a surge of Ponzi schemes that alleged to be investing in phone booths. As the technology for cell phones improved, cell phones became common place eliminating the need for phone booths and causing investments in phone booths to fail.

Just after the Y2K era, began the dot-com era. The dot-com era began in the late 1990s when the use of the internet grew very quickly. There were many technology-based companies that began and failed just after Y2K ended, around March 2000. There was a burst of technology-based Ponzi schemes in the late 1990s, ending with the dot-com collapse in the spring of 2000 (FCIC, 2011, p. 59).

There was a drop in schemes based in technology beginning in about 2007, when the financial crisis began, until about 2011. From this time, 2011, there was a surge in technology-based schemes frequently based in computer parts and in algorithms. The first drone technology scheme was in 2013. As technology progresses, there will be new schemes based on the new technological trends; it is new inventions that primarily drive the technology-based Ponzi schemes (Figure 10.3d).

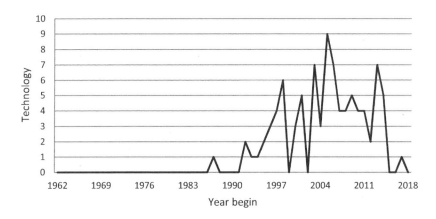

Figure 10.3d Technology by Year Begin.

Real Estate

Real estate-based Ponzi schemes occurred throughout the time frame of the study. Generally, this included investing in real estate businesses or actual properties. The housing boom of 2002–2007 shows a dramatic increase in real estate-based Ponzi schemes from 2004 to 2007, then a decline to 2011 with all Ponzi schemes. There has to be a market in real estate for this form of investment to be enticing. When the housing market is down there is no incentive to invest in real estate. From the time frame of 2009 to 2018, many of the real estate schemes were based in distressed properties (Figure 10.3e).

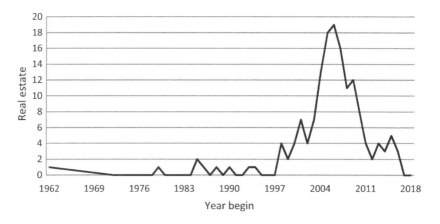

Figure 10.3e Real estate by Year Begin.

Mortgages

It is no surprise that the graph for mortgage-based Ponzi schemes (Figure 10.3f) is very similar to that of real estate-based (Figure 10.3e) Ponzi schemes. Many schemes were both real estate– and mortgage-based. Those that were mortgage-based may have been investing in mortgaged-backed securities, or at least they thought they were. Some were mortgage companies and others were in private funding of mortgages. The primary influence here was the derivatives market in bundled mortgages during the subprime housing boom.

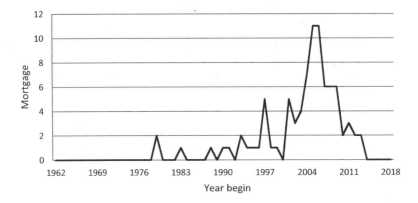

Figure 10.3f Mortgage by Year Begin.

Securities

Securities and equities are the dominant theme in Ponzi schemes. This has been the dominant manner throughout the study time frame. Figure 10.3g demonstrates a sort of zigzag incline until 2007 when securities schemes peaked at 23 schemes in one year, then a decline. In comparison to Figure 10.1, we see that all Ponzi scheme beginnings began to decline in 2007. The securities-based Ponzi schemes were wide ranging, with no particular legislation influencing the trends in securities frauds. Primarily, it was the market itself that influenced the increases and declines the trends in securities-based frauds.

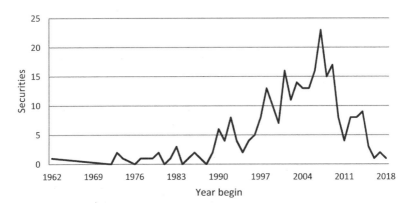

Figure 10.3g Securities by Year Begin.

Commodities

The commodities Ponzi trends have sharper increases and declines than the securities timeline (see Figures 10.3h and 10.3g). However, the commodities schemes are about half of those for the same time periods as the securities schemes looking at the vertical or Y axes. In both securities and commodities there is a low from about 2017 until the time frame of the study January 2020. It is likely that there will be many schemes exposed in the next few years from 2020 on. The vast majority of commodity-based schemes were referred to as commodity pools, not referencing a specific type of commodity as the investment.

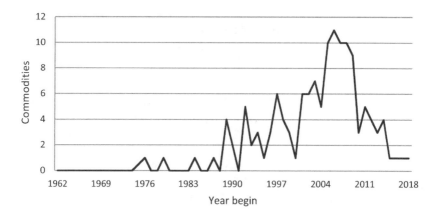

Figure 10.3h Commodities by Year Begin.

Futures

The futures-based schemes show an increase in the 1990 decade overall, with a drop from 1997 until the early 2000 decade. When the dotcom Ponzi schemes were on the increase, the futures Ponzi schemes were non-existent. The futures schemes increased with other market increases from about 2002, peaking in 2009. Securities and commodity schemes peaked in 2007. Many schemes that were commodity pool schemes were also said to be investing in futures as well. Futures Ponzi schemes tend to range from about 2–3 per year, but were non-existent when prime bank schemes were at the height in the late 1990s (Figure 10.3i).

FOREX

The FOREX schemes reached their peak between 2006 and 2008. There was an earlier smaller peak in the early part of the 2000 decade. Basically, the FOREX schemes shot up between 2004 and 2007, then declined just as rapidly (Figure 10.3j).

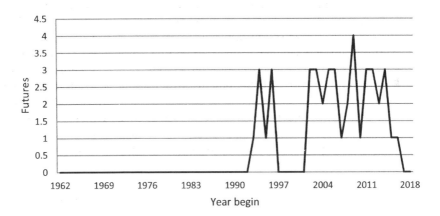

Figure 10.3i Futures by Year Begin.

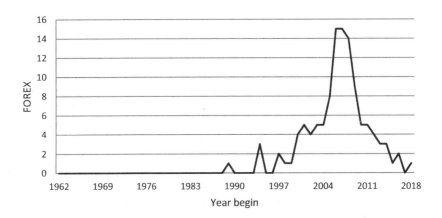

Figure 10.3j FOREX by Year Begin.

Promissory Notes

Ponzi schemes based in promissory notes were common throughout the study time frame, but also peaked in 2007. "Promissory notes" is a catch-all phrase often used instead of "securities," particularly when the investment is being promoted as a private investment as opposed to investing through exchange securities or commodities (Figure 10.3k).

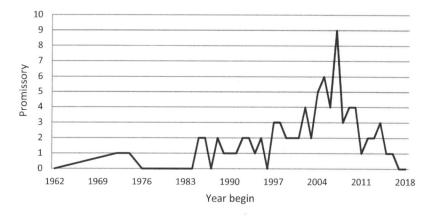

Figure 10.3k Promissory Notes by Year Begin.

Oil and Gas

Ponzi schemes based in oil and gas are one of the earliest manners and means for Ponzi schemes going back to when oil began being used for heating houses, and the use of gas with the early automobiles. What is interesting is that in 1999 when the dot-com bubble was in place and when other Ponzi manners were on the increase, oil and gas schemes were zero for the year. Similarly, there was only one oil-/gas-based scheme in 2009. In the 2020 time frame, with the beginning of the COVID-19 scare, the price of crude oil was as low as $6.50 a barrel on April 21, 2020. The price began to decline from $57 per barrel in January 2020. Any ongoing schemes that may have been based in oil or gas are likely to have collapsed. When the price of crude oil is so low, it is unlikely to attract investors in a Ponzi scheme based on oil, unless there are those who believe they can buy low to make profits (Figure 10.3l).

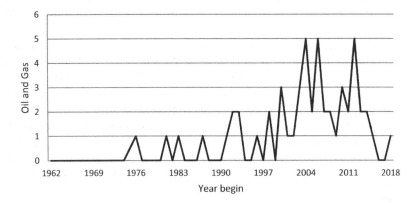

Figure 10.3l Oil and Gas by Year Begin.

Minerals and Gems

Ponzi schemes based in minerals could be any mineral characteristic, from mineral processing, gems, and precious jewelry to copper or precious metals and bullion. All, except for one, were based in falsities, in that there were no actual mining operations or actual investing. There were two schemes based on rare coins and silver, one of which was a legitimate coin shop that could not keep up with the demand. These schemes also demonstrated sharp zigzag trends as far back as three schemes in 1989. There was an increase in 2005 when the housing bubble was on the increase and there was investor confidence. It is possible that investor-victims may be more easily enticed by the notion of investing in gold and other precious metals as a hedge against economic declines (Figure 10.3m).

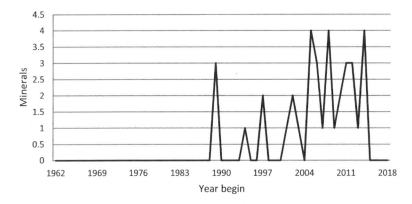

Figure 10.3m Minerals by Year Begin.

Insurance

The year with the greatest number of insurance-based Ponzi schemes was 2008. At this time the economy itself was beginning to falter. Even more curious is that investors thought that investing in insurance entities when the economy is in a down trend was a good idea. In many of the insurance-based cases, the perpetrators were insurance agents. They may have found that selling enough insurance to earn a livelihood proved challenging. Or they may have found that their insurance clients were already established relationships of trust. The two cases that involved viaticals were in 1994 and 2001. The viatical Ponzi in 1994 was one that stated the investment was in purchasing life insurance policies of those with AIDS, a case of profiting from a health crisis. Instead the case was just a Ponzi scheme. This was a time frame when many people were dying as a result of AIDS (Figure 10.3n).

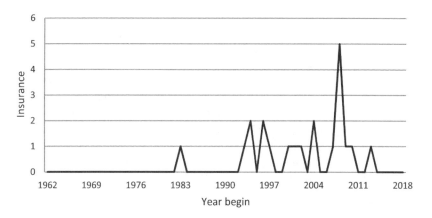

Figure 10.3n Insurance by Year by Year Begin.

General Investment Instruments

General investment instruments are any investment instruments that were not specifically stated as one of the more formal known terms discussed above. These schemes were oftentimes private investment entities, or those that referred to themselves as venture capitalists, warrants, options, and so on. These general investment schemes show a trend similar to the securities trend above (Figure 10.3o) (see Figure 10.3g).

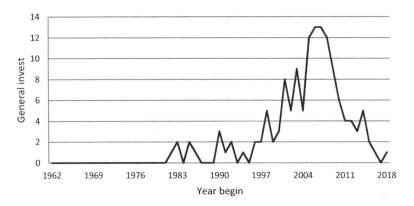

Figure 10.3o General Investment Instruments by Year Begin.

Other

This category encompasses all of the Ponzi schemes that did not fit into investment tools, medical/pharma or technology categories. This includes tractors, farm or business equipment, latex gloves, motorcycle businesses, airplane parts, cleaning products, worm farms, film companies, and other entertainment such as Broadway play and music performance tickets, and, more recently, the cannabis-based schemes. The "other" schemes are comparable in numbers to the securities schemes and spiked at the same time in 2007 (see Figure 10.3g). One thing is very clear from this category, that anything can be a means of inspiring a Ponzi scheme (Figure 10.3p).

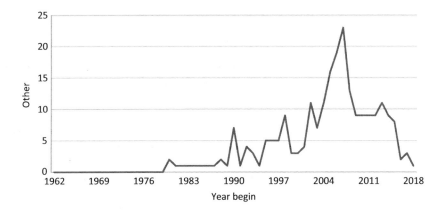

Figure 10.3p Other by Year Begin.

Loans

Loans were differentiated by the specific term of "loan" such as auto loans, bridge loans, and pay-day loans, and are differentiated from other debt instruments such as mortgages or bonds. Some alleged to be debt refinancing programs; no debt re-financing took place in any of the schemes. One commonality with real estate is the schemes based on bridge loans, the practice of taking out a short-term loan to bridge the gap until more permanent long-term financing is secured. This type of loan is sometimes used in real estate when a property owner must wait for the sale of another property before buying a new house. The majority of bridge loan Ponzi schemes were within the time frame of 2003–2009 during the housing bubble and the financial crisis. The peak of loan-based schemes of all types were between 2007 and 2009. Very few of the loan-based schemes provided actual loans at any point; the majority were intentional Ponzi schemes where there were no actual loans made (Figure 10.3q).

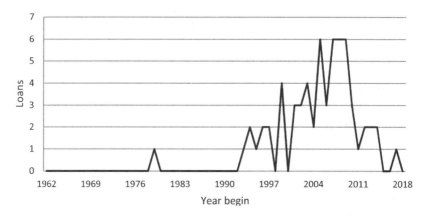

Figure 10.3q Loans by Year Begin.

Bonds

The schemes based in bonds had the biggest surge in 2007 just as the financial crisis was beginning. Just prior to 2007 and in the following year, there were no schemes based on bonds. There was an earlier surge in 2005 at the height of the real estate boom. A smaller surge on schemes based on bonds occurred in 2010 at the height of the financial crisis. During the housing bubble housing values dramatically increased. This meant that municipal governments could increase property taxes; therefore, good for aiding municipalities in paying off their bond debts. As the financial crisis worsened, many homes went into foreclosure; municipal governments were no longer bringing in the planned revenues. Municipal bonds may have had lower ratings at this time. It is likely that fearful investors look toward treasury bonds when other investment instruments are unpredictable, in that bonds are considered a more secure investment, unless, of course, one is investing in a Ponzi scheme based on bonds (Figure 10.3r).

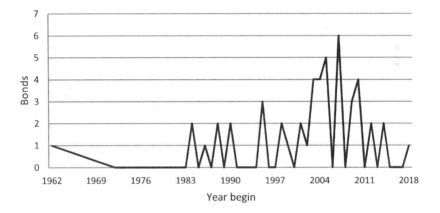

Figure 10.3r Bonds by Year Begin.

Medical Research, Billing, Devices, and Pharmaceuticals

The schemes in this category professed to be investing in medical devices, research, pharmaceuticals, and frequently medical billing. The medical billing schemes were based in factoring medical receivables. The highest number (4) of medical-/pharma-based schemes was in 2007, again at the beginning of the financial crisis. One 2010 scheme stated to be involved in Alzheimer's treatments. This is a time when the US population of elderly is at the highest point in history with the parents of the baby boomers in their 80s and 90s, and when the baby boomers themselves are over 55. More people are living to an age where they are vulnerable to any of the dementias. It is likely we will be seeing more of these schemes in the near future. At the time of writing, COVID-19 is devastating the world population; it is just a matter of time until the first COVID-19-based scheme is caught. Ponzi perpetrators are opportunists (Figure 10.3s).

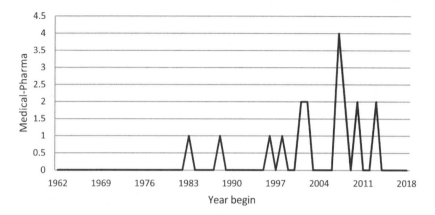

Figure 10.3s Medical-Pharma by Year Begin.

Cryptocurrency

Digital assets/cryptocurrencies came to life as a result of the world financial crisis. The first cryptocurrency was established in 2009: bitcoin. The first bitcoin Ponzi scheme began in 2011. We see the cryptocurrency schemes going up at a time when other Ponzi schemes are going down. We can expect that cryptocurrency Ponzi schemes are here to stay and that we will see an increasing amount of cryptocurrency Ponzi schemes exposed in the very near future (Figure 10.3t).

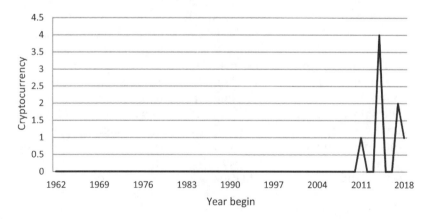

Figure 10.3t Cryptocurrency by Year Begin.

Conclusion

This chapter explained Minsky's economic theory in relationship to Ponzi schemes and the economy. The section on manner and means demonstrated that there are trends in what perpetrators choose as a basis for their schemes. What is chic-and-trendy for the times is more likely to be believable to investor-victims. Additionally, as some technologies go out of market viability Ponzi schemes based on those mechanisms stop, such as pay phones. Mapping out the manner and means of Ponzi schemes by the year they began gives an indicator of how economic events and legislative events can encourage or discourage fraudulent activities. The last phase of Minsky's theory in financial instability is the government intervention. We can now look at government response to financial events and frauds with legislation and regulation in the next chapter.

Notes

1 Harry Markopolos attempted to show the SEC that Madoff was running a Ponzi scheme on several occasions. He was ignored by the SEC, hence his book *No one would listen.*
2 One exception is the Home-Stakes Oil scheme that began in 1954. Documentation was found after the data sets were analyzed.

References

Antitrust Consent Reform Act of 1995.
Banking Act of 1933; Glass-Steagall.
Financial Crisis Inquiry Commission (FCIC). (2011). *Financial Crisis Inquiry Report; Final report of the National Commission on the causes of the financial and economic crisis of the United States.* New York, NY, Public Affairs.
Financial Services Modernization Act/Gramm-Leach-Bliley Act of 1999.
Lewis, M. (2011). Why do Ponzi schemes succeed? *Accounting Forum*, doi:101016/j.accfor.2011.11.002
Markopolos, H. (2005). *The world's largest hedge fund is a fraud.* Retrieved from: https://www.sec.gov/news/studies/2009/oig-509/exhibit-0293.pdf
Markopolos, H. and Fisher, D. (2010). *No one would listen: A true financial thriller.* Hoboken, NJ, John Wiley and Sons.
Minsky, H. (1982). *Can "it" happen again? Essays on instability and finance.* Armonk, NY, M.E. Sharpe Inc.
Santayana, G. (1905). *The life of reason.* New York, NY, Charles Scribner and Sons.
United States v. AT&T (1982) 552 F. Supp.31 226.

Chapter 11

Laws, Regulation and Legislative History

This chapter discusses the government interventions in the form of Acts, laws, and regulations that apply to Ponzi schemes. Minsky's fourth phase is the government interventions to financial collapse; these laws and regulations have been instituted as a response to economic failure and events that have resulted from or enabled economic crimes.

Angry victims often want authorities to "throw the book" at their victimizers. Due process, the rule of law, and the Constitution protect the rights of the accused. Constitutionally there is a presumption of innocence. Investment frauds are such that there are civil regulations and criminal laws that perpetrators can be charged with. In order for a case to have criminal charges there must be adequate evidence to result in a guilty plea or conviction: "beyond reasonable doubt." In civil cases the standard is "the preponderance of evidence." This chapter will discuss the differences between criminal and civil actions, as well as summary judgment and administrative decisions. In civil cases there may be sanctions or penalties while the perpetrator is "neither admitting or denying guilt." In criminal cases the guilty often plead out for a reduced sentence. This chapter will discuss the laws and regulations, and the history of events that necessitated the laws, regulations, and Acts established to protect Americans and their money. This is meant to be a layman's overview, not an in-depth legal interpretation. For a legal resource, readers are encouraged to access *The Ponzi book* (2012), by Kathy Phelps and Honorable Steven Rhodes.

Many of the laws and regulations in effect today came about as a result of the Great Depression. These laws were enacted in the time frame of 1933 and 1934, at least 13 years after Charles Ponzi's scheme. A second phase of legislation was enacted as a result of Enron and WorldCom, resulting in Sarbanes-Oxley (2002, July 3), and then Dodd-Frank was the government intervention after the financial crisis of 2007–2010. Throughout the decades in between, there were amendments to the earlier laws.

A Ponzi scheme is not a specific law that is broken but a name adopted to identify a specific fraudulent act: the act of "taking from Peter to pay Paul." Those charged in Ponzi schemes are charged with specific violations such as mail and wire fraud, and with not being a registered broker/adviser. Those who are required to be registered brokers or investment advisers are a matter of statutory law. There are federal requirements and state-level requirements; the federal laws and regulations are discussed below. The state regulations can be accessed through individual state websites. These laws determine who is required to be registered, among federal and state agencies, and what qualifies for exemptions. For legitimate trading and money managing businesses there are reporting requirements, on state and federal levels based on how much money a broker takes, manages, or invests. This reporting enables authorities to monitor the broker or adviser.

Any investment business or individual carrying out financial investing actions with other people's money and managing more than one hundred million dollars in funds must be registered with the SEC or CFTC. Anyone providing advice on investing for compensation must be registered under the Investment Advisers Act (1940). Each state has its own specific requirements regarding registration with the SEC. Some states, such as New York, require those entities, or persons, managing above 25 million dollars in funds to register with the SEC; each state has its own monetary value requiring registration with the SEC. In many Ponzi schemes the perpetrators were not registered with the SEC or CFTC as required. This information is stated in SEC and CFTC documents.[1] Registration was used, in coding, to determine which of the entities as stated by federal law enforcement and regulatory agencies had been legitimately functioning investment businesses. The United States Investment Advisers Act of 1940 states:

> Section 3(a) (4) (A) of the Act generally defines a "broker" broadly as any person engaged in the business of effecting transactions in securities for the account of others.
>
> All "financial planners, money managers and investment consultants are regulated as 'investment advisers' in the United States under the U.S. Investment Advisers Act of 1940." As such, they are required to register with the SEC.
>
> (SEC)

> The Securities Exchange Act of 1934 defines the Broker-dealer:
> Section 3(a) (4) (A) of the Act generally defines a "broker" broadly as any person engaged in the business of effecting transactions in securities for the account of others.
>
> (SEC)

Of the 1,359 Ponzi schemes in this study, only 12 percent were legitimately registered financial investment entities through the SEC and CFTC. The civil and criminal legal action documents (listed below), within the SEC, CFTC, and databases indicate whether or not the entities have been properly registered, at any point in the duration of the business entity. The SEC, CFTC, FINRA, and NFA websites allow for searching for information on legitimate, registered entities within their websites. These websites have been established for investors, as well as those who manage others' investments to perform due diligence.

The information within agency documents indicates when the entity became a Ponzi scheme, as well as when federal agents or regulatory authorities ended the scheme. This is determined by the investigations by federal regulatory and investigative actions. The IRS, USPS, SEC, CFTC, and FBI designate a scam "Ponzi" through the investigative process. The investigative process by the SEC and CFTC refers to an action (complaint) in a case that has been brought before the respective commissioners, who then determine that the case warrants an official, formal investigation. Many of these cases are turned over to the FBI or the US Attorney for criminal action. Other cases are initiated administratively by the SEC and CFTC without being referred for criminal charges. Some cases are initially investigated with the FBI, the IRS, ICE, the Secret Service, or the United States Postal Inspectors, and are addressed by the SEC or the CFTC after the criminal case.

Legal Framework

This section explains the laws and regulatory violations that determine what the crimes and/or violations that perpetrators have been charged with in the Ponzi schemes. These laws and violations have evolved, and been amended, with the frauds and economic conditions over the decades. The regulatory responses by the SEC and CFTC may be in response to crises or increased frauds. As an example, the development of cryptocurrencies has required both agencies to develop regulations and policies to evolve with the technological trend. A second example: all agencies have recognized that as the baby boomer generation ages, there is increased elder fraud and both agencies and the DOJ have stepped up their vigilance with elder fraud prevention.

The Ponzi Presumption

This "general rule" states that when a Ponzi scheme exists, intent to defraud is implied (Phelps and Rhodes, 2012, § 2.03). This is used in clawbacks and disgorgement when receiver or trustee is pursuing those who have received illegal gains in Ponzi schemes. The use of the Ponzi Presumption enables receivers and trustees to establish more quickly that fraud has been committed and to begin to claw back ill-gotten gains by requesting the court apply the Ponzi Presumption (McDonald and Ploeger, 2011). John McDonald Esq. and Marcus Ploeger Esq. explain that the receiver must be able to satisfy two criteria in order to use the Ponzi Presumption:

1   That a Ponzi scheme has taken place.
2   That the purpose of the transfer of funds was part of the Ponzi scheme.

(McDonald and Ploeger, 2011, p. 81)

The Civil Process

The civil process allows a plaintiff to bring an action against a defendant for monetary damages, when the defendant has failed to carry out a legal obligation. The plaintiff is generally the SEC or the CFTC. Many individuals who are victims are also plaintiffs suing their Ponzi perpetrator in an effort to get their funds back (see bankruptcy, Chapter 5).

In Ponzi cases the primary agent of a company has a legal obligation to be honest with investors concerning the investment risks. Further, these primaries have a responsibility to invest their clients' money in a manner consistent with what they have told investors. Finally, there is a legal obligation of the primary agent to honestly report their credentials, or lack thereof, as well as previous criminal convictions, SEC or CFTC sanctions, and if they have been banned from brokering or trading to their investors and potential investors. In short, they cannot fail to disclose crucial information to investors.

The federal civil process generally enforces only when federal regulation is involved; this applies to jurisdiction. Most Ponzi cases involve multiple states; thus, federal jurisdiction also applies. The civil process generally begins with a cease and desist order, or complaint served on a defendant, presumably the primary agent in a business, a brokerage, or a corporation generally brought forth by the SEC or CFTC. This complaint alleges the facts, violations, and financial damages and equitable relief sought. In some cases, this complaint will state that a jury trial is requested. The burden of proof is much less in civil proceedings. The plaintiff has the burden of proving the case by a "preponderance of the evidence." Generally, this means finding in favor of which party presents the stronger evidence. Civil proceeding records are coded as "cv" in court documents.

The Securities and Exchange Commission's Role in the Ponzi Scheme Investigation

The SEC commissioners comprise five presidential appointees with staggered terms. No more than three of these can be of the same political party. The SEC's mandate:

> The SEC was established in 1934 as a reaction to the Great Depression, it is mandated to:
>
> - Interpret federal securities laws.
> - Issue new rules and amend existing rules.
> - Oversee the inspection of securities firms, brokers, investment advisers, and ratings agencies.
> - Oversee private regulatory organizations in the securities, accounting, and auditing fields.
> - Coordinate US securities regulation with federal, state, and foreign authorities.
>
> (SEC website)

The Investigative Process

The SEC's process for investigation of any suspected fraud generally starts with an investor complaint, market surveillance, an SEC inspection, or a whistleblower. When a complaint is received usually from a victim-investor, there is to be a search performed through the Name Relationship Search Index (NRSI) system to determine if there are any other ongoing examinations or investigations of the subject. In the Madoff case, the NRSI search did not take place. This would have informed all staff of any ongoing inquiries in any division (different divisions had different ongoing inquiries into Madoff's operations at the time (Markopolos and Fisher, 2010). In an investigation, examiners would ascertain the validity of comments and documents from an entity under inquiry, such as determining if stated trades actually took place; this was not done in the Madoff case (Markopolos and Fisher, 2010).

The SEC staff receives a complaint and then opens a Matter Under Inquiry (MUI). This is an initial examination to determine if there is evidence to recommend the matter to the SEC's Enforcement Division. The secondary investigation determines if there is evidence to send the matter on to the Commission, which determines whether there are grounds to open a Formal Investigation. Commission meetings, where decisions to open formal investigations are discussed, are not open to the public nor are there publicly available records of the proceedings. There is no data on how many potential cases are rejected for formal investigations because of lack of evidence of a regulatory or criminal violations.

The criteria for determining if a MUI is worthy of being referred for an investigation recommendation are stated in the SEC *Enforcement Manual*: "Whether the matter involves: particularly egregious or extensive misconduct, potentially widespread harm to investors; if it involves a person of authority; a large number of victims or particularly vulnerable victims" (p.,4 sec. 2.1.1). *The Enforcement Manual* discusses how Regional Directors have flexibility, creativity, and the ability to prioritize their resources. It goes on to give criteria for determining how best to allocate personnel resources. The manual specifically designates the number of attorneys that are to be assigned to significant cases, but it does not mention fraud investigators, forensic accounting experts, or investment specialists (p. 5, sec. 2.1.1). The *Enforcement Manual* was produced after the congressional hearings, the IG and Government Accountability Office (GAO) reports, as well as after the independent Boston Consulting Group (BCG) report.

Section 2.3.1 of *The Enforcement Manual* discusses the MUIs and what the criteria are for recommending a matter for formal or further investigation. The designation is open to the discretion of SEC investigative personnel, but cover such considerations as: if an SEC regulation is in violation, the scope of possible victims, if the issue can be investigated within the statute of limitations, the monetary amount, and is the issue something best referred to another agency or a state authority. Once an MUI has been opened, senior SEC regional officials receive weekly reports on the progress of the inquiry. If the matter has not been closed before 60 days, it then becomes an investigation. An MUI is submitted to the Associate Director of the Enforcement division who is obligated to make a determination to submit an issue to the Commission, for a formal investigation determination, within two days of receiving the MUI. Only the vote of the Commission determines if a formal investigation will take place.

The matter will then go through the Wells process, whereby the suspected individual or entity has the opportunity to explain their actions. The Wells process informs the individual or entity being investigated that a preliminary investigation is being submitted to the Commission, what securities laws are thought to have been violated, and that the individual or entity has the right to communicate with the Commission. In some cases, if the Commission receives information where there is evidence of serious wrongdoing, the Commissioners can issue a cease and desist order or other equitable relief, within the same day, to prevent further loss to victims. The Commission then rejects or refers an MUI to the Law Enforcement Division for a formal investigation. Once the Law Enforcement Division is involved the matter generally results in further criminal legal action by working with the Department of Justice. All criminal investigations are handled by the FBI or DOJ. Some states take criminal action, even though the SEC or CFTC takes civil action. However, the SEC and CFTC administrative judges can institute civil monetary penalties and sanctions.

Commodities Futures Trading Commission Investigations

The CFTC carries out the investigative process in the same way as the SEC. In the CFTC, the different divisions determine that a Commodities Exchange Act violation has taken place or that other relevant federal laws have been violated. A Preliminary Inquiry is begun when there is adequate documentation that there has been a violation. A Deputy determines if a case warrants an investigation. The CFTC personnel then must recommend administrative action to the Commission. Once the Commission has determined civil action is in order, the matter goes before an administrative law judge (ALJ). If the Commission determines that criminal action has taken place the case is referred to the Department of Justice.

Administrative Law Judges

Administrative law judges preside over civil proceedings in securities and commodities cases. These judges are selected internally through SEC and CFTC personnel processes.[2] These federal-level law judges hold public hearings in federal courts.[3] These hearings include the hearing of evidence, determining the facts and rendering legal conclusions. When defendants do not appear, the judge may order a default judgment against them. Administrative law judges can require disgorgement and set civil penalties and issue sanctions against the defendants.

The authority of ALJs has been challenged recently in federal court. David F. Bandimere received a sanction in a Ponzi scheme case in Denver, Colorado. He appealed the sanction based on Article II of the Constitution, the Appointment Clause. In the recent 10th Circuit United States Court of Appeals case, *Bandimere v. SEC*, Bandimere questioned whether ALJs are inferior Officers of the Court or are Officers, as it pertains to Article II, section 2, clause 2, of the Constitution (the Appointment Clause). Under the Constitution federal judges are to be appointed by the president, but the administrative judges are selected through internal processes within the SEC and the CFTC. The issue at hand is that the actions of these judges are more than administrative; they are judgments, including imposing sanctions and penalties, both of which suggest some indication of guilt (Adler, 2016). In short, the *Bandimere v. SEC* case brings into question the constitutionality of ALJs and their decisions, and whether their decisions are a violation of the Appointment Clause because they have not been appointed by the president:

The United States Constitution Article II § 2 clause 2 states in part: "[The President] shall appoint ambassadors, other public ministers and consuls, judges of the Supreme court and all other officers of the United States."

The *Bandimere* case hinged on the *Lucia v. Securities and Exchange Commission* Supreme Court decision (2018). The issue of the appointment of ALJs was resolved with the Supreme Court decision *Lucia et al. v. SEC*. The Court held that the ALJs are Officers of the United States, and subject to the Appointment Clause (138 S. Ct. 2044, 2018) (US Const. Art, II § 2). Executive Order 13843 made an exception to the previously used competitive hiring practice of ALJs. The administrative judges are now classified as members of the excepted service, meaning the agencies can use discretion in hiring based on merit, for specific needed skills and expertise.

Civil Actions: Complaints, Injunctions, and Sanctions

Civil actions listed below are carried out by the SEC and the CFTC. These are differentiated from civil suits filed by investor-victims who have lost money and sue the perpetrators. In some cases, there is a jury trial demand; in others there are only administrative proceedings through an administrative judge.

Complaint

The complaint is the initial pleading beginning a civil action. These documents allege who did what, when they did it, where they did it, generally how they did it and specific details about the defendants, and what regulations were violated. There is usually a "prayer for relief" called a "demand," which is requesting the court for relief against the defendants. A "prayer for relief" is asking for damages, meaning monetary compensation.

Injunctions

Injunctions are orders by the court requiring that a defendant cease some activity, such as taking funds, paying out funds, moving funds, or investing. An injunction may be temporary or permanent. A "Cease and desist order" requires that an individual or an entity stop whatever they are doing that is considered a violation. This may also include a restraining order.

Consent Order

Many consent orders in administrative cases use the phrase "neither admitting nor denying guilt." The accused is taking responsibility and accepting penalties and sanctions without admitting or denying guilt. This allows the defendant to reach a settlement. This is controversial, because it allows the perpetrator to resolve the action without admitting wrong doing, or to simply pay a penalty to resolve a problem quickly. It also suggests that there is wrongdoing for someone who has not pleaded guilty, who might indeed be innocent.

Summary Disposition or Judgment

Summary judgments are often issued in civil cases to come to a decision quickly without the use of a trial. The court determines if there is material fact or if a case is one of the law. Summary judgments are commonly used in securities cases, primarily for determining sanctions.

> Rule 2SO(b) of the Commission's Rules of Practice provides for motions for summary disposition. The hearing officer may grant the motion for summary disposition if there is no genuine issue with regard to any material fact and the party making motion is entitled to a summary disposition. The Commission has regularly upheld use of summary disposition in cases where a respondent has been enjoined or convicted and the sole determination concerns appropriate sanction.
>
> (SEC, 2017, March, 6)

Civil Sanctions

Disbarment, Prohibition, and Suspensions

Disbarment or barring is preventing an individual from trading or being associated with a brokerage, or barring them from being in a supervisory position of those who do trade. Accountants and attorneys can be barred from appearing before the SEC and CFTC. There can be permanent barring, or barring for a few years or months. The recipients of the barring can appeal. The SEC also revokes the registrations of registered investment advisers and other businesses. The CFTC invokes prohibitions on trading.

Both the SEC and CFTC can institute trading suspensions. In the SEC it is generally for ten days (SEC, 2018). Suspensions are generally less than six months in the CFTC. For either agency to suspend trading there must have been actual trading going on in the first place; this is often not the case in most Ponzi schemes.

Settlements

Settlements are a procedure designed to return funds to investors where appropriate and to avoid the cost of litigation. Litigation is manpower-intensive and therefore costly. Sometimes it is in the best interest of the taxpayer and investor-victims to work toward a settlement to make investors whole, rather than to litigate.

Penalties

Both the SEC and CFTC are authorized to impose penalties through the Commodities Exchange Act and the Securities Exchange Act. According to the CFTC *Enforcement Manual* (2020, 6.8., pp. 29–30) the gravity or seriousness of the offence may be considered in determining the penalty amount as well as the number of offenses. Whether or not and how often penalties are actually collected in the Ponzi schemes was not a matter of public record. It is likely that amount is relatively low considering that restitution and legal fees come first, and that most Ponzi perpetrators file for bankruptcy. It is likely that there is very little money left to pay penalties.

The Criminal Process

The criminal process begins with an investigation that could be initiated by the FBI or another federal agency with law enforcement capacity such as the Internal Revenue Service, Secret Service, United States Postal Inspectors, and Immigration and Customs Enforcement. The Department of Justice's United States Attorneys determine if the case should go before a Grand Jury. Related criminal case documents are designated as: "cr" in court documents. This requires that there is evidence that a criminal action has taken place such as mail fraud, wire fraud, and securities fraud.

Informational Report or the Criminal Complaint

An "Information" is also known as a "bill of information." An informational is a "formal criminal charge made by a prosecutor without a grand jury indictment" (Black's law, Garner, 2009). This is a list of the charges signed by the accuser, usually an investigator with the FBI or DOJ. The prosecution may convince a judge that there is probable cause to go forward with a case. In this process, the defendant can agree to plead guilty and waive their right to a grand jury and formal trial in exchange for a lesser sentence. Many cases are processed through this method.

Grand Jury

The grand jury process is enabled by the Fifth Amendment to the Constitution. The grand jury is held in private; the proceedings are not open to the public, nor are the transcripts. If the jury determines that there is evidence of laws being violated, they vote to indict. In a grand jury proceeding the evidence is presented by the prosecutor. The process is very one-sided against the defendant. The jury may ask questions and ask for evidence. The purpose is to determine if there has been a crime committed and, if there is evidence, to go forward with a trial. In grand juries, the deliberations are recorded and transcribed, but are not a matter of public record.

Indictment

The indictment is a legal action, the written accusation, that specifies what laws the individual is charged with violating. This is an affidavit that is sworn to under oath. This applies to felonies. Generally, grand jury indictments are submitted to a magistrate judge, designated as "mj" in court documents. These documents are sealed, until the defendant is arrested.

Federal Judges

Federal judges are nominated by the president and are confirmed by the Senate with lifetime federal judgeships. As stated earlier, the federal judges are authorized by US Constitution Article II § 2 clause 2. This Article gives authority to the president to appoint Supreme Court judges, District Court judges, the Court of Appeals, and Bankruptcy Appellate panel judges. The latter two courts consist of three-judge panels who hear appeals and make decisions whether the law was correctly applied. Article III of the US Constitution establishes the authority of the courts.

The lengthy case of Claud Richard (Rick) Koerber exemplifies the criminal judge's discretion in the due process equation:

- On January 21, 2016, Rick Koerber's Ponzi case was dismissed with prejudice. It was dismissed because of the length of time it took to bring to trial, under the speedy trial clause of the Sixth Amendment to the Constitution (US Const. amend. VI). The original grand jury indictment was in 2009. The judge had also determined that many of the delays had been caused by Koerber himself. There was a large quantity of documents (20 boxes) under discovery; neither side could get through them in the allotted time. The case was initially dismissed with prejudice because of the seriousness of the offenses with which he was charged. Koerber's associate, Gabriel Joseph, was sentenced to 78 months in 2016. On January 18, 2017, in a judgment on an appeal, a ruling by the appellate court overruled the trial judge and ordered the reinstatement of the charges against Koerber. Koerber's scheme was a real estate-based fraud that had taken place between 2004 and 2008 during the housing bubble. Koerber was convicted in September 2018, and received a federal sentence of 170 months (USA v. Koerber, 2017, January 18).

Guilty Plea

The USSC reports that the majority of federal cases, overall 95 percent, are pleaded out (USSC, 2015, Annual Report). When a defendant pleads guilty, many of the facts that would have come out in a trial are not presented. In these proceedings, a more thorough explanation is generally provided in the presentence report. When there is a plea agreement, the defendant agrees not to appeal. There is generally an agreed-upon sentence that is less than would be given in a criminal trial that results in a guilty verdict. Many cases start out going to trial, then the perpetrator accepts a plea of guilty.

More often than not in Ponzi cases, the perpetrators admit their guilt, pleading guilty to the crimes of which they are accused. This process allows for the judge to reduce the length of time in sentencing for saving the court the time and cost of a jury trial. In many cases the co-conspirators plea-bargained in return for their testimony against the primary defendant. These offenders are considered cooperators. In such cases the agreement between the cooperator and the Department of Justice is not made public. While the court docket indicates a plea agreement was made the details are not made public for the safety of the cooperator. In other cases, the primary pleaded guilty before the case was presented to a grand jury. Madoff pleaded guilty, saving the court the cost of a jury trial, although it did not result in a reduced sentence (USA v. Bernard Madoff, 2009, March 12). Generally, these pleas include a clause whereby the defendant will not appeal the sentence.

Appeals

In the appeals process, those criminally convicted, or those who have been found liable in civil cases, can appeal the conviction, or decision in a civil case. In those cases that go to trial and end in conviction, appeals are common. An appeal asks a higher court to reverse a lower court's decision, based on the reversible error of the lower court proceeding.

- R. Allen Stanford was convicted in a jury trial. Stanford then appealed the sentence based on several technicalities (USA v. Stanford, 5th Cir. Ap. 2015, October 29, p. 2). The Fifth Circuit affirmed Stanford's conviction; his sentence of 110 years was affirmed. Stanford then took his case to the Supreme Court arguing that the SEC froze his assets and therefore he was denied the right to an attorney of his choosing. His writ of certiorari was denied in October 2016 (Robert Allen Stanford v. USA S.Ct. 15-1490, 2016).

The Criminal Charges in Ponzi Schemes

In general, the majority of cases are charged under United States Code (USC) Title 18 Part I Chapter 63 Mail Fraud and other Fraud Offenses, Sections 1341-1351, and securities and commodities fraud. Also, Chapter 47 1001-1040 includes frauds and false statements, including loans and mortgages. This may include frauds and false statements, and/or embezzlement, Chapter 31 641-670. A few cases are charged with racketeering under the RICO Act, also under Title 18 Chapter 96 1961–1968. In some cases, the perpetrators are charged with conspiracy to commit one of the crimes discussed herein. In some cases, the investigation is initiated by the IRS and the charges include tax evasion. Other cases are charged under USC Title 15 that covers investment companies, publicly offered securities and activities that may adversely affect investors. Title 15 specifies the responsibilities of investment companies to their investors.

In the cases that were false banks, meaning the perpetrators started their own banks, without the appropriate licensing and authorizations, perpetrators may have been charged under USC Title 12 Banks and Banking Offenses. Laws addressing currency are also under this title. This list has the most common charges but is in no way an exhaustive list of all of the criminal charges in Ponzi schemes.

Frauds and Swindles

This law covers forms of deception, artifice, or intent to defraud (USC 18 ch.63 § 1341). These include frauds committed using the United States Postal Service. This is one of the earliest laws (1909, March 4, ch. 321, § 215, 35 Stat.1130), along with mail fraud (1872). This was the primary law used to prosecute frauds until after the Great Depression when the Securities Act of 1933 was enacted. Mail fraud falls under section 1341.

Mail Fraud

The Mail Fraud Act was enacted in 1872; it includes using the United States Postal Service to mail business and investing materials to prospective investors as well as the sending or receiving of checks or cash through the United States Postal Service. Many Ponzi schemers are charged with mail fraud (18 USC § 1341). This was more common in earlier cases before the internet.

Wire Fraud

The frauds by wire, radio, or television law (18 USC § 1343) are more relevant today because of the internet than when first established in 1950. At this point in time, all Ponzi schemes make use of internet technology and phones, as well as electronic transfer of funds. Wire fraud also includes using radio or television to advertise a fraudulent scheme. All of these mechanisms fall under the Wire Fraud Act. Most Ponzi perpetrators are charged with wire fraud, usually several counts. The Wire Fraud Act was enacted when telephones, radio, and television became common place.

Racketeering

Some cases are charged with racketeering conspiracy under the RICO act. To be considered for racketeering charges a business entity must be a business "enterprise." "An 'enterprise' is defined as: an individual, partnership, corporation, association, union or other legal entity" (RICO Act 18 USC § 1961). Second there must be at least two crimes committed within a ten-year period; this is considered a "pattern of racketeering activity." Under the RICO Act (18 USC §§ 1961, 1962, 1963), the crimes considered prohibited activities include:

1   It is a crime to use or invest any income derived from a pattern of racketeering activity.
2   Collection of unlawful debt.
3   A pattern of racketeering activity; this must be at least two criminal acts within a ten-year time frame.
4   To establish acquire an interest in or operate and enterprise engaged in or affecting interstate commerce.

In addition, the aspect of conspiracy is as follows: "a defendant who conspires to commit a substantive offense under section 1962, (a)(b)(c) can be convicted of a RICO conspiracy even though the defendant does not personally commit or agree to commit the racketeering activity or collection of unlawful debt" (USSC.gov). With this in mind the RICO Act covers many aspects of Ponzi schemes; it is surprising that more defendants in Ponzi cases are not charged under the RICO Act, in addition to the usual charges of mail fraud, wire fraud, and securities fraud. Two cases in which the defendants were charged with racketeering or racketeering conspiracy are:

•   One of the biggest cases where the perpetrators were charged with racketeering was that of PEI. There were several primaries involved; the two most known were James Tyson Jr, and Ramin Amini. Amini is a fugitive; his case can be reopened if he is found. Many of the 92 perpetrators were charged with racketeering conspiracy. This scheme was considered a mortgage fraud scheme. Drew Sharreff-El, considered to be one of the primaries, was charged with fraud with identification documents, among other charges. Among the many co-conspirators the charges were mortgage fraud, money laundering conspiracy, concealment of money laundering, securities fraud, wire fraud, bank fraud, and other charges, depending on what the perpetrator's profession was and position in the "Enterprise," as it was referred to by federal investigators (DOJ, 2014, December 3, p.r.; USA v. Amini et al., 2013, April 18; USA v. Drew Sharreff-El, 2011, July 21; USA v. James Tyson Jr.).

- A second well-known case involving racketeering charges was that of Scott Rothstein. Rothstein was one of the primaries in the Florida law firm Rothstein, Rosenfeldt, Adler. His Ponzi scheme told investor-victims that they were investing civil case settlements. The second aspect of his scheme was bridge-loans to businesses. In his plea agreement Rothstein admitted that his business was a criminal enterprise, one of the criteria to satisfy the RICO charges (FBI, 2010, June 9).

The Racketeering Influenced Corrupt Organization (RICO), established as sections 1961–1968 of the Organized Crime Control Act of 1970, allows for both civil and criminal actions in addressing organized crime activities. The primary criminal definitions are as follows:

- "An 'enterprise' is defined as including any individual, partnership, corporation, association, to other legal entity, and any union or group of individuals associated in fact although not a legal entity" (18 USC § 1961 (4)).
- "Pattern of racketeering activity" requires at least two acts of racketeering activity committed within ten years (18 USC § 1961 (5)).

Government Response and Regulatory History

The purpose of financial laws, Congressional Acts, and regulatory agencies is to protect the financial markets, to keep the American economy stable, and to prevent crimes. Economist Hyman Minsky theorized that the nation's financial instability and the government regulations influence economic fluctuations. In response to the Great Depression (1929–1939), laws were enacted, agencies created, and regulations were put into place to control financial markets. The laissez-faire government oversight during the boom economy in the "Roaring Twenties" was seen as a cause of the depression. Congress responded with legislation to prevent economic catastrophes caused by unfettered financial markets from happening

again. This is the basis for economist Minsky's theory of financial instability (Minsky, 1982).

There were market panics and a few mild recessions throughout the
decades since Glass-Steagall and the Security Acts of 1933. For the most
part, the economy was relatively stable until the Glass-Steagall Act was
repealed by the Financial Modernization Act of 1999. Presidents Reagan and Clinton both favored libertarian economic principles that held
government should not interfere with financial markets. This philosophy
paved the way for the enactment of the financial Modernization Act of
1999. Even before Glass-Steagall and the Securities Acts of 1933, there
were congressional Acts and a Supreme Court decision attempting to
prevent and control fraud and other financial crimes. The following is
a chronological description of regulatory Acts, and how they relate to
current Ponzi schemes and economic trends.

Prior to the Glass-Steagall Act of 1933, there were many mortgage
frauds similar to those that took place just prior to the financial crisis
(2007–2010), during the housing boom created by subprime mortgages
(approximately 2004–2006). These were two periods in history where
regulations were not in effect, or were not effectively enforced, allowing
many mortgage frauds to occur in relationship to a booming economy
and then a financial collapse. In the 1920s there were cases of mortgage
securities fraud whereby the investor/victims were buying securities in
mortgages companies that never actually provided loans to consumers (Frasca, 1931). This was in the time period of Charles Ponzi's fraud
scheme that now is the name sake of this specific type of fraud. At that
time, this specific type of fraud schemes was simply called a "swindle," a
term that applied to many types of frauds.

- The Mail Fraud Act of 1872
  The first legislation to be passed in reaction to fraud was the Federal Mail Fraud Act of 1872. The laissez-faire economics practices
  of the United States in the nineteenth century enabled a wide variety of frauds. The postal service enabled frauds to take place from a
  distance. To stem the tide of increasing frauds perpetrated through
  the postal service, Congress established the Mail Fraud Act of 1872,
  making it a federal offense to commit fraud through the United States
  Postal Service (USPS). The USPS Investigative Agents are the second
  longest established federal investigative unit, to that of the United
  States Federal Marshals. The USPS is involved in most investigations
  because perpetrators often use the mail to carry out their frauds; in
  some cases, the USPS is the agency that first identifies the fraud.
- Taxing Illegal Gains
  In 1927, the Supreme Court ruled that earnings from bootleg-
  ging and other criminal activities had to be reported and that the
  perpetrators were required to pay taxes on illegally gained funds.

This opened the door for prosecutions and enabled federal authorities to prosecute based on tax evasion, when they could not prove other criminal activity. If individuals were legally earning money, they would have documentation to prove the funds were legally obtained. Today, many fraud perpetrators are caught through fraudulent tax documents. At times, it is the Internal Revenue Service (IRS) that identifies the fraud scheme; the IRS is involved in many investigations.

- The Banking Act of 1933, also known as the Glass-Steagall Act

   The Banking Act of 1933, more commonly known as Glass-Steagall, was established in response to the 1929 stock market crash. It was thought that one of the primary reasons for the crash was risky financial transactions between commercial banks and speculating in the stock market.[4] Hence, the intent of this act was a legal block between commercial banks and investment banks. This prevented investment banks from using commercial depositor's funds for investments. Thus, if the financial institution made a bad investment and lost money, the average bank client did not lose their funds. This and the empowering of the Federal Reserve Bank ended the era of laissez-faire economics in America.

- Securities Act of 1933

   This Act primarily had two purposes: To require that potential investors receive information about securities being offered for public sale and to enact laws that prevent fraud and deception in securities investing. Most Ponzi perpetrators are charged under one or more of sections in the Securities Act.

- Securities Exchange Act of 1934

   This Act established the Securities and Exchange Commission, enabling this federal agency to monitor, regulate, and take legal actions in securities markets. This was amended in 1964.

- The Commodities and Futures Exchange Act of 1936

   This Act authorized the Commodities Futures Exchange Commission, allowing it to develop regulations, and to regulate commodities and futures markets. Those perpetrators using foreign currency or commodities are charged with violations under this Act.

- The Investment Company Act of 1940

   This Act defined and classified investment companies and it determined reporting and auditing requirements for investment companies. Those entities that fit the definition of an investment company are required to register with the SEC. These entities must maintain a portion of their assets for investors who want to take their funds. This means a certain percentage must be held in cash so that investors can take their principal as they request. This Act also requires that investment companies disclose their investing policies and practices to their investors. In short, this means they cannot say they are investing in one thing while they are really investing in a riskier venture. The one shortcoming of this Act is that 3 (c) (1) allowed that entities with under 100 investors were not required to register; this allowed hedge funds to avoid registering and monitoring to some degree. This loophole was closed in 2005.

- Federal Deposit Insurance Act of 1950

    This Act ensured that member depository institutions depositor's funds would be protected. Should a bank fail, the customer's deposits in the bank would be guaranteed by the US government through the Federal Deposit Insurance Corporation (FDIC). This Act was to prevent the runs on banks that occurred during the Great Depression when people wanted to get their money out before the financial institution became insolvent. During the Great Depression, fully functioning financial institutions collapsed because their customers panicked and pulled out their funds en masse; even a solvent bank could go under, because its loan portfolio could not be liquidated fast enough to pay all the depositors demanding the return of their money.

- Fraud by Wire, Radio, or Television: The Wire Fraud Act of 1952

    With electricity, phones, radios, and televisions commonly available by the 1950s, frauds committed using phone lines, television, and radio became a problem. Congress responded with the Wire Fraud Act of 1952. Together with the Mail Fraud Act, the majority of charges filed against Ponzi perpetrators fall under these two Acts. As technology developed with time, the frauds adapted to the technology, then Congress developed laws to combat the frauds. Crimes using the internet fall under the jurisdiction of the Wire Fraud Act. Ponzi perpetrators all use phones, and now, usually the internet as well, allowing the majority of perpetrators to be charged under the Wire Fraud Act.

- Community Reinvestment Act of 1977

    The Community Reinvestment Act of 1977 was established to encourage banks to support loans in low-income and moderate-income neighborhoods. Before this Act, it was very difficult for lower-income families to get mortgages. The Federal National Mortgage Association, more commonly known as Fanny Mae, was established in 1938 to help supply affordable home loans. The Federal Home Mortgage Corporation, more commonly known as Freddie Mac, was established in 1970 for the same purpose. Both buy loans on the secondary markets, but the primary difference in the two entities is that Fannie Mae buys loans from commercial bankers and Freddie Mac buys loans from smaller banks. Today, they are both shareholders-owned, functioning under congressional charters, meaning government-sponsored entities, owned by stock holders. The Financial Crisis Inquiry Commission report concluded that Fannie Mae and Freddie Mac mortgages endured losses just as the entire mortgage market did, but their mortgages did not default as severely as the rest of the mortgage markets (FCIC, 2011, p. xxvi). The FCIC determined that Fannie Mae and Freddie Mac were followers in the losses, not the leaders of the losses: not a contributing cause to the financial crisis. Regardless, Fannie Mae and Freddie Mac were put into conservatorship by Congress in September 2008.

- Federal Deposit Insurance Improvement Act of 1991

In the 1980s the United States experienced the savings and loan crisis. Money markets had appeared as an investment product in the late 1970s. When money-market funds became available, people removed their money from savings accounts and put the funds in money market accounts where they could earn higher interest rates. The interest rates on savings and loans were regulated by the federal government, but money market interest rates were unregulated; people earned greater interest in money market accounts. The interest rates being paid were high and the underlying assets were tied to loans with low interest rates; the thrifts did not have the cash flow available to supply the demand of those removing their funds from the savings accounts. This was one contributing cause of many savings and loans collapses in the 1980s.

The federal government intervened in these bank failures with bail-outs; this is when the term "too big to fail" was first used (FCIC, 2011, p. 37). This Act was designed to limit the use of taxpayer funds to rescue financial institutions. The economic principle of moral hazard suggests that when one entity knows that another entity will take responsibility for their financial mistakes, the original entity is not punished for its failure, but instead rewarded. If financial institutions make bad decisions and the federal government bails them out, it only encourages financial institutions to make bad financial decisions. Pontell also refers to this as "gambling resurrection," meaning the savings and loans knew the federal government would bail them out if they failed, so they took on risky investments in the hope of success (Pontell, 2005).

- Financial Services Modernization Act of 1999

This Act was enacted in 1999 and is also referred to as the Gramm-Leach-Bliley Act for its authors. It repealed the Glass-Steagall Act, allowing financial institutions to integrate functions. The most significant aspect of this Act is that it allowed financial holding companies to be established within financial institutions. This enabled large financial institution to spread their risk over several subsidiaries. It opened the door for investing in the subprime-mortgage derivatives that were the primary cause of the financial collapse. More simply, it allowed investment banks and commercial-retail banks to merge their practices.

- Sarbanes-Oxley Act of 2002

    The Sarbanes-Oxley Act of 2002 is also known as the Public Company Accounting Reform and Investor Protection Act in the Senate, and the Corporate and Auditing Accountability and Responsibility Act in the House of Representatives. It was enacted in reaction primarily to the illegal actions of Enron, and Arthur Andersen accounting failure of the Enron audits. Enron (2001, December 2) and WorldCom (2002, July 19) filed for bankruptcy. In both cases, the companies used improper accounting to cover up losses that amounted to billions of dollars. Congress reacted to Enron, WorldCom, and Arthur Andersen's (2002) failure with Sarbanes-Oxley (2002, July 30) to require integrity in public corporations and accounting practices.

- Credit Rating Agency Reform Act of 2006

    Prior to the financial crisis, Congress had established the Credit Rating Reform Act. This Act required the SEC to establish guidelines for the ratings agencies so that their ratings have validity. The problem with the ratings agencies is that it is the companies they rate who pay a fee to be rated, to the ratings agencies: a conflict of interest. The ratings agencies failed to give honest ratings prior to the financial collapse, contributing to a false sense of security among investors. With the 2006 Act, ratings agencies are required to report on marketing practices, to disclose rating methodologies and honest disclosure of performance statistics. More simply they are required to provide credible reports and to be forthright about the relationship with the companies they rate. This was enacted prior to the financial crisis, yet ratings agencies still failed to provide credible ratings of mortgage-backed securities.

- Fraud Enforcement Recovery Act of 2009

    This Act was in response to the many frauds, specifically mortgage frauds, and the major Ponzi schemes that had taken place. The Bernard Madoff and Allen Stanford schemes took in billions from victims, leaving the impression that regulations were ineffective and the federal agencies were not fulfilling their responsibilities. This Act provided federal agencies with more legal tools and funding for staffing to aggressively investigate financial crimes. This Act made it a federal crime to overvalue real estate property. It redefined the term "financial institution" to include mortgage businesses.

- Dodd-Frank Wall Street Reform and Consumer Act, also known as the Financial Stability Act of 2010. This Act echoes Minsky's theory of financial instability in its name. The Dodd-Frank Act is in response to the financial collapse after a boom economy, resulting in government intervention. This Act ushered in a new era of a wide range of regulations affecting all aspects of financial markets and banking industries. The Act itself is 2,300 pages, containing 400 complex financial industry rules in response to the financial crisis. To note just a few:

1   There are greater reporting requirements of asset-backed securities. Securitizers are required to perform due diligence and provide a report to investors.
2   The Act establishes the Financial Stability Oversight Council, which has the responsibility of accountability within the financial industry and to identify threats to financial industries.
3   The Volcker rule restricts banks and holding companies from certain activities related to proprietary funds, hedge funds, and covered funds and equity funds. Banking holding companies cannot participate in proprietary trading and cannot own or be in partnership with hedge funds.
4   Limits on proprietary trading means that bank holding companies cannot be the principal of a company that trades in securities, derivatives, or commodities.
5   Ratings agencies are required to submit reports to the SEC, including the methodologies and data that are used to determine ratings. Each agency must have internal controls and a separation between marketing and ratings functions. These agencies must have board members who are independent, two of which must be users of ratings agencies ratings. The members should not solely come from the companies being rated.
6   Allowing the SEC and CFTC to provide financial rewards to whistleblowers.

Table 11.1 allows us to compare historical, political, and economic events in relationship to financial legislation. The Great Depression lasted for approximately ten years. The result was significant legislation affecting the financial and banking industries.

Conclusion

In conclusion, throughout the decades, since 1872, frauds and swindles have forced Congress to take legislative actions. Some activities may not have been illegal prior to the Securities Act of 1933, but the Great Depression made it clear that laws and regulations were necessary. When some of those legislative Acts put in place to protect investors and the economy were removed, we saw the housing bubble and then the financial

Table 11.1 Table of Financial Events in History and Legislation

Financial/Historical Event	Year	Legislation
	1872	Mail Fraud Act of 1872
Panic of 1907	1906–1907	
Post-World War I	1918–1919	
Great Depression	1929–1939	
	1929	Uniform Sale of Securities Act
	1933	Glass-Steagall Banking Act of 1933
	1933	Securities Act of 1933
	1934	Securities Exchange Act of 1934
	1936	Commodities Exchange Act
	1938	Maloney Act
	1939	Trust Indenture Act of 1939
	1940	Investment Company Act
Post-World War II	1945	
	1950	Federal Deposit Insurance Act of 1950
	1952	Wire Fraud Act
Post-Korean War	1953–1954	
	1956	Uniform Securities Act
Recession	1960–1961	
	1964	Amendments to the 1934 Securities Exchange Act
Recession	1969–1970	
	1970	Securities Investor Protection Act
OPEC oil embargo	1973–1975	
	1974	Commodities Futures Exchange Act
	1977	Community Reinvestment Act
Iranian oil embargo	1980–1982	
	1983	Insider Trading Sanctions Act
	1990	Market Reform Act
Savings and loan crisis	1990–1991	
	1991	Federal Deposit Improvement Act
	1999	Financial Services Reform/Gramm-Leach-Bliley Act
Tech-wreck/Y2K	2000–2002	
	2002	Sarbanes-Oxley Act
	2006	Credit Rating Agency Reform Act
Financial crisis	2007–2010	
	2009	Fraud Enforcement Recovery Act
	2010	Dodd-Frank Act

crisis. Eventually, perpetrators find new ways to commit frauds. As new technology develops, especially electronically, new methods are available for fraud. The legislators and regulators are always behind; they cannot take action until it is clear there is a problem. Cryptocurrencies were just beginning at the time the Dodd-Frank was being written and passed. As this is written, we are in the fourth month of the COVID-19 pandemic. The FBI is predicting a rise in cryptocurrency frauds as a result of COVID-19, as well as overall frauds based on COVID-19 (FBI, 2020, April 13). The legislative actions will always follow the trends; it is impossible to predict what frauds will occur based on technology. Just as Minsky predicted, there will be economic failures; then the government must step in.

Notes

1 This information is standard in all SEC and CFTC complaints.
2 Administrative law judges are appointed pursuant to the Administrative Procedures Act Public law 404-79th Congress, section 11, authority granted in sections 7 and 8.
3 Some proceedings are held in US District Courts; others are held in federal offices.
4 Banking Act of 1933, Public law 73-66 73rd Congress 1933: "To provide for the safer and more effective use of the assets of banks, to regulate interbank control, to prevent the undue diversion of funds into speculative operations, and for other purposes."

References

Adler, J. (2016, December 28). Are the SEC's administrative law judges unconstitutional? *The Washington Post.*

Antitrust Consent Reform Act of 1995 H.R. 1528 104th Congress.

Bandimere, David v. United States Securities and Exchange Commission United States Court of Appeal for the Tenth Circuit (2016, December 27). Chttps://www.sec.gov/news/speech/clayton-keynote-mid-atlantic-regional-conference-2019

Commodities Futures Trading Commission Enforcement Manual, (2020, May 20).

Commodities Futures Trading Commission Civil Monetary Penalty Guidance. Memorandum, (2020, May 20).

Congressional Research Service, (2019, February 11). Mail and wire fraud: A brief overview of federal criminal law.

Credit Rating Agency Reform Act of 2006 109th Congress.

Delaware Title 30 State Taxes, Income, Inheritance and Estate taxes Chapter 19 Corporate income tax. Retrieved on July 14, 2019 from: https://delcode.delaware.gov/title30/c019/index.shtml.

Dodd-Frank Wall Street Reform and Consumer Act also known as: The Financial Stability Act of 2010 111th Congress.

Executive Order No. 13843. (2018). Excepting administrative law judges from competitive service. *Federal Register* Vol.73 No.135.

Financial Crisis Inquiry Commission. (2011). *The Financial Crisis Inquiry Report; Final Report of the National Commission on the Causes of the Financial and Economic Crisis in the United States.* Washington, DC, Government Printing Office.

Frasca, C., (1931). *Stock swindlers and their methods.* New York, NY, Charles Frasca Publisher.

Fraud Enforcement and Recovery Act of 2009 111th Congress.

Garner, B. (ed) (2009). *Black's law dictionary*. St. Paul, MN, Thomson Reuters.

Hertz Corp. v. Friend United States Supreme Court 559 U.S. 77 (2010).

Investment Advisers Act of 1940 76th Congress.

Lucia Raymond v. Securities and Exchange Commission, United States Supreme Court, 138 S. Ct. 2044 (2018)

Markopolos, H. and Fisher, D. (2010). *No one would listen: A true financial thriller*. Hoboken NJ, NJ, John Wiley and Sons.

McDonald, R. Esq. and Ploeger, M. Esq. (2011). Bankruptcy clawbacks: The Ponzi scheme presumption and valuation. *Bankruptcy and Insolvency Insights*.

Minsky, H. (1982). *Can it happen again; essays on instability and finance*. Armonk, NY, M.E. Sharpe.

Phelps, K.B. and Rhodes, S. (2012). *The Ponzi book: A legal resource for unraveling Ponzi schemes*. New Providence, NJ, Lexis Nexis.

Racketeering Influenced Corrupt Organization (RICO) §§1961-1968 of the Organized Crime Control Act of 1970.

Sarbanes-Oxley Act 107th Congress (2002, July 24).

Securities and Exchange Commission. Division of Law Enforcement, (2017, November 28). Enforcement Manual.

Securities and Exchange Commission in the Matter of Joe Lawler, (2017, March 6). Motion for Summary Disposition.

Securities and Exchange Commission v. David F. Bandimere United States Supreme Court 17-475 (2017, September 29).

Stanford, Robert Allen v. U.S.A. Petition for a Writ of Certiorari. United States Supreme Court 15-1490 (2016, October 28).

State of Utah, White Collar Crime Offender Registry. Retrieved from: https://www.utfraud.com/Home/Registry, Retrieved on November 29, 2019.

Utah State Administrative Code Rule R105-3.

Utah State Code of Criminal Procedure Title 77.

United States Code Title 12 Banks and Banking.

United States Code Title 18 Part I Chapter 63 Mail Fraud and other Fraud Offenses, §§1341-1351; Chapter 47 1001-1040 Frauds and False Statements.

United States Code Title 18 Chapter 96 1961-1968. Racketeer Influenced Corrupt Organizations.

United States Constitution Amendment VI.

United States Constitution Article II § 2.

United States Sentencing Commission, (2015). Annual Reports and Source books.

United States v. Amini et al. (2013, April 18) Superseding bill of indictment.

United States v. Bernard Madoff (2009, March 12) Guilty plea transcript.

United States v. Claud R. Koerber aka Rick Koerber (2017, January 18) Indictment.

United States v. Drew Sharreff-El, et al. (2011, July 21) Indictment.

United States v. Robert Allen Stanford, Court of Appeals for the Fifth Circuit 12-20411 (2015, October 29).

Chapter 12

Significant and Unique Ponzi Schemes in History

There have been many scams and scandals that have been highlighted in the general media and that have found their way into the history books. The cases discussed here are but a few. Prior to Charles Ponzi, in 1920, these types of frauds were simply called "swindles" or "taking from Peter to pay Paul." The term "Ponzi" was not yet used, so these types of frauds are not easily found in earlier legal documents. Now, 100 years after Charles Ponzi's scheme, the specific type of fraudulent scheme where the funds of later investors are used to pay the interest and principal to earlier investors is specifically called a Ponzi scheme. The following cases were chosen for the availability of information and the time period that the scheme had taken place, with an effort to find documentation of at least one scheme per decade. In the decades of the 1940s and the 1950s there were few Ponzi schemes showing up in the major media. It is likely that the war was bigger news.

The first case using the term "Ponzi" appeared in the 1944 SEC annual report. Dewitt T. Simpson and his co-conspirators were convicted in 1943 in the case involving industrial loans. Throughout the 1940s, a second case was based on loans, two others were based on mining and another on cigarettes and peanut vending machines. In the time period during and immediately after WWII, there were relatively few schemes simply because discretionary income was less available to much of the population. The war was a time of rationing and war bonds; there was not much in the way of discretionary income for investing. What excess income there may have been probably would have gone to purchase war bonds. Before WWII, the country was still recovering from the Great Depression, entering the war triggered the financial rebound from the Great Depression. There were Ponzi schemes, but they may not have been referred to as Ponzi schemes, making it difficult to find them in court documents and general media. The SEC annual reports for the 1950s showed one scheme based in loans, one on grains, one using promissory notes and another based on insurance. Federal agencies have few documents available through websites for cases that took place before 1973.[1]

The cases prior to 1973 in this study were found in SEC online archives. Hard copies of documents are stored through federal archive sites, making searching for them and through them impractical.

Efforts to access some documents from twentieth-century decades through the Freedom of Information Act (FOIA) process were generally met with patience on the part of SEC employees. At times, accessing the documents was quite a challenge in that the documents were stored in hard copy in file boxes in large storage rooms, not easily retrieved. Prior to the Public Access Court Electronic Records (PACER) system, accessing federal court documents was a costly and time-consuming effort. Federal websites have improved throughout this nine-year research process, enabling access to more cases and documents. It is the electronic access to federal documents that has enabled this research.

It would be ideal to find enough information to look at economic trends and Ponzi schemes for the past 150 years, but the information is not consistently available. Instead, this historical analysis using available case studies looks at the schemes that are known, qualitatively, to discuss the economic conditions at the time period of each scheme and the nature of the fraud committed. The following cases that are discussed herein were outstanding in the media, providing information about the cases. These cases are by no means the only cases, just those available for study because they are well known and in the press. Most cases have at least one book published on them, if not several books. Later cases are discussed herein because they are unique in some way, not the sort of thing one would expect to be a basis for a Ponzi scheme, such as a worm farm.

Most of the securities laws now in place were enacted in 1933 and 1934, primarily in response to the Great Depression, with later amendments. Prior to these Acts, most states had "blue sky laws," enacted in the early decades of the twentieth century. These laws were titled as such because of the intent to keep the unscrupulous from selling investors all but the blue sky; confidence scheme perpetrators were quite willing to sell anything, with no laws preventing them from doing so. Before the Great Depression of 1929, laissez-faire economic principles were the norm (Keller, 1988). It was not yet evident that there was a need for strong federal securities regulation. Before the Great Depression it was thought that securities regulation was a state-level law matter. The collapse of the stock market in 1929, combined with a few Ponzi schemes and other types of financial frauds, made it clear that Congress had to establish federal securities laws. Hence, we now have the Securities Act of 1933 and the Securities Exchange Act of 1934, which established the regulations and the Securities and Exchange Commission, a federal regulatory agency.

The methods used to carry out Ponzi schemes have adapted as technology changes, and in relation to economic and political events occurring throughout time. The following Ponzi scheme cases discuss the nature of the fraud, as well as the economic and technological conditions of the time period of each scheme. Earlier Ponzi schemes did not last long, generally less than a year. These are the Ponzi schemes that are known; there are undoubtedly many more that were not covered in the press.

Economic, political, and technological circumstances play a part in the schemes, such as the OPEC oil embargo in the 1980s, and technological advancements in the 1990s. Peggy Stines' scheme in the 1980s was based on the silver used in processing photography film. Now, with digital photography, the scheme might be based in home printing equipment. We did not see major regulatory changes until there were massive financial declines affecting the entire nation's economy such as the Great Depression of 1929 and the financial crisis/Great Recession of 2007. Just as technology has influenced recent schemes being based in cryptocurrency and Uber, earlier schemes were also based on the technology of the day. The following schemes are discussed with emphasis on the economics of the time, if it is relevant, and the technology that related to the fraud. The economic aspect is discussed because people only have discretionary funds for investing during positive economic trends and because it is indicative of boom economies illustrating Hyman Minsky's theory of financial instability (1982). Second, the discussion of technology is a result of information that has come out with this study: that the manner and means of the fraud are a product of, or influenced by, the technologies of the day.

Significant Ponzi Schemes in History

Sarah Howe 1880 Ladies Deposit Company

During the latter part of the nineteenth century women were basically seen as fragile, gullible, and not capable of handling their own financial affairs. Women were perceived as likely to be a victim of fraud, not a perpetrator of fraud. It was in 1869 that the women's suffrage movement formed organizations to begin to fight for the right of women to vote. The Civil War had just taken place between 1861 and 1865. During the war, women, as they had throughout history, took on the work of the men who had left for war. Women found they could manage their finances and do the physical labor of the men. In the post–Civil war reconstruction period, the economy in the North was growing; women had their own money and wanted to manage it themselves.

In 1878 Sarah Howe established the *Ladies Deposit Company* in Boston. This was a bank run by women, for women depositors. This bank guaranteed women 80 percent interest per year (Robb, 2012). This was an attractive opportunity for women who generally worked as domestic servants, seamstresses, and school teachers. Howe's scheme was an affinity-fraud in that it sought only women as investors and was run by a woman. Howe accepted funds only from single women; those who were widows and spinsters were ideal targets. The bank attracted women who wanted to be self-sufficient. As with all Ponzi schemes, Howe did not actually invest the money given to her in interest paying loans or other businesses; instead, she provided interest payments by paying earlier investors with later investors' funds. The general sentiment of the times was that the business would fail, not because it was thought to be a fraud but because women were thought to be intellectually incapable of running a financial institution (Robb, 2012, p. 448).

In this time period (late 1800s), women were thought to be unsophisticated in the arena of financial matters and incapable of managing their own money. Women had little access to education that imparted financial knowledge and competency. As is typical in Ponzi schemes, the most vulnerable are preyed upon: in this case women who were widowed or spinsters and otherwise single, with no male protector to oversee their finances. When Howe's scheme collapsed in 1880, more than 800 women lost approximately $250,000 (Robb, 2012, p. 447). There may have been more victims who may have been too ashamed to come forward, revealing their naiveté and victimization (Robb, 2012).

Howe was sentenced to three years in prison. When Howe was released in 1884 she started another bank on the same principles, yet another Ponzi scheme. Two years later this scheme also collapsed, but this time she disappeared and was not tried or convicted again. She died five years later, a pauper (Robb, 2012, p. 455).

Ulysses S. Grant and Ferdinand Ward 1884

Ferdinand Ward was the son of a Protestant pastor and missionary. His scheme took place in the early 1880s. He had befriended the son of former President Ulysses S. Grant, eventually establishing a business partnership with former President Grant himself (President 1869–1877). This business venture collapsed in 1884, leaving Grant virtually broke.

Grant and his son returned to New York City in 1881. Buck Grant, former President Grant's son, convinced his father to partner in an investment firm with his friend Ferdinand Ward. The company was called Grant & Ward, Bankers and Brokers. The Grants trusted Ward.

Ward had experience on Wall Street, having worked there in the New York Produce Exchange. Ward eventually worked his way into stock and bond markets. The method of the scheme was legitimate investing, where the investors would buy stocks that were then used as collateral for loans to buy more stocks. Ward borrowed against his clients' accounts. This is paramount to using other people's property as collateral for a loan. In the end clients were paid with later clients' contributions. Whether this scheme was an intentional fraud or whether it was a legitimate business that failed, thus becoming a Ponzi scheme, cannot be determined. But it bears similarity to those schemes that failed during the 2007 financial crisis.

Civil War had taken place from 1861 to 1865. The Transcontinental Railroad had been completed in 1869. There had been a financial panic in 1873, during Grant's term as president. During this time, the New York Stock Exchange was closed for ten days. This panic was the precursor to the depression between 1873 and 1879. This depression was said to be caused by the bankruptcy of Jay Cooke and Co., a banking entity that backed railroads, in 1873. The stock market had plunged in 1879 and then began to rebound in 1880. The stock's values began to rise in 1881; shortly thereafter Ward convinced the Grants to become partners. In 1883, the stock market began a decline; by 1884 there was again a market panic. In the end, the Grants had lost everything. Ward had used the Grants for their name and connections (Ward, 2013).

William Miller and the Franklin Syndicate 1899

In 1899 William Miller established the *Franklin Syndicate*, initially running it out of his candy store in Brooklyn. At first, he worked with a few people he knew in his Bible study class, promising them 10 percent per week or 520 percent per year. This business entity was incorporated, but there was no board of directors or stated type of business. This scheme was an intentional Ponzi scheme with no indication of a proposed or alleged investment mechanism. As with all Ponzi schemes, Miller gladly paid early investors their promised interest and returned the principal to any investor who requested it. Prompt payment built the trust needed to make the scheme work. He started his scheme with people he knew in his church group, making it initially a faith-based affinity-fraud. Once word got out, the scheme expanded to anyone willing to invest. Miller's scheme lasted only a year. Miller was a young man, only 21, when he started his scheme. Miller had a partner who was a professional con-artist, named "Schlessinger." Schlessinger was smart enough to abscond with his share, disappearing to Europe, leaving Miller with the full financial responsibility. Miller received a ten-year sentence that was commuted to five years (Oltmann, 2014). The economics of the times were comparatively good; not quite as good as the boom economy prior to the financial crisis of 2007, but good. Many people were immigrating to the United States; agriculture was increasing; the United States was a very inviting place with economic opportunities.

Charles Ponzi 1920

The term we now use for the specific type of fraud being studied herein comes from Charles Ponzi and his 1920 fraud scheme. This form of fraud was termed a *swindle* at that time. Since that time, this type of fraud scheme is now called a Ponzi scheme. Ponzi's scheme lasted for only about six months. His scheme was discovered and exposed by journalist William McMasters. The memoir of McMaster's interactions with Charles Ponzi is now a manuscript archived at John Jay College of Criminal Justice, City University of New York.[2]

William Henry McMasters was a journalist working independently, initially hired as a press agent for Charles Ponzi. He had taken notes on his experiences with Charles Ponzi throughout a three-week period in 1920. Within a few hours of talking with Charles Ponzi, McMasters quickly knew that what Ponzi said he was doing was impossible. McMasters kept the discussions going with Ponzi, which affirmed his suspicions that Ponzi was carrying out a fraud. McMasters took his suspicions to the local district attorney as well as the state attorney general. In the manuscript, McMasters talks about Charles Ponzi having a phobia about money, stating that "no sane person would do what he is doing" (McMasters, pp. 145–146). McMasters thought that Ponzi was mentally ill, because Ponzi did not seem to grasp that what he was doing was wrong, and that Ponzi had an obsession with money (McMasters, 1962). McMasters wrote the memoir beginning in the 1920s, but finished just before his death in 1962.

Charles Ponzi's scheme lasted a few months, less than one year. His scheme promised a 50 percent profit in 45 days. The basis of the scheme was foreign stamps. He told people the profits were made by the value differences in foreign stamps, similar to the foreign currency markets. However, Ponzi did not purchase even one foreign stamp; his scheme was an intentional fraud from the onset. Many of Ponzi's victims were other Italians, initially making this scheme also an affinity-fraud, but eventually expanding to anyone. Ponzi's scheme primarily took place in the Boston area, eventually moving to New York and New Jersey.

Charles Ponzi had previous convictions for which he served prison terms. Ponzi had been imprisoned in Canada for forging a check. After Ponzi was released, he helped some Italian immigrants come into the United States from Canada, illegally. He was caught smuggling undocumented people into the country. The immigrants told the truth about what was happening and they were freed. Ponzi lied and said he was just helping a friend and was sentenced to yet another prison sentence in the United States. Once he served the federal sentence in Atlanta, he made his way to Boston, where he began his Ponzi scheme in 1920.

When World War I began, the United States was in a recession. The war was being fought in Europe; Europeans were buying their supplies for the war from the United States. This caused a financial boom between 1914 and 1918 in the United States, until it entered the war in 1917 (National Bureau of Economic Research). In 1919, the economic conditions in the

United States were "healthy," an environment that allowed people discretionary funds, enabling them to make investments (Frasca, 1931, p. 9). The United States established "Liberty bonds," which were war bonds in support of the war effort (McMasters, 1962; Ponzi, 2009; Zuckoff, 2006).

Leo Koretz 1921–1923

The first automobiles began to be available in 1908. As ownership of vehicles became more common, there was a need for petroleum products. The early 1920s brought the first oil-based Ponzi scheme: Leo Koretz seized the opportunity. His $2 million scheme purported to be based in land he allegedly owned in Panama. At the time, the Panama Canal was being constructed, Koretz convinced his clients that they were investing in Panamanian oil wells. Koretz's scheme began to fail in the end of 1923. As his scheme began to fail, he began doling out cash to family members, telling them not to put it into bank accounts. One investor had gone down to Panama to see the oil fields that Koretz had touted to his investor-victims. There were none to be found. The land on Koretz's fraudulent surveyor's map belonged to someone else, who knew nothing of Leo Koretz. The intentional scheme was exposed. Koretz received a prison sentence of six years; he died within two months from the complications of diabetes (Jobb, 2015).

From 1919 until 1923, "oil and mining stocks were at their highest boom," said Charles Frasca in his book *Stock swindlers and their methods* (Frasca, 1931, p. 108). During this period of time automobiles were becoming commonplace, creating a demand for petroleum products. With any new technology, the fraud perpetrators were quick to follow. This all contributed to the financial boom of this time period and also contributed to many frauds based on oil and mining.

Ivar Kreuger 1930

Ivar Kreuger developed a business producing matches in the early part of the twentieth century. The economics of the time were good when Krueger came to the United States from Sweden, in 1922, just after WWI. The country was undergoing an economic boom that is known as the Roaring Twenties. Kreuger had come to the United States to make money; the economy was booming at that time.

Matches were still a staple in the early part of the twentieth century. Krueger developed match factories throughout Europe and the United States; he was the "match king." Krueger wanted a world monopoly on match production. While Krueger had several legitimate businesses throughout Europe and the United States, he was heavily in debt and not capable of paying his expenses. He devised a scheme to bring in funds by purporting to be a financier to Europe's governments using a method of: "convertible gold debentures" based on a 20-year maturation with a 6.5 percent interest rate paid at maturity, technically what is known as a bond (Portnoy, p. 42). The "convertible" part meant the bonds could be exchanged for shares. However, rather than the funds being used to fund loans to European governments as investors and banks were told, the funds were used to pay off previous debts. Kreuger's scheme was a business-failure scheme of the largest magnitude, international in scope. Kreuger had cooked his many sets of books, many times, in order to give the appearance of solvency.

The stock market crashed in 1929, putting an end to the Roaring Twenties. By 1930, Kreuger was having financial difficulties and falsifying the profits. Kreuger was also neglecting to report liabilities in his financial reporting. When he realized his difficulties, he had a printer in Europe print counterfeit Italian treasury bills. Krueger had begun moving around shares from his European companies in different countries; he was shuffling the money between companies (Portnoy, 2009). In 1933, when Kreuger's empire was clearly collapsing and he was about to be found out, he committed suicide.

Robert Trippet et al. and Home-Stake Oil 1954–1972

Prior to Madoff and after Charles Ponzi, one of the more known Ponzi schemes was *Home-Stake Oil* (MClintick, 1977). Trippet began his scheme about 1954; by 1972 he had taken $140 million (McClintick, 1977, p. 301). The *Home-Stake* scheme was based on oil-well drilling securities and was an intentional fraud. This scheme purported to be using forced water or steam below the earth's surface to bring up oil, now known as fracking. Trippet's victims were primarily America's rich and famous, bankers, and prominent politicians such as Senator Jacob Javits and several stars: Jack Benny, Liza Minelli, Barbara Streisand, Andy Williams, Bob Dylan; these were the same types of victims as in Bernard Madoff's scheme (McClintick, 1977, 305–306; NY Times AP, 1975, January 15). Trippet's victims were many of the most well-known celebrities of the time period. Trippet took investors to see oil fields that may or may not have been his. He showed investors painted pipelines that investors were told were his oil pipelines but were actually water pipes used for agriculture on someone else's land (McClintick, 1977, p. 130). The SEC permanently enjoined *Home-Stake* companies in 1970 (SEC, 1971, April 28). This did not stop the Ponzi scheme. In 1977, Trippet and five of his twelve co-conspirators pleaded no contest to federal criminal charges and received one-day sentences with one to three years' probation (McClintick, 1977, p. 293). Criminal charges were dropped on the remaining seven; however, they and several others received only civil charges (McClintick, 1977, p. 294).

The political and economic conditions of the time would have enhanced the attractiveness of an oil-based investment scheme. In 1973,
there was an oil embargo instituted by the Organization of the Petroleum
Exporting Countries (OPEC). The Yom Kippur War of 1973 had given
rise to the OPEC countries to reject selling oil to the United States because it had sided with Israel.

James Donahue Hedged Investments
Associates and Broker Services 1980s

Donahue began his investment firm, *Hedged Investments*, in the late
1970s. He invested in stock options and experienced massive losses. He
falsely informed his investors that there were profits. Investors were allowed to withdraw from their accounts assuming that there were actual
profits earned. The funds were actually the contributions of new investors. His intentional fraud scheme began in 1984 and continued until it
collapsed in 1990. Donahue was an unregistered investment adviser and
a broker-dealer. Donahue's scheme took in $316 million. This scheme
would be classified as a false-brokerage, in that he was not properly registered with the SEC but still carried out the practices of an investment
adviser (SEC, 1991, September 6). This scheme was going on during the
savings and loan crisis. At the time investors were taking their funds
from savings accounts and putting the funds into higher-interest money
market funds. It is not known if Donahue marketed his financial entity
as a money market account. Money market accounts were the newest,
trendiest investment tool of the time, everyone wanted in one.

Peggy D. Stines 1980s

Peggy Stines began a Ponzi scheme in 1981 that continued until 1984.
This scheme was based on the extraction of silver from photograph
processing. Stines had no actual silver extraction business entity; her
fraudulent scheme was intentional. She took advantage of more than
a thousand victims, taking in more than $17 million. Peggy Stines re-
ceived a sentence of 99 years, the highest sentence of any female involved in a Ponzi scheme; she was approximately 44 years old when
sentenced (SEC, 1984, December 26). Peggy was released after serving
ten years of her 99-year sentence; her husband Donald served only four
years. Peggy was the primary; her husband was charged with tax evasion and contempt for refusing to divulge where the money had been
secreted (SEC, 1984, November 20). Stines' scheme was perpetrated
using the technology of the times. The scheme was not related to the
economic current of the time period.

A Note on the 1990s

Prior to the 1990s, the stock market crash of 1987 – Black Monday – occurred on October 19, 1987. The crash lasted only a few months and was preceded by a bull market throughout 1987. There was a period featuring inflation, a high rate of growth, corporate mergers, and insider trading; insider trading manipulated the market. A panic among institutional investment managers caused a mass sell-off of securities. The Federal Reserve responded by making funds available to banks. In response, the largest banks doubled their lending to securities investment institutions. This set a precedent for future financial crises. The 1987 crash was short-lived and of the Ponzi schemes in existence at the time,[3] few collapsed but instead all continued to function well into the 1990s; some did not fail until the financial crisis of 2007.

The Ponzi schemes in the 1990s were frequently technology-based frauds. This was an era before cell phones were common place; there were many schemes that revolved around pay phones. The Department of Justice ended the AT&T monopoly in the 1980s. In the early 1990s mobile phones were in the beginning of use, and were very large car phones by comparison to today's cell phones. The era of non-phone company ownership of pay phones was short-lived, but while it existed there were several Ponzi schemes based in pay phones. In these schemes, investors thought they were investing in ownership of pay phones and that they would receive a percentage of the revenues paid into the phones by users. Similar to most Ponzi schemes, there was no actual purchase of pay phones; the funds were only used for Ponzi payments to other investors. As cell phones became quite common in the twenty-first century, pay phones became obsolete. As technology changes the methods of the Ponzi perpetrators adapt.

The 1990s ushered in the dot-com era and the great hype before Y2K. A few successful dot-coms of the 1990s were: Google began in 1996; Amazon began in 1994; eBay began in 1995. But there were many start-ups and many failures, some were legitimate business ventures, some were scams. Many of the emerging technologies were overvalued; eventually the stock values declined, leading to the tech-wreck. Y2K was the concern that at midnight in the year 2000, there would be massive technological failures because of computer programming qualities. The world changed from the twentieth century to the twenty-first century with a snore; the worries were unfounded.

Patrick Bennett 1990s

Prior to Bernard Madoff's scheme, Patrick Bennett's scheme was the biggest in history. His scheme took place from 1990 to 1996 in the Syracuse region of New York State. He is on record for taking $570 million in his leasing Ponzi scheme. The Bennett family ran a legitimate business for many decades; the family business was doing well. This scheme is classified as an intentional scheme. Bennett had taken over certain aspects of the family business and did not let his parents know what he was doing. The basis for his scheme was business equipment leasing. He told investors they were buying office equipment and then receiving a portion of the interest in the leasing of the equipment. However, he had several investors pay for the same piece of equipment, meaning each piece was purchased several times over and the interest paid to the investors were Ponzi payments (SEC v. The Bennett Funding Group et al., 1996, April 15).

There was a recession in the early 1990s that lasted until March 1991. The 1990s were the beginning of the technology boom that fostered a healthy economy for most of the 1990s decade. Patrick Bennett was sentenced to 22 years; his brother Michael received three years' probation.

Allen Stanford 2009

Robert Allen Stanford (herein: Stanford) began his many businesses on the Island of Montserrat in 1985 in the British West Indies, and then moved to Antigua in 1990, establishing the *Stanford International Bank Ltd. (SIBL)*. Establishing his businesses offshore enabled Stanford to avoid many American banking laws that would have brought him to the attention of US authorities sooner.

Stanford had at least 130 business entities, some of which may have been legitimate businesses. The primary business was the sale of securities of the *Stanford International Bank Ltd.*, his international bank. Investors bought securities or certificates of deposit that were to be investments in the bank. The interest paid on these securities and certificates of deposit issued for *SIBL* were Ponzi payments paid to early investors from the funds received from later investors. Stanford's scheme was intentional; however, he appealed his case, believing he did nothing wrong and that his bank and other businesses would have survived had authorities not closed his businesses.

Stanford had registered with the SEC as an investment adviser in 1995 (Kotz, 2014). At the time Allen Stanford was sentenced in 2012, he had at least 29 accounts in other countries. Authorities have tried to reclaim the money from these accounts in other countries (DOJ, June 14, 2012). His scheme included banks in Venezuela and Ecuador; many people in these countries also lost money through placing their funds in his banks. In Antigua, he had his own newspaper so that he could control the press coverage of his activities. He had also owned a cricket team and made sure there was press coverage of his largess.

SEC employee Julie Preuitt knew that Stanford was running a Ponzi scheme as early as 1997. Preuitt tried to convince her superiors of this in 1997, 1998, 2002, and 2004, yet each time the case was turned down for a formal investigation. Stanford used the proof of multiple informal examinations by the SEC with no finding of fault as proof that he was legitimate (Kotz, 2014; SEC OIG, 2010).

David Kotz was the SEC's Inspector General at this time. He investigated the SEC failures in both the Madoff and Stanford cases. In Kotz's Inspector's General report on the failure of the Fort Worth SEC office to investigate Stanford, it was determined that a former head of enforcement, Spencer Barasch, rejected the Stanford case for formal investigation multiple times. After he left the SEC Barasch tried to work for Stanford on several occasions (SEC, 2012, May 24, a.p.). Barasch settled criminal and civil charges that he inappropriately represented Stanford, with the Department of Justice accepting a fine of $50,000 (SEC, 2012, May 24, p.r.).

Kotz found that the Fort Worth SEC office prioritized the quantity of prosecuted cases over quality, meaning the Stanford case would be very time-intensive to bring to action, taking away manpower from bringing a greater quantity of actions in the time it would take to bring down Stanford. Stanford's scheme was offshore and multinational, and he had at least three business entities in the United States; these types of schemes are manpower-intensive to investigate.

On June 19, 2009, Stanford, Laura Pendergast-Holt, Gilbert Lopez, Mark Kuhrt, and Leroy King were federally indicted on charges related to the Ponzi scheme. Pendergast-Holt was convicted and sentenced to three years. Gilbert Lopez and Mark Kuhrt were each sentenced to 20 years in federal prison. James Davis was Stanford's college friend and business partner; he aided authorities in the investigation and was sentenced to five years (DOJ, 2015). Leroy King was the chief financial regulator for Antigua and Barbuda, whose actions enabled Stanford's scheme. King was extradited to the United States to answer to federal charges on November 8, 2019, ten years after Stanford was brought to justice. King pleaded guilty in January 2020. Stanford's scheme is intentional; his business entities and their many practices were knowingly fraudulent.

FBI had an ongoing case involving Stanford. It was thought that Stanford's banks were being used for money laundering operations for other illegal enterprises. Stanford had businesses and branches of his bank on several Caribbean islands as well as in Venezuela. For a time, the SEC deferred to the FBI because of these other money laundering investigations. Once the Madoff scheme came to be public knowledge, the SEC could not afford another embarrassment and brought Stanford to civil action.

Scott Rothstein 2005–2009

Scott Rothstein's $1.2 billion scheme is documented as having taken place from 2005 to 2009 (FBI, 2010, June 9, p.r.). His scheme was operated out of his Florida law firm: Rothstein, Rosenfeldt and Adler. His scheme was based in promissory notes on non-existent loans, which were alleged to support business financing. The Rothstein scheme made use of false online accounts that his victims could access, regularly updated with false information (FBI, 2010, June 9, p.r.). Twenty-two individuals were sentenced in Rothstein's scheme, many of whom were attorneys in his law firm. His firm did practice law, but in the end, the law firm failed because of the Ponzi scheme. This scheme took place during the boom economy of the mid-2000 decade. This scheme is significant not just for the amount of money taken but in the fact that this was a law firm and so many of those convicted were attorneys. Rothstein was convicted of racketeering, money laundering, mail, and wire fraud. This scheme was intentional; it was not a Ponzi scheme out of failed business but in addition to a successful law practice.

Two sources report that Rothstein is in the inmate witness protection program in an undisclosed federal facility (Malkus, 2013; McMahon, 2016). Rothstein does not appear in the Bureau of Prison inmate locator. Allegedly, his cooperation with authorities somehow earned him being in the witness protection program. Both sources report that he had interactions with organized crime. However, after Rothstein's plea agreement he and his wife hid assets, a violation of his plea agreement. His wife Kimberly was sentenced for hiding assets.

Bernard Madoff 1990–2008

At this writing, the Madoff case is the scheme of all schemes. There are at least four movies/documentaries, and at least six books written on Bernard Madoff, his scheme, and family members, as of 2019 (Arvedlund, 2010; Eren, 2017; Henriques 2011; Kirtzman, 2010; Markopolos and Fisher, 2010; Ross, 2009). His scheme began in the early 1990s, to the best knowledge court records could document. Madoff had gone to law school but never finished; his brother Peter was an attorney and is now disbarred. The *Bernard L. Madoff Investment Securities* (*BMIS*) was registered as an investment adviser with the SEC in 2006, but had been an SEC-approved registered brokerage firm since 1960 (FINRA BrokerCheck). Specifically, Madoff told investors that his firm would be investing their funds in securities; however, this was never done. The original amount taken was stated in federal documents as $65 billion with approximately 8,000 victims. At this writing, the final amount taken is considered to be $19 billion. Through clawbacks and disgorgement, some funds have been reclaimed and distributed to the victims; the process is ongoing.

Madoff's business entity was a registered broker-dealer; Bernard Madoff was the primary agent. The entity was formed in 2001, but he had been practicing as an investment adviser for many years prior. Madoff himself had passed the series 63-uniform securities agent exam (1997);

the series 55-limited representative equity trader (2000); and the series 1-registered representative exam (1960). For coding purposes, the business entity was classified as a broker-dealer registered with the SEC; Madoff was a registered broker and investment adviser.

Madoff is Jewish; his victims were primarily Jewish; his scheme is considered an affinity-fraud. The business entity never actually invested the clients' funds. In his sentencing memorandum, he explained that he was not good at trading initially and he thought that he would eventually make up for losses with good trades that never materialized; his was a brokerage-failure scheme. It was not intentionally planned as a Ponzi scheme; it was originally intended as an investment firm. It failed as a result of the financial crisis and was exposed, but the Ponzi scheme began from a financial downturn in the early 1990s. Many feel that his business was fraudulent from at least the 1970s. However, this study relies on what is stated in publicly accessible federal documents.

Madoff's scheme became known in December 2008, through his own admission. His scheme was one of many that were exposed during the financial crisis. Madoff could no longer bring in enough clients to satisfy the guaranteed returns of all of his investors, now victims. It was Bernard Madoff's massive fraud that brought this type of fraud to the forefront of public attention.

Fourwinds

Carlos Uresti was a Texas state senator and an attorney at the time he became involved with *Four Winds Logistics Laredo* and Stanley Bates. Uresti and Stanley Bates carried out their Ponzi scheme while Uresti was in office; his position provided credibility to the business entity. He is now an inmate in the Pollock United States Penitentiary. The manner and means of this Ponzi scheme were based on fracking for oil and gas. Uresti was also held accountable for bribes paid to a Reeves County judge. Uresti clearly had the image of success as a state senator, his status providing the image of success needed to recruit investors (DOJ, 2019, February 12, p.r.; SEC v. Carlos Uresti and Stanley Bates). The scheme was intentional; as an attorney and a legislator, Uresti knew what he was doing was illegal.

Robert Shapiro-Woodbridge

Robert Shapiro had at least 275 LLC entities that were shell companies. This scheme took in at least $1.29 billion from at least 9,000 victim-investors (FBI, 2019, p.r.). Shapiro told investors that the investments were "backed by properties owned by third parties" (DOJ, 2019, August 8, p.r.). What few properties did exist were owned by Shapiro or the shell companies. The *Woodbridge* co-conspirators and employees made use of high-pressure boiler-room tactics. This scheme took place after the Madoff and Stanford cases from at least 2012 to 2017. Shapiro employed at least 130 employees in at least five states. The SEC complaint on this case was filed in 2017; the criminal charges were in 2019. The *Woodbridge* scheme was quite intentional and massive.

The Carpoffs and DC Solar 2011–2018

Jeff and Paulette Carpoff pleaded guilty to their billion-dollar Ponzi scheme in January of 2020 (DOJ, 2020, January 24, p.r.). This scheme was based on manufacturing, leasing, and operating solar-powered mobile generators. This type of investment was made attractive through tax credits for energy-saving solar products. The revenues received from leasers were supposed to be the interest paid to investors. Only a fraction of the mobile generators were actually produced, so the revenues paid to investors were Ponzi payments. There were less than 6,571 of these generators produced, yet investors were told there were 17,600; none of these were found by authorities. Another investment fund managed by the Carpoffs was alleged to have 2,280 generators but only 90 were found (SEC, 2020, January 24, prg. 43). The US Marshals seized 185 vehicles from the Carpoffs' collection, the sale of which netted $8.2 million (U.S. Marshals, 2019, p. 40). The couple also had a private jet valued at $3.9 million and several luxury homes. The Carpoffs had used the funds gained in the Ponzi scheme to purchase a minor league baseball team and to sponsor a NASCAR racecar (IRS, 2020, April 15). The Carpoffs did an excellent job of appearing to be very financially successful; clearly all that glitters is not gold. Jeff Carpoff was licensed as a general and electrical contractor. Federal documents did not indicate that this was a one-time thriving business that failed, but instead a scam from the beginning (SEC, 2020, January 24, prg. 7). This was an intentional Ponzi scheme.

Unique Cases

The manner and means of Ponzi schemes are only limited by the creativity of the perpetrator. They must know something of the alleged investment in order to present a convincing promotion of their scheme. The following cases were unique in that they are not the type of thing one would expect a fraud to be based on.

- Kenneth Dachman owned several business entities titled *Central Sleep* and *Advanced Sleep*; these entities were alleged to supply medical equipment that diagnosed and treated sleep disorders. Dachman also fraudulently claimed that he held a PhD. *Stone Lion* is an entity owned by Scott Wolf that alleged to help start-up companies. Wolf used his company to solicit investors in Dachman's business. Dachman had previous companies that were non-existent sports medicine and rehabilitation (SEC v. Kenneth Dachman et al., 2012).

- One scheme was based on worm farming, that of Robert Dalton. This was a business-failure scheme. The three primaries solicited investors promising more than 250 investor-victims' profits of at least 25 percent. Worm castings are considered an excellent fertilizer; in addition, gardeners like to buy worms to aerate the soil. This was a legitimate business but more than half of funds collected were to bring in new investors and to pay Ponzi payments instead of to run the worm business (SEC, 1999, September 30, l.r.)

- One of the more interesting schemes is the one that was supposed to purchase defaulted pre-World War II German bonds (SEC vs. Integrated Equities., and Jeffrey Weston 2006, prg 1). This case was carried out between 2004 and 2006 in Nevada. The perpetrators must have been very skilled to convince 50 people that there was some value in prewar bonds for a country that lost the war.

- In the same time frame was the scheme of Russell Erxleben who was selling WWI German government gold bearer bonds. Bearer bonds are owned by the holder, not a register owner. This case was 2005–2009 in Texas. Like Weston, it is surprising that he found people willing to invest in the bonds of a government that lost the war, even if they were bearer bonds (FBI, 2014, February 24, p.r.).

- Two separate and unrelated schemes were based on selling event tickets. The first lasted from 2010 to 2016. Ash Narayan's *The Ticket Reserve* allowed ticket buyers to reserve tickets at sports events that were yet to be determined. Investors were investing in the business; the profits were to be made from the ticket sales (SEC v. Narayan, 2018). The second of which is more well known because it is a current one; Four of five perpetrators received criminal sentences. It is the case of *875 Holdings* and *Advanced Entertainment*. This recent case is well known because the perpetrators alleged they were purchasing tickets for high-profile events such as the successful Broadway musical *Hamilton* (SEC v. Joseph Meli et al., 2017). In addition, one of the perpetrators was a high-profile radio personality.

- Another recent case was based on wine. John E. Fox pleaded guilty to running a Ponzi scheme based on European wines. There was actual business of purchasing and selling of wines, but Fox was not able to keep up with what he promised investors and the business turned to a Ponzi scheme. *Premier Cru* wine shop was begun in 1980, but the fraudulent scheme began in the 1990s. In recent years, the wine was never actually purchased. Fox was sentenced to 78 months in 2016 (DOJ, 2016, December 14).

- The Whale Whisperer: when we think we have heard or read it all, there is a new slant on Ponzi schemes that is completely unimaginable. One prime example is that of Paul Gilman, who is also discussed under technology in Chapter 4 on manner and means. Gilman referred to himself as the "Whale Whisperer" (SEC v. Paul Gilman, 2018, p. 4, prg. 12). He is alleged to have made documentaries on whale and dolphin music. Gilman had many technological projects that did not generate income; his was a scheme that began as legitimate businesses that failed, eventually turning into a Ponzi scheme.
- Ronald Rewald was sanctioned by the SEC for a Ponzi scheme that took place in the early 1980s. The company name was *Bishop, Baldwin, Rewald, Dillingham & Wong, Inc.* It was alleged by Rewald that a CIA agent by the name of Cavannaugh used the company as a cover (Wright, 1984, April 26). Media reports from the time claim that Cavannaugh was actually James Bishop, a CIA agent. The media report stated that the CIA acknowledged the business was used as a cover for one agent. Rewald claimed that he was a covert agent for the CIA (Wright, 1984, April 25).[4] Rewald received a sentence of 41 months, and Sunlin Wong received 27 months; there was no further mention of Bishop or Cavannaugh.
- The scheme of Gurudeo Persaud was based on astrology. His company, *White Elephant*, was supposed to be a private equity fund. A private equity fund is a fund made up of accredited investors and institutional investors, differing from hedge funds in that they tend to look for long-term profits. His first investor-victims were friends and family. At the time he was legitimately working for a registered broker-house; he began soliciting their customers for his own investment company. Persaud had series 7 and 66 licenses, and was a certified financial planner; by all appearances he was running a legitimate business, except that his business entity, *White Elephant*, was not registered with the SEC as required. Persaud used astrological principles, meaning he felt that the gravitational pull of planets and the moon affected the emotions of humans, their behavior, and their financial decisions; therefore, he could predict market fluctuations (SEC v. Gurudeo Persaud, 2012, June 25, l.r.; SEC v. Gurudeo Persaud, 2018, June 20). Somehow, he was not able to use astrology to predict that he would receive a criminal sentence of 36 moon cycles, and that both the SEC and FINRA would bar him.
- Hanif Moledina ran a fraudulent coffee bean roasting company. His scheme was based on large contracts to buy coffee beans from growers in South America and then to sell to major coffee corporations in the United States. There were no contracts to buy coffee or to sell coffee. The funds collected that were to be used to buy green beans were instead used for Ponzi payments and Moledina's personal expenses (FBI, 2010, March 5, p.r.).

Latex Gloves

- There were three separate schemes based on latex gloves. One was based on "factoring" of latex gloves manufactured in Malaysia. Factoring is investing in accounts receivable. In the Larry Osaki/ *Wallenbrock* case, there was no actual factoring taking place. This scam was also run through offshore entities in the late 1990s and early 2000s. It was an intentional Ponzi scheme (SEC v. Larry Osaki et al., 2003, August 27, a.p.).
- In another scheme, *SF Capital*/Miguel Salazar, also in the early 2000 decade, also made use of factoring in latex glove manufacturing. It was thought the post-9/11 time frame would require greater latex glove usage. At the time there was fear of biological weapons (the anthrax mailings), hence the assumed need for more latex gloves.
- The third latex glove scheme was alleged to be based in manufacturing and distribution of latex gloves internationally. Deepaul Wannakuwatte told investors that he had contracts with the Veterans' Administration, and that he had a glove manufacturing plant among several businesses (DOJ, 2014, p.r. Wannakuwatte). Previously, Wannakuwatte had owned the Sacramento Capitals tennis team (DOJ, 2014, p.r. Wannakuwatte).

Funeral Arrangement Schemes

- There were two Ponzi schemes based on funeral arrangements. In *the National Prearranged Services Inc.* case, customers paid for funeral services prior to the time of death. This company also sold insurance policies related to the funeral services. This scheme had 97,000 victims in at least 16 states (FBI, 2013, p.r.). The scheme ran approximately 16 years, ending in 2008. When individuals entered into a contract, the funds for the funeral arrangements were supposed to be put into a trust that would make investments. Instead, the actual documents, contracts, and deposits were falsified, including switching what were originally whole-life insurance policies to term policies. It was a very complex scheme that also took advantage of other funeral businesses.
- A more recent scheme, *Financial Visions, Inc.*, was similar in that it was based in insurance policies that would front families' money to pay for funeral expenses and then receive payment once the decedent's insurance policy paid out. The investors were paying into the insurance fund. This scheme was started as a legitimate business that was not able to make profits to pay investors and then became a Ponzi scheme. This scheme was primarily in Colorado (SEC v. Rudden, 2018).

Cattle

There were two schemes based on cattle or livestock. One scheme, *R & K Angus Ranch*, was based on cattle:

- Kevin Asbury had two cattle businesses that promised investors they were investing in cattle that he would then raise and sell, and all would enjoy the profits. Asbury did not purchase the cattle as he had told investors (FBI, 2012, p.r. Asbury). This type of scheme requires knowledge of the business, in this case cattle, in order to present a convincing proposition to attract investors. This case was primarily in Missouri.
- The second cattle-based scheme was in California, and one of three businesses run by Christopher Dougherty. One of the businesses was a cattle and hay broker (SEC v. Christopher Dougherty, 2019, April 26). The other two businesses were a registered investment adviser and a real estate. He did buy and sell some cattle and hay but not enough to make profits, hence the Ponzi payments.

A third cattle-based scheme had come to public light in March 2020; it was the first federal-level scheme Ponzi scheme indicted in South Dakota. It was not brought to trial before January of 2020, and therefore not in the data, but noted here because it is South Dakota's first federal-level scheme on record.

Conclusion

This chapter could have been a book itself. There are a great many more interesting Ponzi schemes that could be discussed. Those included here are a few of the more significant and well-known schemes, with a few unique schemes to conclude the chapter. The takeaway is that a Ponzi scheme can be based on anything investor-victims will invest in, and that in general, technological trends fuel the ideas for the schemes.

Notes

1 Per conversations with PACER employees and federal agency webmasters.
2 *Fraud and Swindles Collection.* [collection of published and unpublished works on subjects relating to fraud and swindles, broadly defined]. Special Collections, Lloyd Sealy Library, John Jay College of Criminal Justice/CUNY, New York City.
3 It is likely there were more schemes but the term "Ponzi" may not have been used. Second, not all federal agency records are available prior to the eGovernment Act, 2002.
4 The newspaper articles are within a "sanitized" copy submitted to the US Department of Justice, April 26, 1984.

References

Arvedlund, E. (2010). *Too good to be true: The rise and fall of Bernie Madoff.* London UK, Penguin Publishing Group

Department of Justice, (2014, March 13). Sacramento businessman indicted for bank fraud. (Wannakuwatte). Press release.

Department of Justice, (2014, May 8). Former Owner of Sacramento Capitals tennis team pleads guilty to 450 million fraud scheme. (Deepaul Wannakuwatte). Press release.

Department of Justice, (2016, December 14). Berkeley wine shop owner sentenced to six and a half years in prison for running a wine Ponzi scheme. (Fox). Press release.

Department of Justice, (2019, August 8). Mastermind of $1.3 billion investment fraud (Ponzi) scheme- One of the largest ever- sentenced to twenty-five years in prison on conspiracy and tax evasion charges. (Shapiro- Woodbridge). Press release.

Department of Justice, (2019, February 12). Former state senator Carlos Uresti sentenced to federal prison for Bribery. Press release.

Department of Justice, (2020, January 24). Top executives plead guilty to participating in a billion dollar Ponzi scheme—The biggest criminal fraud scheme in the history of the Eastern District of California. (Carpoff). Press release.

Eren, C. (2017). *Bernie Madoff and the crisis: The public trial of capitalism.* Stanford, CA, Stanford University Press

Federal Bureau of Investigation, (2010, June 9). Fort Lauderdale attorney sentenced to 50 years in billion-dollar Ponzi scheme. (Rothstein). Press release.

Federal Bureau of Investigation, (2010, March 5). Virginian sentenced to 90 months in $16 million fraud scheme. (Hanif Moledina). Press release.

Federal Bureau of Investigation, (2012, August 23). Former Howard County man sentenced for $88 million cattle fraud schemes. (Asbury). Press release.

Federal Bureau of Investigation, (2013, November 14). *Six defendants sentenced to a total of 36 year in prison in National Prearranged Services case.* (Cassity). Press release.

Federal Bureau of Investigation, (2014, February 24). Russell Erxleben sentenced to 90 months in federal prison for $2 million Ponzi scheme. Press release.

Federal Bureau of Investigation, (2019, August 8). Mastermind of $1.3 billion investment fraud (Ponzi) scheme- one of the largest ever- sentenced to twenty-five years in prison on conspiracy and tax evasion charges. (Shapiro). Press release.

Frasca, C. (1931). *Stock swindlers and their methods.* New York, NY, Charles Frasca Publisher.

Henriques, D. (2011). *The wizard of lies. Bernie Madoff and the death of trust.* New York, NY, Times Books.

Internal Revenue Service, (2020, April 15). Court ordered final forfeiture of over $54 million in connection with billion-dollar Ponzi scheme. (Carpoff). Press release.

Jobb, D. (2015). *Empire of deception: The incredible story of a master swindler who seduced a city and captivated the nation.* Chapel Hill, NC, Algonquin Books of Chapel Hill.

Keller, E. (1988). Introductory comment: A historical introduction to the Securities Act of 1933 and the Securities Exchange Act of 1934. *Ohio State Law Journal* Vol.49 pp. 329–352.

Kirtzman, A. (2010). *Betrayal the life and lies of Bernie Madoff.* New York, NY, Harper Perennial.

Kotz, H.D. (2014). *Why Ponzi schemes work and how to protect to yourself from being defrauded.* New York, NY, Thomson-Reuters/Aspatore.

Mack, S.M. (2012). *The end of normal: A wife's anguish, a widow's new life.* New York, NY, The Penguin Group Plume.

Malkus, C. (2013). *The ultimate Ponzi scheme; The Scott Rothstein story.* Gretna, LA, Pelican Publishing.

Markopolos, H. and Fisher, D. (2010). *No one would listen: A true financial thriller.* Hoboken, NJ, John Wiley and Sons.

McClintick, D. (1977). *Stealing from the rich; The story of the swindle of the century.* New York, NY, M. Evans and Company.

McMahon, P. (2016, March 22). Rothstein associates no longer owe millions to Ponzi victims. *SunSentinel.*

McMasters, W.H. (c1962). *The Story of Ponzi: America's Most Baffling Swindler.* Unpublished manuscript. *Fraud and Swindles Collection.* Special Collections, Lloyd Sealy Library, John Jay College of Criminal Justice/CUNY, New York, NY.

Minsky, H. (1982). *Can "it" happen again? Essays on instability and finance.* Armonk, NY, M.E. Sharpe Inc.

National Bureau of Economic Research. *The Economics of World War I,* Retrieved January 2017. Retrieved from: http://www.nber.org/digest/jan05/w10580.html

New York Times, AP, (n.a.) (1975, January 15). 13 Defendents deny charge of swindling. (Trippet/Home-Stake).

Oltmann, V. (2014). *William "520%" Miller, The Ponzi files.* Fraud Chronicles. com Delaware.

Partnoy, F. (2009). *The match king: Ivar Krueger, the financial genius behind a century of Wall Street scandals.* New York, NY, Public Affairs of the Perseus Books Group.

Ponzi, C. (2009). *The rise of Mr. Ponzi: the long suppressed autobiography of a financial genius.* Austin, TX, Despair Inc.

Robb, G. (2012, December). Depicting a female fraud: Sarah Howe and the Boston Women's Bank. *Nineteenth Century Contexts* Vol.34 No.5 pp. 445–449. New York, NY, Routledge Taylor and Francis Group.

Ross, B. (2009). *The Madoff chronicles: Inside the secret world of Bernie and Ruth.* Glendale, CA, Kingswell.

Securities and Exchange Commission (1971, April 28). Home-Stake Oil program, others enjoined. (Trippet). SEC News Digest 71–83.

Securities and Exchange Commission v. Robert S. Trippet et al. (1974, December 17) SEC News Digest issue 74–243.

Securities and Exchange Commission v. Peggy D. Stines (1984, November 20) News Digest 84–225.

Securities and Exchange Commission v. Peggy D. Stines (1984, December 26) News Digest 84–249.

Securities and Exchange Commission v. James D. Donahue (1991, December 6) SEC News Digest 91–173.

Securities and Exchange Commission v. Bennett Funding Group (1996, April 15) (Patrick Bennett) Complaint.

Securities and Exchange Commission v. Robert J. Dalton, James L. Masini, and George J. Bodlak, (1999, September 30) Litigation release.

Securities and Exchange Commission v. Larry t. Osaki and Van Y. Ichinotsubo (2003, August 27) Administrative proceeding.

Securities and Exchange Commission v. Integrated Equities Inc. and Jeffrey Weston (2006, June 26) Complaint.

Securities and Exchange Commission v. The Bennett Funding Group Inc., Patrick R. Bennett, Bennett management and Development Corporation, Bennett Receivables Corporation and Bennett Receivables Corporation II (2006, July 18) Litigation release.

Securities and Exchange Commission OIG-526, (2010, March 31). Inspector's general report of investigation of the SEC's response to concerns regarding Robert Allen Stanford's alleged Ponzi Scheme.

Securities and Exchange Commission v. Kenneth Dachman, Scott A. Wolf, and Stone Lion Management, Inc. (2012, February 6) Complaint.

Securities and Exchange Commission v. Stanford International Bank, LTD. Stanford Group Company, Stanford Capital Management, LLC, R. Allen Stanford, James M. Davis, and Laura Pendergest-Holt (2009, February 16) Complaint.

Securities and Exchange Commission, (2012, May 24). SEC bars former staffer from practice before commission. (Barasch/Stanford). Press release.

Securities and Exchange Commission v. Spencer C. Barasch (2012, May 24) Administrative proceeding.

Securities and Exchange Commission v. Gurudeo Persaud aka Buddy Persaud (2012, June 20) Complaint.

Securities and Exchange Commission v. Gurudeo Persaud (2012, June 25) Litigation release.

Securities and Exchange Commission v. Joseph Meli, Matthew Harriton, 875 Holdings, LLC, 127 Holdings, LLC, Advance Entertainment, LLC and Advanced Entertainment II LLC. (2017, January 27). Complaint.

Securities and Exchange Commission v. Ash Narayan, the Ticket Reserve Inc. a/k/a Forward market Media, Inc. Richard M. Harmon and John Kaptrosky (2018, January 4) Complaint.

Securities and Exchange Commission v. Paul Gilman (2018, June 4) Complaint.

Securities and Exchange Commission v. Daniel Rudden, Financial Visions Inc., et al. (2018, July 19) Complaint.

Securities and Exchange Commission v. Carlos Uresti and Stanley Bates (2018, September 28) Complaint.

Securities and Exchange Commission v. Christopher Dougherty; C&D Professional Services Inc. dba C&N Wealth Management; JTA Farm Enterprises, LLC; JTA Real Estate Holdings LLC. (2019, April 26) Complaint.

Securities and Exchange Commission v. Jeffrey P. Carpoff and Paulette Carpoff (2020, January 24) 2:20-cv-00180. Complaint.

United States of America v. Robert Allen Stanford et al. (2012, June 14) Closed criminal division cases: court docket number H-09-342.

United States Department of Justice (2012, June 14). *Allen Stanford Sentenced* to 110 years in prison for orchestrating $7 billion investment fraud scheme. Press release. United States Marshals Service FY 2019 Annual Report.

Ward, G. (2013). *A disposition to be rich, Ferdinand Ward the greatest swindler of the gilded age.* New York, NY, Vintage Books Random House.

Wright, W. (1984, April 25). Rewald seeks investors' backing – this time in suit against the CIA. *The Honolulu Advertiser.*

Wright, W. (1984, April 26). CIA Agent who used Rewald firm is a cover identified at meeting. *The Honolulu Advertiser.*

Zuckoff, M. (2006). *Ponzi's scheme: The true story of a financial legend.* New York, NY, Random House.

Conclusion

Concluding Insights

In this concluding chapter, the intent is to provide information for potential investors to educate themselves to recognize red flags and possible frauds, and how to research business entities themselves. This includes understanding how a potential investment's profits are made, how businesses are run, and knowing how to carry out due diligence. The reader should understand that this is not intended to be legal advice; for specific information about securities laws, investors should contact an attorney. This chapter gives an overview of due diligence as it pertains to Ponzi schemes. For a more in-depth discussion of due diligence techniques, Pat Huddleston's book *Vigilant investor* provides a wealth of information (Huddleston, 2012). For those in the legal profession, Kathy Bazoian Phelps and the Honorable Steven Rhodes have provided a significant book on the legal aspects of Ponzi schemes: *The Ponzi book* (Phelps and Rhodes, 2012). Phelps has a second book on carrying out one's own due diligence: *Ponzi-proof your investments* (Phelps, 2013).

One caution to the reader is to be particularly circumspect of investments that cater to the latest trends and newest technologies. As stated earlier, investors want to get in on the newest trends in hope of getting in early to make greater profits. It is expected that soon there will be Ponzi schemes exposed based in COVID-19, and artificial intelligence (AI) exposed. This conjecture is purely based on that there is a massive social and economic need for testing, treatment, and a COVID-19 vaccine, and that AI technologies are the newest in the technology industry, making them attractive investments, with the least information available to determine viability of the business entities.

As this book goes to publish, we are in the COVID-19 outbreak. At this time some jury trials are being postponed because a moratorium has been declared based on COVID-19 being considered a national emergency. Some US District Courts are continuing trials and hearings making use of distancing and teleconferencing. Fraud schemes based on COVID-19 testing and remedies popped up overnight. It is just a matter of time until authorities find someone who has marketed a COVID-19 investment product in research and development, testing equipment, vaccines, or treatment that is a Ponzi scheme. In addition, the virus is causing job loss and economic decline. As the economy declines, we will see many Ponzi schemes exposed, which began prior to COVID-19, as we did during the financial crisis.

For those affiliated with religious organizations, particularly religious leaders, if a church or temple member wants to promote an investment through the religious organization, do your own due diligence before permitting them access to your members. For those who are members of a congregation, if the leader diverts from promoting the faith to promoting investment instruments: do your own due diligence. Far too many people have been taken advantage of based on their faith.

The information that follows are the suggestions developed from reading thousands of financial market cases, not just Ponzi schemes, including but not limited to: affinity-fraud, elder-fraud, faith-based fraud, pyramid schemes, cherry picking, boiler-rooms, pump-and-dumps, binary options frauds, mortgage frauds, real estate frauds, bank frauds, cryptocurrency frauds, microcap cases, prime banking, pension frauds, spoofing, and theft by deception cases. Theft by deception frauds may be the greatest quantity of investment frauds, but there is no unifying term that can be used in search engines to research and find all of the cases. In this type of fraud, there are no Ponzi payments; the perpetrators present themselves as legitimate broker/dealers or investment advisers and take the money from their victims without making an investment or returning any of the funds. The manner and means of deception are as varied as the mind can conceive.

The findings here primarily reflect on Ponzi schemes that are intentional frauds. In the case of brokerage-failure or business-failure schemes, the due diligence is different because the businesses are formed or incorporated properly, the brokers or investment advisers have the appropriate licenses, then something goes wrong that causes the business or brokerage to turn into a Ponzi scheme. The perpetrators may genuinely believe they are going to turn the business around and pay everyone back at some point. When people believe their own lies, they are more believable to others. For this reason, it is suggested that due diligence must be a routine carried out often, not just when considering working with someone initially. This advice of practicing routine, occasional, and random due diligence does not apply only to individual investors, but to all institutional investors, including banks, lending entities, insurers, and pensions. Many schemes gave the appearance of legitimacy initially, but after time the financial reports and documents could no longer hold water.

There is risk in all investing; if the individual you are thinking of investing with cannot articulate that there is risk and what that risk is, then take your money elsewhere. There is no guaranteed profit in investing. Investors should be very suspicious of anyone who says they can guarantee a profit. As Pat Huddleston says, "If it sounds too good to be true, you are talking to an amateur scam artist" (Huddleston, 2012, p. 114). His meaning is that only inexperienced con-artists present frauds that seem to be too good to be true, that more experienced fraudsters are more subtle and believable.

How does one know who they should and should not trust with investments? If you cannot afford to lose your money, be very careful with whom you entrust it. Understand that with all investment there is risk; no one can ever guarantee a profit. Quite simply: "In God we trust," for everyone else, carry out thorough due diligence. Then keep carrying out due diligence; do not assume once is good enough. Some Ponzi schemes developed out of legitimate businesses that failed. Do not take anyone's word for it that they are registered with the SEC, CFTC, NFA, FINRA, or are incorporated; research it yourself. Any deception is a red flag.

Understanding Profits

A business that offers products or services must meet operating costs with a financial gain in order for there to be profits to pay investors. In stocks, the selling price must be higher than the buying price for there to be a profit to pay investors. In bonds there must be interest on the debt for there to be profits to pay bondholders. In order for investors to receive dividends on their invested funds, a company should have means of making a profit. Investors need to look at any perspective investment or business to see if they can determine documentable proof of a profit. If investing in a company that funds start-ups, or is a start-up, there may not be proof of possible profits; there should at least be a sound business plan. This takes some digging; you cannot take anything at face value. The means of making profit should be clearly stated and make sense. If the discussion of how the profits are made is convoluted and loaded with jargon, be suspicious. It may be the emperor's new clothes or empress's new gown syndrome. A company's prospectus should honestly report how the business operates and is managed, and the company's financial status; this should be accurately reported in the company's audited financial statement.

In most Ponzi schemes the "profits," also known as returns, may go on for years and years without reason to attract suspicion, until the scheme collapses. Then it is too late. Prudent investors may want to withdraw their principal periodically just to see if they can still get it out. It was when some investors tried to take their principal out that they found it no longer existed.

Family and Close Friends

The majority of business entities in general start out contacting friends and family for support, investing, and as customers. This is what is common place. How does one determine if they are capable of doing what they say there are? How does one question them about their skill set, competency, and business acumen without becoming the family ogre? If it is a major investment, ask for a business plan. Tell them you need specifics on how the funds will be invested or used. You want concrete documentation of how they expect to earn a profit and how you will be paid. What is the contingency plan for paying investors? Make it clear, by written contract that you want your principal back in full on a written date, even if they are relatives or friends. Even if your friends and relatives have the best of intentions, they may not have the skills or a solid plan to earn profits, and to repay investors. If President Grant can be fooled by an acquaintance, anyone can.

Similarly, when we are looking for a service or business, we ask our friends, family, and religious affiliation members if they know someone they have had good results with. We believe that a personal reference from someone we trust will somehow ensure or increase success. This is what is normal. However, this personal introduction is the primary mechanism used to gain investor-victims in many fraud schemes as well. Potential investors need to ask how the friend or family member met the individual in question. They need to be asked, "What makes them so convinced this business or individual can do what they say they will?"

Understand that Ponzi schemes are started by treating the first investors very well, making sure they get their profits or returns on schedule, in order to build credibility, and to attract other investor-victims. Keep in mind no one ever reports someone to the SEC, the CFTC, or the FBI because they are receiving high rates of returns as promised. It is only when the returns cease to come as promised, or investor-victims cannot get their principal back, that the authorities are contacted. A confidence scam works because victims must be gullible and believe everything the perpetrator tells them. Part of the alleged "exclusiveness" is weeding out those who have the business acumen to recognize fraud.

Technology Trends and International Trends Fostered by the Internet

Financial markets are digitized, meaning transactions are all computerized and move from computer to computer, nation to nation, in a fraction of a second. This allows for sophisticated trading practices that may or may not be legal. Blockchain is the computerized system used in cryptocurrency transactions (Vigna and Casey, 2015). This system time stamps all transactions so that they are carried out chronologically. This system recognizes individual users' accounts and passwords so that cryptocurrency can be used anywhere in the world for any transaction. As this system grows worldwide, illegitimately attained funds can be transferred to cryptocurrency, or originate in cryptocurrency, the usage of which can be easily accessed anywhere in the world. Encryption can make tracking these transactions very challenging for authorities. If an investor cannot understand the technology, they should ask themselves if it is really a good investment.

We have only begun to see the impact of cryptocurrency on the world marketplace. The survey *Regulation of cryptocurrency around the world* (U.S. Library of Congress, 2018) discusses the state of cryptocurrency legislation in 130 countries. Countries have varying standards, some with absolute ban on cryptocurrency as legal tender, some with implicit ban on usage. One country that chose to produce its own cryptocurrency backed by oil, calling it the "petro," is Venezuela. This report lists China as having an implicit ban on cryptocurrencies, while at the same time in the process of issuing its own cryptocurrency (Id., pp. 4 and 6). According to this report, these countries are now, or are in the process of, issuing their own cryptocurrencies (Id, p. 6), as of 2018:

* Anguilla
* Antigua and Barbuda
* China
* Dominica
* Grenada
* Ireland
* Lithuania
* Marshall Islands
* Montserrat
* Saint Kitts and Nevis
* Saint Lucia
* Saint Vincent and Grenadines
* Venezuela.

Increasingly, Ponzi scheme perpetrators and other fraudsters are using social media to solicit their services using YouTube, Facebook, and Instagram. Social media enables fraud perpetrators to be active in several states or countries, as in the case of Chamroonrat. Chamroonrat held meetings with his co-conspirators via Skype (SEC v. Chamroonrat et al., 2017, May 11, prg. 30). The perpetrators in this case lived in Thailand, Israel, Canada, and Nevada, USA.

The internet allows for international registration and incorporation using financial service centers, with opaque reporting standards. It also allows perpetrators to carry out practices and types of trading outside the regulation and monitoring of the SEC, the CFTC, and FINRA restrictions. When schemes are carried out in multiple nations it is challenging for federal law enforcement or regulatory entities to monitor transactions. An action may be perfectly legal in one nation, yet quite illegal in another nation.

286 Laws, Economics, and History

Are They Appropriately Licensed or Registered?

Investors are encouraged to familiarize themselves with the SEC's and CFTC's websites; the links are provided below. The SEC and the CFTC offer a wealth of information for investors to educate themselves. The SEC and the CFTC can come in after a fraud has been committed, but the only preventative means is the individual investor's due diligence and self-education. The Financial Industry Regulatory Authority (FINRA), the National Futures Association (NFA), and North American Securities Administration Association (NASAA) also offer information. National Futures Association provides a service similar to FINRA BrokerCheck, called BASIC. Both systems are user-friendly and allow investors to check business entities, individuals, and pools for appropriate registration. These agency URLs provide investor information:

- https://www.sec.gov/smallbusiness/goingpublic/exchangeact reporting
- https://www.sec.gov/reportspubs/investor-publications/divisions-marketregbdguidehtm.html
- https://www.sec.gov/page/investor-section-landing
- https://www.sec.gov/edgar/searchedgar/companysearch.html
- https://brokercheck.finra.org/
- https://www.nfa.futures.org/basicnet/

The CFTC provides information on who is exempt from registering with the CFTC here:

- https://cftc.gov/sites/default/files/tm/tmcpo_cta_exemptions.htm

The SEC website gives clear guidance on the credentials a legitimate broker, dealer, trader, or investment adviser should have. Make certain to look up the rules on who must be registered with the SEC and why they must be registered. Do not take someone you are planning on giving all your money to at their word, even if they are family or a religious affiliate. Do not assume emblems of federal agencies on their website mean that they are properly registered; these logos can easily be copied and pasted onto a website. The emblems/logos belong to the federal agencies; a private entity is not the agency; if it has them posted on their website it is a red flag. These links above and below provide publicly available information on business entities that are registered or licensed. Readers need to understand that holding a FINRA license or being properly registered is no guarantee of profits. It is merely a way of determining if someone has required licenses, is registered properly, and if they have been truthful about their credentials or their experience. It also enables investors to see if an individual has had previous disciplinary actions against them. However, be warned that 523 Ponzi perpetrators had taken the FINRA and NASAA exams and were licensed at some point. Many used the licensing to present themselves as credible in order to carry out the fraud. These links allow investors to research for themselves:

- SEC Action Look-up Individuals: SALI
  https://www.sec.gov/litigations/sec-action-look-up
- Securities and Exchange Commission, SEC-EDGAR: https://www.sec.gov/edgar/searchedgar/companysearch.html

The Securities and Exchange Commission's Investment Advisor Public Disclosure website allows for ascertaining both SEC and state-level registration and background information. This is required of anyone who actively trades other people's money:

- www.advisorinfo.sec.gov

Securities and Exchange Commission, SEC advanced search options:

- https://www.sec.gov/search/search.htm

The Financial Industry Regulatory Authority is a nonprofit trade organization that regulates and monitors its members. It is funded by members fees; it is not a government agency.

- Financial Industry Regulatory Authority, FINRA: https://brokercheck.finra.org/

Similar to FINRA, the NFA is an industry regulatory entity funded by members fees.

- National Futures Association, NFA: https://www.nfa.futures.org/
- NFA BASIC:
  https://www.nfa.futures.org/basicnet/

State securities: North American Securities Administration Association:

http://www.nasaa.org/

Bonds

The Municipal Securities Rulemaking Board (MSRB) is a self-regulatory organization established by the Securities Acts Amendments of 1975.

The MSRB's purpose is to make rules regarding municipal bond issuers, to regulate those who sell municipal bonds, and to provide consumer education and market information. The Board is made up of individuals who are municipal securities advisers and brokers, and those who may represent institutional and retail investors. The MSRB website states that no entity is allowed to post their logo; this is to prevent the abuse of logos as falsified proof of legitimacy. It offers MUNIEDPRO, courses provided for the public to learn about municipal markets. The Electronic Municipal Market Access system (EMMA) is an interactive website that allows users to access a state and that then provides links to entities that have bond in municipal markets. The MSRB provides a wealth of information that investors can access on municipal bonds through EMMA:

https://emma.msrb.org/

Treasury bonds information can be accessed through the United States Treasury website, which also provides information on scams and frauds associated with Treasury bonds. Treasury Direct: https://www.treasury-direct.gov/indiv/products/prod_tbonds_glance.htm

Nationally Recognized Statistical Ratings Organizations

Nationally recognized statistical ratings organizations (NRSROs) came under fire after the financial crisis because they failed to provide accurate ratings on mortgage-backed derivatives leading up to the financial crisis. It is important to understand which ratings agencies are financially supported by the companies and entities that they rate. Investors need to research how each rating agency is funded and how they arrive at their ratings. This is done by going to each entity's "About us" section on their websites. After the financial crisis some ratings agencies received penalties from the Department of Justice, for failing to provide accurate ratings of securitized mortgages (DOJ, 2015, February 3, p.r.; DOJ, 2017, January 13, p.r.). As a result of the Dodd-Frank Act, the SEC adopted credit rating agencies reforms requiring internal controls, disclosure of how the agency arrives at their statistical ratings, and conflict of interest transparency (17 CFR Parts 232,240,249, and 249b).

Business Formation/Incorporation

Each state has a website where anyone can look up the status of a corporation, generally the Division of Corporations. Government agencies have ".gov" at the end of their web address or URL. Make sure you are not going to a business that will charge you for information that government agencies offer free of charge; a government website will have ".gov" at the end of the URL. Also, research the licensing requirements and incorporation requirements for that state. For state agencies, use a Boolean search in google.com:

- State + Division of Corporations + site:gov

Ask the primary if the business is incorporated, or otherwise formed (LLC, LP, PC), and where the business is incorporated. Just because an entity has "Inc." after the business name does not mean it was actually incorporated. It is important to do a thorough check of incorporation or formation. Sometimes a business entity may have the names as corporate officers other than those the investor is working with. Some securities fraud recidivists have been barred from being the officer of a company, so they get someone else to be the officer of the corporation for them. It is means of hiding a questionable history. This should be a red flag; if the entity is incorporated under someone else's name ask who they are, and ask to meet them.

- Be sure to check the states of Delaware and Nevada for incorporation, regardless of what state the primary is running the business entity from.

The laws and requirements of the different types of business formations vary by state. Professional corporations (PC) are generally used by accountants and attorneys; the legal requirements vary by state. Investors would need to see what the requirements are for the choice of entity for the state they are in or where the investment entity is formed/incorporated:

- Sole Proprietor
- General Partnership
- Limited Liability Company (LLC)
- Limited Liability Partnership (LLP)
- C Corporation
- Sub-chapter S Corporation

- Some individuals have a criminal record, or a bar on being associated with a securities business, or in being an officer of a corporation as a result of previous securities violations; they may have someone else listed as the head of the company. This can be found through the SEC and FINRA websites. Incorporation/formation information is found through state agencies when they are not licensed as investment advisers.

Real Estate and Mortgages

In real estate and mortgage-based investments, investors need to use other research skills. If an investment is said to be in purchasing real estate property or development, go to visit the sites in person, unannounced, ask questions. Find out who the owner of the property is. This can be researched through the municipal offices, title companies, and attorneys. In some cases, the perpetrators use the same real estate property or item of business equipment as proof to many investor-victims. In some schemes the investment is stated to be pooled funds contributing to property investment. Investors should ask for a list of properties that have been purchased with the funds to ascertain who holds the titles on these properties.

Insurance

There were Ponzi schemes that were based in insurance or insurance products. Some of the perpetrators were former insurance agents, some were properly licensed, others only said they were insurance agents. In addition, several perpetrators were licensed insurance agents who found their Ponzi investor-victims through their insurance clientele. To ascertain the professional standing of an insurance agent, check with state agencies. Each state has its own requirements for insurance agents. You can contact the state agency to find out if someone is properly licensed to sell insurance and if there are any complaints against them. Generally, this agency is referred to as the Department or the Division of Insurance.

Annuities are generally purchased through insurance companies. Investors may want to check the rating for the insurance company through the ratings companies to understand how well the insurance company is performing.[1] For example: is the company in good financial condition that indicates the annuity funds will still be there when the annuity is expected to be paid? Investors also need to verify that the salesperson is indeed licensed through the insurance company that they say they are. They can also check with the state licensing board to ascertain if the salesperson is in good standing.

In a Ponzi scheme that was indicted as this book goes to press, the perpetrator was a career insurance broker. He was legally employed and licensed. Yet he had submitted false applications for insurance policies in the names of individuals without them knowing it. He had his clients make premium payments directly to him. He also convinced his clients he was an investment adviser; they trusted him and allowed him to control their funds.

Broker-Dealer Expectations

The SEC guide to broker-dealer registration explains who must be registered with the SEC and what exceptions there might be. All current and potential investors need to be familiar with this information.[2] Basically, anyone who is buying, selling, or trading securities (stocks, bonds futures or commodities, or any other financial instruments) with other people's money must be licensed to do so. The SEC differentiates between brokers, dealers, traders, and investment advisers as each has been defined by the Securities Exchange Act of 1934. There are licensing and registration responsibilities for each and fiduciary responsibilities. The CFTC also explains the requirements and responsibilities for dealers, traders, and pool operators.

The SEC's Form ADV and EDGAR

The Form ADV registers investment advisers with both the SEC and state-level securities agencies. This form requires investment advisers to provide information on their business, their personal qualifications and experience, information on anyone who might be in management, fees, and disciplinary actions. Generally, registered investment advisers are individuals who have taken and passed the series 65 exam with NASAA, who have registered with the SEC and file the Form ADV annually with the SEC. Those registering with the SEC must also file an annual report. The ADV form is public record. Investors can use it to see if the investment adviser's claims and promotions match up with what is reported on this form.

The SEC's Electronic Data Gathering, Analysis, and Retrieval system (EDGAR) is a publicly accessible government search tool that allows anyone to search for information on companies or individuals required to register with the SEC. This SEC website provides tutorials on how to use EDGAR.[3]

Determining the Standing of Attorneys

In the cases where the Ponzi perpetrator was a licensed attorney, the investor can check their standing with their state licensing board. Investors can also determine if an attorney has had disciplinary actions or complaints. It can also be determined if the "attorney" is actually a licensed attorney and not someone illegally presenting themselves as such. The American Bar Association's website offers links to each state's licensing agency:

*   https://www.americanbar.org/groups/legal_services/flh-home/
    flh-lawyer-licensing/

There were Ponzi scheme cases where perpetrators claimed to be attorneys when they were not, in and of itself against the law. In one Ponzi case, the perpetrator adopted the identity of a legitimate attorney. By checking with state licensing authorities, the investor can find the appropriate address for an attorney and other history to determine if the person they are talking to is who they say they are, and a licensed attorney.

How to Determine if an Accountant Is in Good Standing

Check their credentials, education, and experience. Far too many intentional Ponzi perpetrators falsified their experience and education to investors. Some perpetrators said they were CPAs when they were not. The American Institute of CPAs (AICPA) offers a service to determine CPA license verification:

*   https://www.aicpa.org/forthepublic/findacpa.html

The National Association of State Board of Accountancy (NASBA) has established a database on CPAs: https://nasba.org/features/nasbalaunch-escpaverify/ and https://cpaverify.org/
Consumers and investors can also carry out a Boolean search by state using the search terms:

*   Name of state + CPA + License + Verification + site:gov

Different states have different offices that maintain records on licensing; sometimes it is a Board of Accountancy or Board of Licenses; there is no one term for all states.

Insurance Agents

Insurance agents must be licensed with the state they sell insurance in. This generally requires taking a test for specific types of insurance. Investors can go to their state's Department of Insurance to verify the standing of an insurance agent and to ascertain if there are complaints. The perpetrator may have never been licensed to sell insurance products or may have lost their license. The National Association of Insurance Commissioners provides advice on working with insurance agents: www.naic.org.

Banks, FDIC, and SIPC

Banks

A few Ponzi schemes were based on individuals that started their own banks. In order to function as legal banks these entities must be chartered and licensed with the appropriate state and federal agencies. In the United States we have a dual banking system, meaning we have national-level banks and state level banks. The Federal Deposit Insurance Act (12 U.S. Code §1813 (a) (2)) defines state banks as:

(a) (2) The term "State bank" means any bank, banking association, trust company, savings bank, industrial bank (or similar depository institution which the Board of Directors finds to be operating substantially in the same manner as an industrial bank), or other banking institution-
(d) (1) The term "national member bank" means any national bank which is a member of the Federal Reserve System.

The Office of the Comptroller of Currency (OCC) is the only authority to provide national and federal-level banks with charters; this agency provides the rules and requirements for establishing a national bank or a federal savings association. Again, the general public considering investing in what they are told is to be a bank can contact the Office of Comptroller of the Currency to find out if the bank is properly chartered and registered to function as a bank. The OCC has regulatory authority and monitoring over federal banks and savings entities.

The Federal Reserve, through the reserve banks, and the Federal Deposit Insurance Company (FDIC) have supervisory responsibilities over state-level banks and savings entities. The Federal Reserve has responsibility over those state-chartered banks that have FDIC memberships. The Federal Deposit Insurance Company covers all types of deposits with those institutions that are insured. Each individual depositor is insured up to $250,000 per banking institution. The FDIC does not cover stocks, securities, or other investments, nor insurance policies.

Federal Deposit Insurance Company

Some Ponzi schemes claimed to be insured by the FDIC. The FDIC does not insure brokerages, securities, or investments. This agency came into existence out of the financial failure of the Great Depression. Its purpose and responsibility are solely related to banks. Investors need an understanding of what this agency does in order to recognize when someone is giving them false information that states the investment entity is FDIC-insured. Investors can check the FDIC site to see if an entity that claims to be FDIC-insured actually is an insured institution by going to FDIC BankFind: https://research2.fdic.gov/bankfind/index.html.

The FDIC only insures deposits in FDIC member banks up to $250,000 per depositor, per insured bank. It does not insure securities at all, only deposits with insured banks. The FDIC-insured banks are examined for compliance with federal banking acts, as a means of protecting consumers and the economy. Some schemes were based on fraudulent banks that may have falsely declared they were FDIC-insured.

The SIPC

The Securities Investor Protection Corporation was established by Congress: Securities Investor Protection Act of 1970, 15 USC §78ccc. It is not an agency but an organization of members who are registered brokers and traders. The directors are appointed: one by the Department of the Treasury, one by the Federal Reserve, and five members chosen by the President with Senate approval. The members of the SIPC are brokers or dealers that are registered with the SEC, with provisions under the enabling legislation of the SIPC, by law. Investors would do well to check if an entity is a member:

•   https://www.sipc.org/list-of-members/

In order for an investor's funds to be insured through SIPC, the brokerage must be an SIPC member. When a brokerage that is an SIPC member goes out of business the individual investors are insured up to $500,000. The SIPC does not guarantee losses caused by market fluctuations. It is important to make certain a brokerage and its clearing house are SIPC members in order to receive funds in case of a brokerage-failure. In order to receive funds in the case of a brokerage-failure, the individual investors must have documentation of contracts, investments, and transactions.

   In 2010, the SEC warned protentional investors about a fraudulent website, called the "International Security Investor Protection Corporation" (SEC, 2010). This site falsely claimed that it had found Madoff funds in Malaysia. Sites such as this try to victimize Ponzi scheme victims and other victims of frauds, again.

What to Watch for

Through PACER

Public Access to Court Electronic Records (PACER) is a federal website that provides access to federal cases for a minimal fee. This site enables the public to check on previous bankruptcies, current bankruptcy proceedings, civil suits by federal agencies, civil suits by other business entities or individuals, and criminal proceedings. In order to use this service one must establish an account; this is free of charge. However, one must use a credit or debit card to pay for the documents at ten cents per page, with a maximum fee of three dollars per document. Users are encouraged to make sure to have the exact spelling of the name of the primary agent and the region (state) of a legal action to make certain they get the right person in a search. This is a user-friendly website.

•   Check the Public Access to Court Electronic Records, PACER: https://www.pacer.gov/

State-Level Records

Some state-level documents can be found through Boolean searches without a charge. However, many state-level court documents may charge a fee as high as $60.00, per court document; these are accessed through state websites.

Blind-Eye Accounting

The term "blind-eye accounting," sometimes referred to as willful blindness, refers to the practice of accountants intentionally failing to recognize and expose fraudulent acts that they have a professional responsibility to address. In some of the Ponzi cases it was the accountants who were carrying out the fraud. They went to prison and lost their licenses. In other cases, the accountants were employed or contracted by someone who was carrying out the Ponzi scheme.

Madoff employed two accounting firms; both had ethical and legal responsibilities to honest and accurate statements, reports, and audits, at the very least. Konigsberg provided advice to both Madoff's business and to Madoff personally. Madoff provided a relative of Konigsberg with a no-show job in lieu of Konigsberg's payment (DOJ, 2014, June 24, p.r.). Both David G. Friehling and Paul J. Konigsberg were charged civilly with the SEC, and criminally under the Department of Justice.

- Madoff recommended his accountant, Paul Konigsberg, to his investors (DOJ, 2014, June 24, p.r.). When the investors used the same accountant as Madoff, it removed a level of protection and accountability; an outside accountant may have caught on to the falsities in Madoffs financial statements and monthly account statements. Konigsberg admitted helping produce fraudulent statements in Bernie Madoff's scheme. Konigsberg also admitted to backdating trades on client accounts. He was an attorney and an accountant (FBI, 2013, September 26); he had a professional responsibility to know what his client was doing. Konigsberg received monthly investment account statements from his clients who were also Madoff's clients. Those Madoff investor-victims who were also Konigsberg clients may have been lulled into believing their investments were safe because they shared the same accountant as Madoff. Konigsberg was also a minority partner in *Madoff Securities International Limited*. There were many levels of conflicts of interest and unethical behaviors on Konigsberg's part. However, Konigsberg was cooperative with prosecutors and received time served for falsifying records of an investment adviser (USA v. Paul Konigsberg, 2013, September 26).

According to the American Institute of Certified Public Accountants (AICPA), auditors must "obtain sufficient appropriate audit evidence to be able to draw reasonable conclusions on which to base the auditor's opinion" (2019, AU-C §500.04). The auditor has a responsibility to be objective, not assuming that the entity being audited is either honest or dishonest: "In exercising professional skepticism, the auditor should not be satisfied with less than persuasive evidence because of a belief that management is honest" (2019, AU-C §230.09).

- David G. Friehling was Madoff's audit-accountant. Friehling also received time served as Madoff's auditing firm. Friehling was responsible for auditing BMIS' financial statements that were filed with the SEC. He did not follow GAAS and GAAP guidelines for audits, nor did he audit for BMIS' internal controls. Instead he gave BMIS a pass on all auditing practices that would have and should have indicated that Madoff owed billions in liabilities that were not disclosed (SEC, 2009, March 18, pp. 2 and 3). Friehling misrepresented to AICPA that he was not carrying out audits with BMIS, thereby avoiding peer review of his sketchy audits.

Publicly traded companies must file annual audited financial statements with the SEC. The accounting firms would report irregularities only to be replaced by a different firm. There were shell companies that Trippet used to move money out of *Home-Stake Oil* (McClintock, 1977, p. 48). In Trippet's case below, several accounting firms attempted to provide accurate financial reports and audit information that would have made financial discrepancies obvious, but Trippet just switched accounting firms, or had his in-house accountant provide documents. His in-house accountant was not a CPA. The SEC did take action, in a superficial way, by enjoining the company. The DOJ indicted Trippet et al., but the court accepted pleas of nolo contendere and let the perpetrators off with a slap on the wrist.

- In the Trippet *Home-Stake Oil* Ponzi scheme, Trippet went through four different accountants in a five-year period, by 1960, a significant red flag (McClintock, 1977, p. 45). There were shell companies that Trippet used to move money out of *Home-Stake Oil* (McClintock, 1977, p. 48). One accounting firm reported this in the annual report to the shareholders, so Trippet used a different report without the information put together with his in-house accountant that wasn't a CPA. Trippet was selling more drilling units than stated in the prospectus to investors, as well as what was stated in the financial reports to the investors. When *Arthur Andersen* accountants discovered the overselling of drilling units and saw that payments to investors were not being paid from oil revenues, they had the opportunity to expose the Ponzi scheme but didn't; this was 1964–1966 (McClintock, 1977, p. 101).

- In the late 1980s case of Broadhollow, both Rita Baskin of *Baskin Planning* and *ASCO Advisory Services* recommended that their clients invest with *Broadhollow Funding Corporation*, a purported real estate mortgage company, that was actually a Ponzi scheme. Neither ASCO or Baskins properly vetted Broadhollow's financial statements, before recommending investing to their clients (SEC, 1991 December 12).

Search Suppression Services

As technology advances for the good of the consumer, there are always means of using the same tools to aid in fraud. Just as there are search engines to aid in finding information out about a prospective business entity or individual, there are also internet businesses that hide negative information or complaints of customers, and undisclosed information, called search suppression services. Initially, these were designed in helping individuals and businesses to remove false or fraudulent information about themselves.

Red Flags

- Is there a claim of guaranteed high returns? No return can be guaranteed.
- Is there a claim of no risk? All investments hold risk.
- Is there full transparency? A lack of transparency is a red flag.
- Are you being told that their trading practices are proprietary?
- Is the individual unregistered with the appropriate authorities? Make sure you check FINRA, NFA, CFTC, and SEC websites for disciplinary history. Ask if there have been complaints, if they have been barred, or filed for bankruptcy; you can check to see if they provide an honest answer.
- Are you being told an answer that is so full of jargon you cannot understand what they are saying? It may be the "emperor's new clothes" vocabulary being used. The perpetrators may be speaking in jargon to make you feel inferior so that you will assume they know what they are talking about and you do not.
- Can they break down their explanation into laypeople's vocabulary so that you can verify their statements?
- Is there missing information?
- Is the means by which the person promoting the investment will make a profit a percentage or a fee? Is it clearly stated in a contract? How do they support themselves? No one can afford to be in any business without some sort of profit for themselves. How they get a fee for their services, whether it is a percentage of profits or a fee per

transaction must be in writing. No one is giving you investment advice out of the goodness of their heart; no matter what they say, they must have a financial stake somewhere in the mix. You have a right to know honestly what that is, and in writing.

- Is the sales personnel or adviser really pushy, are they very aggressive? Ask yourself why they are so insistent on getting your money. If it is such a good deal why aren't people beating down their door? Their phone should be ringing off the hook. If the investment is that great, they won't need to push it aggressively, people will come to them.
- Was it a cold call? If you would not have considered this sort of investment had they not called you out of the blue, be very suspicious; hang up. Cold-callers pay for lists of people's names, specifically lists of those who are elderly.
- How did they contact you? Was it through a social-based network, language-based radio, or a religious radio advertisement? Was it a hotel meeting event? Whatever the initial contact, you must carry out your own due diligence on their experience, credentials, and employment history, as well as financial history.
- Can you determine that actual trades or investments have been carried out? When a broker carries out a trade in your account, they are required to send you a trade confirmation. Make sure you read them and save them.
- Can you determine if financial statements may be fraudulent? Ascertain the validity of documents; save every document, specifically every account statement. Some are simply fraudulent documents where blue-chip or other securities or commodities are listed, but there were never any trades taking place.
- Ask a third party with auditing experience to review the information provided by the primary or promoter.
- Does the entity have an auditor? Can you get their name and check out their credentials? More than one Ponzi perpetrator had a nonexistent auditor, or an incompetent one.
- Is it a private offering? Generally private offerings require accredited investors. Accredited investors are expected to be financially sophisticated enough to carry out their own due diligence.
- Is it an unregistered security offering? This means it does not have an effective registration statement filed with the SEC. Not having this registration and trying to sell unregistered securities is a felony. Here is the link to the SEC's information on exceptions to unregistered securities: https://www.sec.gov/smallbusiness/exemptofferings
- Verify that their corporate address is a real office in a real building. If they are asking you to send a check to a different address you should be asking why.

- If you are told not to contact anyone else, do contact someone else!
- Is the entity incorporated? If not, why not? Is it otherwise organized such as a limited liability corporation, a limited partnership, or not formally organized at all?
- Where is it incorporated? Delaware, Nevada, Wyoming, offshore? Ask them for an explanation of why they incorporated in another state or with an offshore entity. Many legitimately incorporate in other places for tax purposes. However, these places may also have reduced transparency for corporate officers.
- You need to know who the corporate officers are. If the promoter is not forthright on this be suspicious, do some checking on your own. Recidivists may get someone else to be the executive officer because they may be barred from heading a securities associated entity, or they do not want anyone to know they have previous securities bars or felony convictions.
- It is a red flag if you are being asked to write a check with a different name than the name of the corporation, or to an individual such as a sales agent. The check should be going to a business entity listed in promotions, not to a private individual's account. You need to check that the business entity exists.
- Have they told you their investment strategy is low risk or no risk? There are no such thing as no-risk investments. Ask for proof of low risk, make them explain it. Get it in writing, find out what makes it low risk.
- What is the proof that they can return your principal investment if it is no risk? Have they guaranteed that they have their own funds held in escrow to be paid out in case there are losses? They cannot do that. Check with FINRA:
    https://www.finra.org/rules-guidance/rulebooks/finra-rules
- Have they told you it is FDIC-insured? FDIC applies only to bank deposits in FDIC member banks.
- Have they told you they are SIPC-insured or -guaranteed? This applies only to SIPC members. Brokerages that are not members must inform investors that they are not SIPC members. Check it out with SIPC; do not take their word for it.
- Are you pressured in to rolling over your principal and profits once the maturity date arrives? Insist on taking some, or all out to see how the broker-dealer-adviser responds.

After investors carried out painstaking due diligence, the work is not over. Keep meticulous documentation of every transaction and communication in an organized, chronologic system; it is necessary to recuperate losses in the case of fraud or if the legitimate brokerage goes out of business.

Our federal and state regulatory agencies, as well as self-regulating organizations that are enabled by Congress, serve the purpose of protecting investors and providing them with a wealth of information for investors to educate themselves. These are user-friendly websites that are written in understandable language.

Ultimately, the decision to trust someone else with their money rests with the investor. The SEC, CFTC, FINRA, and NFA can post information on how to avoid fraud and provide means for carrying out due diligence, but the responsibility is on the shoulders of the investor to educate themselves and to carry out due diligence. All investing has risk. If you are going to invest, educate yourself. When you do invest, watch those investments to look for red flags. The majority of schemes made contact through word of mouth; individuals tell their friends and family about the "great deal" they found. Readers should think about how they might feel if their advice caused friends and family to lose everything. Likewise, if a friend or a family member recommends an investment to you, how are you going to feel about them if their advice causes you to lose everything? A little common sense and a lot of due diligence may save some investors from losing everything to a Ponzi scheme.

Notes

1 Investors need to access each ratings agency (NRSRO) to ascertain how they achieve their ratings and to compare different ratings agencies' values. Ratings agencies may have conflicts of interest that investors must educate themselves on.
2 SEC guide to Broker-Dealer Registration: https://www.sec.gov/reportspubs/investor-publications/divisionsmarketregbdguidehtm.html
3 EDGAR: https://www.sec.gov/reportspubs/investor-publications/divisions-marketregbdguidehtm.html

References

American Institute of Certified Public Accountants. (2019). *AICPA professional standards*. Chicago, IL, Commerce Clearing House.

Department of Justice, (2014, June 24). Manhattan U.S. Attorney announces guilty plea of New York Accountant in connection with the massive fraud at Bernard L. Madoff Investment Securities. (Konigsberg). Press release.

Department of Justice, (2015, February 3). Justice Department and State partners secure $1.375 billion settlement with S&P for defrauding investors in the lead up to the Financial Crisis. Press release.

Department of Justice, (2017, January 13). Justice Department and State partners secure nearly $864 million settlement with Moody's arising from Conduct in the lead up to the Financial Crisis. Press release.

Dodd-Frank Wall Street Reform and Consumer Protection Act. (2010). 111th Congress.

Duros, S. (2018, September). *Cryptocurrency and blockchain: Background and regulatory approaches.* Wisconsin Legislative Reference Bureau.

The Federal Deposit Insurance Act of 1933, 73rd Congress.

Federal Deposit Insurance Corporation. Who is the FDIC? Retrieved from: https://www.fdic.gov/about/learn/symbol/index.htmlhttps://www.fdic.gov/about/learn/symbol/index.html

Huddleston, P. (2011). *The vigilant investor: A former SEC enforcer reveals how to fraud-proof your investments.* New York, NY Amacom.

McClintock, D. (1977). *Stealing from the rich; the story of the swindle of the century.* New York, NY, M. Evans.

Phelps, K.B. (2013). *Ponzi-proof your investments: An investor's guide to avoiding Ponzi schemes and other fraudulent scams.* Los Angeles, CA, IRR Publishing.

Phelps, K.B. and Rhodes, S. Honorable. (2012). *The Ponzi book: Legal resource for unraveling Ponzi schemes.* New Providence, NJ, LexisNexis.

Securities Exchange Act of 1934, 85th Congress, Amended 2018, 115th Congress.

Securities Acts Amendments of 1975, 94th Congress.

Securities Investor Protection Commission, list of members. Retrieved from: https://www.sipc.org/list-of-members/

Securities and Exchange Commission, (1991, December 12). Rita Baskin barred; registration of Baskin Planning Consultants LTD. Revoked. News Digest 91-235.

Securities and Exchange Commission v. Naris Chamroonrat, Yaniv Avnon, Ran Armon, G six Trading Y.R. Ltd., and Adam L. Plumer (2017, May 17) Complaint.

United States Attorney, (2009, July 17). Accountant for Bernard L. Madoff Investment Securities, LLC charged in felony information for accounting violations. Press release.

United States Library of Congress, (2018). Regulation of cryptocurrency around the world.

United States v. David G. Friehling (2009, March 17) (Madoff). Information.

United States v. Paul Konigsberg (2013, September 26) (Madoff). Indictment.

Glossary of Terms

Accredited investor: An investor treated under the Securities Act of 1933 as being knowledgeable and sophisticated in financial matters (Garner, 2009). Generally, they are individuals with an income of at least $200,000, or couples with an income over $300,000, with a net worth of $1 million. They are expected to be knowledgeable or sophisticated in investing. They can also be institutions such as pensions, insurance companies, banks, and larger entities that invest over $5 million.

Administrative proceeding: Any of several actions taken by the SEC in a case.

Affiliation: Individuals who self-identify with a group, such as by nationality, ethnicity, by religious groups, profession, sexual orientation, including physical characteristics such as being deaf.

Affinity-fraud: **Also known as community-fraud.** The members of the group self-identify with the affiliation, such as religious groups, professional groups, nationality, or ethnicity, based on whom the perpetrator shares the same self-identifying quality.

Annuity: A contract that is generally with an insurance company. The customer makes a large onetime payment or several payments to an annuity. Usually, they are meant to make regular payments as income at a later date, such as retirement.

Barring: A non-monetary action or remedy by the SEC, CFTC, or FINRA. FINRA may permanently bar or prohibit an individual from associating with a member entity.

Binary options: A method of investing where the investment either pays out based on a date and time or it pays nothing at all.

Bond: A debt instrument, similar to an IOU. When a buyer purchases a bond, they are lending money to the issuer. Generally, bonds are issued by a government entity for capital projects. In return for the loan, the issuer promises to pay the buyer a specified interest rate during the life of the bond and to repay the principal when it matures (SEC).

Broker: An agent who specializes transactions involving in stocks, bonds, commodities, or options for others. They must be registered with the SEC where securities are traded and the CFTC in commodities trades (Downes and Goodman, 2014) (must pass exams and be registered).

Broker-failure/brokerage-failure: A Ponzi scheme that begins when a legitimate broker or brokerage fails.

Business-failure: A Ponzi scheme that begins when a legitimate business fails and turns into a Ponzi scheme.

Cease and desist order: "A court or an agency's order prohibiting a person from continuing a particular course of conduct" (Garner, 2009).

Certificate of deposit: Investors provide a lump-sum deposit for which they agree to leave the amount in the bank or credit union for a set amount of time. In return there is a set interest rate. Generally, there are penalties for withdrawing the funds before the end date. These are debt instruments usually issued by banks.

Clawbacks: This is money taken back (Garner, 2009). This refers to trying to take back the profits to earlier investors that may have been the principal of later investors.

Commodity: This refers to agricultural products of grains, dairy products, eggs, poultry, livestock, food-oils, cotton, wool, coffee, metals, oil, and natural gas that are traded on exchanges.

Commodity pool: An entity that combines the funds of the pool participants to invest in commodities or futures in aggregate, sharing profits and losses.

Complaint (civil): "The initial proceeding that starts a civil action and states the basis for the court's jurisdiction, the basis for the plaintiff's claim and the demand for relief" (Garner, 2009) This is sometimes followed with an amended complaint that adds additional facts, thereby replacing the initial complaint. These are the initial charges brought by the SEC and CFTC.

Criminal complaint: A legal document that explains the facts in a criminal case and is usually used to get an arrest warrant.

Cryptocurrency: Also known as cybercurrencies, digital assets, virtual currencies. Digital currencies that hold no physical intrinsic value and no fiat value. There is no country or agency issuing a physical object that is minted and holds value. Because there is no centralized agency there is no means of regulation, monitoring, or enforcement of value or movement (Downes and Goodman, 2014).

Day Trader: A day trade is an invest cycle that takes place within one day; a day trader is someone who carries out day trading daily.

Dealer: "Any person or company in the business of buying and selling securities for his or her own account, through a broker or otherwise" (FINRA) (must pass exams and be registered). An individual or a firm acting as a principal in securities or commodities transactions (Downes and Goodman, 2014).

Derivative: A financial instrument such as a security that has a value based on an asset. The price is derived from the value of the underlying asset. In the subprime mortgage scandal bundled mortgages were the derivatives. There are over-the-counter derivatives and exchange-based derivatives.

Digital assets: See *cryptocurrency*.

Disgorgement: The act of giving up illegally obtained funds acquired in a Ponzi scheme by legal requirement. This generally refers an equitable remedy denying the Ponzi perpetrator their illegally obtained profits.

Enterprise: Refers to a business or brokerage intending to make a profit.

Entity: An individual, company, partnership that has an identity for the purpose of business.

Equity: This refers to the shareholders' holdings, stock; often used interchangeably with securities as equities. This can also mean the value of an owner or shareholder's holdings if the asset were to be liquidated.

Ethnicity-based: A Ponzi scheme that targets people who are Americans based on a specific ethnic heritage.

Factoring: The process of a billing company taking the responsibility of collecting medical payments. Payments for medical bills can take time to collect because of insurers, the claim submission process, and slow-paying clients. The factoring entity pays the medical business for their receivables and then takes the responsibility of collecting.

Faith-based: A Ponzi scheme or fraud that uses faith to carry out the Ponzi scheme through religious organization connections.

False-brokerage: A feigned broker, brokerage, dealer, or investment adviser that presents themselves as being properly licensed and registered, but are not, in order to perpetrate a Ponzi scheme.

Feeder fund: An investment entity that contributes funds to a larger or umbrella fund or investor. In the case of Ponzi schemes there may be many feeder finds contributing to a larger Ponzi scheme. The feeder fund may be a secondary Ponzi scheme or a legitimate registered investment entity that may or may not know that the umbrella entity is a Ponzi scheme.

Financial service center: Offshore economic centers that support banking, incorporation, investment funds, brokerages.

Flipping: The practice buying real estate usual residential homes for a very low price and then selling them very quickly to make a profit.

Foreign currency exchange/FOREX: The market for foreign currencies. This is one of the largest investment markets with losses and profits based on the values of national currencies as the values fluctuate.

Futures or futures contract: "An agreement to purchase or sell a commodity for delivery in the future: (1) at a price that is determined initiation of the contract; (2) that obligates each party to the contract to fulfill the contract at a specific price; (3) that is used to assume or shift price risk; and (4) that may be satisfied by delivery or offset" (CFTC).

Hedge fund: These are private investment funds that pool funds using more aggressive investing methods that generate higher returns, but also have greater risk. Generally, they require investors to be accredited. Hedge funds are less regulated than other types of investments and funds.

High-yield investment program (HYIP): This is the practice of promising unrealistic, exorbitant high rates of returns on investments.

Incorporation: The formation of a legal corporate entity. It is the act of establishing the corporation as an entity and its assets as separate from its owners or officers.

Indictment: "The formal written accusation of a crime, made by a grand jury and presented to a court for prosecution against an accused person" (Garner, 2009).

Information or informational: Is a formal procedure where an individual is informed of the charges against them. It is a document that spells out the criminal charges without the grand jury process. The defendant appears before a magistrate judge who determines if there is probable cause. The defendant can waive the indictment and proceed on the information alone, without a grand jury indictment, in which case there will usually be a plea agreement.

Initial public offering (IPO): This is the initial offering of a private company's shares as stocks to public investors.

Injunction: "A court order commanding or preventing action. To get an injunction, the complainant must show that there is no plain, adequate, and complete remedy at law and that an irreparable injury will result unless the relief is granted" (Garner, 2009). This action is often taken by the SEC or the CFTC to prevent schemes funds from being moved.

Intentional scheme: A Ponzi scheme that was designed and carried out as a fraud. There was never any legitimacy.

Investment adviser: "An investment adviser is a firm or an individual that, for compensation, engages in the business of advising others to the value of securities or as to the advisability of investing in, purchasing or selling securities. An investment adviser can also be a firm or individual that, for compensation and as part of a regular business, issues analysis or reports concerning securities" (SEC).

Investor: A buyer of a security, commodity, future, bond, promissory note, real estate, or other product with an expectation of profit.

Leverage(d):   Refers to using borrowed capital for an investment.

Liquidate: This is taking a business or an individual's assets and converting them to cash. This may refer to selling property or selling one's shares or other investment instruments.

Liquidity: Is the flexibility of money flow, the ability to have cash in hand.

LLC – limited liability company: A company statutorily authorized in certain states that is characterized by limited liability.

LLP – limited liability partnership: A partnership where some or all partners have limited liability. One partner is not liable for a negligent act committed by another partner.

Money market account: A type of interest-earning account, generally that allows the possibility of limited check writing on funds that are deposited for investment purposes. The liquidity of the deposited funds is limited by federal regulation.

Mutual fund: "The common name for an open-end investment company. Mutual finds pool money from many investors and invest the money in stocks, bonds, short term money-market instruments or other securities. Mutual finds issue redeemable shares that investors buy directly from the fund or through a broker for the fund instead of from other investors" (SEC).

Nationality-based: A Ponzi scheme that targets people from a specific nation or nationality.

Nolo contendere: The defendant accepts a conviction without pleading guilty.

Options: "Options are contracts giving the purchaser the right, but not the obligation, to buy or sell a specified quantity of a commodity" (CFTC), or security in the securities market "at a fixed price within a specific period of time, regardless of the market price instrument (SEC).

Penalty: A monetary fine imposed by an administrative judge for violations in Ponzi schemes. This is generally in addition to disgorgement or restitution, and can be ordered in a civil or criminal action.

PIPE: Private investment public equity.

Plea: The defendant admits guilt or pleads not guilty.

Ponzi: A Ponzi scheme is an investment fraud that pays existing or earlier investors with funds collected from later investors. Ponzi schemers promise to invest the funds, yet that is not done or investments are made minimally.

Primary: The agent in a company or fraud scheme who is the initiator of the company or fraud scheme. In federal complaints, this is the first name listed and is generally indicated as the primary individual in a Ponzi scheme. Sometimes the primary agent is referred to as the principal (in the first degree).

Prime bank instrument: In these frauds, the perpetrator says that they are working with major banks, international banks, and that they have approval of the Federal Reserve and the World Bank, but there is no legitimacy to these claims. This is a term that applies to many types of banking frauds: prime bank debentures; prime bank guarantees; high-yield trading; standby letters of credit; guaranteed bank notes.

Principal: The initial investment, or accrued investment funds. This is the funds invested without the interest.

Principal in the first degree: The primary perpetrator in a Ponzi scheme or other crime.

Principle: "A basic rule or law" (Garner, 2009).

Private equity fund: Thee funds are generally made up of accredited investors and institutional investors. The purpose is usually longer-term investments, such as buying out distressed companies and controlling shares in public companies.

Probation: "A court imposed criminal sentence that, subject to conditions, releases a convicted person into the community rather than prison" (Garner, 2009). In a few cases convicted Ponzi scheme participants have received probation instead of a prison sentence.

Promissory note: "Promissory notes are a form of debt that companies use to raise money. They typically involve investors loaning money to company in exchange for a fixed amount of periodic income" (SEC). Although legitimate promissory notes are an appropriate investment, some fraudsters use this as a mechanism to defraud investors; it is a common term used in Ponzi schemes.

Pyramid scheme: In the classic pyramid scheme, participants attempt to make money solely recruiting new participants (SEC), also known as multi-level marketing schemes. Each level of participant makes a profit on those they bring into the scheme, with amounts trickling upward to previous participants. This is differentiated from Ponzi schemes in that in Ponzi schemes all funds go through the primary perpetrator and are then redistributed, with later investor funds being distributed to earlier investors.

Qualified investor: An investor who is an individual and has an investment portfolio worth at least $5 million, or a company that owns or manages investments worth at least $25 million, sometimes referred to as an accredited investor.

Registered brokerage/broker-dealer:
- **FINRA:** "Firms registered with FINRA or a national securities exchange that acts as securities dealers or brokers, or performs both functions" (FINRA).

- **SEC:** "An individual who acts as an intermediary between a buyer and seller, usually charging a commission to execute trades" (SEC).
- **CFTC:** A person paid a fee or commission for executing buy or sell orders for a customer. In commodity futures trading, the term may refer to: (1) a floor broker, a person who actually executes orders on the trading floor; (2) account executive or associate person, the person who deals with customers in the offices of futures commission merchants; (3) the futures commission merchant (CFTC).

Registered investment adviser: "Any person or firm that: (1) for compensation; (2) is engaged in the business of; (3) providing advice, making recommendations, issuing reports, or furnishing analyses on securities, either directly or through publications. A person or firm must satisfy all three elements to be regulated under the Advisers Act" (SEC) (must be registered with the SEC and state of practice).

Reinsurance: Insurance for insurance companies to reduce the amount of risk that is undertaken.

REIT: Real estate investment trust. Business entities that invest in real estate with pooled funds of several investors.

Restitution: Compensation for loss; especially full or partial compensation paid by a criminal to a victim, not awarded in civil trial for tort, but ordered as part of a criminal sentence or as a condition of probation.

Sanction: "A penalty or coercive measure that results from failure to comply with a law, rule or order" (Garner, 2009). In most cases, the perpetrators of Ponzi schemes receive the civil sanction from an administrative judge, requiring that they not trade or have contact with anyone who trades in the stock or commodities markets. It is likely that they are barred from trading or investing for life.

Securitization: The process of spreading out risk by pooling debt instruments, such as mortgages, into an aggregate, then making it a security.

Security: "An instrument that signifies ownership position in a corporation (a stock), a creditor relationship with a corporation or a government body (a bond), or rights to ownership such as those represented by an option, subscription right or subscription warrant" (Downs and Goodman, 2014).

Sentence: The number of months or years of imprisonment determined by a judge in a criminal conviction.

Stock: An instrument that signifies an ownership position (called an equity) in a corporation, and a claim on its proportional share in the corporation's assets and profits (SEC).

Straw buyer: Someone who presents themselves as a buyer for someone else to circumvent a law.

Time served: Upon a guilty verdict or plea a defendant is given the amount of time already spent in prison awaiting trial.

Trader: Those who purchase and sell investment instruments such as stocks, commodities, and options for their own account.

Transfer agent: A "transfer agent" is defined in Section 3(a)(25) of the Securities Exchange Act of 1934 as any person who engages on behalf of an issuer of securities or on behalf of itself as an issuer of securities in, among other things, countersigning securities upon issuance, monitoring securities issuances to prevent the unauthorized issuance of securities, and recording the issuance, transfer, and cancellation of securities.

Unintentional scheme: A Ponzi scheme that turned into a fraudulent scheme when a legitimate business or brokerage failed.

Viatical: "An agreement in which an investor buys a life insurance policy from a policy holder with a terminal disease with a life expectancy of less than two years at a substantial discount from the death benefit" (Downes and Goodman, 2014).

Warrant: "A type of security generally issued together with a bond or preferred stock that entitles the holder to buy a proportionate amount of common stock at a specified price, usually higher than the market price at the time of issuance" (Downes and Goodman, 2014).

References

Commodities Futures Trading Commission. (CFTC). Glossary. Retrieved from: http://www.cftc.gov/ConsumerProtection/EducationCenter/CFTCGlossary/index.htm#S

Downes, J. and Goodman, J. (2014). *Dictionary of finance and investment terms.* New York, Barron's Educational Series.

Financial Industry Regulatory Authority (FINRA). http://investor.gov/glossary/glossary_terms/?gid=a

Garner, B. (ed) (2009). *Black's law dictionary.* St. Paul, MN, Thomson Reuters.

Government Printing Office. (GPO). Retrieved from: http://www.gpo.gov/fdsys/pkg/USCODE-2011-title7/pdf/USCODE-2011-title7-chap1-sec1a.pdf

Securities and Exchange Commission. (SEC). Glossary. Retrieved from: http://investor.gov/glossary/glossary_terms/?gid=a

Index

Taylor & Francis eBooks

www.taylorfrancis.com

A single destination for eBooks from Taylor & Francis
with increased functionality and an improved user
experience to meet the needs of our customers.

90,000+ eBooks of award-winning academic content in
Humanities, Social Science, Science, Technology, Engineering,
and Medical written by a global network of editors and authors.

TAYLOR & FRANCIS EBOOKS OFFERS:

A streamlined
experience for
our library
customers

A single point
of discovery
for all of our
eBook content

Improved
search and
discovery of
content at both
book and
chapter level

REQUEST A FREE TRIAL
support@taylorfrancis.com

 Routledge
Taylor & Francis Group

 CRC Press
Taylor & Francis Group